Poverty, Social Assistance, and the Employability of Mothers: Restructuring Welfare States

Maureen Baker and David Tippin

Why do some welfare states provide income support for mothers to care for their school-aged children at home while others expect them to find employment when their youngest child is six months old? This study, a fundamental contribution to social policy and social-welfare theory, compares recent efforts to restructure social programs for low-income mothers in four countries: Canada, Australia, New Zealand, and the United Kingdom. While these countries are sometimes classified as 'liberal' welfare states, this book demonstrates that they vary considerably in terms of benefit development, expectations concerning maternal employment, and restructuring processes.

The authors examine changes to income security-programs, discuss the social, political, and economic conditions affecting these programs, and analyse the discourse promoting reform. Using a feminist and political-economy perspective, they conclude that recent, often expensive, efforts to make beneficiaries more employable have not always enabled them to escape welfare or poverty.

While full-time employment opportunities are becoming scarcer, governments are requiring beneficiaries to enter the workforce, often with little social support or improvement in income. Regardless of the impact of employability initiatives on poverty levels, the study concludes that these policies are important ideological instruments in tempering demands on contemporary welfare systems. The result is a more residual welfare state, in which social provision is increasingly presented as a meagre last resort.

MAUREEN BAKER is professor and head, Department of Sociology, University of Auckland.

DAVID TIPPIN is a part-time lecturer, University of Auckland, and a social-policy researcher.

Studies in Comparative Political Economy and Public Policy

Editors: MICHAEL HOWLETT, DAVID LAYCOCK, STEPHEN MCBRIDE, Simon Fraser University. *Studies in Comparative Political Economy and Public Policy* is designed to showcase innovative approaches to political economy and public policy from a comparative perspective. While originating in Canada, the series will provide attractive offerings to a wide international audience, featuring studies with local, subnational, cross-national, and international empirical bases and theoretical frameworks.

Published to date:

1 **The Search for Political Space: Globalization, Social Movements, and the Urban Political Experience** / Warren Magnusson

2 **Oil, the State, and Federalism: The Rise and Demise of Petro-Canada as a Statist Impulse** / John Erik Fossum

3 **Defying Conventional Wisdom: Free Trade and the Rise of Popular Sector Politics in Canada** / Jeffrey M. Ayres

4 **Community, State, and Market on the North Atlantic Rim: Challenges to Modernity in the Fisheries** / Richard Apostle, Gene Barrett, Peter Holm, Svein Jentoft, Leigh Mazany, Bonnie McCay, Knut H. Mikalsen

5 **More with Less: Work Reorganization in the Canadian Mining Industry** / Bob Russell

6 **Visions for Privacy: Policy Approaches for the Digital Age** / Colin J. Bennett and Rebecca Grant, eds.

7 **New Democracies: Economic and Social Reform in Brazil, Chile, and Mexico** / Michel Duquette

8 **Poverty, Social Assistance, and the Employability of Mothers: Restructuring Welfare States** / Maureen Baker and David Tippin

MAUREEN BAKER AND DAVID TIPPIN

Poverty, Social Assistance, and the Employability of Mothers: Restructuring Welfare States

UNIVERSITY OF TORONTO PRESS
Toronto Buffalo London

© University of Toronto Press Incorporated 1999
Toronto Buffalo London
Printed in Canada

ISBN 0-8020-4357-7 (cloth)
ISBN 0-8020-8180-0 (paper)

Printed on acid-free paper

Canadian Cataloguing in Publication Data

Baker, Maureen
    Poverty, social assistance, and the employability of mothers: restructuring
welfare states

(Studies in comparative political economy and public policy; 8)
Includes bibliographical references and index.
ISBN 0-8020-4357-7 (bound)   ISBN 0-8020-8180-0 (pbk.)

1. Mothers – Government policy – Cross-cultural studies.   2. Poor women –
Government policy – Cross-cultural studies.   3. Social policy – Cross-cultural
studies.   I. Tippin, David John, 1952–   .   II. Title.   III. Series.

HV697.B34 1999   362.83'9   C99-931341-X

University of Toronto Press acknowledges the financial assistance to its
publishing program of the Canada Council for the Arts and the Ontario Arts
Council.

University of Toronto Press acknowledges the financial support for its publishing activities of the Government of Canada through the Book Publishing
Industry Development Program (BPIDP).

Canadä

Contents

Tables

Acknowledgments

The idea for this book arose from a research meeting several years ago in Ottawa between Canadian government policy analysts and academic researchers concerning ways to reduce child and family poverty. In this meeting, government analysts placed a heavy emphasis on improving the job skills of individual beneficiaries as a solution to poverty, while downplaying government job creation and the enhancement of social benefits. Subsequently, we came across some Australian government policy reports that used the similar discourse of 'employability' but with different emphases and policy outcomes. Maureen Baker began to think back to her 1995 book, *Canadian Family Policies: Cross-National Comparisons*, to re-examine the discourse of restructuring in these eight countries, and she decided to begin a new project on recent reforms and government rhetoric justifying them in four 'liberal' welfare states.

Human Resources Development Canada generously funded the research for this book, and we would like to thank sincerely Evariste Thériault from the Employability and Social Partnerships Division for his continued enthusiasm for the project. McGill University provided a sabbatical leave to enable Maureen Baker (as principal investigator) to collect data in Australia, New Zealand, and the United Kingdom. Our special thanks to Sara Lederman, from McGill University, who worked on the project as a research assistant. David Tippin soon became co-researcher and joint author of the book.

While in Australia, the Social Policy Research Centre of the University of New South Wales offered space, office support, and intellectual stimulation to Maureen Baker. We want to particularly thank Michael Bittman, Sheila Shaver, Bruce Bradbury, George Matheson, Michael Fine, Marilyn McHugh, Diane Encel, Sol Encel, Peter Saunders, and others at the Centre, as well as Jocelyn Pixley from the Department of Sociology, for their project assistance and their friendship. Peter Whiteford from the Department of Social Security cheerfully arranged a visit to Canberra and a presentation to government policy analysts, and Paul Henman and Judy Raymond from DSS provided valuable data. The Australian Institute of Family Studies in Melbourne also provided office space, a computer, and access to the library, and we especially appreciate the assistance of the late Harry McGurk, the late Kate Funder, Ilene Wolcott, and Ian Winter.

The New Zealand Department of Social Welfare and the Ministry of Women's Affairs invited Maureen Baker to Wellington and gave her important data for the book. We are especially grateful to Susan Rutherford, Lesley Wallis, and Kay Goodger.

In the United Kingdom, the University of Bristol's Centre for Family Policy and Child Welfare offered Maureen Baker an office and institutional support for six months. Hilary Land, the director, offered her own unpublished articles and intellectual discussion, and she, Elaine Farmer, David Quentin, and others helped Maureen to integrate into the centre. Jane Millar from the University of Bath invited Maureen to several conferences, introduced her to many people, and engaged in a useful exchange of ideas. While in the United Kingdom, we also met two New Zealanders: Christine Cheyne from Massey University and Kay Goodger from the Department of Social Welfare in Wellington, who offered us considerable assistance with references and statistics.

We wish to thank Virgil Duff at the University of Toronto Press for his interest in this project and his efforts in publishing the book. The anonymous reviewers provided valuable comments and Curtis Fahey copyedited the manuscript with skill and intelligence. We also appreciate the fact that the editors of Studies in Comparative Political Economy and Public Policy (Michael Howlett, David Laycock, and Stephen McBride) included our work in their series.

Finally, we would like to thank the University of Auckland, which enticed us to New Zealand by offering Maureen Baker a chair in sociology. We also appreciate the opportunity that Ian Carter extended to David Tippin to resume teaching in sociology. These appointments, along with the provision of an office and a computer, enabled us to complete our research and manuscript in Auckland during 1998.

Maureen Baker and David Tippin
Auckland, New Zealand

POVERTY, SOCIAL ASSISTANCE, AND
THE EMPLOYABILITY OF MOTHERS

1

Setting the Stage

Introduction

Depending on where she lives in the 1990s, a low-income mother with dependent children faces different work expectations and approaches to government benefits. The Canadian province of Alberta considers a mother to be 'employable' when her youngest child is six months old. In Australia, the comparable age is sixteen years. Yet both Canada and Australia have ostensibly 'restructured' their social programs in the past few years along neo-liberal lines, to create less state involvement in the labour force and family life, lower taxes and government expenditures, and less generous social programs. This book discusses why cross-national differences and similarities exist in the recent restructuring of social programs for low-income mothers in Canada, Australia, New Zealand, and the United Kingdom.

In these four industrialized countries, conservative politicians and analysts, business groups, and many taxpayers have formed powerful lobbies and expressed concern about the growing cost of social programs and high public debt. Consequently, policy makers are searching for ways to reduce government expenditures and are aware that raising taxes to finance these programs is politically unpopular in most jurisdictions. Governments are also encouraging long-term recipients of social assistance, including mothers with young children, to upgrade their employment skills, to find paid work, and to move off social benefits. New justifications have been created to 'sell' these 'employability enhancement initiatives' to the public. These include arguments about the lack of public money, the moral superiority of paid work over other activities, and the need to reduce 'welfare dependency.'

We will demonstrate in this book that efforts to make beneficiaries more employable have been expensive but have not always enabled beneficiaries to exit from welfare or from poverty. Low-income mothers may have been out of the labour force for years and need at a minimum updated job training and childcare in order to enter and remain in paid work. Wages must be high enough to support themselves and their children, while allowing them to pay for substitute childcare, and statutory leave must be available for family responsibilities. At the same time that full-time secure positions are becoming scarcer in the 1990s, governments are encouraging or requiring beneficiaries to enter the workforce, often with little social support or improvement in income. These employability policies are creating a more residual welfare state, in which social provision is increasingly a last and more meagre resort.

From the 1940s to the 1970s, most industrialized countries developed a range of government programs to guarantee citizens at least a minimal level of income in the event of unemployment, work-related accidents, sickness, pregnancy and childrearing, disability, and retirement. The development of the 'welfare state' was based on the assumption that governments as well as employers, voluntary associations, communities, families, and employees have a role to play in maintaining income security and well-being in the event of business failure, economic recession, or personal misfortune. In addition, welfare states were premised on the idea that governments should assist families at certain stages of the life cycle (such as childbirth and retirement). Welfare states were expected to prevent poverty, counteract negative market forces, create greater equity, or reinforce the social value of childrearing or a lifetime of paid work.

Three broad types of social benefits were developed for families, but governments have tended to favour one type over others, depending on such factors as political philosophies, labour-market conditions, pressure from interest groups, coalitions between interest groups and political parties, and socio-cultural beliefs. Esping-Andersen (1990) labels states such as Sweden or Denmark as 'social democratic' because they established relatively generous universal benefits that are available to all citizens regardless of their income or labour-force attachment. These programs are usually financed through general taxation. 'Conservative' or 'corporatist' states such as Germany or Italy developed social-insurance programs to pool the risk of misfortune among employees, employers, and government. These benefits are financed through contributions and are typically generous for those with a labour-force attachment; those who are not connected to the labour force are left to rely on ungenerous flat-rate benefits. 'Liberal' welfare states such as the United Kingdom or the United States rely mainly on means-tested benefits targeted to those whose private resources have been exhausted. These benefits are financed through general taxation and are usually stigmatized and ungenerous.

Since the 1980s, structural and cyclical unemployment rates have increased in many countries in the Organisation for Economic Co-operation and Development (OECD) and have stubbornly resisted attempts at reduction. At the same time, marriage has become less stable and more mothers need assistance to support themselves and their children without a male breadwinner. Those affected by unemployment, underemployment, and marriage dissolution experienced reduced incomes, which augmented the need for governments to prevent widespread poverty and hunger through social benefits. Yet more people are becoming concerned about the 'high' cost of the welfare state and its inability to sustain itself with an aging population and growing structural unemployment. The political consensus that supported more generous social benefits in the 1960s began to fracture in the 1980s, especially in liberal welfare states that focus on means-tested benefits. When social programs are targeted to a minority of low-income people, it becomes easier for other citizens to argue that they are unnecessary or too generous.

Objective of This Study

The intent of this book is to analyse and compare specific aspects of social-program restructuring in four liberal welfare states – Canada, Australia, New Zealand, and the United Kingdom – which historically have provided mainly means-tested benefits to low-income mothers and their children (Bolderson and Mabbett 1991; Baker 1995; Castles 1996). We analyse recent reforms to social programs for low-income mothers as well as changes in discourse, that is, the ways that government representatives and interest groups talk about social benefits, beneficiaries, paid and unpaid work, and the need for reform. We also discuss the original rationale behind these programs as well as their development over the years, including public debates and actual legislative or policy changes.

Most empirical research on welfare states has been based on employment-related programs that benefit mainly men (Orloff 1996; Sainsbury

1996). For this reason, we have chosen to concentrate on social programs targeted at women, but, to make the project more manageable and focused, we are studying programs that affect mainly low-income mothers. We are including mothers as both beneficiaries and employees because we want to understand and highlight relations between childrearing and paid work. We use feminist and political-economy perspectives to understand why social programs have been established and reformed.

Low-income mothers are the focus of this book because they form a large percentage of recipients of means-tested benefits in the four countries. Because these mothers so often require public assistance, they have also been the object of moralistic criticism concerning their 'dependency.' Yet some lone mothers are less dependent in certain respects than many partnered men who rely upon their wives to maintain a household and raise their children. Both lone and partnered mothers are included in this research because they are subjected to similar ideologies about 'good mothering' and share similar needs when they enter employment, such as childcare and leave for family responsibilities. To understand both the development and the restructuring of social programs, we must analyse political support for reform as well as the economic and cultural context of reform.

The countries included in the research – Australia, Britain, Canada, and New Zealand – are studied together because they initially shared similar social-policy options as well as culture, language, and laws (except for the Canadian province of Quebec, which uses the French language and civil law). These four countries continue to share ideas about the restructuring of the welfare state, as we shall demonstrate throughout this volume. All of them seem to be reading from the same neo-liberal restructuring textbook, but their different interpretations have led to varying outcomes. The specific programs we examine include unemployment and social-assistance benefits as they affect mothers (including employability-enhancement initiatives) but also child benefits, childcare financing, and child-support schemes. In other words, we are discussing programs that influence income security or the ability of low-income mothers to support their children adequately, as well as the social, political, and economic conditions affecting these programs.

One difficulty with comparative research is that program variations are apparent within nations, especially in a federation such as Canada where the provinces have jurisdiction over most of these programs. We address this issue by discussing national averages or trends or by emphasizing specific provincial cases. Another problem is that most social programs are in a state of continual reform, especially those related to moving people off government benefits. We have resolved this problem by keeping the material as up-to-date as possible and by mentioning changes expected in the near future. In addition, comparisons are often difficult because the parameters of the programs differ, eligibility rules vary, and the definitions of terms are often discrepant. When available, we use statistics from international data bases that have been made comparable, or we note the discrepant definitions.

Despite these difficulties, we feel that cross-national policy research is important because policy makers are already looking to other nations for alternative ways of dealing with similar social and political problems. By making explicit the policy options and unique national differences, we hope to expand our understanding of four main questions:

1. Are there important cross-national variations in the original design, implementation, and outcomes of social programs for low-income mothers in these four countries?
2. What political, economic, and social factors have influenced the nature and degree of program restructuring for low-income mothers in each jurisdiction?
3. Why have Australia, New Zealand, and the United Kingdom continued to offer stronger state support than Canada for mothering at home, despite years of neo-liberal restructuring?
4. What implications does this research suggest for theories of welfare-state restructuring?

The Political Economy of Social-Program Development

For much of the twentieth century, Western economies have attempted to influence the size and characteristics of their domestic labour market. The manipulation of fiscal and monetary policy according to the principles of Keynesian economics, along with direct and indirect subsidies to the private sector, was used to alter the supply and mix of jobs to minimize unemployment and smooth out other negative consequences of fluctuations in business cycles. All four governments surveyed here have been involved in job creation and maintenance but have seen themselves as 'employers of last resort.' Citizens, as part of an implicit social and political contract, expected the state to perform these functions but how this was done varied considerably among jurisdictions as the political party in power changed. Especially after the Second World War, governments tended to focus on providing basic education and skills training and ensuring that sufficient workers were available for an expanding labour market. Supplementing the labour supply through immigration was particularly important in Canada, Australia, and New Zealand, which experienced labour shortages during the 1950s and 1960s.

The development of the welfare state was expensive for governments, especially during the 1970s when they created new benefits and expanded eligibility in existing programs. In addition, government bureaucracies were growing, wages were rising, and the cost of supplies was increasing, all leading to extensive annual-deficit financing and accumulation of large government debts. This provided a major structural incentive and premise for the policy reassessments of the 1980s and 1990s. Since then, many governments have been withdrawing from direct influence over the economy and diminishing the public sphere through active policies of privatization, 'contracting out,' and 'downsizing.' At the same time, a political culture emphasizing individualism, choice, fragmentation, and pluralism is encouraging and reinforcing government tendencies to make these cutbacks (Kumar 1995,121).

Neo-liberal governments are now retreating from what they perceive as the 'social engineering' of the past, suggesting that government attempts to influence and alter labour markets are no longer feasible or desirable in the context of globalization of capital and markets and free-trade agreements. The growing emphasis on market forces and paid work is an indication of how these governments are moving attention away from structural causes of unemployment and the concept of income security as a social right (Baker 1996). Maintaining the supply of jobs with adequate incomes and protecting labour standards are becoming less important policy priorities in many countries.

Unemployment rates have been rising since the 1960s in these four nations, but policy makers are now accepting higher levels of unemployment as 'normal' and are encouraging the unemployed to create their own jobs to help resolve structural unemployment. In some jurisdictions such as Canada, employability initiatives have also been accompanied by neo-liberal pressure to reduce statutory minimum wages in order to increase the numbers of low-wage jobs for new labour-market entrants. In the United Kingdom, however, the growing emphasis on employability by Tony Blair's 'New Labour' government is being paralleled by a proposal to develop a minimum wage, which would be a first for the United Kingdom. In all four countries, there has been a shift away from state responsibility for reducing poverty and creating jobs. Traditional government policy tools such as income-security programs are alleged to 'create dependency,' and their funding is subsequently cut.[1] Failure to find work after completing a training program is now considered to be the individual's own responsibility (Deniger et al. 1995).

Since the 1980s, many politicians, supported by employers groups and international financial interests, have undertaken what Peter Leonard (1997, 113) calls a 'discursive shift,' in which the ability to pay for welfare programs while governments are in a deficit financial situation has been called into question. The term 'neo-liberalism' has been used in recent years to refer to many different beliefs about the state, economy, and society. For the purpose of this study, however, neo-liberalism includes 'new right' ideas that the welfare state is too costly and that economic principles should hold more influence in public-policy formulation. Government is often viewed as an obstacle to the attainment of economic objectives and it is argued that taxation rates should fall to enable consumers to spend more and employers to create more jobs. Generally, neo-liberals support the idea that markets can deliver better public-policy outcomes than the public sector. They argue that families normally should be autonomous economic units responsible for their own survival but that government support should be available as a last resort for those in absolute need who are deserving of support. Neo-liberals also view individuals and families as 'clients' or 'customers' rather than citizens with social rights (Pusey 1993; Kelsey 1995; Brodie 1996a). As a result of this discursive shift, social-welfare provision is often regarded as transitional and time-limited assistance rather than as a universal entitlement (Bane and Ellwood 1994).

Before we proceed, the concept of 'restructuring' requires further definition. Pierson (1994, 17) has suggested that government restructuring involves policy changes to reduce expenditures on social provision, structural changes to welfare programs so that the state does less, or political changes to increase the chances of future cuts. Restructuring does not always imply retrenchment in every policy area; it could include protection of the status quo or even expansion of some programs or entitlements. Restructuring usually redefines areas of jurisdiction, the ways in which governments operate, how citizens relate to the state, and consequently the scope of their rights and obligations. The political left typically sees these efforts as cutting social-safety nets, lining the pockets of multinational corporations and the rich, and waging war against the poor and powerless. In contrast, neo-liberals see restructuring as necessary reform, as modernization, and as an attempt to make nations more competitive internationally. Some advocates of restructuring oppose in principle a major role for the state relative to the market or voluntary groups, while others are more reluctant converts, supporting retrenchment as the only feasible means of controlling public finances which they consider to be 'out of control' (Leonard 1997, 113).

The terminology of economic rationalism is being used in all four countries, which means that efficiency, cost-effectiveness, and lower public expenditure are emphasized more than improving services, removing family conflicts, or alleviating poverty. Furthermore, the growing influence of several neo-liberal assumptions is apparent behind the process of reform. The first assumption is that the private sector, using market principles, can often provide more efficient and cost-effective services than government. The second is that providing social benefits to a wider group of citizens has not reduced poverty or unemployment but rather has increased people's willingness to depend on government 'hand-outs.' The third assumption is that receiving social benefits should be perceived not as a social right but rather as a privilege that carries certain responsibilities to the state. These responsibilities may include a promise to search for work, to accept a job when offered, or to perform community service if paid work in the private sector cannot be found.

These neo-liberal assumptions, which we will discuss in more detailed national contexts, have not always been publicly debated but have motivated governments to create a more residual welfare state, with smaller and more targeted social programs. Yet cross-national differences are apparent, which indicates that restructuring is motivated by more than economics. Choices based on political ideology and alliances are still being made (Pusey 1991; Myles 1996). As we will see in the following chapters, some governments have targeted programs for major cutbacks while these same programs are relatively untouched or made more generous in other jurisdictions.

For the past fifteen or more years, the governments of Canada, Australia, New Zealand, and the United Kingdom have been reassessing their social programs, including their goals, design, funding mechanisms, eligibility rules, and benefit levels. This reassessment has been undertaken within the broader process of restructuring the state, ostensibly to make programs and services more efficient and consistent with present financial resources and modern social needs. The four govern-ments have overtly said that they are 'modernizing' social programs and 'improving program effectiveness' when they are restructuring. Our analysis indicates that the expected outcomes are usually designed to reduce the number of claimants for social benefits, to control or reduce public expenditures, to make the host nation more attractive for foreign investment, to limit government deficits, and to offer voters the possibility or reality of lower taxes.

In recent years, public debate about social-program reform has focused on several issues in these four countries. Rising program costs are the major concern, and these are attributed by the political right to the 'generous' benefits developed in the 1970s when national economies were growing and governments and employers could afford to improve benefit levels and to broaden eligibility. In the 1990s, the number and percentage of claimants continue to rise as the population ages, unem-ployment remains high with structural changes to labour markets, and mother-led families become increasingly common as a result of divorce and births outside marriage.

Neo-liberal agendas, which assert the primacy of market forces over state intervention, argue that we cannot afford to maintain the present level of social expenditures and certainly will not be able to afford it in the future. They say that taxpayers are already overburdened and point to high public debt and deficits as 'tying the hands of government' and reducing policy options. If governments must allocate high percentages of public funds to interest payments on the debt, less public money will be available for their operating costs and programs.

The political left is by no means united in its views on these issues. Nevertheless, many social democrats, neo-Marxists, and feminists argue that the welfare state has not been a neutral force but rather represents the interests of a certain segment of the population, namely big business and other powerful interest groups usually dominated by high-income white males. Restructuring is an issue not simply of insufficient money, since governments vary significantly in their priorities for the allocation of public funds, but rather of political choices. Historically, the political left has argued that welfare states have alleviated poverty and suffering just enough to prevent massive hunger and to avoid social unrest but have stopped short of redistributing income or assets in any meaningful way or actually dealing with social injustices (Cuneo 1979; Ursel 1992). The left lobbies for 'real' social reform to provide jobs for the unem-ployed, to guarantee 'living wages,' to help parents combine paid work and childrearing, and to deal more effectively with poverty and violence against women and children. Resolving these social problems, they argue, will cost money but this can be financed through the reallocation of public resources to grant greater political importance to alleviating poverty and inequality and to promoting social justice and citizenship.[2]

We agree that governments should not ignore economic factors such as rising program costs or high debt levels, but we also argue that the development of the welfare state and global restructuring are both profoundly political. Furthermore, restructuring occurs on 'gendered terrain' (Jenson 1996), which means that political decisions are typically made by men rather than women and affect men and women differently because their work and life experiences are often dissimilar. Researchers in all four countries have argued that women and other low-paid workers disproportionately bear the brunt of restructuring (Else 1992; Cass 1994; Connelly 1996; Duncan and Edwards 1996; Larner 1996; Mitchell and Garrett 1996; Armstrong 1997; Evans and Wekerle 1997; Land 1998b). Throughout this book, we illustrate this argument with examples from the four countries.

Mothering, Dependency, and Employability

Especially since the Second World War, government policies in the four countries have encouraged heterosexual marriage and stable nuclear families and have attempted to enhance reproduction and childbearing. Governments recognize that parents contribute to the continuity of a nation by bearing and raising children and reproducing the future population, labour force, taxpayers, voters, and consumers that are necessary for the continuance of capitalist society. In addition, mothers typically provide most of the physical and emotional care and parents offer the discipline needed to enable family members to contribute to society and remain independent of state support.

The four countries have acknowledged the social importance of marriage and reproduction in a variety of ways. One has been to offer higher 'family wages' to married men, that is, a wage high enough to support himself, his wife, and two or three children. Governments have also created income-tax concessions for taxpayers with dependants and established income-security programs such as widows' allowances, maternity benefits, and child allowances. In addition, they have provided direct services, such as public education, health care, and subsidized childcare for low-income families.

Until recent decades, social programs in the four nations typically were based on the assumption that men were or would become family breadwinners, that women were mothers, potential mothers, or care providers for their families, and that marriage involved complementary but different social roles (Cass 1994; Sainsbury 1996). Even when marriage rates were relatively low and not everyone reproduced, social programs assumed that marriage and reproduction were normal stages of the life cycle. Until the 1950s and 1960s, married women were excluded from certain kinds of employment (such as night-shift and public-service positions). Middle-class mothers were encouraged to care for their children at home because their caregiving or 'motherwork' was considered essential for child development and their domestic labour was seen as important for their partners' well-being and continued ability to remain in the labour force. If mothers did not 'have to work' because of financial need, it was considered better if they provided domestic services within the home and left the paid jobs for men and unmarried women.

Some governments (such as Australia and New Zealand) historically supported the male-breadwinner family by regulating wages and maintaining higher pay rates for married men (family wages). In addition, all four governments offered a social-safety net for men who could not support their wives and children on their own. Programs were also provided for mothers without male partners, originally only for the 'deserving' poor and excluding deserting wives and never-married mothers. By the 1970s, the distinction between different categories of mothers was removed and program coverage was expanded. In liberal welfare states, unlike social-democratic ones, support for mothering has been targeted mainly to those in financial need. Furthermore, liberal states have not provided as much public support for women as employees. Cross-national comparisons of family policies demonstrate that both motherhood and work are social as well as physical constructs. In other words, the meanings given to these terms are defined by culture and social policies, varying among nations as well as over time (Baker 1995; Sainsbury 1996).

When the economies of the four countries expanded in the 1960s and 1970s, more opportunities were theoretically available for women to remain in the labour force after marriage or motherhood. As the service sector of their economies grew, labour shortages offered opportunities for married women to take up the slack. The expansion of higher education also enabled more women to enter paid employment – both short-term jobs and careers with future promotional prospects. Many women took advantage of these opportunities, but the development of part-time work encouraged mothers to accept paid work without jeopardizing what was viewed as *their* family responsibilities. Yet ideologies of 'good mothering' in some nations (such as Australia and New Zealand) discouraged many middle-class women from entering paid work at all.

In the 1960s, post-war prosperity was creating a growing gap between the rich and the poor. All four countries were pressured by the 1970s to offer a single social benefit for low-income mothers to care for their children at home, regardless of their route to lone parenthood or poverty, especially if those mothers had no male breadwinner supporting them. The rationale, which differed from policies in some Scandinavian countries, was that it was more beneficial for children and less expensive for the state to pay low-income mothers to care for their children at home than to encourage these mothers to find (low) paid work and to provide public childcare. We demonstrate that, throughout the 1980s and 1990s, governments in Australia, New Zealand, and the United Kingdom continued to promote mothering at home while Canadian governments encouraged mothers to enter the full-time labour force. Nevertheless, at the end of the 1990s, all four governments, in varying degrees, are encouraging or requiring mothers with dependent children to enter the paid labour force. In doing so, they are suggesting either that caregiving work is less important than they once thought or that governments can no longer afford the 'luxury' of paying a social benefit for this kind of work.

Employability Programs and the Concept of Dependency

In all four countries, governments are attempting to increase work incentives and to move beneficiaries off social assistance and into the paid workforce. As we will illustrate for each country, governments say that they are doing this in order 'to reduce dependency.' What we will show is that the concept of 'dependency' in this context is ideological, since it constrains discourse in particular ways that serve specific interests. Many former welfare recipients, especially lone mothers, are no better off financially when they are working for pay because their jobs tend to be short-term or part-time and their wages are typically low (Lord 1994; Armstrong 1996; Lewis 1997). Furthermore, we will discuss in more detail in chapter 2 that dependency is conceptualized in such a way that it does not include married women's reliance on their husbands' income. Reducing dependency does not mean that fathers are encouraged to share caregiving work, which would enable mothers to enter the labour force with fewer home responsibilities. Nor does it always imply more government subsidies for childcare services. This indicates that much restructuring is designed to lower public expenditures rather than to reduce dependency or poverty, to create gender equity, or to make people more self-sufficient. In fact, the new rhetoric implicitly views greater dependence on unpaid family caregivers as desirable or at least superior to reliance on state benefits (Fraser and Gordon 1994; Duncan and Edwards 1996a & b).

One way to reduce dependency on government is to nudge people off social benefits and into the labour force, but, if jobs are not available, this option could raise unemployment rates. Governments could attempt to create jobs, as they did in the 1970s, or they can try to persuade employers to do this by offering lower taxes and subsidized wages. The least expensive government option is to encourage individuals to become more employable, to make them feel personally responsible if they do not find paid work, to rely on private rather than public job creation, and to expect parents to find their own childcare. Yet these sorts of policy efforts have not been very effective in moving people into the labour force (Torjman 1996).

The concept of employability is used in varying ways in the four jurisdictions yet it generally encompasses initiatives that prepare individuals to enter the paid job market – either as first-timers or after an interruption in their employment. If they are already in paid work, the intent is to increase their attractiveness to employers or to upgrade their skills to enable them to find more lucrative positions or become self-employed. Employability initiatives may be voluntary and offer services to help beneficiaries retrain or enter the labour market, or programs may be compulsory 'workfare' that reduces social benefit levels if the 'client' fails to participate or accept a job.

The main feature of employability programs is their focus on individual characteristics, such as educational level, job-seeking skills, work habits, the ability to write résumés, interviewing skills, interpersonal presentation and interaction, self-esteem, and general attitude and demeanour (presenting oneself as a confident, enthusiastic candidate for a job). In some jurisdictions (such as Australia), there is more acknowledgment that structural constraints, such as lack of jobs or shortage of childcare services, can be barriers to finding and maintaining paid work. Consequently, employability programs are often supplemented by institutional services for career planning, counselling, and training. They are also supplemented by wage subsidies and sometimes by childcare subsidies, but these are usually time-limited (Lord 1994; Evans 1993 and 1996).

Low-income mothers are sometimes included in employability programs, depending on the age and number of children, but mothers with pre-school children (though not fathers) are often exempted on the assumption that mothering is different from parenting. Mothers in Australia, New Zealand, and the United Kingdom are typically expected to care both physically and emotionally for pre-school and school-aged children at home rather than to seek paid employment. If they find paid work in these countries, it is usually only part-time employment that is low-paid, insecure, and offers no employer benefits (Cass 1994). Part-time employment reduces the need for public childcare and for changes in the household division of labour. In Canada, low-income mothers with pre-school children have usually been exempted from employability programs, except in jurisdictions such as Alberta where they have been expected to find a job shortly after the birth of their child. Recently, however, several provinces and territories have reduced the age of the youngest child from six or seven years to two or three (Freiler and Cerny 1998, 67).

In different ways and at different paces, each of the four countries has moved towards adopting employability-related discourse, policies, and practices, as we will show in the country-specific chapters of this book. This has been reinforced by the enthusiastic and sustained attention that the concept of employability is receiving in international social-policy discussions. The annual economic summits of the G8 have had employability on their agendas since 1996, as the governments of the largest industrialized nations seek solutions to perplexing problems of unemployment, rapidly aging populations, and social alienation.

Tony Blair's 'New Labour' government in the United Kingdom, as we will see in chapter 6, is a particularly keen supporter of employability. This was reflected in the preparatory discussions leading to the G8 summit hosted by Britain in Birmingham in 1998. Two ministerial-level conferences on jobs in late 1997 in Japan, followed by a London meeting in early 1998 on 'growth, employability and inclusion,' were remarkable both for what they emphasized and for what was omitted. Of particular concern was how those outside the paid-job market (such as youth, the long-term unemployed, lone parents, people with disabilities, and those of retirement age) could be brought into paid work. Ministers at the Japanese conference stressed the importance 'of improving employability through intensive training and educational programmes' (Japan, Ministry of International Trade and Industry 1997). The London meeting reasserted two of the pillars of employability philosophy concerning poverty and spending reductions: 'programmes that encourage benefit recipients to enter or re-enter the labour market, and that make work pay, can raise employment and earnings while reducing overall benefits spending' (Group of Eight 1998a). The G8's vision of a modernized social-welfare system is one in which tax and benefits are reformed to 'foster growth and employment and to enable and encourage those people who are unemployed or excluded from the labour market to look actively for work and find suitable employment, while protecting vulnerable groups.' The policy objective is a 'successful transition from welfare to work' (ibid.). These principles were strongly endorsed by the G8 leaders at the Birmingham summit (Group of Eight 1998b).

Older citizens, including the 'retired,' are not exempt from the employability net. The Birmingham summit reaffirmed the G8's support for an 'active aging' policy that would encourage the elderly where possible to engage in paid work and/or participate in what were categorized at the Japan conference as 'socially useful activities' (Japan, Ministry of International Trade and Industry 1997). The barely concealed implication is that citizens' rights to current levels of public-pension benefits could be called into question as they become more 'active' and self-supporting.

One striking aspect of the G8's employability vision is its gender-neutral nature. Women, with diverse needs and circumstances arising out of inequalities in families and workplaces, do not appear as specific objects of policy. Instead, the G8 portrays citizens in androcentric terms, motivated by economic considerations and with identities governed primarily by their relationship to labour markets. Issues of how reproduction and caring fit into employability policy are not considered, beyond vague references to 'addressing the underlying reasons for exclusion from the labour market' (Group of Eight 1998a). The national-level policy limitations and contradictions arising from the absence of a gendered analysis of employability are fundamental themes throughout this book.

The historical origins and genealogy of the concept of employability in the four countries will also be discussed. The assumptions, inconsistencies, and contradictions underlying this concept as a viable policy option are in many cases related to broader socio-economic changes.

These include the historical assumptions and ideologies behind social programs, the growing participation of mothers in the workforce, the shortage of full-time full-year jobs, the paucity of high-quality childcare services, and pressures on couples to create a more egalitarian division of labour at home.

Low-Income Mothers and Their Income Sources

Low-income mothers are not a homogeneous social grouping. Indeed, post-structuralism cautions against generalizations about these mothers that do not take into account the different experiences and self-identities derived from their economic position, their marital and family structure, their sexual orientation, and their racial or cultural backgrounds. In this book, we are focusing on women with below-average incomes who live with children under sixteen or eighteen years old, the age at which children are considered to be 'independent' in most official statistics (despite much evidence to the contrary). The children's ages may vary, and they may or may not be fathered by the mother's current partner. The mothers may be living alone with these children or they may live with another adult as well; this partner might be a male or a female, a legal husband, a 'common-law' husband, or a less permanent partner. They may also be living with family or friends. The identities, experiences, and capabilities of these low-income mothers are highly diversified. The social circumstances and outlook of a low-income mother living in rural New Zealand in a Maori extended family (*whanau*) is not necessarily the same as a mother living with her children in downtown Toronto. Nevertheless, there are sufficient commonalities to warrant grouping low-income women together for the purposes of cross-national analysis.

The income of such mothers could be derived from government or other benefits, earned income, child support, or a combination of these. If the income is derived exclusively or partially from government, the benefits will tend to be means-tested and are often below official poverty levels in liberal welfare states (Baker 1995; Eardley et al. 1996a & b; Hunsley 1997). Government benefits may include social assistance (welfare) benefits, family or child benefits, pensions for sole parents to care for their children at home, widows' pensions, maternity benefits, unemployment insurance or assistance, tax rebates, and housing assistance. Some of these benefits have kept up with inflation rates in recent years while others have not.

Child support is an important income source for some lone mothers. In addition to the well-documented difficulties of enforcing fathers' legal obligations to pay court-awarded support on a consistent basis, child support paid is usually deducted from a mother's benefit income. This means that her poverty may not be influenced by the father's payment of child support. Child-custody arrangements can further affect a low-income mother's situation. Although terminology differs among the countries, child custody and guardianship remain contentious issues. Many mothers shoulder the daily burdens and enjoy the pleasures of childraising, which makes full-time employment difficult. Increasingly, mothers share legal decision making or guardianship with the children's father after divorce, which can further limit their employment opportunities if they are unable to relocate without his permission (Drakich 1988).

Increasingly, the total income for low-income mothers is derived from a combination of state benefits and earnings from work. The work may be part-time or full-time, can be either inside or outside the home, and the earnings may be reported or unreported (Taylor-Gooby 1997). Labour markets are never static, but in recent years they have undergone significant changes in many countries. These changes include (Banting and Beach 1995; Edwards and Magarey 1995; Van den Berg and Smucker 1997):

1. the increasing globalization of capital, free trade, and common-market agreements;
2. the shift of previously unionized and well-paid manufacturing jobs outside the borders of Western economies;
3. the growth in service-sector employment; and
4. the impact of information and communications technologies.

These factors have altered the jobs available to low-income mothers. Some jobs are relatively stable and long term, but many others are insecure, seasonal, or temporary, lack union protection, require irregular working hours, or lack employment benefits (Myles 1996; Jenson 1996). These labour-market changes, however, do not affect only women. Men's employment patterns increasingly resemble those more typical of women, as lifetime careers with one employer become more elusive and time between jobs lengthens for the unemployed (Armstrong 1996).

Government efforts to move more beneficiaries into the labour force are occurring in a period when capitalist labour markets are becoming increasingly two-tiered: full-time and well-paid secure jobs primarily for those already employed; and part-time, precarious, and poorly paid jobs mainly for new entrants to the job market. This is accompanied by growing income and wealth disparities in many jurisdictions, the relative decline of real income against inflation and taxes, and a structural erosion of the traditional 'family wage' (Castles and Shirley 1996; Millar 1996). Consequently, in all four countries there has been a growth of two-income families in order to meet necessities. This means that one-parent families are relatively disadvantaged, especially if they are led by mothers.

Part-time and irregular work typically remains the domain of mothers, students, and retirees, and women's continuing responsibility for caring work helps perpetuate the availability of part-time employees (Cass 1994). Traditional assumptions about the gendered division of labour within the family, including who assumes primary responsibility for caring of children and other dependants, shapes the 'choices' women have to care or not to care (Jenson 1996; Lewis 1997). Consequently, women's engagement with paid work has been more variable than men's, as women have moved in and out of the job market for marriage, childbearing, childrearing, and their husbands' career changes (Davies 1993, Townson 1996).

Women's labour-force participation rates and government encouragement of two-earner families vary considerably by country, as Table 1.1 indicates. At a societal level, women's entry into paid work is influenced by many factors. These include the level of men's wages relative to the cost of living, the prominence of feminist ideologies concerning the importance of paid work for women's self-sufficiency, and rising rates of marriage breakdown. Paid work is also influenced by the extent of government support for childrearing at home versus employment support, such as pay equity, maternity benefits, and childcare. Re-entry into the workforce after maternity and childraising continues to be a problem for mothers, with the growing competitiveness of job markets and the rapid obsolescence of skills and experience. This is exacerbated by 'male' work cultures and assumptions that are incorporated into labour legislation and social programs, including the idea that paid work can be separated from personal and family life. These assumptions, as well as structural barriers such as lack of childcare, augment problems for women seeking employment and promotion, especially mothers with young children (Baker 1996).

TABLE 1.1
Labour-force statistics, 1994

	Participation rates		Part-time employment	
	M	F	M	F
Canada	78.9	65.1	9.3	25.9
Australia	85.8	62.5	10.6	43.3
New Zealand	82.2	63.2	10.3	35.9
United Kingdom	84.5	64.8	6.3	45.0

Source: OECD, *Employment Outlook: July 1994* and *Main Indicators*, various years. Extracted from Eardley et al. 1996a.

The low income or 'poverty rates' of one-parent households tend to be high in the liberal welfare states, regardless of their income sources (Bradshaw et al. 1996). In the four nations in this study, about half of lone mothers live slightly above or slightly below nationally defined poverty levels, as Table 1.2 indicates. This table also indicates that lone mothers in social-democratic nations (such as Sweden and Finland) tend to have low poverty rates. In liberal welfare states, by contrast, a large proportion of the income of lone parents must be devoted to daily subsistence such as food expenses and housing.[3] In all four countries, over 80 per cent of lone-parent families are headed by women, with much higher percentages for those with children below the age of five (Webb, Kemp, and Millar 1996). These families have the highest incidence of poverty. Many low-income mothers do not have the benefit of a second income, and when they do, it tends to be sporadic and unreliable since male unemployment rates remained higher in the four countries in the 1990s than in the 1960s and 1970s. Furthermore, many non-resident fathers fail to pay child support unless the state enforces it (Richardson 1988; Millar and Whiteford 1993; Funder 1996a & b).

We cannot say exactly what percentage of mothers live on low incomes in the four countries because government statistics do not use this categorization. Instead, governments keep statistics on low-income families, lone mothers, and welfare recipients as a percentage of the population. But they do not usually focus on the same combination of gender, family status, and income level that we include in this book.

Pay can be 'low' compared to the wages of other workers in the job market, or low relative to the cost of subsistence needs (Webb, Kemp,

TABLE 1.2
Poverty rates,* after taxes and transfers, *c.* 1990

Country	Poverty rate	
	Households with children	One-parent households
Canada	13	48
Australia	14	56
New Zealand	18	46
United Kingdom (1987)	17	56
Sweden	2	3
Finland	6	2
United States	22	53

Source: Bradshaw et al. 1996, Stephens and Waldegrave 1995,
Ross, Scott, and Kelly 1996.
*Below 50 per cent of median disposable income, adjusted for family
size. For New Zealand, we have used 60 per cent median income,
since disposable income is defined less generously there (conversa-
tion with R.J. Stephens, senior lecturer at the Victoria University of
Wellington, New Zealand, 11 June 1998).

and Millar 1996). The increasingly casual nature of low-wage work
means that there is little career advancement possible but considerable
competition for these jobs. With a flood of new entrants to the lower end
of the job market, wages are depressed and employers can easily retain
some employees on short-term contracts or part-time hours while making others redundant. Many low-wage jobs are being made more 'flexible,' typically to the advantage of employers and the disadvantage of
employees. As a result, the 'working poor' are a growing phenomenon
in many countries.

Webb, Kemp, and Millar (1996) have suggested a gender-neutral
definition for 'low pay' that is less than two-thirds of the gross hourly
earnings of all workers (including overtime). The OECD defines 'low-
paid employment' as two-thirds of the median income from full-time
employment. Table 1.3 indicates the incidence of low-paid employment
in each of the four countries in this study for males and for females,
indicating that low-paid employment for women is the highest in Canada (34.3 per cent) and the lowest in Australia (17.7 per cent) in 1994–5.
We added two Scandinavian nations (Sweden and Finland) to this table
to indicate that the comparative incidence is much lower in those two
social-democratic countries.

TABLE 1.3
Incidence of low-paid employment* in 1994

Country	Total	Men	Women
Canada	23.7	16.1	34.3
Australia (1995)	13.8	11.8	17.7
New Zealand	16.9	14.4	20.7
United Kingdom (1995)	19.6	12.8	31.2
Sweden	5.2	3.0	8.4
Finland	5.9	3.3	8.7
United States	25.0	19.6	32.5

Source: Freiler and Cerny 1998, 24.
*Low-paid employment is defined as less than two-thirds of the median wage for full-time employment.

We are defining 'low income' mainly as a percentage of median income from all sources, as is done in national statistics and in most international databases such as the Luxembourg Income Study.[4] The percentages typically used are below 50 or 60 per cent of median income. The lack of official statistics on low-income mothers means that it is difficult to determine whether national patterns are changing significantly. Indirect evidence, such as numbers of benefit recipients, growing income disparities, and declines in real income, suggests that low-income mothers are a significant and enduring socio-economic category but with many variations in their social situation. The daily struggle of low-income mothers, including securing a job, obtaining an adequate income, gaining employment-related fringe benefits, and finding affordable childcare, is not necessarily consistent with the assumptions behind recent policy reforms related to employability. Clearly, policy makers must confront the impact of poverty, gender, and family status on employment opportunities and outcomes.

Choice of Countries

The research behind this book is based on four nations that we view as case studies of restructuring: Canada, Australia, New Zealand, and the United Kingdom. The countries were chosen because they share some elements of a common background: an initially dominant English-speaking culture and legal systems based upon English common law. In the past, these countries have implemented similar policies and discussed similar policy options. For example, they all created universal child allowances and unemployment programs in the 1940s. Canada modelled its unemployment-insurance program after the existing program in the United Kingdom. The four nations continue to share policy ideas. Canada, New Zealand, and the United Kingdom have all looked to Australia for inspiration when creating new child-support enforcement schemes. In the late 1980s, Canada looked to New Zealand in designing its Goods and Services Tax. In the late 1980s and early 1990s, the governments of all four countries attempted to target their family allowances, and only the United Kingdom was unable to do so. Now, they are all introducing programs to make beneficiaries more employable and to reduce their state dependency.

All four nations have also seen their policy needs and political ideologies as different from those of other countries. These include the 'corporatist' European nations (such as Italy, France, and Spain) that rely mainly on social insurance, and the social-democratic nations (such Sweden and Denmark) that are seen as overly statist and expensive (Esping-Andersen 1996b; Stephens 1996). We will show that theorists, however, have sometimes masked the differences among these four countries by classifying them all as similar.

Although some of the rhetoric used to promote and encourage employability and work incentives in all four countries are similar, the process through which restructuring has been conceived and implemented is different. In fact, similar rhetoric has sometimes been used to justify opposite policies, especially for caring work. Explaining the reasons for these policy variations is one of the major objects of this book and involves consideration of many factors. These include the original design of social programs in each country, including the underlying assumptions regarding work and family inherent within them. We must also discuss the nature of their respective labour markets, the strength of competing interest groups and political ideologies, and the structure of decision making in each country. The substance and balance of such factors – particularly the balance between the structural and political on the one hand, and the ideological on the other – require detailed explanation.

The timing and public image of restructuring in each country involve both similarities and differences. Major Canadian reforms began with the election of the Conservative government under Brian Mulroney in 1984 and coincided with the signing of the free-trade agreement with the United States in 1988 and several constitutional crises involving disputes over Quebec's status in the early 1990s. Yet more lasting structural reform and deeper cutbacks were implemented after 1993 by the Liberal government under Jean Chrétien – from the same political party that established many of the basic principles of the Canadian welfare state in earlier decades. Although Canada originally modelled its welfare state after Britain's, we argue that it is now moving towards an American-style system emphasizing individual responsibility, in which everyone is expected to work for pay regardless of family responsibilities.

Australia also began restructuring in the mid-1980s but we contend in this book that Australians held on to their welfare state more tenaciously than the other three countries. Australia and New Zealand were the only OECD countries that had not developed state-run social-insurance programs by the 1960s but instead relied on a centralized system of wage arbitration, high wages, and full employment for men to stabilize income. In Australia, the welfare state was sustained and even improved, in part because the trade unions exercised considerable power there longer and were able to force successive governments to consider their interests. In fact, Australian reforms were negotiated in a quasi-corporatist way between the trade unions and the Hawke-Keating Labour governments of 1983 to 1996 (Castles 1996). Although the National-Liberal coalition government continued to make lasting changes to the 'male wage-earners welfare state' (Bryson 1992), Australian official discourse still emphasizes the 'social wage' and the importance of public support for women's unpaid caring work. We show that other factors also influenced this discourse, such as ideologies inherent within early social programs, perpetuated by a low percentage of women in the population and the labour force, and a fragmented feminist movement.

New Zealand is often regarded as an example of a nation that began, in 1984 under a Labour government, a wrenching transformation from a highly protected, secure, and regulated society into one increasingly ruled by harsh market forces (Kelsey 1995). Yet, although New Zealand privatized many state functions and cut social-assistance benefits, by 1998 employed low-income mothers typically worked part-time rather than full-time. The government still pays a benefit to care for their children at home until their youngest child reaches the age of fourteen. Although the government announced in the May 1998 budget that this age will be reduced to seven in 1999, this proposed policy reform was later rescinded after opposition within the cabinet and from the public. These initiatives, discussed in chapter 5, were expected to encourage more full-time work by low-income mothers in the future.

Finally, the United Kingdom is viewed in some respects as the forerunner and the political inspiration for restructuring, dating from the election of the Thatcher Conservatives in 1979 and their policies of privatization and user fees for health and social services. Yet Britain is the only one of the four countries that has retained universal child allowances, and until 1997 it offered post-secondary education to citizens and permanent residents without requiring tuition fees. Ironically, it is now the New Labour government under Tony Blair that has introduced tuition fees. The Blair government has also initiated a controversial Welfare-to-Work program, although mothers with pre-school and school-aged children are not required as of mid-1998 to participate in this program.

The four countries have been grouped together because they focus on ungenerous means-tested benefits rather than universal benefits or social insurance to protect low-income mothers. Yet, as we illustrate below, important differences are apparent in social trends and social programs for low-income mothers in the four countries. In the next section, we will compare the four nations in terms of several demographic and economic variables. In chapter 2, we will develop further the theoretical underpinnings of this book and then devote a chapter to policy reform in each country.

Comparing the Four Countries

Population and Family Trends

The four countries differ considerably in terms of population, ranging from the United Kingdom with about 60 million people to New Zealand (which is similar in geographic size to the United Kingdom) with only 3.5 million people in the early 1990s. Canada's population is nearly double that of Australia, as Table 1.4 indicates. Over the past three decades, all four countries have experienced similar demographic trends, such as a decline in fertility, an aging of the population, a decline in legal marriage, a rise in divorce rates, and an increase in mother-led families. Yet substantial demographic differences continue to exist among these nations. Most noticeably, New Zealand has the highest percentage of one-parent families, the highest birth rate (which is especially high among Maori and Pacific Island women), and the highest rate of teenage births and births outside marriage. These national statistics are influenced by ethnicity and culture, for 20 per cent of the New Zealand pop-

TABLE 1.4
Population and family trends, early 1990s

		Canada	Australia	NZ	UK
Population (millions)		28.8	17.7	3.5	58.1
1-parent families		20%	18%	24%	22%
Birth rate (per 1,000 population)		13.5	14.7	16.8	13.5
Teenage births (per women aged 15–19)		25.0	20.7	32.2	28.9
Births outside legal marriage		29	24	37	31
Total fertility rate		1.7	1.9	2.0	1.9
Divorce rate (per 1,000 population)		3.1	2.5	2.7	2.9
Women as percentage of lower	1987	10	6	14	6
house of parliament	1993	14	9	21	9

Sources: Bradshaw et al. 1996, NZ, Statistics New Zealand 1994, Australian Bureau of Statistics 1995, Baker 1995, *UN Demographic Yearbook* 1992.

ulation comprise Maori and Pacific Island peoples (NZ, Statistics NZ 1997). Of the four countries, Canada has the highest divorce rate but its birth rates are moderate. The countries also vary on the percentage of women members of parliament in the lower house, with New Zealand showing the highest percentage in both 1987 and 1993.

Canada is often studied together with the United States, yet in many respects Canada is more similar to Australia, as illustrated in Table 1.4. Canada and the United States are widely discrepant in terms of most demographic trends (except labour-force participation rates of women) and in terms of social-policy development. The U.S. divorce rate was 4.6 divorces per 1,000 population in 1992 and the rate of teenage births was 58.9. In Canada the divorce rate was only 3.1, while the rate of teenage births was only 25.0. The total fertility rate is also higher in the United States, especially among blacks and Hispanics. This helps to explain the greater preoccupation in American society with low-income single mothers. In terms of politics and social policy, Canada is a parliamentary democracy with an appointed Senate while United States is a republic with an elected Senate. Canada developed universal child allowances and an unemployment-insurance program in the 1940s and government medical insurance in the 1950s and the 1960s. The United States developed none of these social benefits. Despite such differences,

TABLE 1.5
Women's share of part-time employment, 1973–92

	1973	1979	1989	1992
Canada	68.4	72.1	71.6	70.0
Australia	79.4	78.7	78.1	75.1
NZ	72.3	77.7	76.7	73.3
UK .	90.9	92.8	87.0	85.4

Source: OECD 1994d.

Canada's economy, culture, and politics are strongly influenced by its neighbour to the south, as we will discuss in chapter 3.

Labour Force and Economic Statistics

Tables 1.5 and 1.6 concern labour-force comparisons among the four countries in this study. Women's labour-force participation rates are the highest in Canada, and Canadian women are more likely than women in the other countries to work full-time. Since the 1970s, women's share of part-time work has fallen in both Australia and the United Kingdom as more men work part-time. Yet Table 1.5 indicates that women's share of part-time work is still much higher in the United Kingdom than in the other countries. This reflects the predominance of a cultural belief that British mothers should not work full-time when their children are young. In addition, there is a lack of public childcare services, and students do not have the same need to work during the school year because tuition and living expenses have been provided by government.

   If we examine the employment rates for mothers rather than all women, the differences become more apparent. Table 1.6 indicates that Canadian mothers are more likely than those in the other countries to be employed, and those who are employed are far more likely to be working full-time, whether they are lone or partnered mothers. On the other hand, British mothers are most likely to work part-time, especially if they are partnered. The reasons for these cross-national variations will discussed in more detail in chapter 7.

   In the 1960s and 1970s, official unemployment rates were higher in Canada than in the other countries. This partly reflects the fact that mothers have been encouraged to enter the labour force in Canada and

TABLE 1.6
Comparing employment rates for mothers (1994–5)

	Sole mothers			Partnered mothers		
	Employed	F-T	P-T	Employed	F-T	P-T
Canada	57%	32%	25%	74%	41%	33%
Australia	43	22	21	51	27	24
New Zealand	27	17	10	58	31	27
United Kingdom	41	17	24	62	22	40

Sources: OECD 1996, Bradshaw 1997, Statistics NZ, Australian Bureau of Statistics, Statistics Canada, UK Employment Department 1994.

therefore are included in official statistics either as employed or unemployed. In the other three countries, mothers with dependent children tend to remain outside the labour force, caring for their children at home. In New Zealand, for example, the government pays the Domestic Purposes Benefit to low-income mothers to enable them to care for their children at home, but these women are technically not looking for work and therefore are not classified as 'unemployed.' Higher Canadian unemployment rates since the 1960s reflect the greater expectation that mothers work for pay, but they may also indicate the relative lack of union protection for Canadians over the years as well as the seasonal nature of many jobs that are influenced by harsh winter conditions. Over the past two decades, unemployment rates have increased and by 1992 remained close to 10 per cent in all four countries, as Table 1.7 indicates. By 1996, rates had fallen again but remained the lowest in New Zealand and the highest in Canada. Projections for 1998 indicate that United Kingdom's rate may fall below that of New Zealand.

Table 1.8 shows government debt as a percentage of Gross Domestic Product (GDP). The government of New Zealand used the rising debt during the 1980s as the major justification for restructuring the state and cutting welfare benefits, as we discuss in chapter 5. Yet, even when the New Zealand debt was reduced and the government enjoyed an operating surplus, welfare benefits continued to be slashed. In Canada, the high level of public debt still dominates policy discussions even though the deficit (the difference between annual government expenditures and government revenue) was eliminated in 1998. Since late 1997, Canadian debates have related to whether government surpluses should be used to pay off the accumulated debt or to improve health-care services,

TABLE 1.7
Unemployment rates, 1964–98

	Canada	Australia	NZ	UK
1964	4.3	1.6	1.0 (1966)	1.4
1970	5.6	1.6	1.4 (1971)	2.2
1984	11.2	8.9	6.8 (1986)	11.2
1987	8.8	8.1	6.8 (1986)	10.3
1992	10.2	10.1	10.4 (1991)	9.9
1996	9.7	8.5	6.1	7.4
1998	9.1*	8.4*	7.7	5.6*

Source: OECD *Employment Outlook. July 1994*, also
1996, 1997; Baker 1995, 75; Easton 1997, 196.
*Projections

TABLE 1.8
Government debt as a percentage of GDP

	Canada	Australia	NZ	UK
1980	44.3	24.9	50.6	54.0
1985	64.1	26.2	72.9	58.9
1990	72.5	21.3	59.7	39.3
1995	99.1	43.8	50.9	57.6
1997*	96.7†	40.0	–	60.8
1999*	87.9	34.4	–	58.2

Source: OECD economic surveys of each country, various
years; 1997–9 figures from *OECD* 1997.
*Estimates and projections.
†According to Mendelson (1998, 2), the Canadian debt was
actually 72 per cent of GDP in 1997.

social programs, and community infrastructure. Australia's debt has been comparatively low compared to the other nations, which may partly explain why neo-liberals were less successful in persuading governments to restructure quite so dramatically in that country.

Table 1.9 compares social-security benefits paid by government as a percentage of GDP from 1960 to 1995. For the three countries for which data are available from 1960, it can be seen that social spending has generally increased as a share of GDP. By 1995, social spending was at similar levels in each of the four countries. Table 1.10 indicates that GDP per

TABLE 1.9
Social-security benefits paid by government as a percentage of GDP,
1960–95

	Canada	Australia	New Zealand	United Kingdom
1960	8.0	5.5	–	6.1
1970	8.1	5.5	–	8.0
1980	10.1	9.1	–	10.6
1990	13.2	10.5	17.5	10.7
1995	14.9	13.0	15.7	13.7

Source: OECD 1996b.

TABLE 1.10
GDP per capita in U.S.$, 1950–95

	Canada	Australia	New Zealand	United Kingdom
1950	8,400	8,200	7,700	7,200
1960	9,500	9,800	8,900	9,000
1970	13,400	13,900	11,400	11,400
1980	17,800	15,800	13,400	14,400
1990	21,800	18,200	15,400	18,000
1995	18,915	19,957	16,689	18,799

Source: Easton 1997, 27; OECD economic surveys. November 1997.

capita was similar in the four countries in the 1950s. Since then, it has
steadily increased in Canada but increased more slowly in the other
countries, especially New Zealand.

Social Programs and Beneficiaries

Table 1.11 compares the years in which social programs were first introduced in each country, indicating that the United Kingdom and New
Zealand established many of their programs before Australia and Canada. Yet neither Australia nor New Zealand developed statutory maternity benefits for all employees, and other benefits to help women
employees integrate their paid work and childbearing were slow to
develop. In the late 1980s and early 1990s, several governments began
targeting or attempted to target benefits that were formerly universal.
We will discuss the details of these cutbacks in the country chapters.

Table 1.12 shows the availability of benefits for mothers to care for

TABLE 1.11
When social benefits were established

Program	Canada	Australia	NZ	UK
Child allowances	1945–93 universal 1993 converted to targeted tax benefit	1941–50 universal (excluded 1st child) 1950–87 (included 1st child) 1987 targeted	1926 targeted 1946–91 universal 1991 targeted	1945 to present – universal
Old age pension	1926–51 targeted 1951–2000 universal	1908 (old age and disability) – means tested	1898 means-tested 1938 universal	1908 universal
Widows pension	Varies by province	1942 means-tested	1911 means-tested	1908
Benefit for lone mother	No federal benefit Provinces provide 'welfare' to all low-income individuals and families (some pay lone mothers at higher rate)	1973 Sole Parents Pension	1936 deserted wives (means-tested) 1973 Domestic Purposes Benefit – means-tested	1977–97 one-parent benefit
Unemployment benefits	1941 (social insurance)	1944 (social assistance)	1938 (means-tested)	1911 (social insurance) 1934 (social assistance)
State-funded medical benefits	1958 hospital insurance 1966 medical insurance (Medicare)	1948 national health program 1973 Medicare	1938, 1941	1946 National Health Service (universal)

TABLE 1.11 (concluded)
When social benefits were established

Program	Canada	Australia	NZ	UK
Maternity benefits	1971 (unemployment insurance)	No statutory benefits 1912–78 universal maternity allowance 1985 multiple birth payment (employer-sponsored benefit)	No statutory benefits	1975 (both social insurance and social assistance)
Equal pay/ pay equity legislation	1956 equal pay (federal employees) 1984 employment equity Pay equity laws vary by province	1972 equal pay 1986 Affirmative Action	1962 (equal pay – public sector) 1972 (equal pay – private sector) 1990 employment equity (repealed same year by National Party)	1970 equal pay

Source: Australia DSS 1992, Baker 1995, Cheyne, O'Brien, and Belgrave 1997, Harding 1996, Shirley et al. 1997.

TABLE 1.12
Comparing programs and beneficiaries, mid-1990s

Country	Special benefit for mothers at home	Sole mothers on social benefit (%)
Canada	None at federal level but provinces offer needs-tested benefits to mothers	44
Australia	Sole Parent Pension (1973) Parenting Allowance	94
NZ	Domestic Purposes Benefit (1973)	89
UK	Family Credit Lone Parent Benefit (abolished 1997) Supplement to Income Support (abolished 1997)	79

Source: Government documentation from each country, Dooley 1995.

their children at home. Although we will discuss the details of these benefits within the country-based chapters, we should note here that Canada has no federal benefit for mothering at home. Nevertheless, the provinces offer social assistance to all low-income individuals and families that are 'in need' and pay a higher amount to parents for each additional child in the household. Also, some provinces pay lone mothers a family benefit that is higher than other rates of welfare. Yet, unlike the other countries, there is no special nation-wide benefit for lone mothers caring for their children at home that offers a uniform amount of money across the country. A much smaller percentage of Canadian lone mothers rely on government benefits, partly because they are required to search for work when or before their youngest child enters school. Consequently, more low-income mothers in Canada work full-time in the labour force.

These four countries provided different levels of income support to low-income mothers to care for their children at home both before and after restructuring, as we will argue in the following chapters of this book. According to Eardley et al.'s calculations based on 1992 data, net disposable income (after housing costs) for both two-parent and one-parent families was the highest in Australia and the lowest in New Zealand, as Table 1.13 indicates. Social-assistance replacement rates (after housing costs) as a percentage of net disposable income for families with average earnings and one child (aged seven years) were the highest in Australia for both two-parent and one-parent families, and

TABLE 1.13
Families* on benefits: net disposable monthly income in U.S.$, 1992

Country	Before housing costs		After housing costs	
	1-parent families	2-parent families	1-parent families	2-parent families
Canada	806	909	481	585
Australia	677	951	544	758
NZ	628	742	380	472
UK	506	639	499	626

Source: Extracted from Eardley et al. 1996a, 125, 126.
*Parent(s) aged thirty-five, with one child aged three.

TABLE 1.14
Social-assistance rates for families with one child* expressed as a percentage of net disposable income at average earnings, 1992

Country	Before housing costs		After housing costs	
	Lone parent with 1 child	Couple with 1 child	Lone parent with 1 child	Couple with 1 child
Canada	42	47	36	44
Australia	44	60	47	64
New Zealand	49	58	42	54
United Kingdom	32	42	37	49

Source: Extracted from Eardley et al. 1996a, 160.
*Aged seven years.

were the lowest in Canada, as Table 1.14 indicates. This indicates that families on social assistance are likely to be living in poverty, especially if they are lone-parent families in Canada or the United Kingdom. The four countries also vary in how they encourage mothers to seek paid employment and to find alternative care for their children.

Outline of the Book

As the new century approaches, these four countries are well into the second decade of reforming and modernizing their systems of social provision. After expanding on the theoretical framework of the book in chapter 2, we examine the process of reform in each country, to see whether and how social rights have been eroded that formerly helped mothers to support and raise their children. For each country, we provide a brief history of the development of social programs for low-income mothers and recent efforts to restructure these programs since the 1980s. The restructuring is explained, including how governments justified the reforms and which interest groups supported and opposed the changes. Finally, we consider how social policies and programs for low-income mothers are influenced by political structures, pressure group activities, and economic and labour-market changes.

This study in sociology and comparative social policy uses concepts, debates, and theories drawn from feminist studies of the welfare state. Feminists are united in their determination to highlight the importance of gender as a core analytical concept, despite substantial areas of divergence in emphases and interpretation. Recent literature within this perspective continues to demonstrate the usefulness of making more precise the processes and outcomes of welfare-state development in terms of gendered ideologies and practices within work and family.

2

Gendering the Analysis of Restructuring

Introduction

The key theoretical and empirical goal of this book is to find ways to incorporate gender and caring – two relatively invisible features of much of welfare-state theory – into more mainstream analyses that have focused on the state and labour market. We argue that political alliances, processes, and conflicts have been and remain crucial in determining the shape of social-welfare programs. In addition, welfare states have also ensured that capital accumulation can proceed and that citizens view social and economic institutions and processes as legitimate. Although the welfare state is not a neutral arbiter between competing interest groups, neither is it necessarily the enemy and controller of women. Our view, consistent with that of Siim (1988), Watson (1990), and Du Plessis (1992), is that welfare states have sometimes helped women to find and keep paid work, to take employment leave for childbearing, and to maintain their incomes when they had no paid work or no partner. At the same time, liberal welfare states have not encouraged women's autonomy as workers or their economic equality with men.

The analysis of social-program restructuring must focus on reforms to government benefits but also requires a broader understanding of political and economic forces influencing decision making. Understanding recent social-program reforms affecting low-income mothers requires some knowledge of how social policy is formulated, the reasons why some interest groups are able to influence policy formulation, and how governments legitimize their actions. In addition, explaining recent reforms requires an understanding of the broader policy context, including changing labour markets, employment patterns, family structures, gender relations, economic and political ideologies, and the relations between paid and unpaid work. All these factors have influenced the formation and growth of interest groups and the recent preoccupations of governments.

The objectives of reforming social programs are usually presented in economic or benevolent terms in official government discourse and the mass media, such as 'the need to increase market flexibility,' 'to reduce the public debt,' 'to help people back into work,' or 'to encourage people to become independent.' Yet underlying this rhetoric are policy choices based on assumptions and beliefs about political priorities, human motivations, and the nature of work and family. These assumptions often receive little scrutiny by politicians and the media and therefore remain largely uncontested. In fact, the public is often told that we have 'no choice' in our public policies, which is clearly untrue. To understand the outcomes of social-program reform, it is important to analyse not only the constraints on policy making but also the implicit assumptions behind the choices that are available.

Our theoretical approach in this book is to use an analysis that is both gendered and based on the political economy of the restructuring process, to help provide insights into the assumptions and contradictions of these efforts. We emphasize the importance of interactions amongst economic and social changes, interest groups, ideologies, social identities, and political action and actors (Leonard 1997; Jenson 1993; Connelly and MacDonald 1996). In the forefront of our approach lie the classic tools of the study of inequality – including notions of subordination, power, social exclusion, and legitimation (Young 1990, 1997).

In this book, we demonstrate that the ways of viewing paid and unpaid work, dependency, and social provision are 'socially constructed' and can both coincide and vary across jurisdictions (Berger and Luckmann 1967). That is, they arise from cultural understandings and social interaction and have specific social meanings that exclude some alternatives while promoting other interests and outcomes. As we shall see, an appreciation of the social contexts of both mothering and employment-enhancement programs is helpful in explaining national variations in the restructuring of social programs. These contexts tend to be oversimplified, misrepresented, or discounted by some policy makers and advocates of welfare reform.

This chapter is divided into several sections. First, we briefly outline mainstream or 'malestream' approaches to the development and restructuring of welfare states. Second, we develop in more detail feminist responses that include gendered conceptual frameworks and more precise understandings of recent relations among families, the state, labour markets, and interest groups (O'Connor 1993; Orloff 1993; Goetz 1994; Oakley and Williams 1994; Pringle and Watson 1996; Nelson 1997; Smart 1997). We then present a critical review of the rhetoric of 'dependency' and discuss some of employment-enhancement approaches designed to coerce or persuade beneficiaries into the labour force. And finally, we examine the state discourses within which employability programs are presented and evaluated, and their ideological implications for low-income mothers.

'Malestream' Theories of the Welfare State

Social programs are costly to the state and require massive public support. Consequently, they were not developed until industrialization and wage labour created a basis of economic prosperity for both governments and most citizens, allowing for the expansion of the public sector. In the four countries, the development of social programs dates from the turn of the last century. New Zealand created a means-tested old age pension in 1898 (McClure 1998). Australia began the family-wage policy from 1907, the United Kingdom developed an old age pension in 1908, and widows' pensions were initiated in 1908 in the United Kingdom and in 1911 in New Zealand (see table 1.11 in chapter 1). Nevertheless, most social programs in OECD nations were created between the 1940s and the 1970s during a period of economic expansion. Yet prosperity did not translate into generous social programs in all industrialized countries. The United States, for example, became one of the most prosperous countries in the world but it did not develop child allowances, a public health-care system, national unemployment insurance, or paid maternity benefits (Baker 1995, 20).

During the 1970s, theorists such as Titmuss (1974) and Mishra (1977) began to contruct typologies of welfare-state provision and focused on variations among nations (Sainsbury 1996, 1). Since then, theories to explain the uneven development of welfare states have focused mainly on economic and political variables. Considerable effort has been devoted to analysing and classifying welfare-state development and creating 'ideal types,' sometimes based on several axes of variation (Korpi 1983; Esping-Andersen 1990 and 1996; Mishra 1984 and 1990; Kangas and Palme 1992–3; Drover and Kerans 1993).

One of the most widely used classifications is by Esping-Andersen

(1990), who has identified three main types of welfare state based on the quality of social rights, the pattern of stratification resulting from welfare-state policies, and the nature of the state-market nexus. The nations he classifies as 'liberal' tend to focus on means-tested benefits and modest social-insurance benefits, market solutions in the form of occupational welfare and private insurance, and services by voluntary associations and family, giving the state a residual role in welfare provision. 'Conservative' or 'corporatist' welfare states rely mainly on social-insurance programs for those in the labour force and their dependants, and these programs share the risk of income loss among employers, employees, and government. Social-insurance programs offer differential benefits, based on class and income. For those outside the labour force, ungenerous and means-tested benefits are available but social services tend not to be provided by government. Instead, families and charitable organizations are expected to provide support and services for the poor and unfortunate (Esping-Andersen 1996b). In contrast, 'social democratic' welfare states prefer to offer universal programs to all citizens regardless of income or labour-force attachment. Esping-Andersen (1990) contends that social-democratic welfare states are the most highly developed and egalitarian, since they make a large public investment in social provision, 'decommodifying' it to enable citizens to maintain their incomes apart from paid work. We will discuss the concept of decommodification further in the section on feminist responses, where we also note that Esping-Andersen discusses the differences among these three categories of welfare states but not the variations within each category (Sainsbury 1996, 12).

Plough and Kvist (1996) have further developed this typology in order to understand the practices and underlying philosophies of welfare states prior to restructuring. One type of welfare state, heavily influenced by political conservatism, is 'selective' because it focuses on the replacement of lost earnings through unemployment, sickness, or retirement while leaving differentials of status and class untouched. Attachment to the labour force is the major driving force behind this kind of social provision. A 'residual' welfare state takes a more active role in attempting to alleviate poverty, to promote the work ethic, and to enhance economic efficiency. Its ideological basis is political liberalism, as expressed in the reforms advocated by Keynes (1936) and Beveridge (1942) in the United States and the United Kingdom, and its aim is to provide social assistance or social insurance in the form of legally based minimum benefits. A third category is a more comprehensive welfare state, such as Sweden, that is based upon social-democratic principles of income redistribution, prevention of need, and promotion of equality. In this category, social provision is seen as a right based on citizenship or permanent residence.

Explanations of the development of welfare states as well as their restructuring tend to be dominated by the 'power resources' approach (Korpi 1983; Castles 1985; Mishra 1990; Esping-Andersen 1990; Saunders 1994). This approach explains the development of social rights, income redistribution, and welfare provision primarily in terms of the alignment of social classes and interest groups in the political arena, as well as the roles of competing and collaborating institutions (Folbre 1994; Sainsbury 1996; Plough and Kvist 1996). The power-resources approach tends to focus on benefits for paid workers, the power of labour unions as interest groups, coalitions between interest groups and governing political parties, and state provision (Orloff 1996). Power-resources researchers, however, tend to have little to say about social programs for families or how welfare states deal with caring activities (Sainsbury 1996; Pascal 1997; Knijn and Kremer 1997).

A political-economy variation on this approach argues that there is a close and reciprocal relationship among dominant forms of economic production, employment patterns in nation-states, and their systems of social provision. Shields and Russell (1994), for example, contend that the family-wage principle was undercut by the absence of increases in real wages. Coupled with this are the changes in economic activity arising out of Western capitalism's needs for more flexible specialization and part-time labour. In response, the welfare state changes, and this might include restricting social provision and changing eligibility requirements to ensure an adequate supply of low-wage workers. Greater state and business emphasis upon employability programs would be a logical policy response to these requirements. The problem with this argument is that it is not sufficiently sensitive to national conditions, including the interplay of interest groups and ideologies concerning family and caring.

Mainstream theorists have tended to assume consistency among social programs within a particular country (Orloff 1993; Bussemaker and van Kersbergen 1994; Lewis 1997). Yet, while recent research has indicated that nations that offer generous programs for families with children also tend to provide generous programs for workers injured on the job or for old age pensioners, the reverse is not always true (Wennemo 1994; Baker 1995). Furthermore, malestream typologies fail to differentiate between welfare states that promote women's autonomy and equality and those that encourage women's dependence on male family members (Orloff 1996; Sainsbury 1996). Within each of Esping-Andersen's three types of welfare states, both extremes exist (Baker 1996). From a feminist viewpoint, this is a serious criticism.

Mainstream researchers have spent considerable time and effort measuring and comparing social spending, the relative generosity of welfare states, how well they reduce inequality among income groups, and their relative financial cost (Bradshaw et al. 1993 and 1996; Saunders 1994; Whiteford and Kennedy 1995; Eardley et al. 1996a). Yet researchers are still arguing about whether generous social benefits encourage low productivity and high unemployment rates. Many economists contend that social-democratic welfare states have been too generous, making their economies uncompetitive and creating more state dependency. Yet political scientists and sociologists such as Stephens (1996) argue that welfare entitlements have made little if any direct contribution to current economic problems. Instead, problems are caused by political decisions to create free-trade links with other countries and to promote the globalization of labour markets, which leads to higher unemployment. Social-democratic welfare states are premised upon full employment and low unemployment rates, and when unemployment rises, as it has in the 1980s and 1990s, social benefits become expensive.

Theories explaining the timing, prevalence, and focus of restructuring are not as numerous as those that concentrate on welfare-state development (Pierson 1994). Mishra (1990) has studied restructuring in several countries and compared two policy responses to crises in the economy and welfare: neo-conservatism (retrenchment) and social-democratic corporatism (maintenance), which both represent a cluster of values and interests. Using ideology and social class as key variables, he shows that, contrary to theories of the irreversible state, the welfare state has unravelled considerably under neo-conservative regimes.

Mullaly (1994) has argued that the social contract and historic compromise between capital and labour as embodied in Keynesian welfare states have been overturned by the ability of business groups to increase their power resources at the expense of labour and other interest groups. Business is better organized, more articulate in its visions of economy and society (partly owing to well-funded policy think-tanks), and influences decision makers more effectively. He notes that restructuring has class-based targets in the sense that reform has concentrated on low-income and vulnerable groups dependent on public funds. The gendered nature and outcomes of restructuring are not a focus of Mullaly's analysis, nor does it provide a precise explanation for the national variations that we will see in this book among reforms that affect low-income mothers.

In an important elaboration of the power-resources approach, Pierson (1994) argues that retrenchment is a process distinct from expansion and not just the latter's mirror image. His analysis of the successes and failures of the Thatcher and Reagan governments in the 1980s to contain and reduce social expenditures yields a number of insights. First, successful retrenchment is dependent upon its proponent's ability to divide supporters of social programs and to prevent effective interest-group mobilization, as well as upon the prevailing strength of those interest groups. Success also depends upon compensating those who are negatively affected, concealing what is being done from potential critics, and obscuring responsibility. Furthermore, the political battles over social policy during restructuring increasingly concern the ways in which information is provided about why policies should be changed and the consequences of those changes.

Social programs must be disaggregated when analysing retrenchment, since substantial variation is apparent in the vulnerability of individual programs to reform efforts (Pierson 1994). Some programs have experienced relative stability while others have undergone radical changes. Moreover, Pierson argues that universal programs are not necessarily more resistant to change than means-tested ones, because the former have the potential to yield larger savings while the latter may raise perceptions of unfairness and inhibiting work incentives. In the United Kingdom, for example, housing, unemployment insurance, and pensions proved much more vulnerable to restructuring than medical care and targeted welfare programs.

Institutional reforms can contribute significantly to retrenchment in social programs, even when they are not directly linked to specific program cuts (ibid.). These reforms include changes in internal decision making which place more power in the hands of budget-cutters in treasury or finance departments, tax cuts which weaken revenue bases, and changes which reduce the power of the labour movement. These conclusions are particularly relevant for our discussions of Canada and New Zealand.

Pierson has also suggested that welfare-state restructuring has a 'policy feedback loop' based on previous political choices in the expansionist period. This influences prospects for change by creating coalitions of supporters for the status quo or for minimal change, and by changing the resources available to defenders and opponents of the existing welfare state. In other words, the political context has changed. Studies of restructuring, therefore, must go beyond an examination of spending and focus on institutional change, program structure, and the culture of organizations.

Pierson downplays the role of labour movements and the political left as key actors in restructuring processes, but he acknowledges the importance of cultural and institutional factors in shaping each country's policies. His work can be considered as a sophisticated elaboration of the power-resources approach rather than a rejection of it, but as such, it shares some of the deficiencies. Scant reference is made to gender as an important factor in explaining the process and outcomes of restructuring, and the roles played by political discourse, social ideologies, and moral agendas are also unclear.

Feminist Approaches to Welfare Reforms

Feminist researchers argue that a crucial determinant in understanding welfare provision is the gender-based division of labour inherent in the provision of care, access to paid work, and marriage and family relations (Orloff 1993; Hobson 1994; Marshall 1994). Gendered ideologies – ideas about how men and women should behave – have permeated social programs. In liberal welfare states, men's entitlements tend to be based on their attachment to the paid labour force while women's entitlements are often derived from their husband's employment rights or from their status as wives or mothers. If mothers are not affiliated with a male breadwinner or are living in poverty, the state usually offers income support but at a lower level (Orloff 1993). Increasingly, women's entitlements are also obtained through their own attachment to the labour force, yet their employment-related benefits tend to be lower than men's. Women's attachment to the labour force, and therefore their wages and promotional opportunities, are affected by their caring duties, social expectations, and gender-based discrimination. 'Gender-neutral' social policies that ignore these differences become gender-blind and discriminatory in their consequences.

Welfare states have always made some provision for caring work, but this work has been understudied by malestream researchers. Historically, liberal welfare states have supported paid and unpaid caring activities in several ways. Since the last century, they have required employers to pay a 'family wage' to male breadwinners to enable their wives to perform unpaid domestic work. Governments have also paid token allowances to mothers, which have contributed, both financially and morally, to the cost of childrearing. As well, governments have regulated, subsidized, or financed voluntary organizations and private individuals involved in the provision of caring services. Some jurisdictions have provided market-based wages to professionalize and commodify caring work, although this policy has been promoted mainly by social-democratic governments. Governments have provided some compensation for family members who forfeit wages or incur expenses through childbirth or caring for children, disabled persons, or frail elderly (Knijn and Kremer 1997; Knijn and Ungerson 1997). Many of these programs are invisible or downplayed in malestream research, yet how restructuring affects caring work is an important topic of study. Feminists such as Aronson and Neysmith (1997) argue that the 'retreat of the state' in recent years has augmented the cost of care for families as well as the amount of caring work done within the home mainly by women.

The Family Wage and the Male-Breadwinner Family

A primary focus of both social policies and labour negotiations during the expansionary years of liberal welfare states was the male worker/ citizen in the paid-employment market (Orloff 1993). The social rights and employment benefits of the male breadwinner were of paramount concern as he was considered to be sole financial provider for the nuclear family. The male-breadwinner model of family had already been institutionalized into social policy by the turn of the century in the form of the family wage, which paid men enough to support themselves and 'their dependants.' The 'independent' male's position was directly related to how the 'private' sphere of the family was organized along gendered principles. Men were given priority to paid jobs and a privileged position within the family, accompanied by a moral duty to be good providers but with little responsibility for 'private' domestic tasks. Women were expected to marry, to procreate, to care for their husbands and family, and thereby to gain indirect access to a man's wages. These idealized roles may appear to be archaic and somewhat irrelevant in an era when legislation and social attitudes promote gender equality. Nevertheless, these ideologies cannot be ignored or underestimated in analysing the development or restructuring of welfare states. Vestiges of the family-wage concept are still apparent in the United Kingdom, Australia, and New Zealand.

The family-wage concept meant that wage earners were also divided implicitly into two groups – those who supported 'dependants' and those who were supported by others (or were likely to be in the future). In this latter category were mainly unmarried working women but also some partnered women and lone mothers whose wages were regarded by politicians and policy makers as little more than supplemental income or 'pin money' (Webb, Kemp, and Millar 1996). The policy of paying a family wage allowed governments in all four countries in this study to exclude married women from certain segments of the labour force until well into the 1960s. In reality, however, the family wage did not always meet family needs, which was a source of continuing political debate and trade-union protest. Yet the assumption that married women were men's 'dependants' and therefore should be excluded from the labour market helped to bolster the wages of the male working class. For that reason, the trade-union movement supported the family wage and was not particularly interested in promoting women's employment rights (Land 1980; Baker and Robeson 1981).

The male-breadwinner model of family was accompanied by the differential treatment of paid and unpaid work, which subsequently influenced the rewards received by men and women in the social-welfare system. Some liberal welfare states (such as Canada and the United Kingdom) tended to create 'dual social welfare systems' (Sainsbury 1993). One is contributory, earnings-related, relatively generous, and based on social insurance, while the other is non-contributory, related to need, designed for those unattached to the labour force, and based on social assistance. Women have tended to be the beneficiaries of less generous social assistance while men rely on more generous and less punitive social-insurance programs.

Feminists agree that welfare states have helped to reduce income inequality aggravated by unemployment and market forces, but they argue that these same states have perpetuated gender inequality through social programs premised on gender divisions or through their unwillingness to promote gender equality. At the apex of welfare-state expansion in the 1970s, the gap between the rich and the poor became smaller but women remained economically disadvantaged relative to men, especially women from cultural minorities and lone mothers. Women more often than men have been marginalized in part-time or low-paid jobs. They tend to move in and out of the labour force more frequently and, regardless of their marital or labour-market status, to be allocated lower levels of social benefits. Their contributory benefits are less than men's because they are based on lower average earnings. Furthermore, women's social-assistance benefits are meager because their unpaid caring activities are undervalued and not seen as real market-based work.

The legacy of the family wage cannot be underestimated because its discourse and associated practices formed the basis of social programs in many jurisdictions. For example, the male-breadwinner model of family was incorporated into Australian wage policies in 1907 through the *Harvester* judgment (Higgins 1922). It was imbedded in British social policy in the 1940s through the Beveridge report, and the social-security and tax systems consequently assumed a gendered division of responsibilities (Land 1979). Second, the legacy of the family wage solidified gender roles and acted as an official sanction of relations in families and civil society. That is, it approved the idea of the heterosexual nuclear family with the husband/father as principle breadwinner and the wife/mother as care provider. However, wives found themselves in a precarious situation if the family wage was not shared equitably, their husband died prematurely, or their marriage dissolved. Lone mothers with young children were especially vulnerable and experienced difficulty maintaining autonomous and independent households (Orloff 1993). The male-breadwinner model of family has been challenged by women's greater participation in paid work, the increasing insecurity in men's employment, and some renegotiation of gendered roles within families. Yet its continuity and residual power remain, reinforced by male-dominated job hierarchies (Pascall 1997, 45).

The Concept of Decommodification

Feminist researchers have also criticized the concept of 'decommodification' for containing a male bias. Esping-Andersen (1990, 21) has used this concept to indicate that welfare states have provided benefits or services that enable citizens to maintain their incomes outside the domain of paid work. He notes that welfare states vary on a continuum of decommodification; some provide only means-tested benefits for those outside paid work, while others offer more generous benefits based upon universal rights or citizenship (Orloff 1993). Yet cross-national comparisons of decommodification say little about the fact that, when mothers care for their children on government benefits, they tend to be impoverished, unable to establish independent autonomous households, and often dependent on their families. Paying mothers a social benefit to care for their children at home has not been emancipatory. In fact, women are more likely to be able to establish independent autonomous households when they are employed full-time and have access to state-funded childcare and leave for family responsibilities. Lone mothers who are not employed are much more likely to live in poverty (or have incomes less than 50 per cent of the national average) than lone mothers who are employed (Bradshaw et al. 1996, 9). For example, 71 per cent of Australia lone mothers who are not employed are 'poor' compared to 22 per cent who are employed (ibid.).

The concept of decommodification cannot deal adequately with those outside or on the margins of the labour market. As Orloff (1993) indicates, 'gendering' this concept is needed to understand women's access to paid employment and to services that enable them to balance employment and home responsibilities. Throughout this study, we use the term 'gendering' to call attention to the different circumstances, roles, and responsibilities of women and men and the problematic nature for women of many aspects of the welfare state. As gender differences are apparent in both paid and unpaid work, the social programs that decommodify labour can affect men and women differently. For example, parental benefits (a form of decommodification and income replacement at childbirth) have helped women remain in the paid labour force. Although these benefits were created to be gender-neutral, the policy outcome tends to be gender-specific (Baker 1997c). Fathers fail to use parental leave and benefits because they are encouraged to be more concerned than employed mothers about the appearance of job commitment and future promotional possibilities, as well as lost wages and benefits (Orloff 1996; Baker 1997c). Furthermore, when women take parental leave, the division of labour in the home tends to become more traditional.

The commodification of childcare has had little effect on fathers' employment patterns but has enabled some mothers to remain in paid work and contribute to support themselves apart from their families. Researchers need a better understanding of commodification to know when it is emancipatory and when it promotes dependency. In addition, they need to understand the mechanisms and institutions through which access to employment is guaranteed, and whether recent restructuring has eroded these guarantees. With this background, we can now review some of the major analytical insights gained from feminist approaches.

Insights from Feminist Research

We agree that explanations of variations in the development and restructuring of welfare states require an understanding of the influence of interest groups and their alliances. In addition to labour unions and political parties, however, researchers also need to examine the influence of women's groups and their coalitions, as Pedersen (1993) and Bashevkin (1998) have done. Hernes (1987) notes that the relatively greater participation by women in political institutions, social movements, and corporate politics of Scandinavian countries has given a higher political profile to women's issues and created smaller gender inequalities. We also agree with Sainsbury (1994a) that research must consider who receives benefits, under what circumstances, and for what purposes, since social benefits are often differentiated by gender.

Structural inequality based on gender is apparent in households and families in all four of the nations in this study. As women enter paid work, more are experiencing a 'double day' of employment and unpaid domestic work. Employed women continue to take responsibility for housework (especially if they work part-time), to be the predominant caregivers of both children and adults, and to be responsible for maintaining social well-being and family ties (Armstrong and Armstrong 1990; New Zealand, Statistics NZ 1993, 100; Bittman and Pixley 1997). These responsibilities tend to interfere with employment opportunities and influence promotion and income.

More mothers with young children are entering the labour force in all four countries, but this has not necessarily led to an escape from poverty. Some jurisdictions began creating employment-related programs in the 1970s to promote gender equality (such as pay equity and parental benefits), which have helped women become employees and to remain in the labour force. Though such programs have not led to equality of outcome (Baker 1997c), paid work remains important for women because it potentially gives them greater economic freedom, independence, and leverage within their families as well as new or better access to employment-related benefits.

Governments have varied in their encouragement of paid work for mothers. Orloff (1993) proposes that the degree to which welfare states promote or discourage women's access to paid work should be considered as a useful analytical category. In fact, it can be a way of making Esping-Anderson's comparisons of welfare states more gender-sensitive. The affordability and availability of childcare has been seen as a major reason for cross-national variations in labour-force participation rates of women. Comparisons between lone mothers' employment rates in different countries, for example, have identified cost differentials in childcare as the single factor that discriminates unambiguously between countries with high and low labour-force participation rates (Bradshaw et al. 1996). Yet lack of affordable childcare is not the sole barrier to employment: illness, disability, and the belief that children are too young to be cared for by anyone other than the mother are also important (Ford and Millar 1997; Ford 1997). The question remains why women's groups in some countries (such as Canada) have pressured governments for childcare subsidies, while women's groups in other countries (such as New Zealand) have not done so as vigorously.

Social attitudes and their ambivalence and contradictions must also be considered in understanding the restructuring of social programs for low-income mothers. The nature of dominant social attitudes about employed mothers and the extent to which social policy should encourage or compel women to alter their existing arrangements are important factors, although divergent opinions are apparent within any society. Should the state be neutral or more activist with respect to women's employment and childcare? Should welfare mothers be expected to work for pay while middle-class mothers are encouraged to care for their children at home? Many people feel that mothers' primary concerns should be the well-being of their children, but this conflicts with the neo-liberal view that all citizens should support themselves financially (Millar 1996, 185).

Social policy has never been a neutral instrument for well-being but has always been subservient to economic demands, such as maintenance of labour discipline (Dominelli 1991; Maclean and Groves 1991; Edwards and Magarey 1995). Women's needs as employees were considered less important in the development of welfare states than their needs as wives and mothers, with the result that patriarchal relations were left unchallenged or actually reinforced by policy. Recent efforts to reform social programs have often been gender-blind, treating women as genderless citizens or workers and leaving untouched the gender biases built into social programs. Sometimes programs make the opposite and false assumption that men and women experience similar constraints in their work activities and earning potential (Morton 1988). The data we provide in the following chapters indicate that the lives of low-income mothers are not necessarily the same as those of their male counterparts. When gender is ignored in the restructuring process, unexpected and inequitable consequences often occur. We examine reforms in the four nations to see if they ensure that women have a right to income maintenance as independent citizens rather than or in addition to their status as family members.

Feminist approaches have contributed new elements to the analysis of welfare states but they also have limitations. Until recently, they have concentrated upon critiquing malestream theories of welfare-state development and of 'gendering' these approaches. Only recently have feminists begun to analyse the restructuring process (Edwards and Magarey 1995; Sainsbury 1996). Feminist research has also focused on women's historical entitlements as mothers, especially lone mothers (Strong-Boag 1979; Little 1995; Silva 1996; Kiernan, Land, and Lewis 1998), rather than as employees or wives. This research has also centred on the United Kingdom and Europe (such as Lewis 1993; Pedersen 1993; Hantrais and Letablier 1996; Thane 1996) and the United States (Abramovitz 1989; Sidel 1992; Wexler 1997), and much of this research deals with single countries rather than cross-national comparisons (Harding 1996). Furthermore, feminists have not always given sufficient weight to the larger economic and political variables influencing welfare states, including international and global forces in financial markets. Consequently, there was a paucity of comparative research on social policy and welfare-state restructuring from a feminist perspective until the 1990s. Since then, there have been numerous comparative studies using a feminist approach.[1]

Especially since the 1970s, welfare states have provided greater legal protection and rights for women as citizens. At the same time, however, traditional ideologies imbedded in social policies (especially in Australia, New Zealand, and the United Kingdom) have helped keep women within a domestic and dependent role and denied them their full rights as citizens. Currently, neo-liberal governments are cutting back on or tightening entitlement to the very programs that were beginning to give some women greater autonomy from their families and to allow them somewhat more equitable competition in the labour force. Furthermore, the new employability programs are propelling low-income mothers into labour markets that are producing mainly low-wage jobs and do not acknowledge the importance or efforts involved in caring work. These policies and the governments that initiate them tend to assume a separation between work and family and a dichotomy between the public and the private (Armstrong, Armstrong, and Connelly 1997).

Dependency and Social Assistance

The rhetoric of restructuring emphasizes the economic need to reduce government spending and the number of people relying or dependent on social benefits. Provision of 'generous' social benefits is thought to keep taxes high and thereby reduce the possibility of private-sector job creation. It is also considered to be an indication of a malfunctioning welfare state that discourages able-bodied people from accepting paid work and becoming self-sufficient. Long-term reliance on government benefits is thought to lead to both financial and psychological dependency, and the recipients themselves are blamed as suffering from personal inadequacies or motivational problems (McAll et al. 1995; Duncan and Edwards 1996). Policy concern focuses on the length of time spent on benefits, the time between 'welfare spells,' and rates of 'recidivism.' In some countries, lone mothers on social benefits have been viewed as a growing social problem, a drain on the economy, a social underclass, and poor role models for their children (Hardina 1997; Duncan and Edwards 1996). Providing benefits for low-income mothers is also said to encourage women to reject marriage and nuclear-family living.

The neo-liberal notion of dependency carries considerable ideological weight and has been a powerful theme of political mobilization. Especially in societies with strong individualistic cultures such as the United States, the language of dependency provides much of the organizing logic and discourse surrounding welfare reform. Contrasts abound between entitlement and charity, and who is deserving and undeserving (Gordon 1994). The language of dependency also presents social problems as individual and moral issues, and marginalizes those who are so labelled (Fraser and Gordon 1994a). It targets particular groups outside the norms of a self-reliant citizenship and places them under new and more intense forms of state surveillance and control (Brodie 1996). Within this ideological framework, notions of interdependence, community, and social solidarity are downplayed (Leonard 1997).

One strand of American conservatism is concerned that high levels of 'welfare dependency' break the link between social assistance and morality, resulting in demoralization and a loss of discipline and self-control (Himmelfarb 1995). Yet conservatives in many countries hold contradictory views, exhorting middle-class mothers to stay home and perform childcare and domestic duties while also supporting legislation to force mothers on benefits to work for pay and hire someone to care for their children (Piven 1990; Millar 1996). Dependence is acceptable when middle-class wives rely on their male breadwinners, when husbands depend on their wives for personal care or childcare, when employees draw on social-insurance benefits for which they contributed, when business people take advantage of tax concessions, or researchers depend on government grants. Dependence on government social assistance by poor and working-class people, however, is considered to be unaccepable (Cass 1994; Fraser and Gordon 1994a).

Within neo-liberal discourse, 'independence' is associated with wage labour, male breadwinners, and the family wage, and it coexists comfortably with imagery stressing social autonomy, separation, and control over one's destiny (Leonard 1997). In contrast, 'dependence' is associated with receiving income support from the state. Fraser and Gordon (1994a & 1994b) suggest that there is a need to distinguish between socially necessary dependence, related to the provision of care for fellow human beings, and dependence that is related to unjust social conditions and institutions. Neo-liberals often argue that paid work and unpaid care are both socially acceptable; the difference is that unpaid care is a family or 'private' matter that should not require supplemental financial support by the state. Yet feminists claim that the distinction between the private and the public is a false one with dangerous implications for the safety and well-being of women and children. Until recently, the concept of family privacy has minimized state intervention and the protection of women and children even when violence was being perpetrated against them.

The encouragement and glorification of paid labour and the moral obligation to engage in it implies a shift in dominant political and popular discourse from social citizenship to market citizenship. This shift, in effect, represents a further commodification of citizens since they are increasingly viewed as customers, clients, and consumers (Goetz 1994). At the same time, unpaid work such as caring for children or persons with disabilities is devalued and presented as less legitimate and less socially useful (McAll et al. 1995). The elevation of paid work into an ideal to which all should aspire also represents a transition from a model of social policy based on the male-breadwinner family to a more gender-neutral (or gender-blind) one that focuses on the individual earner. The problem is that gendered work inside the home has not changed much over the decades, but more mothers are now expected to work for pay while retaining their caring roles.

The solutions offered to reduce welfare dependency are variable. Bane and Ellwood (1994) suggest that in the American case the solution should involve a multifaceted approach:

1. targeting never-married young mothers who have not used the welfare system for very long;

2. tough enforcement of child-support responsibilities by non-custodial parents;
3. adequate pay for low-wage workers; and
4. improved support mechanisms such as child and health care and information/counselling services.

In some European countries, the emphasis remains on guaranteed annual incomes, universal childcare programs, and government job creation and training programs (Baker 1995; Bradshaw et al. 1993).

The solutions in our four countries include better enforcement of child support, targeting social services and benefits to low-income families, and initiatives to encourage beneficiaries to move into paid employment. Social benefits are sometimes reduced if recipients do not accept counselling, training, or a job offer, to alter the balance between income derived from social assistance and paid work (Duncan and Edwards 1996). Consequently, social assistance is increasingly becoming conditional on community service, paid work, or enrolment in employability programs (Shragge 1997). 'Work,' which is now defined primarily as paid employment, is becoming a focal point and central criterion of modern forms of citizenship (Cass 1994).

Employability Programs

Employability is not a new concept. In contemporary policy discussions, it refers to schemes designed to improve job-seeking abilities, such as writing résumés, preparing for job interviews, developing better work habits and demeanour, and upgrading educational and job qualifications. These improvements are expected to enhance the prospects of finding a paid job but without necessarily guaranteeing one. Employability is sometimes referred to as a human-resources approach (Torjman 1996).

Since the mid-1980s, all countries in this study have created employment-enhancement initiatives as part of their social-welfare or unemployment programs, either as pilot projects or permanent program reforms. These projects include changing eligibility rules to require beneficiaries to seek or accept paid work earlier than they used to. In addition, some governments (such as U.S. states) are limiting benefits to specified time periods and capping the financial amount of benefits (Millar 1996). Central to employability schemes is the expectation that, with some government assistance, beneficiaries must accept personal responsibility to improve their chances of finding and keeping paid work.

While all four countries have always expected unemployed youth and men to find paid employment as soon as possible, the level of compulsion and the involvement of mothers with pre-school and school-aged children varies by jurisdiction. None of the four countries has created rules as drastic and coercive as those set in place in the United States in 1996, where 50 per cent of the welfare mothers in each state must be working for pay by the year 2002 (Baker 1995, 111–12). In the United States, 'job readiness' programs are popular and involve a significant broadening of the past emphasis on education and job training (Hardina 1997). Improving the economic situation and overall life-chances of welfare recipients such as low-income mothers is viewed as an important policy goal but is also defined primarily as an individualistic labour-market issue. That is, these mothers tend to have poor education and skills for existing job vacancies. If their qualifications are improved, it is assumed that participants will move into paid jobs, increase their family incomes, place fewer demands on state-benefit provision, and escape from poverty. Direct or indirect coercion may be used as an added 'incentive' to accelerate or ensure that the outcomes are deemed 'successful,' as in the reduction in the size of welfare rolls.

Employability programs often reinforce or redefine existing class, race, and gender inequalities, transferring them from the household to the workplace (Leonard 1997). They also alter the accepted boundaries between spheres that used to be considered public and private, and between the state and civil society. The concept of employability encompasses many of the major dilemmas and choices faced by modern welfare states as they respond to pressure groups: should provision be public or private, universal or selective, oriented towards income maintenance or improving life-chances (Ginsborg 1995; Esping-Andersen 1996)?

Voluntary employability programs are based on several assumptions about human motivation and the effects of existing policies on behaviour. Foremost among these is the assumption that people want to work and that accepting paid work is the primary goal of 'rational economic man/woman' (Duncan and Edwards 1996). This assumption is in contrast to the view that welfare recipients, as products of a 'dependency culture,' are lazy, poorly motivated, do not want to work, and therefore need to be encouraged or coerced into doing so (Millar 1996; Le Grand 1997). In the state discourse on voluntary employability programs, motivations of the poor have magically changed: now it is claimed that they *do* want to work but just require encouragement and assistance to do so.

The gender-neutral assertion that 'people want to work' is of great significance in this study. Its achievement is to legitimate a male-centred discourse about what are normal and socially acceptable life patterns and priorities, which happen to revolve around what men have traditionally done – paid work outside the home. As Nancy Fraser (1997, 54) has observed, 'the ideal-typical citizen here is the breadwinner, now nominally gender-neutral.' Caring activity is marginal and residual, to be fitted in around the requirements of paid employment. Women's decisions to receive social welfare or participate in paid work are regarded primarily as economic choices, which can be influenced by adjusting the levels of benefits (Lacroix 1997). Economists, the majority of whom are male and who dominate much of contemporary social policy analysis and discussion, tend to share these assumptions.

In all four countries, employability initiatives increasingly assume that a greater number of citizens have a responsibility to look for or engage in paid work, to pay taxes, and to support their families. The degree of emphasis on this responsibility varies among the countries, and the concept of a universal non-gendered breadwinner is by no means the same in each. Yet there is widespread agreement that citizens need to rely on the state for assistance and that benefits should be temporary and conditional on upgrading skills and making an honest effort to find paid work. 'Clients' are classified according to their willingness or ability to participate in job programs, are directed towards work experience and employment-subsidy programs, and are encouraged to draw up 'action plans' to move off social benefits (Evans 1995). Programs to move people off social benefits and into the workforce, however, can also be compulsory.

Compulsory 'workfare' programs assume that welfare recipients do *not* want to work and so should be compelled to seek job training, community service, or paid employment in return for their welfare cheques. If beneficiaries refuse to participate or to accept a job, their benefits are cut or withdrawn altogether. Historically, the degree of public support for workfare tends to rise during times of high unemployment. It was high during the 1930s Depression (Struthers 1996), and it is once again high in the 1990s. A 1994 Gallup poll reported that 86 per cent of Canadians favoured making welfare recipients accept paid work (Torjman 1996).

The United States has been a recognized leader in workfare programs, with legislation such as the Omnibus Reconciliation Act of 1981 and the Family Support Act (FSA) of 1988 that views benefits as transitional to paid work (Nightingale, Smith, and Haveman 1994). The Personal Responsibility and Work Opportunity Reconciliation Act of 1996 limits welfare benefits to a maximum of five years and requires adults to work or accept job training after two years of welfare. It also expects teenaged mothers to live with their parents and stay in school in order to receive benefits and offers no additional funds for children born to mothers on benefits (Hardina 1997).

The idea behind compulsory employability or workfare programs is that they distinguish between the deserving and undeserving poor. Mothers caring for infants, the injured and the sick, and persons with severe disabilities are usually permitted to rely on government benefits, but others are expected to support themselves with paid work and are considered unworthy of public support. It is assumed that paid work will make welfare recipients independent and will increase their self-respect. Paid work is aggressively promoted as a means of material and moral improvement. Workfare advocates argue that accepting government benefits imposes work obligations on recipients, but their approach also involves an apparent desire to punish welfare recipients for their alleged abuse of the system (Lightman 1995).

Workfare programs are designed to reduce welfare costs, increase the incomes of welfare recipients, create a 'deserving' clientele for public assistance, and draw participants into mainstream society (Evans 1993). Workfare is a form of contract, combining fiscal and work-discipline objectives with a desire to improve social integration. These programs, however, involve expensive monitoring and policing because they tend to hold welfare recipients personally responsible for their own unemployment rather than recognizing that jobs are scarce or difficult to find (Torjman 1996). They also assume that welfare recipients are unaware of their best long-term interests and need assistance or coercion to improve their skills and incomes (Lightman 1995).

Several features set employability-enhancement schemes (both voluntary and compulsory) apart from previous policy responses to unemployment. First, the policy preoccupation with skills training has coincided with increased evidence of the structural barriers to finding paid work, such as the decline in full-time jobs and wages resulting from technological change and globalization of labour markets (Banting et al. 1995; Armstrong 1996; Boyd 1997). By focusing on the improvement of individual skills, governments are implicitly admitting that they will not or cannot deal effectively with the lack of jobs with living wages and the shortage of affordable childcare. Also, the pool of people considered employable has been broadened once again to include persons with disabilities and mothers with young children. At the same time, the government and general public are aware that family circumstances make it difficult for mothers to accept and to retain full-time employment (Beaujot 1997; Ghalam 1997; Matthews and Beaujot 1997).

Second, entitlement to social provision has become increasingly conditional on the beneficiary's willingness to retrain, to search for paid work, and to participate in some type of temporary or permanent-job placement scheme, as it was before the Second World War. During the 1960s and 1970s, there was greater recognition that unpaid work, such as caring for family members or performing voluntary community service, was socially important and should be acknowledged and directly rewarded by governments. Now paid work, governed by the rules and discipline of the capitalist labour market, is considered to be morally and practically superior to receiving entitlements through social programs. In some jurisdictions, especially in Canada, paid work of any kind and at any price seems to be considered superior to caring for one's children at home. While it is acceptable to care for other people's children for a fee, it is not acceptable to care for one's own children out of love or duty and to receive public support. As we will demonstrate in the following chapters, policy priorities in Canada and New Zealand, more than in Australia and the United Kingdom, have focused on lowering benefit levels as well as moving beneficiaries off social-assistance programs.

Third, the rhetoric used by governments to justify social provision has been changing. In the 1990s, eligibility for social benefits is less likely to be based on citizenship or residence or to be considered a social right. Instead, eligibility is now viewed as temporary and contingent, designed to encourage self-sufficiency and employability. Underlying this shift is an increasing emphasis upon market governance and individual responsibility rather than social rights (Pusey 1991; Baker 1997d; Larner 1997).

The Effectiveness of Employability Programs

Reviews of seven voluntary employability programs that grew out of American Omnibus Reconciliation Act of 1981 show that these programs generally led to a modest substitution of earnings for welfare and that they were cost-effective in areas of high job growth. For those without recent market-employment experience, however, the effects on work and earnings were small, although some welfare savings were apparent for the governments. Those who moved off welfare were still poor (Gueron 1990, 1995; Gueron and Pauly 1991; Evans 1992, 1993; Torjman 1996). We should emphasize that these programs were not aimed at lone mothers but welfare recipients in general, and 96 per cent were *not* mandatory 'workfare' but involved voluntary clients.

Shragge (1997) argues that compulsory employability or workfare is a punitive policy with moral overtones and mixed results. In the United States, workfare programs in the 1980s did not have a substantial impact upon overall standard of living, skills development was limited, and the most job-ready individuals were not helped greatly (Gueron 1995). The effects on poverty or welfare dependency were also limited (Nightingale, Smith, and Haveman 1994). Torjman (1996) cites a recent review of U.S. workfare programs that shows little success in improving the quality of employment in schemes that involve mandatory work with little training. When jobs are scarce, workfare programs help create a pool of cheap labour and marginalized workers, who displace existing employees (ibid.). Furthermore, Hardina (1997) notes that workfare programs tend to place people in jobs that do not permit them to escape from the welfare system because these programs necessarily involve low-skilled poorly paid work with few long-term prospects, performed by people with few skills. Self-respect cannot be increased if the job leads nowhere and mandatory work cannot give people more control over their lives (Jacobs 1995). Freiler (1996) also argues that forcing low-income mothers off social benefits and into low-paid work can increase child poverty.

Workfare advocates tend to ignore the barriers to finding and keeping a job. Yet a longitudinal study based on intensive interviews in four U.S. cities has shown how the socio-economic situation of low-income mothers affects their decisions and ability to move into paid work (Edin and Lein 1996). Neither social assistance nor low-wage work provided sufficient funds to meet the subsistence needs of these mothers and their children. Therefore, they made ends meet through a set of survival strategies that included unreported income from side jobs, illegal underground activities such as selling of sex and drugs, and loans and exchanges from their social networks. These activities, however, did not necessarily help them to move into the legitimate labour force. When they accepted low-wage work, it often cost them more than they received from social assistance, since the extra costs for childcare, transportation, clothes, and food outweighed the advantages of accepting a job. Moreover, paid jobs outside the home reduced opportunities to share childcare with neighbours or exchange other services, placing them at a disadvantage within their personal networks. Furthermore, the paid jobs available to these mothers usually devalued their previous life experiences, failed to offer sick leave or paid vacation, and provided unstable income.

Canadian studies by Gorlick and Pomfret (1993) and Lero and Brockman (1993) also indicate the importance of social-support networks, especially the encouragement and assistance of female friends, in influencing economic survival and welfare-exit strategies. Although most low-income mothers wanted to become financially independent and find paid work, they were not all able or prepared to do so immediately. Two-thirds of Canadian lone mothers with children under thirteen did not want to take a job immediately because they felt that they should care for their child at home, they were studying to improve their qualifications, or they had difficulty finding or paying for childcare. Similarly, Oliker (1995) found that the personal lives of low-income single mothers affect their responses to incentives while also shaping their economic decisions and actions. Low-income mothers make decisions about paid work within the context of their family responsibilities and economic constraints.

These studies suggest that expecting beneficiaries to move into paid work is often complicated and risky for low-income mothers and may result in a net financial loss for them and their families. Such complications, which are not always recognized by policy makers or politicians, call into question the insecurity and low pay of available jobs, the shortage of training positions to allow workers to move to better positions, and the psychic damage caused by dead-end and low-paid work. Recognition of these facts also requires an acknowledgment of the lack of child support paid by some non-resident fathers and the inaccessibility of affordable public childcare.

Hardina (1997) notes that lone mothers receiving government benefits have been portrayed as an urgent social problem in the United States. Their presence and numbers were used to justify mandatory work for beneficiaries with young children, limits on benefits for any additional children born into a family on welfare, and the elimination of benefits for teenaged mothers (Goertzel and Cosby 1997). Although the most prevalent components of U.S. workfare are job-readiness programs (such as interviewing skills and résumé writing), there is no empirical evidence that education, job training, job search, or workfare programs are effective in putting people in jobs that help them leave the welfare system (Hardina 1997). Most jobs obtained by former welfare recipients are temporary positions with low wages and do not allow mothers to move off welfare permanently. In recent years, welfare reforms in the four countries have been influenced more by American ideology about employability than by the actual effectiveness of the programs.

Employability Policy: Implications for Low-Income Mothers

Employability as Programs and Practice

Employability initiatives pose difficult questions for low-income mothers, many of whom rely on income-security programs to help raise their children. By the 1970s, governments in the four countries had created social benefits to enable all categories of low-income mothers (including those who had never married) to care for their children at home. Governments now seem less willing to continue these programs as the cost rises. The question remains: Will earned income improve the economic prospects of mothers or will it simply make their lives more difficult? What is a reasonable balance between the rights and responsibilities of citizens who are also mothers with low incomes?

Implicit in employability schemes is the notion that the family with at least one employed parent is the best model of citizenship and thus the one that receives maximum social approval, rights, and benefits. Beneficiaries are being portrayed as willing but frustrated participants in the labour market. This implies that there is a large unsatisfied demand by poor people to move off income-security programs and into paid work, and that mothers place a higher value on paid work than unpaid caring activities. The evidence, however, is inconsistent.

Eligibility for paid employment is, and has been in the past, politically defined and socially constructed, but who is eligible has changed over the years. Although able-bodied adult men were always considered to be employable, both children and married women were legislated or encouraged out of the labour force in the late nineteenth century. Child-labour laws restricted children's access to most paid work, and protective legislation kept women from jobs that were considered dangerous to their health or potential maternity but were also lucrative. Middle-class mothers and low-income widows have been expected to care for their children at home, especially in Australia, New Zealand, and the United Kingdom.

The pool of potential workers is once again growing. In the 1960s and 1970s, students were encouraged to delay entry into the labour force through scholarships, grants, and loans in order to pursue post-secondary education. In the 1990s, however, students are increasingly expected to finance their own education. Many persons with disabilities, considered throughout the 1970s to be unable to work for a living, are now encouraged to take paid work, often with the assistance of comput-erized technologies and supported by new ways of viewing disabilities. In addition, more mothers have been entering the labour force over the past few decades and those who remain at home are seen as the new candidates for employability initiatives.

Given their domestic circumstances, low-income mothers are pre-sented with 'gendered moral rationalities,' that is, decisions based on the various identities and responsibilities they have as paid workers and full-time mothers/homemakers (Duncan and Edwards 1996). In their decisions about paid work, low-income women must consider the avail-ability and cost of transportation and day care, moral beliefs about mothers working, and their own motivations and perceived opportuni-ties (ibid.). Furthermore, they realize that reducing the barriers to labour force entry or re-entry does not necessarily increase the demand for workers.

Rank (1994) reports that social-assistance recipients in Wisconsin repeatedly emphasized their desire to work and to control their own destiny, although this finding could be influenced by social expecta-tions. In Edin and Lein's (1996) American sample, 85 per cent of female respondents wanted to leave welfare for paid work, but only 13 per cent were ready to do so immediately; the rest believed that, given their present circumstances, the costs of going back to work would be too high. About 80 per cent of a sample of 150 Canadian single mothers aspired to leave welfare within five years (Gorlick and Pomfret 1993). Yet they were aware that passage from state support to self support involves considerable risks, such as a lower disposable income and a less secure income for themselves and their families.

Employability discourse assumes that paid employment is the best route out of welfare and will reduce individual and family poverty. Yet a recent review of the evidence in the United Kingdom suggests that get-ting a job does not necessarily guarantee an escape from or even a major alleviation of poverty (Webb, Kemp, and Millar 1996). Labour-market models that make this assumption contain a male bias. Getting a job involves additional work-related expenses that swallow a larger portion of after-tax income for low-wage workers than for higher-wage workers (Pearce 1990). Furthermore, the assumption that paid work will reduce poverty ignores current trends in labour markets in which most new jobs are temporary or low-paid and in which low-wage work does not necessarily lead to better jobs with higher wages (Lochhead 1997). In a competitive and low-wage labour market, women with family responsi-bilities and limited mobility are at a disadvantage compared to other potential employees. A recent multi-country study of lone parents con-cludes that, unless lone mothers can earn an above-average income, they are better off financially receiving social assistance. Marriage, not paid employment, is the more realistic way to improve economic status substantially (Hunsley 1997).

The integration of local economies into global requirements, coupled with the growth in the service sector (especially in part-time jobs), has meant that the market is creating more 'women's jobs' for both men and women, that is, temporary positions with low pay and few employment benefits (Armstrong 1996; Boyd 1997; Larner 1997). Employability schemes such as the one now in place in the United Kingdom ('Welfare-to-Work') can be negated by a 'revolving door labour market' in which employees are shuffled between temporary dead-end jobs and spells on government benefits. In fact, a recent British study found that two-thirds of people on government employability schemes end up back on benefits within nine months (Denny and Elliott 1997).

Some countries (such as the Netherlands and Australia) encourage women to remain at home with their children for extended lengths of time, while others (such as Sweden and the United States) expect that women will enter the labour force as soon as possible after childbirth (Baker 1996). These are two substantially different models for defining the employability of mothers, yet within each model one can find juris-dictions that provide high levels of public support and others where social provision is minimal. Whether or not mothers are considered to be 'employable' does not determine their poverty rates, for these rates differ substantially between Australia and the Netherlands, as they do between Sweden and the United States (ibid.). Instead, women's pov-erty rates can be reduced by generous and comprehensive cash transfers and tax concessions for families with children. They can also be lowered by high wages and statutory employment benefits such as pay equity, parental benefits, and leave for family responsibilities, as well as the availability of childcare, public health insurance, and unemployment benefits (Wennemo 1994; Baker 1996).

Employability discourse contains the implicit assumption that participating in paid work will generate common orientations towards the value of work, shared identities with the larger community, and an enhanced sense of social integration. Yet the adequacy of jobs and the provision of childcare shape and constrain people's thoughts, strategies, choices, and actions. Designers of employability programs assume that positive attitudes and strong work motivation is enough, but, even if these assumptions are correct, how to maintain motivation over time remains a challenge.

Julian Le Grand (1997) has observed that the contemporary transition in many countries towards quasi-markets in social provision and away from high taxation and social security is underpinned by a philosophical shift in assumptions regarding how and why people behave. Citizens are assumed to be self-interested economic actors who will make decisions that maximize their economic advantage. Employability combines moral and material work incentives for the individual: work is good for you, and work provides you with a larger income. This can be considered as a very top-down and male perspective that has little supporting evidence.

To what extent and how people respond to incentives and disincentives is more assumed than proven (ibid. 149). This assumption is linked to the elevation of working for pay outside the home as a principal societal value, to be highly esteemed and rewarded. Paid work outside the home (done primarily by adult men) is superior to unpaid work within it (done primarily by women), and the former contains elements of self-discipline and moral superiority lacking in the latter. There is little acknowledgment that incentives and disincentives vary by socio-economic circumstances, the nature of informal support networks, women's own identities, and their sense of responsibility as mothers providing resources for the household.

Employability programs also contain implicit assumptions about the composition of families, the nature of family dynamics, and what constitutes 'good mothering' and 'responsible family behaviour' (Millar 1996). While there is great diversity of views in every country concerning what is acceptable, dominant views are embodied in policy. These include views on gender-appropriate work and how it is to be supported by government. In countries such as the United Kingdom, Australia, and New Zealand, with strong histories of male breadwinners and female caregivers, it has been increasingly acceptable for mothers with school-aged children to be employed part-time. Full-time employment is still thought to interfere with childrearing and homemaking responsibilities (Millar 1996, 185). New Zealand announced changes in its benefit rules in 1998 to encourage greater employability among beneficiaries, but those changes related to low-income mothers were later rescinded.

Employability programs assume, too, that the economic savings from unpaid welfare benefits will not be exceeded by other costs paid for or subsidized by the state, such as upgrading basic education, skills training, and childcare services. Governments can avoid this problem by requiring others to provide these services: such as informal networks, voluntary organizations, or the market. Yet researchers have concluded that employability programs without sufficient training and without childcare services have not been effective (Torjman 1996).

Employability advocates tend to assume that labour markets will be amenable to the needs of job seekers, yet these schemes tend to idealize or misrepresent the realities of job markets (Deniger et al. 1995; Nightingale, Smith, and Haveman 1994). Many advocates of greater employability assume that the market will provide what is needed, and that a detailed analysis of the current job market and future opportunities is secondary to improving individual qualifications. This last assumption raises the issue of the political economy of employability. Candidates for employability programs tend to be among the most socially marginalized, and these programs can be seen as new mechanisms for managing marginalization and enforcing social control rather than fully integrating beneficiaries into the workforce (Lord 1994; Deniger et al. 1995).

Feminist research indicates that neither caring for children on a state benefit nor working for pay allows many low-income mothers to escape from poverty (Doherty, Friendly, and Oloman 1998). In order to deal with women's poverty, policies need to improve the availability and subsidization of childcare services. Minimum wages and wage supplements need to increase, and policies of full employment need to be reinstated. The unemployed require better information and community-development schemes to support them in their search for work. Communities and voluntary organizations are limited in the amount and kinds of assistance they can offer, but mothers who receive family and community support tend to do better in employment-enhancement programs than those without this support (Conseil de la famille 1997). Greater participation in caregiving and housework by men needs to be encouraged. Women require better training opportunities leading to full-time employment (Pearce 1990; Gorlick and Pomfret 1993; Evans 1993; Lero and Brockman 1993; Cass 1994; Torjman 1996). Programs also need to be tailored to respond to the diverse circumstances of participants, including community work and personal-development courses (Gorlick 1996; Conseil de la famille 1997).

The evidence suggests that a focus on enhancing the employability of individual beneficiaries would make good policy sense in a thriving economy creating many new jobs with living wages, with low unemployment rates, extensive public childcare, preventive social services, and minimal wage inequalities between men and women. Yet these conditions are not currently present in any of the four countries of this study.

Employability as Ideology

Employability initiatives also contain ideological elements in that they intersect with the neo-liberal vision of a greater role for private markets in social decision making, reduced citizen's rights and expectations of state assistance, and increased responsibility on the part of each individual for his or her own life (Jenson and Phillips 1996). A complex relationship exists between political ideologies and social practices (Ginsborg 1995, 251), especially in conditions of social change. As we shall see, each of the four countries has different ideological legacies that influence how their policies are conceived, articulated, and implemented. These legacies relate to socially acceptable family structures, ideas about good mothering, appropriate roles for women and men, and how these concepts are justified and reinforced through policy and practice.

In restructuring efforts, the nature and the role of 'the public' is being gradually yet persistently altered on the ideological level. Long-standing ideas of the collective interest are being supplanted in official political discourse by notions that citizens are individual consumers with no a priori claims on social provision from the state, and that they increasingly should look to private support such as the family, community, and voluntary organizations (Baker 1997b, 18). This is reinforced by the view that social spending must now be justified, not in terms of fairness and income redistribution, but in terms of its potential for human capital investment and its ability to increase opportunities for individuals (Taylor-Gooby 1997). Liberal welfare states become more residual in influencing social outcomes, and social class and inequality are no longer regarded as significant constraints on improving life chances and market status. Instead, the guiding ideological themes are personal responsibility for success and failure, and individual abilities and efforts.

Employability initiatives can also be examined from the perspective of their possible effects, intended or unintended, upon the personal and social identities of participants. Identities are socially constructed and partly reinforced within the realm of political discourse (Jenson 1993). The identities of mothers on benefits are frequently tied to the traditional idea that women can be 'good mothers' only when they remain in the home to care for their family. At the same time, government support for these caring activities is shrinking. Indeed, in countries such as Canada, childcare is considered to be work only when it is done outside families (Baker 1996). This low value placed on caring diminishes the identities of mothers at home.

As early as the 1960s, the United States changed its policy to prevent low-income mothers from receiving state support to raise their children at home. The means-tested Aid to Families with Dependent Children (AFDC) program was modified in 1967 to encourage mothers to enter the labour force through participation in training programs. Workfare to end 'welfare dependency' was made widespread by the Omnibus Reconciliation Act of 1981 and was pushed farther by the 1988 Family Support Act. Even in its early phases, the AFDC was defined in many states to classify most mothers as 'employable' regardless of job opportunities (Abramovitz 1989). These policies began to change ideas about good mothering so that it now includes the ability to support one's children financially as well as emotionally. Yet poverty rates remain high among lone mothers.

How are the identities of women 'mobilized discursively' so that they will view getting and retaining a paid job as a driving force in their lives? Larner (1997), in a discussion of New Zealand's neo-liberal reforms of the 1980s and 1990s, has suggested that the emphasis upon market governance 'involves the formation and reformation of the capacities and attributes of both collective and individual forms of self.' The increased emphasis on pulling or pushing low-income mothers into the workforce through employability schemes encourages low-income women to change their self and social identities, reinforced by prevailing economic contexts. That is, low-income mothers are invited to see themselves less as recipients of state aid to support a household with dependent children and more as self-supporting members of the labour force.

Employability programs portray mothers at home as potential and actual burdens on the taxpayer and the state, and encourage these mothers to be seen and to define themselves as potential workers who must support themselves and their children (Brodie 1996b). Once women are defined as employable individuals and not solely as mothers, then they become 'welfare dependants' in need of therapy and rehabilitation by the state so that they can become 'productive' members of society (ibid.). In addition, employed mothers are encouraged to see themselves as making a valid societal contribution, rather than being engaged solely in childcare at taxpayer expense (which is not 'real' work). Employability, then, is another arrow in neo-liberalism's quiver by which governments seek to redefine their roles and obligations towards their citizens.

Identity is related to social circumstances and is shaped through thought, discourse, and practice. In fact, people have multiple identities that can be contradictory and transitory and do not necessarily make sense to outsiders. Employability programs ask low-income mothers to assume new identities as employees too quickly without adequate social support, for they often must deal with emotional and physical responsibilities which many men do not have to shoulder by virtue of their lack of involvement in domestic chores (Larner 1997). A transition in identities is assumed to be something that can be accomplished if one has the will and aptitude to do it, yet many of these mothers have limited job skills and work habits and lack confidence (Conseil de la Famille 1997).

How should mothers allocate their time between paid and unpaid work? What choices do they have and what support will they receive from state, community resources, and their own networks for various options? Inequalities of power and opportunity between mothers and fathers and parents and non-parents abound in the absence of employment-equity programs, leave for family responsibilities, and childcare services. In employability programs, little consideration is given to mothers' views and values, such as the importance that raising their own children at home might have for their sense of self-worth and the opportunities that childrearing provides for autonomy and self-affirmation (Deniger et al. 1995). Low-income mothers are objects for policy, increasingly required to behave in ways dictated by governments.

Conclusion

A recurring theme in this chapter is the pervasiveness of gender inequality within families, workplaces, and policy initiatives. When social programs either assume that women are men's economic dependants or base eligibility upon labour-force participation, then women without male partners and women without employment are at a structural disadvantage (Lewis 1993; Baker 1996). Furthermore, the outcomes of employability programs tend to be different depending on gender, age, and work experience.

The neo-liberal view of the 'modernization' of social provision contains some misrepresentations about the daily life experiences of women and men, the nature of family life, and the labour market. Beneficiaries are viewed as dependants who may or may not be unwilling to work, but many are already working hard to raise their children. An alternative view, arising from an understanding of the gendered division of labour in both paid and unpaid work, would question why low-income mothers – whether partnered or not – can seldom support themselves and their children without government assistance. The answer to that question would lead back to difficult historical questions:

1. Why are there so many jobs that do not pay a living wage?
2. Why are childbearing and caring granted a lower social value than paid work?
3. Why do inequalities exist between men's and women's wages?
4. Why is work that is performed by women so often undervalued?
5. Why do women form the bulk of the part-time workforce? and
6. Why do disparities remain virtually unaltered between men and women in household labour despite the influx of mothers into the labour force? (Baker 1996).

All four countries are encouraging beneficiaries to leave social assistance and enter paid work, yet there are significant national variations in ideology and practice. In this book, we explain why certain models and policies arose and have become accepted at particular times in the different countries, and what ideologies and assumptions support these policies. Employability schemes exist in each country within a complex and diverse set of social-assistance programs, which have a bearing on the lives of low-income mothers. The next four chapters will analyse recent policy developments in Canada, Australia, New Zealand, and the United Kingdom and how they have affected the economic well-being of low-income mothers.

3

Government Debt and Policy Choices: Restructuring in Canada

Introduction

In this chapter, we discuss attempts, mostly successful, to restructure the Canadian welfare state by both Conservative and Liberal governments[1] since 1984. These reforms were largely justified by neo-liberal arguments that Canada had no choice but to reduce government expenditures because the public debt was so high that interest payments were crippling government efforts to finance present and future programs (Courchene and Stewart 1992). The restructurers of the Canadian welfare state suggested that high public debt was caused primarily by the expansion of social programs throughout the 1960s and 1970s. Yet many other factors contributed to government debt and deficit than the expansion of social programs.

The Canadian public debt (both federal and provincial) grew substantially from the 1970s because of several factors. The Canadian tax structure was reformed by both Liberal and Conservative governments, which reduced public revenue. Global changes in labour markets created higher unemployment rates and government policies tolerated high inflation and high unemployment (Mimoto and Cross 1991). In addition, debt increased as the aging population generated more pensioners, more lone-parent families required income support, and ineffective child-support programs failed to enforce support payments by separated and divorced fathers. Nevertheless, a remarkable degree of political consensus has cut across party lines, focusing on 'generous' social programs as the main cause of high debt. The solution is thought to be smaller government, social programs targeted to the most needy, and more reliance on families and voluntary organizations for caring services.

Employers' groups, business organizations,[2] financiers of government debt, and other adherents of the political right have used the ideology of economic rationalism to promote global trade and higher profits for the private sector. Furthermore, these groups have successfully persuaded governments and right-wing opposition parties (such as the Reform Party of Canada) that unemployment is voluntary, that the private sector can create more jobs if taxes are low and capital can move freely across borders, and that public policies that benefit the business sector also help to keep the entire nation prosperous (Cameron 1997). Neo-liberals continue to argue that Canadians have become too dependent on state benefits and need to become more self-reliant. Within this ideology, the solution to 'welfare dependency' is the promotion of 'employability,' social programs to train welfare recipients and encourage them to make the transistion to paid employment.

Although both Conservative and Liberal governments have used economic rationalism to justify program reforms, dismantling social programs has been motivated by far more than concern about high public debt and welfare dependency. We demonstrate in this chapter that political reasons such as disputes between the federal and provincial governments and fear that the Quebec separatist movement will shatter the Canadian federation have also been motives in program reform. Yet, rather than focusing on the political necessity for reform, both Conservative and Liberal governments have often used 'objective' economic arguments to gain greater acceptance for their policies. By using the discourse of economic rationalism and through careful timing of reforms, the federal government has been able to make dramatic changes to Canadian decision-making structures and popular social programs.

We argue in this chapter that further restructuring will be hastened by several structural changes to the state and to funding arrangements between the federal and provincial governments. Especially important for low-income mothers is the 1996 change in the way that social assistance is funded, from matched funding to block funding. This will lead to further decentralization of decision making or 'constitutional change by stealth' (Battle 1995), the elimination of national program standards, and further cuts in services and benefits which will disproportionately affect low-income individuals and families. Reducing federal grants will also decrease the possibility of future program expansion promised by the Liberals in their 1993 election campaign. Although the Liberals eliminated the annual federal deficit by 1998, both the rhetoric and the cuts continue.

This chapter will illustrate that the growing assault on 'welfare dependency' under the banner of social-program reform does not take sufficient account of labour-market conditions or gender relations in paid and unpaid work.

Debt and the Canadian Welfare State

As we noted in chapter 1, Esping-Andersen (1990) classifies Canada, Australia, and Britain (along with the United States) as liberal welfare regimes, emphasizing their similar reliance on means-testing, modest benefit levels, and a residual welfare state. Baker (1995), however, argues that this classification might be less appropriate for family-related programs than for retirement pensions or labour-market programs. Other researchers have noted substantial differences in the social programs of welfare states classified as 'liberal' (Mitchell 1991 and 1992; Eardley et al. 1996a; Saunders 1994; Castles 1996). Australia and New Zealand created a male wage earner's welfare state while the Canadian government limited poverty and inequality through social transfers from the federal government to both provincial governments and to individuals (Myles 1996).

Several national programs were developed in Canada, most when the Liberals were in power, involving social insurance or cost-sharing with the provinces to deal with unemployment, sickness, maternity, disability, retirement from paid work, and low income (Guest 1997). The constitution had to be changed to enable the federal government to become involved in provincial jurisdiction (McGilly 1998). Until recently, the federal government also paid universal old age security and family allowances directly to individuals and families as citizenship entitlements. This system of 'fiscal federalism,' which was based on attempts to promote national unity and alleviate regional disparities through federal transfer payments, became the foundation for the construction of the welfare state in post-war Canada (Banting 1987; Jenson 1990).

Canada's physical proximity to the United States has the potential to enable the easy flow of ideas, products, and capital between the two countries. Historically, however, Canadians modelled their social programs after Britain's and distinguished themselves from Americans by their more generous welfare state (Guest 1997). Political Toryism in Canada regarded the state as a major participant in economic development and as a mediator between citizens and the full impact of the marketplace, and accordingly it accepted the establishment of national social programs to provide health services and protect people from loss of wages through unemployment, sickness, and maternity. At the same time, while trade barriers and immigration laws limited the flow of products and people, skilled labour, capital, and manufactured goods always moved easily from the United States to Canada. In return, Canada exported raw materials to be processed in the United States.

Since the 1980s, ideas and capital from the United States to Canada flowed even more freely with the continental and global approach to trade and business of the Mulroney Conservative government. The appearance of the Reform Party, based in western Canada, on the national political stage in the late 1980s further buttressed the political right by acting as a conduit for American-style anti-state ideas. During the same period, the influence of trade unions declined and the political left, traditional supporters of a national economy and a strong welfare state, was eroded.[3] Large corporations placed strong pressures on governments to reduce business costs and to create an 'equal playing field' with harmonized rules for employers in both countries (Banting 1992; Cameron 1997). One result of this pressure was the signing of a free-trade agreement between Canada and the United States in 1988, later enlarged to include Mexico. Another result has been widespread acceptance of the neo-liberal view that any government regulation of employment, including social-security contributions ('payroll taxes'), minimum wages, and pay-equity legislation, is bad for business.

The organizing themes and discourses of the American new right, concerning the destructive dependency of the welfare state and citizens' responsibilities, were popularized and made more acceptable by Canadian conservatives, especially those in the Reform Party (Brodie 1996a). These themes complemented continentalist economic policies of free trade, presented as a necessary reform to deal with globalization and international trading blocs. Moreover, the United States placed substantial pressure on Canada to 'harmonize' many of its welfare-state policies, using the argument that welfare-state generosity can be a form of unfair economic subsidy.

Over the past two decades, Canadian governments (both Liberal and Conservative) have reformed the tax structure in an attempt to make the country more conducive to business investment. In these reforms, governments have reduced corporate taxes but raised personal income taxes for the middle class, thereby limiting the growth of tax revenue (Mimoto and Cross 1991; Banting 1992). This has been done during a period of increasing unemployment (that has hovered around 10 per cent), growing poverty among women in the wake of rising divorce rates, and mounting concern about 'child poverty,'[4] all of which revealed the market's failure to provide income security (Myles 1996). The increasing need for social protection required higher levels of social spending (Myles 1996). In addition, governing costs rose with inflation throughout the 1970s and 1980s, and high interest rates required more resources to finance the growing federal debt and deficit. This growing deficit encouraged the Conservative government to introduce a goods and services tax (GST) in 1989, despite widespread opposition from small business, the Liberal Party, the New Democratic Party (NDP) and anti-poverty groups.

Throughout the 1980s and early 1990s, a consensus was apparent among centre and right parties (Conservative, Reform, and Liberal), which dominated the federal Parliament, that the most important policy priority was to control and reduce the deficit. Canadians received several well-publicized visits from New Zealand politicians, officials, and experts who lectured Canadians about the dire consequences of 'hitting the debt wall.' The 'New Zealand Experiment' quickly became a model to be studied closely by Canadian conservatives. Although there was general public acceptance that the deficit had to be reduced, the main debate was over how this should be accomplished and at what pace.

By the 1990s, Canada's government debt and deficit were still higher than those of most other OECD countries. In the period to 1983, the Canadian public debt was similar to that of other OECD nations – about 50 per cent of GDP. By 1994, the public debt had reached 95 per cent of GDP (Armitage 1996; OECD 1994, 44), but, after major government cutbacks (and lower interest rates), the debt declined to 72 per cent by 1997 (Mendelson 1998). The government deficit (expenditure minus revenue) was only 1.8 per cent of GDP in 1961, had increased to 6.8 in 1985, and by 1992 had fallen only slightly to 6.7 (Richards 1994, 41). After several years of economic growth and severe cutbacks by the Liberals, the federal government's deficit was eliminated in 1998.

The political right insisted on social-spending cuts and viewed the cost of social programs as the main reason why spending was 'out of control.' Yet, compared with other OECD countries and even to the United Kingdom and New Zealand, social spending in Canada as a percentage of GDP was not particularly high in the 1980s or 1990s. For example, Canadian social spending in 1980 was about 13 per cent of GDP but it was over 18 per cent in New Zealand and the United Kingdom. In 1992 Canada's social spending was nearly 20 per cent while the

United Kingdom's had increased to nearly 23 percent (OECD 1996a). However, compared to countries such as Sweden (Rehn 1985), Canada has always spent more on 'passive' employment programs such as unemployment insurance than on job-creation and training programs.

The political right believes that the private sector, functioning in self-regulating and efficient markets, would create more new jobs if payroll and income taxes were kept low, although evidence on this point is not yet compelling. Furthermore, it believes that Canadian employees would work harder and be more willing to accept certain jobs if they could not rely on 'generous' social programs. In making this argument, the right points to relatively low unemployment rates in the United States.

The political left, on the other hand, has argued that Canadian social spending and tax rates are both moderate compared to many European nations. The left admits that, although social spending has not grown as fast as it has in countries such as Sweden, it has increased since the 1960s. But the programs created in the late 1960s (Medicare, the Canada Pension Plan, maternity benefits, and so on) have provided a social safety net for unemployed people or those unable to work because of old age, disabilities, or childcare responsibilities. Further, while both income tax and payroll tax rates are moderate in Canada compared to many European nations (Baker 1995, 133), the left points out that in the last decade taxes have increased for middle-income Canadians but not for high-income earners. The left wants tax reforms to 'make corporations and the rich pay their fair share.' It has also argued for government job-creation programs and publicly funded childcare services to increase employment and therefore tax revenue.

The feeling is widespread that Canadians are 'taxed to the max.' Canada is deftly and frequently compared to the United States, which has among the lowest taxes of OECD countries. Indeed, it is striking that, in the Canadian political and ideological arena, comparisons with the United States and less frequently with New Zealand are virtually the only ones that are considered relevant. Alternatives drawn from other countries (especially European ones) are sharply circumscribed and considered irrelevant to the North American context (Baker 1997e). This transition from a national to continental North American context in the last ten years is an important aspect of the structuring of Canadian public-policy discussions.

In the 1993 federal election, the Conservatives were soundly defeated and were left with only two seats in the House of Commons. The victorious Liberals, who won the election with the slogan 'Jobs! Jobs! Jobs!,' immediately began a social-security review, widely consulting experts and advocacy groups from the left and the right. Government departments were reorganized; the welfare (or income security) component of the Department of Health and Welfare was linked with employment issues in a new department called Human Resources Development. The new Minister (Lloyd Axworthy) appeared genuinely interested in reducing child poverty and family violence and improving childcare services, but his objectives were overridden by a Cabinet decision to cut social spending. Just when many Canadians believed that social programs would be improved and modernized, the social-security review was shelved and the cuts began. The public surprise with this policy turn was similar to that which occurred in New Zealand following Labour's election in 1984 (Kelsey 1995).

Before we analyse the details and implications of this development, we should first outline the history of Canadian social programs. This brief outline will reveal that, although the Mulroney Conservative government initiated considerable reform from 1984 until 1993, the subsequent Liberal government continued and augmented this approach, all with little change in political rhetoric (Pulkingham and Ternowetsky 1997b, 15).

A Brief Overview of Federal Social Programs

Under the Canadian constitution, jurisdiction is divided between the federal and provincial governments. Labour legislation (including minimum wages and employment leave), job training, social-assistance programs, social services,[5] education, health services, and family law (but not divorce law) are provincial jurisdiction. Unlike in Australia, where collective bargaining used to be centralized and the federal government remains responsible for income-support programs, Canadians may receive quite different levels of wages and benefits in one province compared to another. Yet the Canadian constitution has allowed the federal government to maintain 'spending power' in areas of provincial jurisdiction. This means that, if the provinces accept federal money, they must abide by federal restrictions on how this money is spent. This aspect of the constitution has led to numerous disputes over jurisdiction, which continue to the present (Guest 1997; McGilly 1998).

Although employment was initially considered provincial jurisdiction, the constitution was amended in the 1930s to allow a national unemployment-insurance program (UI) (Guest 1997). This program began in 1941 with contributions from the federal government, employers, and employees, but it is now based only on contributions from employers and employees, paying up to 60 per cent of previous wages to a maximum amount. In 1971 the Liberals amended the UI Act to include sickness and maternity benefits. In 1985 the Conservative government added adoption benefits, and, after a Supreme Court challenge based on equality rights,[6] it added ten weeks of parental benefits for either parent employed at childbirth. Major restructuring has taken place with UI in recent years under the Liberal government, as we show later.

The first mothers' allowance in Canada was established in 1916 in Manitoba, but only for 'morally upright' women with dependent children (Ursel 1992). Other provinces soon followed in providing such benefits (Evans 1992; Little 1998). In 1945 the Canadian government created a federal family allowance for all families with children under sixteen (later raised to eighteen) that was paid monthly to mothers, regardless of their family income or labour-force status. There was also a child-tax deduction, originating in 1918 when the federal Income Tax Act was passed. This deduction was revised over the years and additional child-tax concessions were developed by the Liberal government during the 1970s (Baker 1995). The Conservative government made major changes to federal child benefits in December 1992, outlined later in this chapter.

In 1951 Canada created a universal and federal old age pension, which also required a constitutional amendment relating to jurisdiction. Since 1926, there had been a means-tested old age pension administered by the provinces but cost-shared with the federal government. The 1951 Old Age Security (OAS) was financed through general revenue and administered by the federal government, and in 1967 the Liberal government added a means-tested Guaranteed Income Supplement (GIS) for low-income seniors. Both OAS and GIS have been indexed quarterly to the Consumer Price Index. In 1996, the Liberals announced that old age security would be replaced with targeted benefits (discussed in the section on restructuring later in this chapter), but they were later forced to rescind this proposal after public opposition.

In the late 1950s and early 1960s, Canada's Medicare program was developed by the Liberals, after recommendations from two royal commissions and considerable pressure from the social-democratic Co-operative Commonwealth Federation (CCF; later the NDP), especially in the province of Saskatchewan. This program initially involved national guidelines and federal-provincial cost-sharing for provincial hospital and medical services. Yet in 1977 this cost-sharing was changed to block grants from the federal to provincial government, regardless of provincial costs. In 1996 funding for Medicare was merged with social services and post-secondary education.

Although social assistance and social services were always provincial jurisdiction, the Canada Assistance Plan (CAP) was established in 1966, which was a cost-sharing agreement between the federal and provincial governments. In this agreement, the federal government agreed to match, dollar for dollar, eligible social-assistance expenditures as long as programs were based on financial need rather than any work requirement, offered an appeal procedure, and allowed beneficiaries to move between provinces without penalty. When the original agreement ended in 1996, however, CAP was replaced by the Canada Health and Social Transfer (CHST), the new funding arrangement for medicare, social assistance, and post-secondary education. We will discuss the details of these changes later in this chapter.

The Canadian welfare state was developed from the 1940s until the 1970s but since the late 1970s there have been no new national programs except those created from merging (and reducing) existing ones. Although the Liberal Party formed the government when all these social programs were introduced, they have played a major role, along with the Conservatives, in restructuring them. The Reform Party has pressured both governments in recent years to reduce public spending and 'balance the books,' while the NDP has argued to retain and improve the 'social safety net.' At the same time, the Parti Québécois has pressured the federal government for more control over social programs. In the next section, we will discuss details of provincial social-assistance programs and how they have affected low-income mothers.

Provincial Social-Assistance Programs

Social-assistance programs are designed and operated by the provincial, territorial, and municipal governments with financial assistance from Ottawa. These programs, known as 'welfare,' include benefits for the long-term unemployed and the 'unemployable,'[7] usually between the ages of eighteen and sixty-five, and have been based on a needs test. This test compares the budgetary needs of an applicant and any dependants with the assets and income of the household (National Council of Welfare 1997b).

Although each province was assigned responsibility for its own programs of public assistance from the beginning of confederation, the provinces originally passed many of these costs on to the municipalities and to private charities. In 1913 the municipalities paid about 53 per cent of public-welfare costs (excluding 'relief' or unemployment benefits), the provinces paid about 30 per cent, and the federal government paid about 17 per cent (Ursel 1992, 170). Benefits were minimal and highly stigmatized, based on a residual notion of the welfare state, namely, the idea that the state should not interfere with family life unless it was clear that the family could not or would not provide and protect its members. By the 1930s, the division of expenditures was nearly equal among the three levels of government.

Responsibility for funding social programs gradually shifted from 1900 to the 1970s from local and provincial governments to cost-sharing arrangements between the federal and provincial governments (ibid). As marriage breakdown and unemployment became more prevalent, living costs increased, and social-service costs rose, the provinces pressured the federal government for more financial assistance. As noted above, in 1966 the Canada Assistance Plan was signed, in which the federal government agreed to pay 50 per cent of provincial welfare costs if they fit into federal guidelines of eligible expenditures. Provinces were required to base social assistance solely on financial need and could not ask beneficiaries to perform community service or work for their benefit. The provinces were also required to provide an appeal procedure.

CAP was designed to provide income to meet the cost of basic requirements of a single person or family when all other financial resources have been exhausted. Most provinces created a single unified program, but three provinces[8] retained a two-tiered system where long-term benefits (such as for sole-support parents) are paid by the province while short-term and emergency aid is paid by municipality (in these cases, there is a residence requirement). The development of CAP allowed the provinces to expand social-assistance programs to include low-income seniors, persons with disabilities, unemployed persons ineligible for federal unemployment insurance, and lone parents (Baker 1995). Childcare subsidies for low-income families were also included in CAP, but throughout the 1980s childcare advocates argued that more spaces and higher subsidies were needed (Friendly 1994).

In 1987, several months before an expected election call, the federal (Conservative) government proposed a National Strategy on Child Care, including higher tax deductions for employed parents and a new national program which would 'take child care out of welfare funding' (CAP). Initially, this appeared to be an exception to the Conservative agenda of cutting social expenditures. The tax increases were implemented but the new funding arrangement for childcare failed to pass through the Senate. It became apparent that fewer subsidies would eventually be available in those provinces currently spending the most money on childcare (Ontario and Quebec) and that public money would be used to finance for-profit care. When the 1988 election was called, the Child Care Bill died. Critics argued that the government had no intention of allowing it to pass but were trying 'to score political points' with women voters before the election (Baker 1995, 202).

By the end of the 1980s, most provinces had also tightened their child-support enforcement procedures, especially for welfare recipients, focusing on 'making fathers pay' and catching 'dead-beat dads' or fathers who defaulted on their payments (Mackie 1994). The rhetoric surrounding these reforms stressed both 'enforcing parental responsibilities' and 'reducing child poverty,' but there was little discussion why some parents fail to support their children, and what is the best solution to family poverty. In reality, programs to enforce child support were designed to save social-assistance money. Unlike in Australia but similar to Britain, none of the new enforcement schemes in Canada allows mothers on social assistance to keep any of the child-support money paid by the father. This means that, although the provincial government saves money, welfare women and their children are no better off financially and child poverty is not reduced (Zweibel 1993, 1995).

Despite the establishment of CAP, welfare rates have always varied substantially by province and fall well below poverty lines[9] in all jurisdictions. For example, couples on social assistance with two children would receive 48 per cent of poverty-line income if they lived in New Brunswick in 1996, but up to 69 per cent in Prince Edward Island or Ontario. Welfare incomes varied as a percentage of average provincial income for couples with two children from 26 per cent in New Brunswick to 35 per cent in Prince Edward Island (National Council of Welfare 1997b).

The lack of welfare generosity in some provinces relates to high unemployment rates, low economic growth, and a lower per-capita tax base, but also to a more punitive philosophy about why people need assistance and what role the state should play in personal life. Controversies continue about how to fund growing welfare costs, how to help those in need without dampening work incentives and encouraging dependency, how much income recipients really need, and how to ensure that they do not abuse the system.

Between 1974 and 1990, the real value of 'welfare income' (including provincial social-assistance, the federal Family Allowance, and federal and provincial tax credits) grew by 32 per cent. At the same time, social-assistance income (which accounted for 88 per cent of 'welfare income') grew at an average of 27 per cent in all of Canada. Yet the per-capita income of Canadians increased by only 20 per cent over the same period, leading to a public perception that welfare recipients in Canada are relatively well-off. Yet in 1990 a lone mother solely dependent on government transfers still had a cash income equal to only three-quarters of the poverty-line income (Dooley 1995).

From 1986 to 1995, welfare benefits fluctuated considerably by province. In Alberta (with a Conservative government), benefits declined by 41.6 per cent for a single employable person, by 22.4 per cent for single parents with one child, and by 17 per cent for a couple with two children. In Ontario (with Liberal and NDP governments), benefits increased by 15.3 per cent for a single employable person, by 16.7 per cent for a single parent with one child, and by 20.7 per cent for a couple with two children. Yet, from 1994 to 1995, after Ontario voters elected a Conservative government, benefits fell by 7.1 per cent for a single employable person, by 7.2 per cent for single parents, and by 7.8 per cent for couples with two children (ibid.). In 1995 welfare benefits, including those for sole mothers, were cut once again by 22 per cent (Evans 1996).

Throughout the 1980s, the taxback rate for welfare recipients who earned above their small exemption varied from 75 per cent to 100 per cent (Battle and Torjman 1993; NCW 1993). This meant that they could not increase their earnings and still continue to receive social assistance. It was difficult for low-income individuals to escape 'welfare dependency,' especially if they had to pay for childcare services. Many researchers saw this as a deterrent to moving welfare recipients into the workforce and an encouragement of black-market earnings. Yet conservative critics felt that allowing recipients to keep more of their earnings was too generous and was giving them a 'free ride' compared to low-income earners not receiving government benefits.

Although many Canadians see welfare rates as 'generous,' cross-national research confirms that they are not, as we indicated in table 1.13 and 1.14 in chapter 1. If we compare the net disposable income of lone parents with one child living on social assistance (after housing costs), their 1992 income was lower in Canada than in Australia, New Zealand, and the United Kingdom (Eardley et al. 1996a, 126). If we make the same comparison for two-parent families, Canadian families on social assistance have lower disposable incomes than comparable families in Australia and the United Kingdom but higher than in New Zealand. Nevertheless, Canadian benefits are considerably lower than those of many European countries (Baker 1995; Eardley et al. 1996a).

For families on social assistance, housing costs are factored into welfare payments, but most recipients must obtain private rental housing. Several provinces (such as Quebec and Manitoba) have provided cash assistance for the housing needs of families with children. However, 35 per cent of all renting households in Canada spent more than a third of their income on shelter costs in 1991 and only 5 per cent of households received rental subsidies. Mother-led families are more likely than others to pay rent and more likely to spend over a third of their income on housing costs. Yet only 11 per cent of lone mothers received housing subsidies in 1990. During the 1960s and 1970s, federal housing programs rapidly expanded, but in recent years such funding has been reduced. Consequently, many low-income families must spend a disproportionate amount of their income on housing (Baker and Phipps 1997, 171).

Mothers, Employment, and Social Assistance

The categorization of low-income people into employable and unemployable has a long history in Canada. As early as 1920, some Canadian provinces[10] began paying mothers' allowances to low-income widows and deserted mothers who were considered to be 'morally worthy' or 'deserving' (Little 1995). These women were considered to be unemployable because they had childrearing responsibilities, but benefits were low by today's standards. If a woman lived with a male partner, her welfare benefits were discontinued because he was assumed to be financially responsible for her and her children.

Before the 1960s, few policy efforts addressed women's employment aspirations or needs because her job was considered to be childrearing and homemaking (Lord 1994). Female labour-force participation rates were low, especially for mothers with pre-school children. Furthermore, lone-parent families formed a small percentage of all families until the divorce law was liberalized in 1968 and until more single women began keeping their babies in the 1970s and 1980s (Baker 1993). Also, few part-time jobs or childcare services were available to enable mothers to combine childrearing with paid employment. Consequently, low-income partnered mothers accepted paid work at home (such as taking in laundry or dressmaking) or found part-time employment. When lone mothers were employed, they tended to work full-time but were expected to make their own childcare arrangements (Lord 1994).

Canadian divorce rates skyrocketed throughout the 1970s and, as poverty rates grew among mother-led families, so did concern about the 'feminization of poverty.' More lone mothers came to rely on social benefits despite increases in married women's labour-force participation, higher average wages, the growth of service industries, and greater general prosperity. Low-income mothers with pre-school children were permitted to accept social benefits and social-service workers classified them as unemployable, permitting them to receive a higher benefit than those expected to find paid work. Yet these benefits remained well below the poverty line (National Council of Welfare 1995b).

From the 1960s to the 1980s, many mothers entered or remained in the labour force as the service sector expanded and more part-time jobs were created, but lone mothers experienced difficulty finding work and caring for their children. Women's average wages remained about two-thirds of men's and federal family-allowance benefits (paid to all mothers of dependent children since 1945) were too low to raise incomes and keep mothers out of poverty. Some low-income mothers were able to find subsidized childcare after 1966 (when CAP was created) and after 1971 many employed mothers could deduct part of the cost of childcare from their taxable incomes (if they paid income tax). Pregnant employees became eligible for statutory maternity benefits in 1971 but these were restricted to women who worked full-time for the same employee for a year (Baker 1995). No other leave for family responsibilities was entrenched in law. Consequently, many lone mothers lived in poverty and relied on social assistance. These mothers sometimes worked part-time but usually did so in the underground economy because tax-back rates on welfare payments were typically high (Dooley 1995). Furthermore, the enforcement of court-ordered child support was left to the custodial parent (usually the mother) with little government assistance.

From 1973 to 1991, lone mothers increased from 8 per cent of all mothers to 14 per cent, while married mothers declined from 56 per cent to 44 per cent. Throughout the same period the average age of lone mothers dropped, but the percentage under the age of twenty-five has remained stable at 10 per cent (ibid.). The poverty rate of lone mothers fell from 67 per cent in 1971 to 60 per cent in 1991 as social-assistance rates and wages were increased. Yet the percentage of lone mothers on social assistance actually rose from 40 per cent to 44 per cent, as the composition of lone mothers changed to more divorced and never-married mothers and fewer widows (ibid.).

Lone mothers are not a homogeneous category and substantial differences are apparent in employment status and income by age, as well as in the path to lone parenthood. Dooley (1985) notes that for older lone mothers (thirty-five and over), social-assistance income and full-time earnings grew at the same rate between 1973 and 1991. Furthermore, older lone mothers increased their schooling and bore fewer children, which meant that they did not need to rely so much on social assistance. The percentage of older lone mothers on welfare actually declined (ibid.). Yet 37 per cent still relied on social assistance in 1991 (ibid.). On the other hand, labour-market opportunities have been declining relative to social assistance income for younger lone mothers (under thirty-five), and 58 per cent were on welfare in 1991. While lone mothers had a higher chance than married mothers of being employed in 1973, they did not in 1991.

Lone mothers are now less likely than married mothers to be employed, despite their greater need for employment income. This relates to the fact that employment growth has been in part-time jobs, but only those with a second income can survive on part-time earnings. Lone mothers can receive more income from social assistance than from part-time wages, and many decide to maximize their income by accepting welfare benefits or by working full-time. Until 1996, welfare rules did not allow them to work for more than a few hours a week while receiving benefits.

Although politicians in the United States have expressed considerable concern about 'welfare dependence,' there was no explosion of welfare usage among Canadian lone mothers from 1973 to 1991. Lone mothers as a percentage of all welfare recipients declined as more young individuals and couples could not find work and relied on social assistance.

Reliance on social assistance is higher in times of economic recession. Numerous studies also indicate that those with low levels of schooling, who earned low wages in the past, who have high numbers of children, whose children are pre-school age, and who are never-married have higher welfare rates (Evans 1984; Prescott et al. 1986; Allen 1993; Charette and Meng 1994). This indicates that welfare rates are influenced by labour markets, demographic factors, and policy (Dooley 1995). While new policy reforms in Canada tend to assume that more welfare recipients should be in the workforce, the other nations in this study have placed a higher value on state support for mothering at home. We will examine some Canadian policy reforms in detail in the next section.

Restructuring Canadian Social Programs

CAP and the Canada Health and Social Transfer

Perhaps the most important changes to the Canadian welfare state have been the indirect ones affecting funding arrangements between the federal and provincial governments. As Paul Pierson (1994) has noted, governments that choose indirect or disguised reforms, and especially reforms that involve structural changes to the 'rules of the game,' are often more successful in restructuring the welfare state. This is precisely the case in Canada.

From 1966 until 1996, provincial social assistance and social services were funded through the Canada Assistance Plan, and from 1977 to 1996 health-care services and post-secondary education were funded through Established Programs Financing (EPF).[11] In 1996 both of these programs were combined to form the Canada Health and Social Transfer. This reform has important implications for the design and delivery of social services, as we will see when we will discuss the details that led to the CHST.

The Canada Assistance Plan was an agreement between the federal and provincial governments to share the costs of social assistance and social services. The federal government entered into this program to help the provinces (especially those with a lower tax base) to provide basic social services that otherwise might not be affordable. CAP stipulated that the provinces must base these programs on 'need' (defined by needs tests for the household), make services available for all eligible residents, establish an appeal procedure, and require no community or other work in return for social benefits.

Throughout the thirty years of CAP's existence, the program was controversial. From the viewpoint of the federal government, cost sharing became less acceptable as provincial costs increased. The federal government could not predict future expenditures because the provinces determined them. On the other hand, some of the provinces wanted to experiment with social-service delivery and eligibility rules for social assistance but were restricted by federal regulations. This was perceived as interference in provincial jurisdiction.

The recession of 1981–3 created higher social-assistance caseloads and costs, and the Neilson task force on program reform recommended major restructuring (Lord 1994). In 1985 the Mulroney government and the provincial governments agreed to modify CAP to increase employment-enhancement initiatives. The provinces were permitted to add work incentives to social-assistance programs, and the federal government, through the Canada Job Strategy program, provided money for skills training that formerly had been channelled through provincial governments to the private sector (ibid.).

Reducing tax-back rates on the earnings of welfare recipients was one change that was expected to increase work incentives. British Columbia and Ontario reduced these rates but later evaluations of this policy change proved inconclusive. Lone mothers on welfare increased both their working hours and their earned income (Low 1993; NCW 1992), but the welfare spell of lone mothers did not decrease in British Columbia (Bruce 1994).

In a further attempt to limit expenditures, the federal government placed a 5 per cent ceiling on CAP to the three 'wealthier' provinces (Ontario, British Columbia, and Alberta) from 1990 to 1995. This 'cap on CAP' simply 'off-loaded' the rising costs of welfare to the provinces and augmented the inequalities in federal spending among the provinces. British Columbia, for example, was spending over 70 per cent of provincial expenditures on social assistance and social services while Quebec and many other provinces were still spending 50 per cent (Goldberg 1994, 22). The Conservative government in Alberta responded by cutting welfare benefits and introducing job-search requirements even for mothers with pre-school children, and the new Conservative government in Ontario cut welfare benefits by 22 per cent in 1995 (Evans 1996). In violation of CAP regulations, British Columbia introduced residence requirements, arguing that thousands of welfare recipients were arriving from Alberta each year, placing an untenable burden on welfare funding.

In 1995 the federal Liberal government made the decision to end the Canada Assistance Plan when it expired in 1996 and to replace it and EPF with the new Canada Health and Social Transfer. This program offers lower levels of federal funding to the provinces, given as one block grant. The total amount of federal money was reduced from $29.4 billion in 1996 to $25.1 billion in 1998, with the expectation of greater cuts in the future as cash transfers are replaced by tax points (Mendelson 1995).

Several important ideological issues are inherent in the changes associated with the CHST. The federal government and economists placed a high value on stability and predictability of funding for social programs, as well as on the need to reduce social spending in order, as they said, to prevent 'hitting the debt wall.' Conservative parties and provincial leaders emphasized the importance of decentralized decision making in social policy, which is seen as 'closer to the people.' They also argued that the federal government should gather and redistribute tax money but should no longer tell the provinces how to spend it in areas of provincial jurisdiction. The days of popular support for a strong federal government (such as the Trudeau years in the 1970s) appear to be over, but decentralization has allowed the federal government to shift the blame to the provinces for cutbacks.

Politically, the provinces can now decide freely how to spend federal grants for social assistance and social services. Although funding regulations associated with Medicare were retained, all regulations associated with CAP were removed with the exception of the ban on residence requirements. The CHST is designed to provide federal predictability in transfer payments, but critics from the left are concerned that health, social agencies, and universities will be forced to compete for diminishing resources. Furthermore, some provinces (especially those with Conservative governments) are expected to reduce welfare benefits further and introduce workfare programs, engaging in a 'race to the bottom' in terms of welfare generosity.

Under the new program, the provinces can no longer spend more money during an economic recession and have the federal government cushion the cost. This suggests that the CHST is not as responsive as CAP to fluctuations in the economy. Critics of the CHST are also concerned that the unequal funding formula inherent in CAP has been retained in the new program rather than being made more rational. As CAP was based on provincial spending for persons 'in need of assistance,' the amount of money the federal government transferred to a province under this program was unrelated to the population of the province or to the degree of poverty. Federal funding was entirely dependent on provincial spending whereas it might be fairer to use a per-capita basis. Furthermore, it is clear that the new funding arrangements will mean considerably less federal money for social programs at a time when unemployment and financial need are increasing (Mendelson 1995; Steinhauer 1995).

One of the reasons why this legislation passed so easily was that the Canadian government successfully pitted interest groups against one other and thereby diminished opposition. Provinces were competing with one other for funding and were divided over the wisdom of decentralizing program control and giving up national standards for social assistance. Social-service agencies were competing against hospitals and universities, all of whom were struggling for survival after extensive funding cuts. But, most important, this legislation was designed to offer the provinces more autonomy in the design and administration of their social programs. This decentralization was expected to be one factor that might help persuade the province of Quebec to remain in Canada. From our perspective, this off-loading to the provinces provides the structural incentive for the provinces to create employability programs designed to reduce government expenditures.

Child Benefits

After the Mulroney Conservative government came to power in 1984, child benefits became a focus of restructuring (Kitchen 1997). At this time, child benefits included an income-tax deduction for families with children (established in 1918), the universal Family Allowance (FA) that was established in 1945, and a refundable child-tax credit established in the 1970s for low-income families. (The childcare-expenses deduction from income tax was considered to be an 'employment expense' rather than a 'child benefit' and was not included in child-benefits reform.) The government argued that the FA was no longer affordable or needed by many families and that scarce government resources should be targeted to poor families to reduce 'child poverty.' Discussions of poverty focused almost exclusively on 'child poverty,' since children were always the 'deserving poor' whereas adults were often suspected of defrauding the welfare system (Baker 1995).

   Family benefits began to be cut in the early 1980s, when the Mulroney Conservative government came to power, but these reforms coincided with the surge of mothers entering the labour force. At that time, women's groups and the child-welfare lobby argued that the universal Family Allowance should be retained. They noted that the FA gave the clear message that government and society valued childrearing and that reproduction was important for the nation, as well as for individuals and families (Child Poverty Action Group 1986; Kitchen 1990). Furthermore, they argued that the FA was the only family income over which some mothers had exclusive control. Researchers and anti-poverty groups noted that a monthly allowance was more advantageous than an annual income-tax credit for low-income families. Furthermore, they argued that the child-tax deduction was worth more to higher-income families and therefore should be converted to a refundable tax credit to make it more advantageous to the poor (Battle 1992).

For several years, parliamentary committees discussed restructuring family benefits but eventually the Mulroney Conservative government reduced the value of the child-tax deduction and then changed it to a credit in 1988.[12] Furthermore, it lowered the threshold income of the refundable child-tax credit that was established by the Liberals in the 1970s to assist low-income families with children. Finally, in December 1992, the Conservative government rolled the three child benefits into one targeted benefit: the Child Tax Benefit (CTB). Unlike many other OECD countries, including the United Kingdom, Canada no longer offers a universal benefit for families with dependent children. Australia had targeted its family allowance in 1987 but added a supplement for low-income families. No supplement was added in Canada.

The taxation department administers the CTB rather than the department responsible for social services,[13] reflecting the growing influence of economic rationalism within the federal government. This benefit initially delivered about $85 a month to the mother or guardian, about the same amount that was received under the previous system of family allowance and tax benefits. Yet the CTB was targeted to middle- and low-income families, initially with a $500 per year Working Income Supplement (WIS) for the 'working poor.' Kitchen (1997, 66) notes that: 'its introduction reflected the growing uneasiness in government circles and among their political advisors about the poverty wall which left some families better off living on welfare than working in a low-wage job. They ignored the fact that a web of bureaucratic rules and regulations of provincial and territorial social assistance systems governing eligibility, benefit levels and high tax-back rates created the poverty wall in the first place.' Yet, in 1994, only 23 per cent of families receiving the CTB also received the WIS (ibid.). Kitchen argues that the WIS originates in Victorian morality and the ideology that the poor do not want to work, and that it has no place in a child-benefit program.

Despite the 1989 all-party resolution in the House of Commons to attempt to eliminate 'child poverty' by the year 2000, poverty rates increased during and after the 1990–1 recession. Furthermore, the percentage of children in low-income families increased by 41 per cent between 1989 and 1995, or from 15.3 per cent to 21.0 per cent of all children (Battle 1997). By 1996 the poverty rates had not declined, despite the 'improvement' announced by Statistics Canada in the economy (NCW 1997a, 2). A recent study by Kapsalis (1997) shows that between 1986 and 1996 the social-assistance rates (in constant dollars) for single parents with one child under sixteen have fallen in seven out of ten provinces, as have their employment rates.

In 1996 the federal government announced changes to the CTB, again designed to 'reduce child poverty' and to 'provide work incentives' to low-wage earners with children. This policy was based on a model suggested by the Caledon Institute of Social Policy in Ottawa to 'take children off welfare' and was recommended in the report to premiers of the Ministerial Council on Social Policy Reform and Renewal in March 1996. This report proposed to put aside past differences among the federal, provincial, and territorial governments and to seek a new framework for cooperating on problems of common concern (NCW 1997a).

Beginning in July 1997, WIS was increased and restructured to take into consideration the number of children in the family. As of July 1998, the enriched WIS payment and the CTB formed one new payment: the Canada Child Tax Benefit (CCTB). These new arrangements will add $850 million a year in the 1998–9 fiscal year to the $5.1 billion that the federal government now spends on the Child Tax Benefit. Of the total new spending, $250 million was announced in the 1996 budget speech and the other $600 million in the 1997 budget speech (ibid., 5).

The CCTB provides a maximum annual amount of $1,625 for the first child and $1,425 for each additional child for families with net incomes up to $20,921 (a lower threshold than previously). Families who do not claim the childcare-expenses deduction receive an additional $213 for each child under seven, the same as they did under the previous CTB. However, the WIS and the $75 supplement for the third and subsequent child in a family both disappear under the new system (ibid., 6).

Critics argue that the 'new' money that will fund the enhanced CCTB was actually the same money that was cut from federal transfers to the provinces for social assistance just before and at the time that the CHST replaced CAP. Furthermore, this payment will be based not on the financial needs of children but on the working status of their parents, since the provinces will be allowed to deduct the working supplement from beneficiaries. This reinforces the old dichotomy between the deserving and undeserving poor, as well as the newer emphasis on paid employment. In addition, the maximum WIS cannot be claimed by people earning less than $10,000 (or more than $20,921), which means that many part-time or low-wage workers will be penalized (Kitchen 1997; Pulkingham and Ternowetsky 1997b). Finally, 'taking children off welfare' does not address their parents' economic problems, and it is difficult to see how the poverty of children can be isolated from the poverty of their parents.

A more optimistic assessment is offered by the Caledon Institute of Social Policy, which considers the CCTB budget announcements for 1997–8 a 'worthy but limited advance in social policy' because the changes 'launch what promises to be a major structural reform of both the child benefit and welfare systems' (Battle 1997). If the federal government continues to raise the value of the benefit over the years, it will have created a de facto guaranteed income that will significantly reduce the risk of poverty among children (ibid., 15).

The income-tax deduction for childcare expenses ($7,000 per preschool child in 1998, and $4,000 for children aged seven to sixteen) can be seen as a 'child and family benefit' rather than an employment expense. If we view it this way (although the government does not), then the Canadian government is providing more generous benefits to high-income families than to modest- and low-income families (Kitchen 1997). Furthermore, the federal government now spends less money on direct income support for families with children than it did in 1985, when the Mulroney government began restructuring child and family benefits (ibid.). From 1971 to 1990, there was a 10 to 16 per cent increase in government-regulated child care spaces every year. After 1990, however, this growth fell and by 1996 spaces were growing at only 5.5 per cent (Canada, HRD 1997, 9). The federal government's retreat from cost sharing since 1996 will further reduce public resources for childcare services (Doherty, Friendly, and Oloman 1998).

Since 1974, the province of Quebec has supplemented the federal Family Allowance, and since the late 1980s it has also paid an allowance for pre-school children and an allowance for newborn children (Canada, HRD 1994). This benefit for newborns was particularly controversial because it paid much more money for the third child than for the first child in a family and was introduced with pronatalist and nationalist rhetoric by the Bourassa Liberal government (Baker 1994). When the federal government abolished the FA in December 1992, Quebec retained its own allowances. In October 1997, however, it rolled these three programs into one targeted family allowance, based on family income, number of children, and the number of parents in the family, and combined it with provincial social assistance (Quebec Government 1997). The cash payments for larger families, which had not been effective in raising fertility rates, quietly ceased with little publicity despite the fact that they were introduced with a flourish in 1988.

In July 1996 British Columbia also created an integrated child benefit when it replaced welfare benefits for children with the BC Family Bonus, an income-tested program that serves low- and modest-income families with children (Battle 1997). In the September 1997 speech from the throne, the federal government announced its intention to double the amount of money allocated for the Canada Child Tax Benefit.

Although the federal government has directed resources at poor families since the mid-1980s, this strategy has not improved the lot of children (Freiler 1996). The Child Poverty Action Group argues that Canadian public policy condemns women to poverty as either mothers or workers, and that the absence of strong family policies remains a major barrier to the social and economic equality of women. They argue that the federal government needs to play a leadership role to ensure adequate and consistent standards of living for all children, women, and families across Canada, noting that the CCTB, negotiated between the federal and provincial governments, offers some promise. Yet they criticize this initiative as being too narrowly focused on welfare reform and low-wage work and offering no long-term commitment to resolve child poverty (Freiler and Cerny 1998).

For low-income mothers, recent changes in the child-benefits system will place greater pressure on them to alter their balance between paid work and caregiving, since paid work and full citizenship rights are becoming increasingly linked. We would argue that the amount of money allocated to resolve child poverty has been too little and that it has been counteracted by labour-market trends and government policies that promote unemployment and underemployment and at the same time restrict entitlement to benefits.

Old Age Pensions

Although this book focuses on low-income mothers, eligibility for certain old age benefits tends to be influenced by social circumstances and choices made earlier in the life cycle. In nations with social-insurance programs (like the Canada/Quebec Pension Plans), those who remain in full-time paid employment throughout their lives are likely to experience greater income security in old age than those outside paid work. Many wives and mothers remained dependent on their husbands' income or social benefits for a portion of their lives. Old age pensions that are based on citizenship or residence are most beneficial to low-income mothers.

Since 1951, Canada has provided a universal flat-rate pension for seniors that was worth about $406 a month in 1997 and indexed quarterly to the Consumer Price Index (Clark 1998). In the social-program expansion of the mid-1960s, the Liberal government lowered the age for Old Age Security from seventy to sixty-five and introduced the Guaranteed Income Supplement for low-income seniors, mainly women who had been homemakers and therefore unable to save for their retirement. The Spouses Allowance was also added in 1975 to provide an income for those aged sixty to sixty-four (usually women) who were married to an old age pensioner. These public pensions were designed to reduce poverty among seniors, which had been a serious problem in the 1950s and 1960s.

By the mid-1980s, poverty among seniors had been substantially reduced although 62 per cent of unattached women over sixty-five were still living in poverty in 1983 (Baker 1993, 294). Yet the population was aging, pension expenditures were rising, and the federal government was searching for ways to reduce costs. The Mulroney Conservative government continued to privatize the pension system, using tax concessions to encourage higher contributions to registered retirement savings plans so that people could 'be responsible for their own retirement.' This program clearly benefited those with higher disposable incomes (men rather than women, and those employed full-time rather than those caring for children). In addition, the Conservatives encouraged employers to provide or extend work-related pensions plans, which then covered only a small portion of the workforce (and few women especially).

Gradually, government and public rhetoric shifted away from viewing income security in old age as the government's responsibility towards seeing it more as a private responsibility with a government safety net. The old age pension was no longer deemed to be a social or citizenship right earned from lifelong contributions to the nation. Instead, government rhetoric focused on 'wealthy seniors' enriched by inflated real estate holdings, who were and should be self-sufficient and therefore did not need a 'public handout.' Yet, since the 1970s, when public pensions became well established in Canada, poverty rates among seniors have dropped even though they have increased for younger families and individuals. National old age pension programs have been one of the great success stories of the twentieth century (Myles 1995).

In 1985 the Mulroney government tried unsuccessfully to deindex partially the OAS, but this move was opposed by angry seniors' groups. After winning a second term of office in 1988, however, the Conservative government began taxing back all of the OAS from higher-income earners, which was called 'the clawback' by critics. This change was greeted with less opposition because the government had continued to emphasize that public money was being spent on 'wealthy seniors' who did not need it. In effect, the clawback was the beginning of the end of universality for the OAS. By 1995, seniors had lost some of their pension if their net individual income was over about $53,000 and all of it if their income was over about $84,000 (NCW 1996a & b).

In 1995 the Chrétien Liberal government continued in the same vein as the Conservatives by proposing to combine the OAS and GIS into a new Seniors Benefit. In addition, it eliminated the income-tax deduction for people sixty-five and over and the tax credit on the first $1,000 of pension income (NCW 1996a). The proposed Seniors Benefit was eventually dropped as policy in 1998, but it was expected to be effective in 2001, non-taxable and based on family income. Those with a family income below $26,000 would have received the maximum benefit, partial benefit would have been paid up to $52,000, and those above $52,000 would have received nothing. Although this was presented as a policy to reduce poverty among seniors, it would have offered low-income seniors only about $120 more per year (ibid.). In addition, it would have removed public-pension rights from many low-income women who are married to men with incomes above the threshold. Considerable federal money would have been saved.

In addition to the proposed overhaul of the OAS, the Canadian government announced reforms in 1996 to the contributory Canada Pension Plan (CPP). When it was established in 1966, the contribution rate was set at 3.6 per cent of contributory earnings (1.8 per cent from employees and 1.8 per cent from employers). This was increased gradually to the 1996 contribution rate of 2.8 per cent from each or 5.8 per cent of earnings, but maximum pensionable earnings are set at only $35,400. In 1997 reforms were being considered that would raise contribution rates over five years to 9.9 per cent of earnings, cut the maximum retirement pension, and reduce the drop-out clause from seven to five years. The drop-out clause has enabled people to leave the labour force for up to seven years without jeopardizing the level of their future pension, and this has largely been used by mothers who leave paid work to raise children. Any reduction in this drop-out period would have disproportionately affected mothers.

The government argues that the Canada Pension Fund is insufficient to cover the future pension costs of an aging population without premium increases, but employers' groups argue that higher premiums will 'kill jobs.' Poverty among seniors has been reduced over the years, yet public pensions are being cut at a time when unemployment rates remain high and savings are more difficult for the average Canadian.

Critics argue that the proposed changes to the Canada and Quebec (QPP) pension plans would disproportionately affect women because they are more likely to depend on public pensions. Women tend to occupy jobs without pension plans and lose private pension credits when they interrupt their employment for family reasons. The CPP/QPP has been important to women because it is portable, offers a drop-out clause for caring activities, covers everyone in the paid labour force, allows for a flexible retirement age, and is fully indexed for inflation (Caledon Institute of Social Policy 1996).

The 'war of attrition' on Canadian old age pensions has continued for over thirteen years. Strong public opposition prevented some cutbacks, but other reforms have been successfully introduced. Despite a change in government from Conservative to Liberal, no policy reversals were made and the ideological shift away from universal public pensions has continued.

(Un)Employment Insurance

Unemployment Insurance was established in 1941 as a federal social-insurance program to pool the risk among employees, employers, and government of involuntary short-term unemployment. Over the years, governments, employers, and employees have used UI for training, job creation, regional-income redistribution, and income supplementation (Canadian Council for Social Development [CCSD] 1996). Consequently, it has moved away from its original goal of protecting employment earnings from temporary and involuntary unemployment (Cuneo 1979). Yet the program has always reinforced earning inequalities and offered greater protection to men than to women because benefits are paid only to contributors who are employed continuously with the same employer and are based on a percentage of previous earnings. This kind of social-insurance program discriminates against those who do not work full-time throughout their lives.

The Trudeau Liberal government expanded UI in 1971 to include more categories of employees (especially seasonal workers) and to offer sickness and maternity benefits. These changes were particularly useful to low-income women, who formed a large segment of temporary workers, but also enabled pregnant women to maintain some employment income during pregnancy and to return to their positions after giving birth. In the 1980s, however, the Conservatives began tightening eligibility and federal contributions to the UI fund were reallocated to resolve regional disparities in unemployment. In 1990, 23 per cent of unemployed workers were ineligible for UI but by 1996 this had increased to nearly one-half (CCSD 1996).

After the 1993 election, the Liberals continued to attack UI. Although the fund had a surplus of $5 billion, employers' groups successfully pressured the government for lower payroll deductions. The government cut benefits and added new eligibility restrictions. In 1996 UI was renamed 'Employment Insurance' (EI), which involved an important ideological shift with greater emphasis on the personal characteristics affecting 'employability' and with less emphasis on structural unemployment and job creation (ibid.).

EI, like the former UI, is financed through payroll taxes but employers' contributions have never been based on the total wage bill. Before 1995, employers did not have to pay premiums for contract workers or employees who worked less than fifteen hours a week. This policy encouraged employers to replace full-time employees with part-timers or contract workers. The new EI legislation, effective January 1997, requires employers to pay premiums for all employees (but still not for contract workers). This reform is an attempt to dissuade employers from converting full-time jobs to part-time jobs. The new legislation also bases eligibility for benefits on hours rather than weeks of work. Yet this system still means that those working overtime (men) will qualify for benefits sooner than those working part-time (women) (CCSD 1996). Furthermore, employees must work longer to qualify, especially if they are recent entrants to the labour force (such as mothers returning from childrearing duties), or what the government calls 'repeat users' (low-wage workers). Benefits continue to be based on the level of previous earnings, which on average are lower for women than men.

For the first time, the new EI also introduces a Family Income Supplement (FIS) that allows low-income claimants who receive the Child Tax Benefit to receive a 'top-up' of up to 80 per cent of insurable earnings to a maximum of $413 a week. Although this was introduced as a policy 'to alleviate family poverty,' it means an average increase of only $30 a week for these claimants. But the greater concern is that this top-up could open the door for further income-testing in a social-insurance program that has always been based on individual contributions and previous earnings. In addition to these changes, the previous Conservative government taxed back up to 30 per cent of unemployment benefits and this 'clawback' has increased under the Liberals (ibid.).

The 1996 reforms to EI were portrayed as an attempt both to modernize UI and to return it to its original intent, but it is clear that a smaller percentage of unemployed people will qualify for benefits at a time of high unemployment. These reforms can therefore be seen as efforts to reduce program costs and prevent the rise of 'payroll taxes.' Yet more Canadians are now working in temporary and low-paid positions ('nonstandard' jobs) and a higher percentage of Canadians now experiences some unemployment throughout their working lives.

Employability-Enhancement Schemes

Canadian unemployment rates have hovered around 10 per cent for over a decade, yet eligibility for federal unemployment benefits has been tightened, forcing more people to rely on provincial social assistance. Furthermore, divorce rates have remained high, over 40 per cent of lone mothers rely on social assistance, and governments now acknowledge the need to provide social benefits to women and children from abusive homes. These factors have increased welfare costs and have led provincial policy makers, inspired by the general ideological assault on 'welfare dependency,' to modify programs to move more people off benefits and into the paid workforce.

Not all provinces specify when they considered a welfare mother with dependent children to be employable, but most encourage mothers into the labour force by the time their youngest child reaches school age (six years old). Yet there is considerable provincial variation. Alberta's Conservative government specifies that mothers are 'employable' when their youngest child is six months old; in British Columbia (with a left-leaning government), a welfare mother was, until 1997, 'employable' when her youngest child was twelve years old, but since then the cut-off has been reduced to seven years (Freiler and Cerny 1998, 67). Generally, the provincial governments led by conservative parties are limiting eligibility and cutting benefit levels. Ontario's Conservative government, for example, cut benefits by 22 per cent in 1995 (Evans 1996). These cutbacks coincided with rising provincial welfare caseloads.

One motivation to increase work incentives relates to the fact that, in the early 1990s, a lone parent would receive a higher income on welfare than from full-time market work at the minimum wage in all provinces except Quebec (NCW 1993). This does not mean that welfare benefits are generous, but rather that Canadian minimum wages have not increased as fast as either average wages or social-assistance rates. Another concern is that lone mothers remain on social assistance longer than other categories of able-bodied recipients and often experience 'repeat spells' of welfare. While the median spell on welfare in recent years has been six months for lone mothers, it was only three months for couples and four months for single individuals (Evans 1987; Barrett 1994; Cragg 1994). Although policy makers in Canada consider these welfare spells to be too long, we note in chapter 6 that lone mothers in the United Kingdom remain on social benefits (Income Support) for an average of four years at a time (Finlayson and Marsh 1997).

In the 1980s, several provinces (Nova Scotia, New Brunswick, Quebec, Ontario) initiated employability-enhancement programs. These were driven by a joint federal-provincial initiative linked to changes in cost sharing under the Canada Assistance Plan, which committed governments to increase the employment opportunities for welfare recipients (Lord 1994). The federal government's objective in these agreements has been 'to assist social assistance recipients to make a successful transition from welfare to work (Canada HRD 1994c, 7), a goal that includes turning some recipients into self-employed entrepreneurs through small business start-up schemes. The focus is on individual attributes: pre-employment counselling to help beneficiaries assess their employment needs and goals, training through courses and project work, wage subsidies to employers, internships, and community service for young people (ibid., 30–2).

Lone mothers have been exempt from the requirements to look for paid work in some provincial schemes. In Nova Scotia, the programs remained voluntary because of the small numbers of training spaces and the large number of applicants, but participants were provided with counselling in life skills, job-search skills, and budgeting and financial management, supervised by 'coaches.' Lord (1994) concludes that assessment, information, and referral infrastructure give some hope to clients eager to leave welfare at any cost but that the programs do little to improve women's position in the labour market. Furthermore, they do not address other pressing concerns of women on social assistance, such as the need for subsidized day care, adequate financial resources, and better access to education (ibid.).

Ontario's Supports to Employment Initiative (STEP), introduced in 1989, allowed welfare recepients to earn more income without losing benefits, and it also included life skills and job-search counselling, information and education on employment-training programs, an employment plan, and partial reimbursement for transportation, supplies, and childcare. According to various assessments, STEP seemed to work in the short term, but long-term effects were less encouraging. STEP clients exhibited a higher exit-rate from social assistance than members of control groups, but a higher rate of recidivism as well. In 1992 this program was cut back because of rising costs and concern that it was drawing people into social assistance (Evans 1995; Klassen and Buchanan 1997).

The Ontario employability scheme illustrates in some detail the origins of contemporary employability discourse and its evolution through three successive governments: Liberal, New Democrat, and Conservative. The provincial Liberal government initiated an independent review of Ontario's social-assistance programs in the mid-1980s. The subsequent report, suggestively entitled *Transitions* (Ontario Government 1988), proclaimed that 'rather than serving as a safety net that can ensnare people, a future social support system should function as a springboard. It must buffer a fall while automatically propelling people upward again' (ibid., 88). Paid work was not only the basis of individual self-worth, it was a key contribution to collective provincial health; a paid job's transforming power meant both 'self-reliance and community integration.' Employment, it was confidently asserted, could also provide 'self-esteem ... and emotional and psychological fulfillment' (ibid., 89–90). The hierarchy of valuable paid work and less useful unpaid work was set in place, but one is left to wonder about the emotional and psychological state of women providing care in the home. The report contains neither a gendered analysis nor acknowledgement of the unique circumstances of most low-income mothers. Employable individuals are the unit of analysis and poverty is an individual matter, rectified by improving an individual's labour-market attributes. The notion of mutual responsibility of state and citizenry is emphasized. The *Transitions* report, while opposing compulsory work for all beneficiaries, recommended 'opportunity planning' for most welfare recipients, with obligations to participate for some (ibid., 206, 228–9).

The New Democratic government produced a subsequent report, *Time for Action*, which reasserted the transforming and empowering capacity of paid work as a means of overcoming 'dependency' and income insecurity. This report argued that the demand from recipients to move into paid work would be so overwhelming that coercion would be unnecessary: 'We expect recipients will be lined up at the door of opportunity planning' (Ontario Government 1992, 83).

In the 1995 election, the Ontario Conservatives, under the banner of Mike Harris's 'Common Sense Revolution,' replaced the New Democratic Party in power. Harris spoke of 'workfare' – compulsory employment for welfare recipients – with strong right-wing rhetoric suggesting Draconian changes but with few details about how the proposed program would work (Lightman 1997). In 1997 the Ontario government introduced the program called 'Ontario Works' but it is expected to take two years to implement across the province. Furthermore, many people were initially excluded from the compulsory component of the program, including single mothers with pre-school children, persons with disabilities, and those who had been unemployed for less than four months (Philp 1997). By 1998, however, Ontario was expecting some lone mothers whose youngest child is three years old to find paid work (Freiler and Cerny 1998, 67).

Individuals participating in 'Ontario Works' have three options: to perform community service for up to seventeen hours a week, to enrol in skills upgrading, or to sign on with a broker who is paid a fee for every person matched with a job.[14] Critics argue that this program is not much different than existing back-to-work or skills-training programs in Ontario, although some of these had been terminated when federal training funds to the provinces were cut in 1996 and other programs were always underfunded (ibid.).

Researchers and social-service workers argue that most unemployed people do not need to be coerced into paid work but are already desperate to find employment. Yet too few jobs prevent them from doing so. In other cases, the jobs that welfare recipients find are so insecure and wages are so low that they are afraid of being worse off in the workforce than on social benefits (Gorlick and Pomfret 1993; Lord 1994; Mullaly 1994 and 1995; Deniger et al. 1995; Sayeed 1995; Evans 1996). Furthermore, Lochhead (1997) indicates that low-wage work is not necessarily a stepping-stone to better jobs and wages. Ontario welfare offices have shifted their focus to such an extent that they appear similar to employment offices, although few welfare recipients have actually lost benefits under the new program (and few have also found permanent positions). The Harris government, however, revised welfare legislation in November 1997 to make it easier to cut the benefits of those who refuse a job or training position (Philp 1997).

In New Brunswick, 'NB Works,' introduced in 1992, was a six-year pilot project designed to provide participants with education, training, and subsidized work experience that may lead to permanent paid work. Although it was advertised as completely voluntary, Mullaly (1997) argues that participants were selected who had the most potential for success. Over 80 per cent of participants have been women and the public-relations arm of NB Works portrayed these working mothers as positive role models for their children. Yet the mothers in the McFarland and Mullaly study (1995) said that they felt guilty because they did not have the time and energy for their children. If the children were sick and mothers took too many days off work, the mothers sometimes were asked to leave the program. Two-thirds of participants had dropped out of the program after thirty months; 39 per cent returned to social assistance. Initially, self-esteem was high because mothers thought they were 'getting off welfare,' but esteem dropped when it became difficult to reconcile family responsibilities with program demands and uncertain job prospects. Mullaly (1997) argues that NB Works fails to recognize or to value the crucial work of childrearing unless a person is paid to perform this task in someone else's home.

In 1993 Alberta began a workfare program called 'Alberta Job Corps,' in which lone parents with children over six months are required to look for work. At the same time, the government cut supplementary benefits (such as payments for school supplies and school transportation). Previously, the age limit for the youngest child was two years old, which is still comparatively young. Alberta welfare recipients have always been motivated to find paid work, because the gap between benefit levels and the provincial minimum wage is significant. Murphy (1997) provides short vignettes of the effects of new employability policies on the lives of several single mothers, demonstrating that those with childcare responsibilities and those who have experienced long absence from the workforce face serious problems in finding and keeping employment.

Quebec had negotiated different funding arrangements than the other provinces for welfare and in the late 1980s introduced workfare through L'Extra program. Recent welfare reforms have made benefits more selective and introduced concepts such as 'individual responsibility,' which are basic principles in American-style workfare programs (Shragge 1997). The Quebec reforms also define unemployment as an individual deficit or pathology rather than an international and structural problem (Shragge and Deniger 1997). Employability programs, especially in Quebec, create a new structure for 'managing marginalization' rather than actually integrating the jobless into the labour force. These programs can be particularly destructive to individuals if there is no job at the end of the program because they give false hope and make the jobless feel personally responsible for their lack of work (Deniger et al. 1995). New welfare rules in Quebec now expect a lone mother to find a job when her youngest child is two years old (Freiler and Cerny 1998, 67).

Despite government rhetoric about assisting people to exit from poverty and become self-sufficient, the political goal of employability initiatives appears to be to reduce provincial welfare expenditures (Lord 1994). The success of these programs has been measured by reduced reliance on social assistance rather than finding permanent full-time work. In some cases, the financial position of clients is not improved when they move from welfare to work because they tend to occupy part-time, insecure, and low-paid positions (Lord 1994; Evans 1995; Armstrong 1996; Hardina 1997). Skill training usually allows only for low-wage jobs and the duration of these programs is too short to enable clients to find permanent full-time work that pays enough to support their families. Consequently, these programs provide few prospects for the kind of upward mobility that could eventually lead women out of poverty (Callahan et al. 1990; Lord 1994, 202).

Although employability programs encourage women as well as men into the labour force, the expectation remains for women, even when employed, to maintain primary responsibility for home and family (Ghalam 1997). The 1995 General Social Survey investigated whether the attitudes of Canadians are still shaped by a gendered division of labour or whether they reflect the reality of women's work in the labour force. In this study, 59 per cent of men and 51 per cent of women agreed or strongly agreed that a pre-school child is likely to suffer if both parents are employed. Yet the data also indicated that 73 per cent of women and 68 per cent of men agreed or strongly agreed that both spouses should contribute to household income (ibid.). Furthermore, men and women aged twenty-five to forty-four who worked full-time and had children under the age of nineteen each spent an average of ten hours in paid and unpaid work activities in 1992. However, the women devoted 1.6 hours more per day on unpaid work than their male counterparts (Frederick 1992). These surveys indicate that Canadians' attitudes about women, work, and family remain ambivalent and somewhat contradictory (Ghalam 1997).

In contrast, employability programs tend to project certainties, particularly that paid work is the best means for beneficiaries to escape from poverty and welfare dependence. The middle-class bias of this assumption is apparent. In the late 1990s, there are growing public doubts about the negative effects of employed women's 'double day' for marriage and children. Yet the message to beneficiary women is that a paid job will lead to prosperity, high self-esteem, and social acceptability, regardless of the consequences for their children and personal lives.

The Enforcement of Child Support[15]

While the federal Divorce Act, 1968 expected married fathers to pay child support, the Divorce Act, 1985 recognized that both mothers and fathers have an obligation to support their child. Child support, however, is provincial jurisdiction and is still awarded and enforced through an adversarial court process in the Canadian provinces. The majority of cases are settled out of court but formalized in a court hearing (Richardson 1996). Two major problems have been apparent in awarding and enforcing child support: in the past judges have been allowed considerable discretion in assessing the amount of awards and the custodial parent has been expected to sue the non-custodial parent if the payment was not made. These have resulted in low awards with very high default rates (Richardson 1988; Finnie 1993).

The existing divorce legislation (updated in 1985) states that child support should be divided between spouses according to their ability to pay, although property can substitute for regular support (Galarneau 1992). When deciding on the award, judges consider any economic advantages or disadvantages arising from marriage breakdown, the financial consequences to the children, the length of the marital relationship, functions performed by the spouse during cohabitation, and any other order or agreement relating to the support of the child (ibid.). The level of child support has historically depended on judicial discretion and effective advocacy, with no assessment formulae or periodic updating (Garfinkel and Wong 1990).

Since 1987, federal law has allowed the provinces to track defaulting parents by using federal tax files and to garnish federal money owed to the parent, such as income-tax refunds (Morton 1990). Despite these changes, the national default rate on child-support payments (defined as not paid at all, not paid on time, or only partially paid) was estimated as 50 to 75 per cent in the 1990s (Fine 1994), down from 50 to 85 per cent in the 1980s (Finnbogason and Townson 1985). This figure includes parents who cannot pay as well as those who do not wish to pay.

The Canadian government gathers statistics from the provinces on divorces, custody arrangements, and court awards of child support, but separating partners who make private arrangements are excluded from these statistics. As more couples live together without marriage certificates, especially in Quebec,[16] the dissolution of more relationships will be unrecorded by any level of government. Furthermore, private child-support arrangements are difficult to enforce.

Evidence collected by Pask and McCall (1989) indicated that child-support orders neither adequately reflected the cost of raising children nor equitably shared the costs between fathers and mothers. They noted that many non-custodial parents (mostly men) could afford to pay more than the courts required them to pay. Most child-support awards have been set arbitrarily, such as $200 or $400 a month, which does not suggest careful consideration of either the actual cost of raising a child or the tax implications of the award (Richardson 1996, 240). In 1988, child-support payments comprised 7 per cent of the payers' median income but 12 per cent of the custodial parent's income (Galarneau 1992).

Over the past decade, major changes have been made in the enforcement of child support in Canada (Finnie et al. 1994). All provinces have developed new enforcement programs but they vary in scope, effectiveness, and jurisdiction. Most automatically impose a payment order only when there is the first sign of default ('first default principle') (Richardson 1996, 241). In contrast, Ontario and New Brunswick assume that all people paying child support are potential defaulters, so enforcement procedures are in place from the beginning. Court-awarded support payments are deducted from pay cheques in the same manner as unemployment-insurance premiums or income taxes, thus removing the possible stigma of garnishment. A few provinces (such as British Columbia) limit their programs to welfare recipients, while others (such as Manitoba and Nova Scotia) monitor all child-support orders in the province (Vanier Institute of the Family 1993, 11).

In a New Brunswick study, Lapointe and Richardson (1994) indicated that there was full compliance in 58 per cent of child-support cases, while the percentage of fathers who clearly refuse to pay ('dead-beat dads') was only about 10 per cent. Other defaulters were temporarily unable to pay, caught in administrative disputes, or were in the process of having the award adjusted in court.

About 40 per cent of Canadian women with child-support orders are receiving 'welfare' or income assistance from their provincial government. This means that any child-support payment made by their former husbands does not benefit them but rather reduces government expenditures on income assistance (Richardson 1996, 242). In fact, many low-income divorced mothers would prefer to receive welfare from the government rather than child support from the children's father, since child support requires them to maintain a relationship with their former partner. This is especially a concern when there is a history of abuse. Increasingly, provincial governments are requiring mothers to identify the children's father, provide information about him to the state, and officially request child support before receiving social assistance.

After years of discussing the assessment and enforcement of child support, a joint federal-provincial-territorial family law committee recommended in 1995 a formula to standardize child-support awards across Canada, as well as ways to address other weaknesses in the current system (Canada, Federal/Provincial/Territorial Family Law Committee 1995). Yet this is an area of provincial jurisdiction, which means that the Canadian government could not require a national assessment formula or enforcement procedure. In the March 1996 budget speech, however, the federal government announced a comprehensive child-support strategy that has received provincial government approval. This included the introduction of guidelines to establish 'fair and consistent awards' in divorce cases, new tax rules for child support, and stronger enforcement procedures to help provincial and territorial enforcement agencies ensure that support obligations are respected. Legislation for the guidelines and new tax rules came into effect in May 1997 (Canada, Dept. of Justice 1996). The guidelines take into account the average cost of raising a child and include rules for calculating child-support payments based on the payer's income, the number of children, and the province of residence. There are provisions for adjustment to recognize a child's special expenses or to prevent financial hardship in certain circumstances. The legislation strengthens enforcement by giving provincial and territorial enforcement agencies access to federal records and databanks and allowing the suspension of passports. Child support paid under agreements or court orders after May 1997 will no longer be deductible for the payer or included in the income of the recipient for tax purposes (Canada, Status of Women 1997).

Child-support payments are especially important to lone mothers who work in low-paid jobs. For those who must rely on social assistance, however, whether or not the father pays does not affect the income of the mother and children.

Advocacy Groups, Child Custody, and Support

Reforming legislation always involves compromises among political ideologies and competing interest groups. Although many groups have advocated reform to marriage and divorce laws, men's rights groups (such as Fathers for Justice) have argued that divorcing fathers are treated unfairly in the courts with respect to the division of matrimonial property, as well as child custody, access, and support (Bertoia and Drakich 1993). In 1987 a number of men's groups joined together to form the Canadian Council for Family Rights. This group lobbied for paternity benefits, joint custody, and more liberal access by divorced fathers to their children.

Men's rights groups frequently argue that lack of access or visitation rights inhibits fathers' willingness to pay child support. They claim that mothers sometimes make access difficult and that the courts systematically deny child custody to divorcing fathers (Crean 1988; Dulac 1989). The government's own research, however, has failed to support the alleged inequalities in the law. Canadian courts almost never deny the non-custodial parent some access to the children, although it may be closely supervised if there is a history of abuse, violence, or insanity (Richardson 1996, 233). Furthermore, fathers are more likely to receive sole or joint custody when they ask for it (Price and McKenry 1988; Richardson 1996). Despite their efforts, men's groups have not been effective in curbing the widespread trend to reform legislation on child-support enforcement. Also, child custody laws have not changed and the basis of custody decisions remains 'the best interests of the child.' Sole custody, nevertheless, is declining for both mothers and fathers while joint custody is becoming more prevalent. One could not argue, however, that the trend towards joint custody has resulted only from political pressure by the fathers' rights movement. It also reflects the growing understanding that children benefit from two parents, the belief that men with custody are more likely to support their children, and the desire by mothers and fathers to share the burden as well as the joys of childrearing.

The advent of joint custody has generated considerable controversy and research in North America about how custody decisions are made and the impact of various forms of custody on children and mothers. Although most people agree that children need continued emotional and financial support from their fathers after divorce, some men's groups have argued that Canadian law should assume joint custody unless it is proven in court to be ill-advised. Guidelines such as 'the tender years doctrine' and 'the best interests of the child,' they argue, have really been based on invalid assumptions about women's superior abilities to care for young children. In contrast, some feminists have been advocating the 'primary caregiver presumption,' namely, that custody of children after divorce should normally be granted to the parent who provided the primary child care during marriage (Boyd 1989, 1997a). Yet, given the child-care arrangements in most families, this would be tantamount to returning to the presumption of maternal custody (Pulkingham 1994).

Some feminist researchers also argue that court-ordered joint custody could be detrimental to mothers, especially if they are forced to maintain a continuing relationship with an abusive husband (Drakich 1988). But fathers' rights activists claim that women use accusations of physical and sexual abuse to keep men away from their children. Federal research indicates that fathers who are granted joint custody are more likely to pay court-awarded child support (Richardson 1996). However, mothers may actually be awarded less money each month if the children also live with their father even though her expenses may not be reduced. This is consequential for low-income mothers attempting to enter paid work while shouldering the responsibilities of childcare.

Perhaps the most compelling argument by feminists is that joint custody usually means that fathers gain the right to make legal decisions for children who continue to live most of the time with their mother. This arrangement requires complicated joint decision making that could impede her daily caregiving and mobility. Joint custody would certainly restrict her opportunities to relocate for a better job or improved lifestyle, yet the same may be true for the father. These issues continue to be argued in courts across the country.

Another controversial issue relates to the payment of income tax on child support received (Finnie 1996). Until recently, the Canadian government allowed divorced parents (usually fathers) to receive an income-tax deduction for both child and spousal support paid while simultaneously requiring tax to be paid on support received (usually by the mother). These regulations were designed to motivate fathers to pay and to provide tax relief for 'the divorced family' by taxing the mother, who is usually in a lower tax bracket (Zweibel 1995). Feminist groups responded that this tax relief to the 'divorced family' was really a benefit only to the husband/father who in most cases needs the money less than the mother. Therefore, this taxation regulation further undermined the ability of custodial mothers to support their children. They noted that the tax deduction for men has never been an effective incentive to pay but that taxing lone mothers has contributed to their high rates of poverty. Furthermore, married fathers do not receive a tax deduction on money given to their wives for the children, so a deduction should not be granted to divorced fathers.

These tax regulations were contested in the Federal Court of Appeal in 1994 and the Supreme Court of Canada in 1994 and 1995, in the case of Suzanne Thibaudeau, a lone mother from Quebec. In May 1995 the Supreme Court of Canada overruled the lower court decision and concluded that asking custodial parents to pay income tax on child support received was not a violation of the Canadian Charter of Rights and Freedoms. Feminist groups strongly opposed this decision. After considerable public pressure in 1995–6, the federal government eliminated both the income-tax deduction and the requirement to pay tax on new child-support awards after May 1997 (Canada, Department of Justice 1997). Yet the tax regulations remain unchanged for spousal support even though the same principle holds that married men do not receive a tax benefit when they share their income with their wife (unless she has no earnings).

To some extent, divorced fathers in Canada have become scapegoats for the poverty of both their children and their former wives. It is now more cost-effective and politically acceptable for governments to hunt down 'dead-beat dads' than to guarantee full-time employment for parents, to ensure pay equity for women, or to provide subsidized childcare for working parents. There is no question that, if more fathers supported their children after divorce, the children's household income would improve and public expenditures would be reduced. Yet gender-neutral laws and more rigorous child-support enforcement procedures are not sufficient to raise lone-parent families out of poverty. Furthermore, the emphasis on 'making fathers pay' detracts public attention from the need for employment-equity strategies, job creation, and income-security programs and reinforces the stereotype of men as breadwinners rather than caregivers. At the same time that the Canadian government was encouraging the provinces to strengthen the enforcement of child support to 'reduce child poverty,' it was cutting transfer payments to the provinces for social-assistance programs.

Further Restructuring

In March 1996 the provincial premiers released the *Report of the Ministe-*

rial Council on Social Policy Reform and Renewal. This report was man-
dated by the premiers to 'formulate common positions on national
social policy issues' and to 'draft a set of guiding principles and underlying values for social policy reform and renewal' (Mendelson 1996, 1).
Quebec was not involved in the consultations that led to this document,
since it refused to participate.

The report contained four proposals:

1. A consolidation of income support for children into a single national
   program, referred to as an integrated child benefit, an idea that had
   been suggested by many previous documents (including the 1943
   Marsh report). The council wanted this program to be managed by
   both levels of government and delivered by either, but it would
   involve the consolidation of existing funding with no new money.
2. A national income-security program for persons with disabilities.
3. A consolidation of income-security programs for the working-age
   population within a single jurisdiction, as opposed to the current
   division between federal responsibility for employment insurance
   and provincial responsibility for welfare. This would involve joint
   management with options of federal or provincial delivery.
4. A resumption of 'federal responsibility for all programming for
   Aboriginal people, both on and off reserve, with a gradual transfer of
   authority to Aboriginal Communities' (Canada, Ministerial Council
   1995, 2).

The report, while attempting to 'up-load' some costs back to the federal government (Torjman 1997), argues that constitutional responsibility for social programs is provincial jurisdiction. This point remains
debatable, however, since the constitution has been changed several
times to accommodate national social programs such as unemployment
insurance and old age security. A clause was also written into the constitution giving the federal government 'spending power' in provincial
jurisdiction if the provinces accepted federal money. Furthermore, the
federal government has jurisdiction over income tax and since 1918 has
used the tax system to provide benefits for families with children. The
federal government also offered a family allowance from 1945 until 1992
for families with dependent children. It has retained responsibility for
Employment Insurance since 1941, and it was jointly responsible for
social programs under CAP for thirty years. Yet many politicians (especially from Quebec) and conservative interest groups across the country

argue that social programs are provincial jurisdiction and that the federal government should withdraw from them. This misconception is seldom corrected publicly. In fact, opposition to actual restructuring and to new proposals has been weak in Canada. In the next section, we will examine some of the reasons why this is so.

Opposition to Restructuring

Pierson (1994) argues that opponents of the welfare state have been most successful in their attempts at retrenchment when they have been able to divide the supporters of social programs, compensate those negatively affected, or hide what they are doing from potential critics. Furthermore, certain institutional reforms continue to place pressure on the welfare state, including politics that strengthen the hands of budget cutters, weaken the government's revenue base (such as tax cuts), and undermine the position of pro-welfare-state interest groups (such as reducing the power of the trade unions). This is precisely what has happened in the Canadian case.

Although Canadian governments faced organized opposition to their reforms, especially by anti-poverty groups, feminist organizations, the political left, and some provincial premiers, this opposition was diffused or weakened by several political events and government strategies. First, there has been a political shift to the right since the 1980s so that the Liberal Party and the Progressive Conservative Party are relatively close to the centre-right in terms of ideology while the Reform Party on the far right has been a growing force from western Canada.

After 1993, the Reform Party became a powerful force in Parliament. Reform argued for ten equal provinces rather than special status for Quebec, but it also wanted massive decentralization of political power from the federal to provincial governments. This presented a dilemma for the governing Liberals under Jean Chrétien (who is from Quebec), since they wanted to restore Quebec to its status as a Liberal stronghold. One option was to give special powers to Quebec, but this was opposed by most other provinces and conservative interest groups. Accordingly, Prime Minister Chrétien offered all the provinces more power over social programs with the CHST. This policy change received support from the conservative governments in Ontario and from Quebec (as well as conservative economists and business groups) because it reduced social spending. Decentralization also was popular in Quebec because it reduced the power of the federal government and disrupted the 'fiscal federalism' that had formed the basis of Canadian social programs since the 1960s. The result in the late 1990s is that, as federal grants and spending requirements diminish, the federal government has reduced power to demand provincial adherence to national program standards in such areas as Medicare. While the federal-provincial Social Union Agreement of February 1999 (which excludes Quebec) is expected to result in a reinjection of some previously cut health-care funding, the federal government's ability to enforce national program guidelines remains in question (*Globe and Mail* 1999).

In the June 1997 election,[17] the Reform Party became the Official Opposition. The results of this election might eventually change the focus of policy discussion to western-based issues but could weaken the power of Prime Minister Chrétien to unify the country, since he won a majority only in Ontario. The Bloc Québécois (BQ) continues to speak for Quebec's francophone majority, which suggests that Canada is becoming even more balkanized (Greenspon 1997).

The major left-wing party, the New Democratic Party, has been declining in power at the national level. The NDP's political statements have, more clearly than other parties, supported the welfare ideal of redistributing income, wealth, and power. Furthermore, the CCF-NDP was the first political party to insist on the need for public pensions, medicare, public housing, and income-security programs in Parliament, and its efforts had a significant influence on the development of the Canadian welfare state (Armitage 1996). However, the NDP experienced a significant reduction of parliamentary seats in the 1990s, from forty-three in 1988 to nine in 1993. The decline of the NDP was hastened by the erosion of the labour movement that accompanied economic restructuring, as well as by internal divisions sparked by Free Trade Agreement with the United States, constitutional issues, and native self-government.

National unity has always been precarious in Canada. The Quebec sovereignty movement began to gain greater power in the late 1960s and in 1976 the first separatist government was elected. Although the sovereignty referendum of 1980 was unsuccessful, the Parti Québécois (PQ) vowed to regroup and try again. In 1982 the Liberal government under Pierre Trudeau 'repatriated' the Canadian constitution from Britain and added to it a Charter of Rights and Freedoms and an amending formula for jurisdictional disputes. Although nine provincial premiers signed their consent, the PQ premier (René Lévesque) refused to sign. After the Conservatives won the 1984 election, Prime Minister Brian Mulroney made it a principle goal to ensure that Quebec saw itself as an equal partner in confederation and in order to do this he believed that the constitution had to be amended to incorporate Quebec's concerns. Each attempt to change the Canadian constitution seemed to augment national unity concerns, as the irreconcilable differences between Quebec's image of Canada (two founding nations) and the view especially from the west of the country (ten equal provinces) became more apparent. Ironically, each national unity crisis was used by the Mulroney government to pass unpopular legislation and to disguise the restructuring of important social programs (the Family Allowance, Unemployment Insurance, and the Canada Assistance Plan).

The BQ, which was the official opposition in Ottawa from 1993 to 1997 even though it elected MPs only from Quebec, focused on gaining more powers for Quebec and decentralizing decision making on social and economic policy. Its view of confederation is that Canada has always been based on two founding nations (the French and the English) rather than ten equal provinces and that Quebec must retain control over its own social programs.[18] Allowing Quebec powers not enjoyed by the other provinces has been called 'asymmetrical federalism.' In practice, the BQs Official Opposition status meant that a disproportionate emphasis was placed on Quebec sovereignty and decentralization of decision making in parliamentary debates, diverting attention and discussion away from other social-policy issues.

With a diminishing left-wing opposition, rising concern about the break-up of Canada, and a national acceptance of neo-liberalism, it became easier for conservative governments (both the Progressive Conservatives and later the Liberals) to begin dismantling the welfare state. The cap on CAP occurred in 1990 during the debates concerning the Meech Lake Accord (an attempt to amend the constitution so that Quebec would sign.)[19] The abolition of the universal Family Allowance was passed during the debates on the 1992 Charlottetown Accord, a second attempt to bring Quebec into the constitution. And the demise of CAP and the development of the CHST coincided with the 1995 sovereignty referendum in Quebec (in which the 'yes' vote lost by one-half a percentage point). If a new sovereignty referendum occurs before the year 2000, as some have predicted, the threat to national unity may intensify still further.

In the present political and economic climate, social policy appears to be driven by economic policy (Banting 1992; Battle and Torjman 1995), as well as by shifts in power between the federal government and the provinces and concern over national unity. Although the restructuring has just begun, some of these reforms will undoubtedly lead to future dismantling. Removing the administration of social programs from welfare departments and placing them in taxation or revenue departments vests social policy in the hands of economists, who are more likely than sociologists or political scientists to be concerned with work incentives and economic rationalism. Once social programs are converted to tax benefits, governments can modify them more easily, without the necessity of public hearings and parliamentary debate. In addition, merging federal departments that deal with employment issues with those providing income support (as the Liberals did after the 1993 federal election) will hasten the focus on employability-enhancement programs and workfare in the future. This interdepartmental shifting of responsibilities was also a feature of New Zealand restructuring (Kelsey 1995).

Changing fiscal arrangements from matched grants to block funding will provide considerably less federal money for future social services, requiring the provincial governments to make additional cutbacks. Furthermore, without CAP restrictions, provinces can make new program changes to save money, such as basing programs on willingness to perform community-service work or other low-paying jobs rather than on financial need. Or 'need' can be defined at a higher level of income or family/personal problems. Once taxes are reduced, as several governments have promised, subsequent governments will be unable to improve social programs because the funding will simply not be there. In this way, the Liberal government has strengthened the hand of the budget cutters.

The Canadian case has indicated that universal programs are not necessarily more resistant to dismantling than means-tested programs, although public support for old age pensions and Medicare remains high. Certainly more money can be saved by targeting universal programs such as Family Allowance than by attacking means-tested programs for the most unfortunate in society (Pierson 1994). Consequently, Canadian family-related programs based on citizenship rights were eroded first. Yet the federal government also helped to dismantle means-tested programs for the poor by reducing federal contributions and eliminating cost sharing, thus off-loading the cost of social services and the blame for cutting these services to provincial governments. Furthermore, they have disguised their dismantling efforts by passing complex taxation and funding changes at a time when Canadians were preoccupied with national unity and high unemployment.[20] The 1999 Social Union Agreement, although heavily cloaked in the discourse of improving social programs and new Canada-wide initiatives, does not preclude further retrenchment and rationalization under the guise of readjusting federal and provincial responsibilities for social-program funding and delivery.

Conclusion

The implementation of governmental-policy agendas is tempered by the political need to ensure re-election. Yet, although cutbacks often result in lost elections, several strategies and structural conditions can make unpopular reforms more palatable or feasible. If governments can convince their citizens that there is little alternative but to cut social programs, then they may be more successful (Pierson 1994). This has been an important strategy employed by ruling federal political parties. Using the same language as the National and Labour parties in New Zealand in the 1980s, the Canadian Conservatives in the 1980s and the Liberals in the 1990s argued that tough policy decisions needed to be made to eliminate the deficit and to allow the nation to become more competitive internationally. Only the private sector, they argued, could create jobs and government must allow employers to do so by reducing both payroll and corporate taxes and by promoting freer trade. Many Canadians accepted these justifications, partly because few policy options were ever discussed. Neo-liberal politicians consulted neo-liberal interest groups[21] and advisers (mainly economists) to the neglect of other 'experts.' In addition, comparisons were continually made with the United States, which presents a hostile picture of the state's social role, rather than with more social-democratic models of the welfare state. The Canadian case illustrates the mobilization of political power to effectively marginalize opposition and alternative visions of welfare-state change.

The timing of reforms is also crucial. When the Canadian government wanted to pass controversial legislation that restructured social programs, it ensured that the introduction of the legislation coincided with another important political event, thereby disguising its actions. In this case, major reforms to social programs were made when Canadians were preoccupied with national unity.

Changes have also been apparent in the provinces that have strengthened the conservative agenda. Political opposition to neo-liberal policies has been weakened in recent years since the (Harris) Conservative government won the 1995 election in Ontario (the province with the largest population) and the Klein Conservative government was re-elected in Alberta in 1997. Furthermore, political opposition from the left has also diminished at the federal level since the 1993 election, when the NDP retained only nine seats in Parliament. Social-democratic lobby groups remain discouraged as they struggle with both a conservative mood from the electorate and funding cuts from governments. In the 1997 election, the NDP won twenty-one seats in Parliament, but these were mainly concentrated in Atlantic Canada.

Throughout the restructuring process, there has been a gradual redefinition on the ideological level of the nature and role of 'the public.' The notion of collectivity and collective interest – inherent within Canada's major social programs – is being replaced by the neo-liberal concept that citizens are individual 'consumers' with no inherent claims on public revenue. 'Consumers' are told that, in the future, they should look to non-state mechanisms of support (such as family, community, and voluntary organizations) rather than to government. Furthermore, although 'the public' is still being consulted by parliamentary committees, current governments feel less of an obligation to listen to their views than they did, for example, during the 1970s when there was greater acceptance of the notion of citizenship rights and participatory democracy.[22]

Canadians have now experienced fifteen years of economic rationalism led by the federal government, with no indication that it will soon diminish. Canadian governments have accepted some of the same ideological positions as New Zealand, the United States, and the United Kingdom in restructuring the welfare state. Yet neo-liberalism's success in influencing policy has been dependent on a series of structural and political variables distinctive to Canada. These include a shifting of political power from the federal to the provincial governments, the weakening of left-wing political parties and interest groups, and the unique demands posed by the Quebec sovereignty movement.

We have seen in this chapter the multiplicity of forces that can affect low-income mothers as a welfare state undergoes restructuring. The policy thrust towards employability is a gendered process that is not yet fully recognized as such by Canadian governments, which are unable to appreciate the relationship of their restructuring initiatives to labour-market conditions, patterns of unpaid work in the home, and the taxation system. We have also seen that the Canadian experience is conditioned by the legacy of previous social programs and ideas of appropriate mothering, struggles among interest groups around policy priorities, needs to legitimate and justify change, and the influence of new right ideologies concerning 'dependence.' These all occur within a nation made structurally vulnerable by high government debt loads and continuing concern over national unity.

In the next chapter, we will examine the structure of Australia's social-security system and recent efforts there at restructuring. Although both Canada and Australia were initially colonies of Great Britain, their political structures and interest groups developed differently. This influenced the development of social programs, including those for low-income mothers.

4

From Public to Private Dependency?
Reforming Policies in Australia

Introduction

Theorists such as Esping-Andersen (1990) have classified both Canada and Australia as similar welfare-state regimes, yet substantial differences are apparent in the structure of their social programs. Australia has never created national social-insurance programs with contributory benefits, such as Canada's unemployment insurance and national pension plan, preferring to fund programs out of general taxation revenues, based on need rather than work history. Another difference is that social security (including what Canadians call 'welfare') is federal jurisdiction in Australia. In addition, the Australian government pays a special benefit for low-income parents (mothers) to care for both their pre-school and school-aged children at home (Sole Parent Pension), while the Canadian government offers no comparable social benefit.[1] Australians express widespread support for the idea that the state should pay for some form of additional income support to parents and other caregivers, although there is less consensus on the form it should take or the major reason for this support (Bradbury 1996).

Since the early 1980s, Australian legislation and social policy have moved towards treating men and women more alike (Shaver 1995). At the same time, government rhetoric also emphasizes the contribution that caring activities make to the nation, and government ministers continually reiterate that mothers (but not fathers) should be given a choice to enter the labour force or to care for their children at home. Yet, we demonstrate that, in reality, this 'choice' is a false one since the infrastructure and social attitudes provide little support for women to engage in full-time employment if they are also mothers with young children. Lack of public childcare, paid maternity leave, and leave for family responsibilities make it difficult for mothers to compete with childless wage earners. Furthermore, the unit of entitlement for most Australian social programs has been the male-breadwinner family rather than the individual, as we will discuss below. This augments the difficulty that women beneficiaries experience when they try to break out of their domestic roles. Employability programs in Australia exist within a unique legacy of social benefits, combined with widespread and persistent assumptions about appropriate caregiving and labour-force roles for men and women.

Overview of Social Programs in Australia

Australia's approach to social protection has always involved guaranteeing a minimum level of protection to those in the labour force while providing a residual safety net for the unemployed or those unable to work for pay. Historically, most social-security benefits were income-tested and Australia and New Zealand were the only OECD countries after 1960 without any form of contributory social insurance. The Australian trade-union movement was politically stronger far earlier[2] than its counterpart in Europe and the movement ensured high levels of male employment and wages by pressuring governments to protect domestic markets and workers (Castles 1996, 92).

At the turn of century, the Australia government (with pressure from the trade unions) established courts of arbitration that set wages and made them subject to forces outside the market, such as the marital status of the (male) employee, the number of dependants he had, and 'community standards.' The *Harvester* judgment of 1907 established the parameters of a 'fair and reasonable' wage which should meet the 'normal needs of the average employee regarded as a human being living in a civilized community' (Higgins 1922, 37). This 'family wage' was expected to be high enough to cover the living costs of the employee, his wife, and two or three children. In fact, the concept of the family wage and programs linked to household incomes have been at the heart of social and wages policy since the first quarter of the century (Jamrozik 1994; Castles and Shirley 1996).

In 1912 Australia introduced a universal maternity allowance to increase the (white) birthrate, to assist with childbirth expenses, and to help lower infant mortality rates (Bradbury 1996, 3). This lump-sum payment was later succeeded by two tax concessions. In 1915 the government began allowing tax filers with children under sixteen an income-tax deduction. In 1936 a deduction was introduced for dependent spouses and for widowers who required a relative to care for their dependent children. These deductions, however, benefited the taxpayer in the family, usually the father, rather than the person caring for the children. Conservatives saw the family wage as sufficient to cover family costs and thought that there was no need for additional government benefits. Consequently, the debate about offering regular payments to mothers had been a political issue long before the introduction of family allowances in 1941 (ibid.). In the 1940s the Australian government also introduced unemployment benefits and widows and sickness benefits, but, except for child allowances, these benefits were selective, flat-rate, and ungenerous (Castles 1996).

Government support for full employment involved protective tariffs on goods produced outside Australia, in order to foster domestic manufacturing. It also involved a 'white Australia' policy, which placed controls on immigration to exclude low-wage (Asian) labour and to keep population growth low enough to maintain a tight labour market. Consequently, Australians felt that they did not need social insurance or contributory benefits and the government offered a very limited sense of 'welfare citizenship' (Castles and Pierson 1995). Unlike many European nations, Australian governments viewed poverty and unemployment in the 1930s and 1940s as a problem of low wages rather than of lack of state expenditure on welfare (Castles 1996). Australian unemployment rates were also relatively low and economic growth rates high until the 1980s, as Table 4.1 indicates.

Despite low rates of national unemployment, Australian married women have not been full-time breadwinners to the same extent that they have been in countries such as Canada, the United States, or Sweden. Historically, this can be partly explained by the family-wage policy that legally institutionalized female dependence on men. The Australian system has been called the 'male wage-earner's welfare state' (Bryson 1992), yet this system of centralized wage-setting and arbitration-award decisions has not been entirely negative for women's equality. It was more effective in raising women's pay relative to men's than pay-equity legislation in other countries (Castles 1996). Generous male wages and low dispersion of earned income led to high rates of home ownership, assisted by subsidized and interest-regulated loans, and this system provided a functional alternative to social-security transfers (Saunders 1994). The government also established a progressive income tax, but

TABLE 4.1
Economic indicators in Australia

Decade	Unemployment rate	Economic growth
1960–70	1.7	5.3
1970–80	4.1	3.5
1980–90	7.5	3.2

Source: Saunders 1994, 131.

the tax burden on average working families was relatively low (Castles 1996).

By the late 1970s, however, it had become clear to Australia's governments that traditional economic strategies would not be feasible in the future. External trade with Britain had declined, commodity prices were falling, and the country was subjected to the deregulating trends of the international economy (Castles and Pierson 1995). Yet restructuring was initiated in a different way in Australia than in other liberal welfare states and the ideology of economic rationalism has been less pronounced and pervasive there (Castles 1996).

To be sure, economic rationalism has affected Australian social-policy debates. The rising cost of social programs, their 'generosity,' and the growing 'dependency' of low-income beneficiaries on the state have been concerns of conservatives. About 27 per cent of the Australian population relied on targeted social benefits in 1993 (Jones 1996, 1). Social security and welfare benefits increased in real terms by 4.5 per cent a year between 1983–4 and 1993–4 (years of Labor government), but family benefits increased 6.1 per cent and childcare benefits 18 per cent. Conservative researchers, such as Jones (1996), argue that the growth of government spending on children over the past few decades has been a compensation for the 'weakening of families.' In contrast, feminists argue that government benefits have helped lone mothers to establish autonomous households and support their children (Sainsbury 1996).

Considerable public support remains for the Australian social-welfare system, for 'social justice,' and for a 'fair deal' for all citizens. This support is partly explained by the fact that each category of beneficiary (including old age pensioners) receives the same basic amount, in contrast to other countries' social-insurance systems where benefit levels vary by type of benefit as well as by income and contribution rates.

Also, compulsory voting means that a government's political calculations must recognize the nearly one-third of voters who receive social benefits (ibid., 230). This makes it politically difficult to cut social programs.

Longstanding gender inequalities have created unresolved interpersonal tensions in much of Australian family life. These inequalities, such as the historical discrimination against women in the labour force, bring the so-called 'public' and 'private' spheres together. While there appear to be widely shared ideas about what family life should be, yearnings for intimacy can be compromised by structures and practices that provide men with greater marital power and enable employers to evade the costs of raising children. Women primarily accept these caring responsibilities (Bittman and Pixley 1996).

The nature of the contemporary Australian welfare state has been shaped by many factors, none more important than the historical alignment and relative effectiveness of three broad categories of interest groups within the political and state systems. These include the trade-union movement as the representative of the organized working class; pro-market business forces and their intellectual and bureaucratic allies; and various groupings of feminist, aboriginal, ethnic, social welfare, cultural, and immigrant organizations. The interplay of these interest groups has been especially important in the restructuring period dating from the election of a Labor government in 1983.

Restructuring in the Hawke/Keating Labor era of 1983–96 was in part conditioned by and negotiated within a unique formal quasi-corporatist relationship between the government and the Australian Council of Trade Unions (ACTU). Many analysts working in the power-resources tradition cite the arrangements and understandings of the 1983 Accord as key factors setting the discursive and policy parameters for the refashioning of the Australian welfare state (Castles, Gerritson and Vowles 1996; Bray and Neilson 1996; Frankel 1997). This tripartite agreement (among government, employers, and unions) shaped economic policy in Australia and included a trade-off of price and wage stability in return for job security, the continuation of employment-related benefits, and no goods and services tax.

These parameters were three in number. First, Labor governments relied upon market-inspired solutions to meet economic problems that had arisen partly as a result of recession-induced stagnation, the floating of the Australian dollar, finance-sector deregulation, and further integration into global markets. Second, jobs were maintained and modest wage increases permitted. Third, social-policy changes involved a combination of liberal initiatives in matters of individual sexual orientation, health insurance, and occupational health and safety; enhancement of some benefit levels; restriction and targeting of entitlements and eligibility; and increases in the monitoring of recipients. Throughout, the role of organized labour was tempered by ongoing internal policy splits and its reluctance to be perceived as being too close to government (Castles and Pierson 1995, 238; Frankel 1997, 15–20).

The policies flowing out of the Accord reflected, at times, sustained mediation and negotiation of competing left-right interests through coalitions, and at other times the defeat of one partner (such as in the new right's victory on financial deregulation and a floating exchange rate). Instead of introducing a consumption tax (as did the United Kingdom, New Zealand, and Canada), the Australian Labor government reduced the highest marginal tax rate while initiating a capital-gains tax, a progressive fringe-benefits tax on business expenses, and limited government spending (Castles 1996). The government also reduced the role for the centralized negotiation of wages and working conditions, which is likely to generate a greater dispersion of income in the future (Castles and Pierson 1995). Yet the drive towards economic and managerial rationalism did not conflict seriously with the Labor government's traditional commitment to social protection. During the 1980s, Labor restored the national health system (Medicare), which had been eroded by the former Liberal government, and enhanced social benefits for families with children, as we will discuss in detail later in this chapter.

The role of Australian organized labour in recent social-policy issues of concern to the women's movement is decidedly mixed. The ACTU was a major player in both the process of decentralizing wage-setting and the linking of wage claims to productivity growth, which benefited male workers in traditional industries (Bray and Neilson 1996). Historically, the labour movement concentrated on the level and conditions of male employment, as well as the precepts of the male-wage-workers' welfare state, and excluded women from powerful union posts. The accession of women to senior union positions and the rapid increases in women's labour-force participation pushed the protection and promotion of the rights of women workers onto the agenda. The ACTU is now gradually, if reluctantly, coming to grips with some of its internal policy contradictions. It now advocates policies similar to those of the women's movement for improved childcare, gender-neutral private-sector parental leave, leave to care for sick children, benefits for part-time workers, and more flexible working hours. ACTU has also been able to protect centralized wage arbitration for low-wage workers, many of whom are women (Cass 1995; Curtin and Sawer 1996). Yet the links between paid and unpaid work and the redistribution of caring tasks from women to men remain unaddressed, and the overall wage system favours full-time male workers in industrial employment (Cass 1995; Nightingale 1995).

The new right and its allies in business and government filled the policy terrain that was partly ceded by organized labour. Yet Australian business groups were by no means united in purpose. The historical disunity of employers' groups on both policy and organizational matters meant that they did not participate formally in the Accord. Nevertheless, they were powerful lobbyists within government (Bray and Neilson 1996, 81) and had the support of the opposition Liberal-National Party coalition that was firmly in the grips of new right ideology. The Australian right was led by such organizations as the Business Council of Australia and the Australian Confederation of Commerce and Industry. Invigorated by Thatcherist progress in the United Kingdom and also by the growth of international networks of think-tanks, media, politicians, and lobbyists, it vigorously promoted economic-rationalist solutions to the country's problems. The governing Labor Party, dominated by pro-market activists and leaders and working with sympathetic bureaucrats, was receptive to many neo-liberal ideas, including freer trade, reduced regulation of the market, decentralized wage bargaining, and cuts in the public sector (Pusey 1991; Frankel 1997).

Demands for women's equality fit uneasily into this mixture. Institutionally, the women's movement had sufficient strength in the Commonwealth government bureaucracy to launch both a defence of existing programs and demands for expanded ones. The Office of the Status of Women was located after 1983 in the Department of the Prime Minister and Cabinet, and it had responsibility for coordinating a network of women's units in line government departments, providing policy advice, and promoting women's interests (Curtin and Sawer 1996; Bryson 1995). This policy machinery had both substantive and symbolic impact, which was reinforced by similar units at the state level. Bureaucratic strength of women and other advocacy groups on the social-policy side was, however, offset by political weakness within the Australian Labour Party itself, despite the efforts of the Women's Electoral Lobby. Furthermore, women were underrepresented and marginalized in the economic-policy departments, from which flowed an increasing number of decisions with social implications. Adding to the problems were the ongoing differences between the ACTU and many feminists on such issues as the funding of the commercial childcare sector (Curtin and Sawer 1996; Bryson 1995).

The policy outcomes for low-income women stemming from this decision-making and interest-group structure are mixed. Growing female labour-force participation and the undermining of the fair-wages policy called into question many other assumptions about the nature of social provision in Australia (Castles and Pierson 1995, 237). Feminist concerns resulted in several important achievements not on the new right agenda. The regressive Goods and Services Tax (GST) proposal was defeated, tax cuts were expanded to include low-income mothers, and funded childcare spaces grew substantially. Initiatives were taken in such areas as employment strategy, violence against women, health services, rape-crisis centres, anti-discrimination, and neighbourhood and community services (Curtin and Sawer 1996; Bryson 1995). Yet universality of benefits was not retained. An important question remains, which we shall address throughout the remainder of this chapter. What was the women's movement's response to the question of increasing mothers' participation in the labour force? And to what extent did this response reflect the ambiguities and contradictions which Australian feminists have about women in paid and caring work, women's traditional 'decommodified' sphere in the household, and the artificially elevated position of men in paid employment?

Australia provides a contrasting example to New Zealand of the importance of political structures and the organization of interest groups in restructuring the welfare state (Castles 1996). While trade unions and the Labor government negotiated changes to the economy, tax structure, and labour force in Australia, the New Zealand Labour government (and later the National government) pushed reforms through with a minimum of consultation, creating considerable anger from opposition parties and community groups. However, social-security changes introduced by Labo(u)r governments in both countries created a political and ideological climate that made further reforms possible by subsequent conservative governments in the 1990s. Let us now examine the details of restructuring social programs for low-income mothers and their families in Australia from the 1980s to the 1990s.

The Social Security Review and its Aftermath

In 1987 the Hawke Labor government initiated a social-security review led by Professor Bettina Cass, a feminist and pro-Labor university professor. The final report recommended measures designed to reduce child poverty and to improve the link between benefits and the labour market. The report noted that lone parents, especially those with low education, those outside the workforce, and those working part-time, tend to live in poverty (Vrielink 1996). Several new social programs were recommended and implemented as a result of this review, including the Child Support Scheme (1988), Sole Parent Pension (1989), and Jobs, Education and Training (JET) (1989). Before we discuss these initiatives, we should review what was happening to programs established earlier in the century, such as the Family Allowance and unemployment benefits.

Family Allowances

All four countries in this study established universal family or child allowances in the 1940s, and Australia developed such a program in 1941 (Australia, Department of Social Security 1992). The Family Allowance program attempted to create horizontal equity between families without and families with children by providing a universal benefit for all families with children under the age of sixteen. In 1987 the Hawke Labor government introduced an income test for this allowance, as a cost-cutting and targeting measure. Feminist groups and the Office of the Status of Women opposed this reform, arguing that the Family Allowance is sometimes the only money a mother can call her own and that single-earner husbands do not always share equally their income with their wives and children. These arguments did not prevent the government from making the change (Curtin and Sawer 1996). To some extent, opposition was diffused because the government targeted the new benefit to middle-income families as well as low-income ones and also created a substantial supplement for poor families. By contrast, the New Zealand Labour government attempted unsuccessfully to target the family allowance in the same year and again in 1990, although the (conservative) National government was eventually successful in doing so in 1991 (ibid.).

In January 1993 the Australian Family Allowance was renamed the Basic Family Payment (BFP) and the age limit was raised for students. The term 'payment' eliminates the connotation of universality that the former allowance held, but in fact universality had already been removed in 1987. The BFP is now paid to low- and middle-income parents with a least one child under sixteen or a child who is a full-time student under twenty-four and not in receipt of the education allowance (Bradbury 1996, 7). Also in 1993, the former Family Allowance supplement was renamed Additional Family Payment, but it remains a benefit designed for low-income working families not receiving a pension or benefit (Bradshaw, Ditch, Holmes, and Whiteford 1993).

Employment Trends and Unemployment Benefits

In 1944 Australia developed an unemployment-assistance program for people who lose their jobs involuntarily, are registered as unemployed, and are available for work. This benefit differed considerably from Canada's unemployment-insurance program that had been developed a few years before. Australian unemployment assistance has been paid to unemployed men aged sixteen to sixty-four and women aged sixteen to fifty-nine, to coincide with the lower retirement age for women. Supplements have been available for claimants with children or a financially dependent spouse, but the additional income was not paid directly to the spouse. Since entitlement was based on family income and the husband was considered to be the 'head' of the family, he typically received the payment. Unlike Canada's contributory program, the Australian program is financed through general revenue and is means-tested. Unemployed people must demonstrate to the Commonwealth Employment Service that they are looking for work (unless they have disabilities, dependent children under sixteen, or are over the age of sixty), and they may do up to twenty hours of voluntary work a week[3] without forfeiting their benefit (Eardley et al. 1996a, 149). Beneficiaries are also permitted to earn a small amount per week before it is deducted from benefits, but these rules were made more flexible in 1995 (ibid., 155).

The unemployment-benefits system, whose basic structure was designed primarily to assist men who lost their 'family wage,' operates against a historic backdrop of low labour-force participation rates for women, especially when compared to countries such as Canada, the United States, and Sweden. Yet, as Table 4.2 indicates, Australian women, especially those who are married, have been entering employment in considerable numbers since the easing of the recession in the early 1980s. In 1975, about 38 per cent of married women with dependent children were in the paid workforce; by 1992 this had increased to 61 per cent. Dual-income households are now much more prevalent, as in the other countries in our study. Sole mothers with dependent chil-

Table 4.2
Labour-force participation rates of Australian
women, 1966–95

Year	Married women	All women
1966	29.0	36.3
1971	36.4	40.0
1976	41.5	43.0
1981	42.2	44.4
1986	47.1	47.6
1991	52.6	51.5
1995	55.2	50.8

Source: Australian Bureau of Statistics, *The Labour Force (Australia)*, catalogue #6203.0; ABS 1994c, *Labour Statistics Australia*, catalogue #6101.0 (1966–93).

dren increased their workforce participation during the same period from 48 per cent to 52 per cent, although their participation rate dipped as low as 39 per cent in 1983 during the height of the recession (Edwards and Magarey 1995, 266). By 1991, 57 per cent of employed mothers with partners were working part-time, while 44 per cent of employed sole mothers worked part-time (Cass 1995, 51–2). Despite this increase, Australian mothers are much less likely than Canadian mothers to be employed on a full-time basis, as we noted in chapter 1.

In 1983 the Australian Labor Party platform included a commitment of affirmative action within both private and public sectors, and the requirement of equal-opportunity programs was included in the Public Service Reform Act of 1984 (Curtin and Sawer 1996). Because Labor correctly perceived that business would oppose affirmative action, the government gradually introduced these programs into the private sector with considerable consultation, pilot projects, and a working group composed of employers and the ACTU. In 1986 the Labor government passed the Affirmative Action Act, granting equal-employment opportunities to men and women in companies with more than 100 employees. Yet the legislation had little enforcement power until contract compliance was added in 1992 (ibid.). Furthermore, many Australian mothers remained at home to care for their children.

The Hawke/Keating Labor governments encouraged women to become part-time workers while leaving unchallenged the division of labour within the home (Johnson 1996). While gender differences in workforce participation and wages may have been narrowing, repeated surveys reveal wide and persistent gender disparities in the amount of time devoted to housework and caregiving within families (Bittman 1991; Cass 1995; Bittman and Pixley 1997). The double burden for many Australian women, especially low-income women who cannot afford to hire domestic help, affects the time they can spend in paid work. More women in the workforce was primarily viewed by the Labor government as a way of improving economic growth (Johnson 1996), but these initiatives have also helped render more complex the identities of many Australian mothers.

Sole Parent Pension

Australia has provided a widow's pension since 1942 and a supporting mother's benefit since 1973, based on the assumption that a woman who is engaged in the full-time care of children should not be forced into the labour force because of the absence of a breadwinner (Stanton and Herscovitch 1992, 160). Women with partners, however, did not have the same right to leave the workforce and receive a government benefit (Cass 1995, 47), although the wives of unemployed men were indirectly entitled to a benefit through their husband's eligibility. These two benefits were combined in 1989 to create a gender-neutral benefit called the Sole Parent Pension (SPP).

The basic rate of the SPP is equivalent to one-quarter of average weekly earnings – not a generous benefit by Scandinavian standards but one linked to the Consumer Price Index. Prior participation in paid work is not required for eligibility and about 90 per cent of lone parents receive the full or reduced-rate pension (Australia, DSS 1996). The SPP is targeted to low-income sole parents, 86 per cent of whom are women and two-thirds of whom are divorced (Australian Bureau of Statistics 1991). The amount of income permitted before the pension is reduced varies by its source. If a sole-parent pensioner also receives child support from the children's father, a portion of the support money may be retained without losing the pension. This contrasts with the British scheme, which requires lone parents to forfeit their social benefits pound for pound if they also receive support from the child's father (Maclean 1997b). The SPP also requires an assets test that varies for homeowners and renters but it is set at a relatively high level. The SPP is paid until the youngest child reaches the age of sixteen, but it is not payable if a parent is living in a de facto relationship because that person is considered to be married. A lone parent living in privately rented accommodation is also eligible for rent assistance, and this allowance has been increased markedly in recent years (Castles and Shirley 1996, 97).

SPP recipients began to increase their labour-force participation before the introduction of employability programs such as JET, which we will discuss in the next section. The percentage of female pensioners receiving reduced pensions rose from 16.4 per cent in 1982 to 43.7 per cent in 1992, which parallels their greater participation in part-time work. In 1982, 12.5 per cent of sole-parent pensioners worked part-time compared to 22.7 per cent in 1990 (Edwards and Magery 1995, 275).

Over the years, the SPP has generated considerable controversy despite beneficiaries' greater participation in the workforce. The program is seen by many social conservatives as a disincentive to marriage, an incentive to divorce, an encouragement for births outside marriage, and a drain on the social-security budget (Lambert 1994). Lone-parent families are about five times as likely as one-parent families to be in the lowest quintile of income (Australian Bureau of Statistics 1991). Many feminists see the SPP as an important material and symbolic assertion of women's social citizenship rights. Yet constraints on eligibility reduce the value of women's caring work and force sole mothers into the paid labour force in middle age, often with outdated skills and limited job experience (Cass 1995; Shaver 1995; Bryson 1995).

Employability Programs

The Australian labour market changed considerably throughout the 1980s and 1990s, as did labour markets in the other countries. More women and mothers entered the workforce but mainly on a part-time basis. By 1994, 42 per cent of women and 10.5 per cent of men worked part-time (Shaver and Fine 1995, 10), and by 1992, 31 per cent of females and 16 per cent of males were employed casually, mostly in low-skilled jobs with few employment benefits. At the same time, the Australian government began to move away from treating women as different and dependent and towards gender neutrality in more social benefits. This offered fewer provisions for the distinctly female life course shaped by marriage and motherhood (Shaver 1993a, 1995; Cass 1995).

Public discourse on employability was influenced by the major debates on a guaranteed income for all citizens in the 1970s and work-for-the-dole proposals in the 1980s. Both these debates involved political and mass media commentary and attacks on 'dole bludgers,' people who drew government benefits but were unwilling to work. In the 1970s, guaranteed income schemes, designed to break the existing links between work, welfare benefits, and poverty, floundered on a combination of interest-group politics and the constitutional crisis surrounding the dismissal of the Labor government in 1975 (Pixley 1993). A decade later, after the hardships of the early 1980s recession, the Labor government's work-for-the-dole proposals effectively altered the Australian balance between state and individual responsibilities and the conditions under which unemployment benefits would be granted (ibid., 210–13). The idea of compulsory community work in exchange for benefit was abandoned, but, linked with the intensifying 'dole bludger' debate and the growing moral concern over the high percentage of lone mothers on benefits, it formed an important backdrop for the emerging results of the government's social-security review.

The social-security review in 1987 emphasized 'active employment strategies' and new policies to integrate benefits and labour-market policies, an approach strongly endorsed by the ACTU (Bolderson and Mabbett 1991, 166). Most important for sole mothers was the employability initiative called Jobs, Education and Training, introduced in March 1989 and phased in over three years. This voluntary program provides counselling to sole-parent pensioners on the availability of education, training, and employment, as well as access to childcare. Priority has been given to teen mothers, mothers whose youngest child is approaching sixteen, and mothers with children over six who have been receiving the SPP for more than twelve months (Saunders and Matheson, 1991). Internationally, this program has been considered successful because employment rates have increased for lone mothers, yet they have also increased for partnered mothers not receiving any social benefit. Nevertheless, JET influenced the design of the British Welfare-to-Work program in 1996–7, which we will discuss in chapter 6.

In July 1991 the Labor government abolished the unemployment benefit and replaced it with the Job Search Allowance (JSA) for those unemployed for less than twelve months and a NEWSTART allowance for those unemployed for twelve months or more. Under these programs, the unemployed are compelled to undertake retraining and demonstrate that they are actively searching for work in order to receive a government allowance (Lambert 1994). In addition, the government initiated a wage-subsidy program (JOBSTART) which provides a six-month subsidy to employers who hire people from targeted groups, including lone parents (Baker 1995, 93).

From September 1994 until July 1995, several important changes were made in unemployment benefits which heralded a new view of the wife of an unemployed person as eligible for benefits in her own right. This differed from the previous practice of paying an unemployed man extra benefits for 'his dependants.' In the past, the treatment of the married couple/household as the unit for assessing income meant that women whose partners relied upon benefits did not have strong incentives to enter into paid work (Cass 1995). This policy was changed so that women over forty years of age, caring for the home but without children, unable to find work but living with an unemployed man, were directly paid a Partners Allowance while those with dependent children were directly paid a Parenting Allowance. In addition, a lump sum Maternity Allowance was initiated once again in February 1996 for mothers on the birth of their child, which is equivalent to six weeks of the Parenting Allowance (over $A800) (Bradbury 1996). These new benefits were announced in time to solicit the women's vote in the 1996 election (Bittman and Pixley 1996). However, Labor lost the election to the National-Liberal coalition.

In the May 1997 budget, the coalition government announced a pilot 'work-for-the-dole' scheme targeted at unemployed young people who would work in community-based projects in rural areas with high unemployment. In order to make this pilot project a regular part of Australian employment programs, social-security laws need to be changed, and at the time of the program's announcement this issue was being studied by a Senate committee. A portion of the pilot project's budget was intended to cover the participants' childcare expenses ($519,000 out of $21.6 million), but this amount was calculated on only six hours of childcare per day rather than a full workday (*The Australian*, 14 May 1997). Clearly, the Australian government is moving towards greater employability for beneficiaries, but in 1998 low-income mothers with children under sixteen remained exempt from these programs.

Wolcott and Glezer (1995) argue that Australian women more than men organize their work time to suit family needs. Based on research from the Australian Institute of Family Studies[4] (AIFS), they note that, although women express moderate satisfaction with working conditions and hours, they make more family-related accommodations than men by working part-time and taking time off work with sick children. Behaviour has changed very little towards egalitarian sharing of work and family, though there has been more rhetorical change. Policies emphasize 'choice' when it comes to how families will combine work and family, but only women are offered this choice. Furthermore, real or perceived constraints shape the choices of both genders. Flexible work arrangements are still based on the premise that it is women rather than men (and not those in senior positions) who will take advantage of work flexibility (Wolcott and Glezer 1995).

Scrutiny of Beneficiaries

Despite the controlled and measured reductions in provision of benefits by the Australian state, Baldock (1994) argues that intervention, regulation, and intrusion continue in the daily lives of low-income mothers. Yeatman (1990) has characterized this as the development of the 'complex interventionist state.' Some mothers have been encouraged into the private sphere of paid employment, but this does not necessarily mean the disappearance of the government's presence since many are still receiving social benefits. Family circumstances are scrutinized, especially the finances of other family members and cohabitants. Advanced computer technology has assisted the detection of fraudulent behaviour by welfare recipients and, since 1990, applicants for social assistance have been required to give their income-tax file number in order to ensure payments. Another example of the interventionist state is the plethora of mediation, counselling, and conflict-resolution services which have come into being in last few years and which are sometimes compulsory for people seeking social assistance.

Privatization and state intervention have a specially pronounced effect on women, for women form the majority of sole parents, aged pensioners, caregivers, and welfare workers (Baldock 1994). Not surprisingly, women form a substantial proportion of social-security offenders, and the punishment of women offenders is more stringent than for men (Wilkie 1993). The move from state to voluntary-sector services involves an element of 'charity,' emphasizing individual responsibility and employability. Clearly, rolling back the Australian state has had negative implications for women, both as welfare recipients and as welfare workers (Baldock 1994).

Divorce and Spousal Support

Another strategy affecting the income of mothers is the privatization of child support by stricter enforcement of court awards. In 1975 the Family Law Act introduced a unilateral 'no fault' divorce into Australian law. Under this act, the new ground for divorce was 'irretrievable break-down of the marriage,' evidenced by one year of marital separation, but judges retained their discretion in decisions about dividing property to make it 'just and equitable' (Funder and Harrison 1993). Child-support awards tended to be small and non-compliance was considerable; spousal support was considered to be 'rehabilitative,' a 'bridge between marriage and employment,' and was based on the principle of a 'clean break,' as in Canadian law. Legal divorce was seen as offering the freedom to begin again and to enter into new unions with no lingering guilt, financial obligations, or ties between former spouses. Yet, by the late 1970s, this law was seen as arbitrary: men felt that they were 'taken to cleaners' by wives who did not contribute to assets, and many wives saw that their non-financial contributions to the home were undervalued. This led the Commonwealth government to refer the issue of matrimonial property reform to the Australian Law Reform Commission and to ask the Australian Institute of Family Studies to study the economic consequences of divorce (ibid., 26).

AIFS initiated a series of research projects on the impact of divorce on families. In 1984 McDonald (1986) directed a longitudinal survey of over 500 divorced couples with children (two to five years after separation) which focused on the economic consequences of divorce, the division of family property, changing residence, and sources of income. The researchers found that, after divorce, child-support payments were low, sporadic, and poorly enforced, yet many couples were able to divorce and 'settle up' without undue conflict, cost, and pain for the children. In fact, the majority of couples settled out of court. Staying in the matrimonial home rather than moving out increased the odds of retaining it as part of the property settlement. Unexpectedly, women from higher-income marriages were more likely to turn to social-security benefits than those from less well-off marriages because their work skills had atrophied over time. Yet women's sense of well-being after divorce was typically higher than men's, even though their economic status was considerably lower. The researchers related gender differences in living standards to patterns of family repartnering and access to earnings; men were more likely than women to remarry but they also had higher earnings. The researchers noted that child support and other economic transfers did not adequately redress the gender balance.

In a second project sponsored by AIFS, the experiences of the same 500 divorced men and women were monitored from five to eight years after the final separation (but divorcing before the new Child Support

Scheme was introduced) (Funder 1993). The researchers found that differences in living standards persisted between resident mothers and non-resident fathers. Non-partnered mothers experienced a high risk of poverty, and, even though they tended to return to the labour force within five years of the final separation, they still required a 'social security bridge.' Children continued to be a high priority and source of satisfaction for resident mothers, but a diminishing priority for fathers. Yet both men and women tended to 're-equilibrate' after divorce. Private-income transfers, which were infrequent and inadequate in the early years of separation, later became trivial to both, and moving away from the matrimonial home was the norm for both residential and non-residential parents. The study concluded that the issue of private and public responsibility for children in all family types is central to any consideration of the economic remedies for children after divorce.

Common law traditionally considered family issues to be the province of family members rather than an area subject to state control (Harrison 1993, 35). Used in all four countries of this study (except the Canadian province of Quebec), common law is based on judicial discretion, a minimum of legislative prescription, and separate property regimes. Spouses are treated as separate individuals with regard to their property dealings and retain control and ownership of property acquired before marriage. Yet judicial discretion in the division of matrimonial property tends to lead to unpredictability and variation in outcomes, even though it allows consideration of the individual merits of each case. This involves assessment of past and present contributions during married life and then a consideration of whether the outcomes should be equal or varied because of differences in 'need.' The AIFS studies, however, concluded that serious deficiencies were evident in the structure and impact of Australian law related to support (Harrison 1993).

In all four countries, spousal maintenance used to be paid to full-time homemakers or simply to assuage guilt. Now, divorce in Australia terminates marital rights and obligations in all senses of the word. In divorce law, women are no longer considered to be the dependants of men (although they continued to be viewed as dependants in the unemployment-benefit system until 1996). Spousal support need not be based on dependency but rather on the reparation for losses incurred, but the conceptual step was not made in Australia from seeing spousal support as some sort of 'favour payment' to viewing it as an 'entitlement to remedy economic disadvantage' (Harrison 1993, 45). Instead, the Family

Law Act enables a spousal-maintenance award to be made where it is 'proper'; where payers can afford to pay; where payees cannot support themselves because of age, the care of children, disability, or illness; or for 'any other adequate reason' (ibid., 46).

Few Australian judges now require men to pay spousal support after divorce, and when they do so, the court award is not always enforced. Although 25 per cent of separated husbands were required to pay spousal support (or maintenance) in the 1980s, only 7 per cent of separated wives received payments two years after the separation (McDonald 1986). In 1987, five to eight years later, only 2 per cent of former wives were receiving payments (Funder, Harrison, and Weston 1993). Maintenance was rarely paid because the economically stronger spouse could support only himself, a property settlement eliminated the need to pay spousal support, and extra resources went into child support (ibid., 47).

Poverty among children has been seen as a more important policy priority than poverty among mothers, even though research in Australia (as well as in the other three countries) demonstrates that an exceptionally high percentage of lone mothers live in poverty. In 1989 the United Nations Convention on the Rights of the Child became a binding international legal agreement, and well before then political leaders started preparing their statements about their country's achievements in this area (Baker 1995, 68). In 1987 the Australian (Labor) prime minister promised to attack child poverty on every front. Research by AIFS had demonstrated that child-support payments were too low and seldom paid and that families with children had experienced declining living standards (Harrison, Snider, and Merlo 1990). One policy strategy was to revamp child benefits through the social-security system and the other was to revise the child-support scheme.

Child Support

In 1988 a new two-staged policy on child support was introduced (the Child Support Registration and Collection Act), designed to 'help resolve child poverty' but also to 'reduce public expenditures' (Millar and Whiteford 1993). In 1988, Stage One established a Child Support Agency (CSA) within the Taxation Office where support money was collected and deposited in a trust fund from which the Department of Social Security made payments to the residential parent (usually the mother). This shared jurisdiction proved to be cumbersome, as we will discuss later.

Stage Two took the assessment of child support out of the courts and placed it in the hands of the CSA, with a formula for calculating the amount payable. Unlike the British legislation in 1993, the Australian system was not retrospective and covers only those separations occurring after October 1989. The formula is based on the absent parent's gross income (before taxes) from two years before, updated by the Consumer Price Index to the current year. Both married and unmarried parents are included. Living expenses for the parent and any natural or adopted children living with him are deducted, and these expenses are calculated with reference to the value of the government unemployment benefit. The amount of child support payable then varies by the number of children: 18 per cent of remaining income for one child, 27 per cent for two children, 32 per cent for three, 34 per cent for four; and 35 per cent for five or more. The maximum income level for the father's assessment was set at 2.5 times average full-time earnings. Further modifications are made for split or shared custody, non-cash payments, and the mother's earnings (ibid.).

Since the introduction of the Australian scheme, the proportion of lone parents receiving child support has increased and awards are about one-third higher. Yet registration with the CSA does not guarantee that the mother will receive support money for her children, since less than three-quarters of the money due is actually collected. The likelihood of making payments is higher for the formerly married rather than the never-married, for those still in contact with their children, and for those recently separated (Harrison 1993).

The Australian legislation has proved to be controversial, but less so than the comparable legislation in the United Kingdom, as we will see in chapter 6. Although the Australian public agreed that reforms were needed in the setting and enforcement of child support, the legal profession opposed the new scheme because it took away their discretion in setting the amounts of child-support payments (Harrison 1993). The scheme is also perceived to lack flexibility because it does not take into consideration recent changes in parent's income, repartnering, or exceptional expenses. About half of absent parents (fathers) reported that they were 'unhappy' or 'very unhappy' with the scheme (Harrison et al. 1991) and objected to paying for children when there was no access or if they thought their former partner was better off than they were. Absent parents also objected to the 'high' amounts they were expected to pay and to paying through the income-tax system. The main reason absent fathers gave for non-payment was unemployment (Millar and Whiteford 1993).

Lone mothers have reacted against the scheme primarily because payments have been delayed, but 21 per cent expressed concern about potential violence from their partner, saying that registration in the scheme 'opened up old wounds' (ibid.). Nevertheless, the collection rate is better than it was before the introduction of scheme. Furthermore, child-support assessment has been removed from the courts, standardized, and paid indirectly to avoid continued contact with the former spouse. This new process also minimizes under-reporting of child support by welfare recipients (Alexander 1995).

The scheme has also been criticized because the CSA has not improved the collection rate as substantially as people had expected. About half of the mothers who are registered are not receiving payments, and, among those who are, half were already receiving them before the introduction of the scheme. Yet short-term gains are real even though they are modest (Millar and Whiteford 1993). As expected, the scheme has been more successful enforcing support among affluent middle-class men who can be more easily traced and can afford to pay (Jones 1996, 97).

Although CSA claims a 73 per cent collection rate, a parliamentary committee has challenged the calculation method, which does not compare the total amount collected with total amount owed, but rather the total amount collected with the 'estimated collectable amount.' The assumption is that child support cannot be retrieved from parents who have no income or from those who cannot be located. Furthermore, the agency's calculations include amounts collected privately by the residential spouse (Alexander 1995).

Another problem with the scheme is its failure to deliver efficiently the payments it collects. The process remains cumbersome since it is split between two bureaucracies: the Taxation Office and the Department of Social Security. These two bureaucracies experience the expected liaison and logistics problems that tend to occur when jurisdiction is divided. Poor communication also exists with clients. The Taxation Office allegedly sends computerized pro forma letters and does not always not answer correspondence, while clients experience difficulty reaching the office by telephone (ibid.).

The Australian Child Support Scheme is not retroactive, which can be viewed both as a disadvantage and as an advantage. Children born before 1989 are not included in the scheme, which means that they tend to receive lower amounts of child support. In contrast, the British Child Support Scheme (1993) is retroactive, but this has created numerous problems when previous agreements to trade cash or property settlements for child support were overturned.

To coincide with changes to child-support legislation, the Family Law Act was amended in 1995 (effective June 1996). Parental responsibilities used to be defined by which parent was granted custody, guardianship, and access, but the 1995 amendments remove these concepts and any connotation of ownership. Now each parent has joint custody and guardianship of the child, although the courts continue to make parenting orders relating to residence, contact, and other issues. The new focus is on various measures of obtaining agreement, such as counselling, conciliation, and mediation. Parenting plans must be provided, reflecting the parties' agreement on the child's care and upbringing, and the new law emphasizes parents' responsibility for making these plans. Furthermore, the Family Court has streamlined procedures and will not accept escalating disputes until all other avenues have been exhausted. The language of the new Family Law Act is clear and client-friendly, requiring minimal paperwork (Funder 1996b).

Other jurisdictions have used the Australia Child Support Scheme as a model, including the Canadian provinces, New Zealand, and the United Kingdom. Yet the legislation has neither reduced child poverty nor substantially reduced the number of lone mothers on social assistance. The majority of sole parents still depend on government benefits, but this cannot be blamed entirely on child-support payments since full-time employment rates for lone mothers remain low by international standards (Bradshaw et al. 1996).

In the May 1998 budget, the amount of money a lone parent can earn before her ex-partner's child support payments are reduced was cut to $29,500 a year, $2,000 lower than the previous year. Sole parents can earn up to $40,000 before it offsets their ex-partner's child-support payments. Yet only 6 per cent of custodial parents earn more than $30,000 per year (Lamont 1998). Women's organizations (such as Women's Electoral Lobby) criticized this budget change, arguing that it will discourage women from entering the labour force.

Caring for Children and Dependent Adults

Since the Child Care Act in 1972, public day-care centres have been funded through cost-sharing arrangements among federal, state, and local governments but parents must pay fees for these services (Ergas 1990). The federal government pays an operating grant for each approved childcare place and, since 1988, has also offered tax deductions to private companies providing childcare services (Ochiltree 1992). The Australian Council of Trade Unions supported public funding for private centres, but this was opposed by the community childcare lobby[5] and other supporters of universal access who want all care to be not-for-profit (Curtin and Sawer 1996; Kaplan 1996, 54). The number of private day-care centres has increased since they became eligible for government assistance, yet a shortage of childcare spaces exists in Australia (Australia, Child Care Tax Force Interim Report 1996).

Although the Child Care Act initially focused on children 'in need,' the Labor government established a policy of universal access to childcare when it assumed power in 1983. Despite this policy, priority continued to be given to employed lone parents, two-income families, and children with special needs (Ergas 1990). Childcare became a more political issue with higher employment rates for mothers throughout the 1980s, and funding increased steadily (Ochiltree 1992). Commonwealth-funded childcare places were increased from 46,000 in 1983 to 253,000 by end of December 1994 (Wolcott and Glezer 1995).

Before the 1993 election, the Labor Party had promised a social benefit to recognize the loss of income experienced by parents who forgo full-time employment to care for their children at home. Clearly, this policy was designed to capture the conservative women's vote. However, in 1994, after Labor's victory under Paul Keating, the government first introduced the Child Care Cash Rebate (CCCR) to help families meet work-related childcare costs. This rebate, providing $28.80 per week for one child and $62.55 for two or more children, covers both formal and informal care (including care by a family member) and payments are made through the Medicare office. The Labor government also introduced a new childcare-accreditation scheme in the same year (Curtin and Sawer 1996).

Several conservative women's groups (such as Women's Action Alliance) continued to lobby for a payment for mothers at home, reminding the government that the Lavarch report (*Report of the Inquiry into Equal Opportunity and Equal Status for Women*) had recommended it in 1992. In response to this lobby, the Keating Labor government replaced the Dependant Spouse Rebate (DSR) with the Home Child Care Allowance (HCCA). The HCCA was a non-taxable allowance means-tested on the caregiver's income, while the DSR had been a tax rebate paid to the husband based on family income. The maximum HCCA was $60 a fortnight, a very small increase over the former DSR, but the money was directed to mothers as caregivers rather than fathers as the principle tax filers in the family (Henman 1996).

Although both the HCCA and the CCCR successfully captured the women's vote, the allowance remained quite controversial with other interest groups. In earlier years, for example, the trade unions had objected to the idea of converting a tax benefit for (male) breadwinners into an allowance for (female) caregivers, since this would represent a loss of income and power for male wage earners. Yet, as women's labour-force participation and union membership increased and economic globalization forced unions to make concessions to government, the unions eventually supported Labor's childcare reforms. In fact, the unions placed greater emphasis on the 'social wage' to counter the loss of income due to declining real wages under the 1983 Accord (ibid.).

Lobby groups continued to argue about these new childcare benefits. Conservative groups (as well as the opposition parties) argued that the Labor government was favouring employed women over homemakers. Furthermore, they noted that the tax rebate for childcare was distributed at Medicare offices, while the allowance was directed through social security, giving it a different connotation. The conservative Women's Action Alliance objected to the fact that the HCCA but not the CCCR was targeted to lower-income families. The National Council for the International Year of the Family argued that the two benefits should be amalgamated and targeted to families with a child under six, but it also wanted the payment increased. The Australian Council of Social Service (ACOSS) recommended that the allowance be directed to caregivers of pre-school children rather than targeted to lower-income families (Henman 1996).

Because of this controversy, the HCCA lasted for only nine months before the government replaced it with the Parenting Allowance. The Parenting Allowance offers all parents caring full-time for children at home a benefit of A$61.20 per fortnight, but low-income families are entitled to up to $272 per fortnight. In creating this benefit, the Labor government argued that the Parenting Allowance recognizes the value of the caring work performed by parents who choose to stay at home to care for their children (Henman 1996).

Despite these initiatives, Australians have been slower than Canadians to accept the idea of non-family childcare to enable mothers to enter the labour force. Traditional gender-segregated views persist, personal independence is still highly valued, and employed mothers tend to work part-time and retain the major responsibility for housework and childcare. Any convergence in men's and women's time spent in house-work and childcare since the 1980s has occurred because women are spending less time on housework and not because men are spending more (Bittman 1995).

In their 1996 budget, the coalition government (conservative) intro-duced additional changes to the funding of childcare. These included the removal of operating subsidies from community day care beginning July 1997 but with the guarantee that four years of funding would be available for family day care, occasional care, outside-school-hours care, multifunctional services, and multifunctional aboriginal services. The government also extended accreditation to family day care but offered no new funds (Australia, NFDCC 1996). This announcement repre-sented a move from subsidizing group care to privatization by giving parents a tax rebate to purchase their own care. The government ratio-nalized this reform as necessary 'to support choice for parents,' but it also accompanies a devolution of childcare support from the Common-wealth government to state governments.

As in Canada, the state premiers, represented by the Council of Aus-tralian Governments want social services (including childcare) to be delivered by states and territories rather than by both levels of govern-ments. In 1996 family day care[6] was regulated by the Commonwealth government but this will be devolved to the states in the future. Organi-zations such as National Family Day Care Council of Australia (NFD-CCA) objected to these changes because they want common federal goals to be retained to help the states administer services. The NFDCCA believes that it is in the 'best interest of Australia's children for the Com-monwealth government to maintain responsibility for delivery of child care services, that the National Children's Services Program be main-tained and expanded, and that there be allocation of sufficient resources to enable the delivery of high quality care to all those children requiring it' (Australia, NFDCC 1996, 11). The NFDCCA also argues that more government support for one-earner families with the mother at home sends a double message to women. On the one hand, women are being told that they do not need to work for pay yet there is more emphasis on 'employability' in other social benefits (such as the SPP). The Labor shadow minister for aged, family, and community Services (Jenny Macklin) recently asked: 'Is this an attempt to solve unemployment problems by removing women from labour force?' (ibid., 13).

A continued focus on deficit reduction remained a priority for the Australian government, despite opposition from community groups and the political left. Yet, in the October 1996 budget, the coalition government allocated $36.7 million more than in 1995–6 for caregivers, established a National Respite for Carers Program, and announced the creation of Carers Resource Centres across the country. The government also increased the number of respite days available to carers from forty-two to fifty-two days per year and carer pensioners can now spend twenty hours a week (up from ten) in work or study without losing benefits. Furthermore, the government announced an allocation of $31 million more for children with high levels of need (such as children with disabilities) who would normally be placed in federally funded childcare services.

In 1996 the Carers Association of Australia (CAA 1996) noted that there were 1.5 million carers in Australia who saved the government an estimated $8 billion annually by providing these important services, but the majority lived in poverty, their health was poor, and family relationships were near the breaking point. The executive director of CAA stated that the government relied more on these women as it moved ahead with policies of deinstitutionalization, early hospital discharges, and rapid changes in field of community care. (In fact, 75 per cent of the frail elderly and persons with disabilities are now reliant on informal home-based care.) CAA argued that the community health-care system would collapse without the contribution of carers, but, with middle-aged women now entering the workforce and families more mobile, fewer people were willing or able to become carers. Furthermore, the Medicare system contained contradictions: some disability aids are covered under Medicare if the person is cared for in an institution but not if the person is cared for at home. The executive director of CAA claimed that 'carers are shaping up as *the* major social policy issue of the decade' (Carers Association of Australia 1996). Apparently CAA lobbying paid off because in October 1996, during 'Carers Week,' the minister for family services announced that $24,800 of federal money was to be given to CAA. This money was for a study to improve the quality of life of young carers and those they care for, and especially to investigate the role of children under fifteen who serve as carers.

In the May 1997 budget, however, the same coalition government announced further cuts to childcare expenditures. A limit was imposed on new private-sector places in 1998 and 1999, which is expected to save $206.9 million over four years (Gunn 1997). As the level of unmet need among children under five years old is estimated to be about 72 per cent, this announcement is unlikely to win support from parents who cannot find a place for their child. Despite the emphasis on employability, the coalition government also announced that it would limit to twenty hours a week access to Childcare Assistance for parents who are studying or searching for work. If parents required more hours, they would have to use their own money. The government also reduced operating subsidies for after-school care in centres. After 1 January 1998, all funding for childcare outside school hours was paid directly to low-income parents (with family incomes under $26,000) in the form of an enhanced childcare assistance payment (Gunn 1997). Despite these cuts, the coalition government has promised to increase the number of family daycare places by 2,500 from 1997 to 2001, primarily to alleviate pressures in rural and remote areas. In the May 1998 budget, the two-year freeze on childcare-assistance payments was extended for another year despite an increase in centre fees (Allard 1998).

Maternity Allowance

In the 1995–6 budget, the Labor government announced the establishment of a Maternity Allowance to take effect February 1996 (Wolcott and Glezer 1995, 143). Like the original maternity allowance of 1912, this is a one-time payment at the birth of a child. But, unlike the original universal allowance, the 1996 benefit is income-tested to low- and middle-income families.[7] It is worth an equivalent of six weeks of the Parenting Allowance and is non-taxable. The allowance, which is not based on workforce attachment, recognizes the extra costs occasioned by childbirth (such as cots and prams) as well as mothers' lost earnings. In March 1996 the allowance was worth A$857.40 and is payable with the first instalment of Basic Family Payment after the birth. About 85 per cent of women giving birth are eligible for this payment. The introduction of the Maternity Allowance was supported by groups such as ACOSS and the National Council for the International Year of the Family (Henman 1996).

Leave for Childbirth and Family Responsibilities

Since 1973, twelve months of *unpaid* maternity leave have been available to all Commonwealth government employees (temporary and part-time as well as permanent). In addition, these employees receive twelve weeks of paid leave if they have one year of continuous service. In 1979 this entitlement was extended to many private-sector workers when the

Australian Council of Trade Unions brought its maternity test case to the Australian Industrial Relations Commission (AIRC) (Wolcott and Glezer 1995, 145).

In 1990, the AIRC's parental leave test case replaced gender-specific maternity leave in most awards with twelve months of unpaid leave shared between parents (with one week at birth overlapping). In addition, provision was made for parents to work part-time until the child's second birthday, if the employer agrees. By 1992, parental leave had been inserted into 280 federal awards and adopted by most state awards and legislation (ibid., 146). The Industrial Relations Reform Act (1993), proclaimed in March 1994, prohibits termination because of family responsibilities. Employers are now required to provide twelve months of unpaid leave (which can be shared between parents) as a minimum employment entitlement, although casual and part-time employees who have not worked for the employer for twelve continuous months are exempt.

In August 1994 the first stage of the test-case decision on family leave by the AIRC stated that employees can use their own sick leave for the care and support of sick family members. This decision allowed greater flexibility in the workplace for family needs and formally recognized caring responsibilities within households. Yet it did not grant any additional leave time. Stage two of the personal-carers test case in 1995 allowed employees to combine sick leave and bereavement leave for family-leave purposes and provided a maximum of five days of carers' leave that can be accumulated. It also allowed carers' leave to be taken as a portion of the work day rather than an entire day (Australia, Department of Industrial Relations 1996). Many employees, however, are ineligible for carers' leave. This includes the 23 per cent of employees and 30 per cent of women employees who were 'casual' workers in 1994. Also, 24 per cent of women have been in their jobs less than twelve months and are therefore ineligible for paid parental leave (Australian Bureau of Statistics 1994b).

Australian statistics (like those from other jurisdictions) indicate that mothers rather than fathers are taking parental and family leave, even though it was meant to be gender-neutral. Among workers with children under twelve who have been absent in last the two weeks, 9 per cent of women and 2 per cent of men were on maternity or parental leave. There is no special sick leave to take care of family members except for the decisions of the ACTU test cases in 1994 and 1995, noted above. Whatever advances have been made could be halted in the future by the recent move from centralized-bargaining towards more enterprise-level negotiations, even though the award system has been retained (Wolcott and Glezer 1995, 147).

The Australian Bureau of Statistics studied the incidence of long career breaks (defined as six months or longer) as part of a career-experience survey in 1993. The majority of job holders taking a break were between the ages of twenty-five and forty-four, half were employed in the community-services sector, and two-thirds were women. Most of the women cited childbirth and childcare reasons for their long breaks from paid work (ABS 1994). In a separate study of dependent care by the Australian Institute of Family Studies, 64 per cent of workers took time off work to provide care for a parent during an illness or to help them cope with a medical emergency (VandenHeuvel 1993).

In 1994 the National Council for the International Year of the Family lobbied unsuccessfully for a universal twelve-week maternity/parental leave paid through the social-security system, to which all taxpayers would contribute (Wolcott and Glezer 1995, 143). It argued that eligibility should not depend on labour-force status but should recognize children's needs and provide choice for women (and men). Legislation on this point has never been passed. Instead, the Maternity Allowance was introduced in 1996.

The Australian government has made some efforts to acknowledge that women workers are not identical to men workers. Two pieces of legislation have provided the foundations to improve women's position in the labour force. The first was the Sex Discrimination Act (1984), which prohibited discrimination based on sex, marital status, and pregnancy, and in 1992 the Labor government added 'family responsibilities' to this list. The second was the Affirmative Action, Equal Employment Opportunities for Women Act (1986). In 1990 Australia ratified the International Labour Organization Convention 156 (Workers With Family Responsibilities) and United Nations Declaration on the Rights of the Child, both of which strengthen the concept of parental sharing of work and family responsibilities through the provision of childcare (Wolcott and Glezer 1995, 145).

Yet other nations have made greater efforts than Australia has to combine work and family life through social policy. Norway and Sweden, for example, have legislated more equitable sharing of parental leave by stating that the father must take four weeks of leave or those weeks are forfeited. In the Netherlands, all secondary students must take a 'caregiving' subject, introduced in 1992. Even these policy changes, however, have not always created gender equality in the workplace. Danish research indicates that female-dominated workplaces have allowed more 'family space' (defined as flexibility for family leave or interruptions for family concerns) than male-dominated workplaces (Holt 1993). The United States has created few policies to alleviate work/family conflicts, yet labour-force participation rates are high for women. Both managers and fellow employees tend to express concern about job advancement when either men or women take family leave, and the workplace 'culture' tends to discourage the use of this leave (Zackin 1994, 7). Wolcott and Glezer (1995) have used these studies to recommend equitable sharing between men and women for both earning and caring.

Studies of employer attitudes to work and family in small and large Australian businesses (Wolcott 1991, 1993) confirm that many employers still see family concerns as a problem for women and the solution to be part-time work. Attitudes of middle and senior management are an obstacle to integrating family-supportive policies into the workplace, for the managers themselves have wives at home. Wolcott and Glezer (1995) argue that the implementation of flexible workplace policies depend on the corporate ethos but that we need to differentiate between what is merely convenient for the corporation and what is necessary for the job. Waiting until more women enter executive positions is not the solution. A study of 500 women executives found that these senior women were hardworking, ambitious, and happy in their careers, and two-thirds worked more than fifty hours a week. Yet only two-thirds were married and 55 per cent remained childless (Maloney 1994). This suggests that many Australian women still feel that they must make a choice between career and family.

Attitudes are becoming more egalitarian yet behaviour remains traditional. In fact, Australians seem to be ambivalent about egalitarian gender roles; women do not want to relinquish control of childrearing because so much of their identity is connected with it and there is little indication that men want to work part-time. In research studies, Australian women say that they prefer part-time to full-time work (Wolcott and Glezer 1995), yet this personal 'preference' clearly is influenced by traditional attitudes in the larger society and the reality of the division of labour in most homes. Women are still expected to care for the home and children regardless of their employment status.

Part-time work is seen as a solution to women's 'double day,' but part-time workers often work more than thirty-six hours a week in order to get the job done without earning an income sufficient to support their family (Catalyst 1993). At the same time, the average full-time work day in Australia increased from forty to forty-two hours between 1981 and 1993, despite the emphasis on family-friendly working conditions. Furthermore, the percentage of employed men who worked more than forty-nine hours a week increased from 19 per cent to 27 per cent in the same period (ABS 1993). This increase certainly has implications for the gendered division of labour at home.

Globalization has encouraged employers to argue for greater flexibility in the labour force, but this often means that employees are 'on call' to work unpredictable hours, leading to problems with caring arrangements. Furthermore, the 'new technology' and the opportunity to 'telework' in Australia and the other three countries could mean that work will intrude into people's lives all hours of the day, leading to increased pressure and guilt. Despite the trend towards contract work and part-time employment, the Australian social-security system continues to be based largely on full-time employment.

Wolcott and Glezer (1995, 181) believe that integrating work and family can be resolved by mothers working part-time, since 'the majority are satisfied with this solution.' Yet they acknowledge that workplace arrangements have assumed that women rather than men make the necessary adjustments. If this pattern continues, gender segregation will be perpetuated in the labour force and women will continue to receive lower earnings, reinforcing their dependence on both their male partners and the state.

'Choice' and Government Rhetoric

Several recent statements by Cabinet ministers of the National-Liberal coalition government have emphasized 'giving women the choice' to stay at home with their children or to accept paid work. In August 1996, for example, Jocelyn Newman (minister for social security) declared: 'The Government is committed to policies which provide women with greater freedom of choice, particularly in relation to their involvement in the paid work force' (Newman 1996, 1). No mention was made of giving men a similar choice. Newman continued: 'The Government acknowledges women's major role in maintaining family life, a task which is increasingly challenged. As a result, the Government has developed a Strengthening Families Strategy which will assist families to deal with these pressures' (ibid., 5). This strategy included money for 'relationship education services,' parenting education, funding for emergency relief aid to social agencies, and funding for a pilot project for the homeless. In this speech, the minister also announced the National Respite for Carers program, in which the carer 'pension' was renamed a 'payment' and the number of respite days and work or study hours was increased. In the same speech, she also reiterated the government's commitment to maintaining the Sole Parent Pension, the JET program, and the Education Entry Payment (money to defray the academic expenses of those returning to school).

In October 1996, during 'Carers Week,' Judi Moylan, minister for family services for the coalition government, said: 'The family is the core unit in our society. For generations the family has endured as the primary and most effective provider of assistance and support for people of all ages and from all backgrounds. The Coalition is absolutely committed to ensuring that the needs of families remain at the centre of public policy. One of our highest priorities as a government is to relieve the financial pressures on low and middle income families bringing up children' (Moylan 1996b, 1). The minister assured Australians that the government 'recognizes that providing an economic and social environment in which families can achieve their full potential is crucial to maintaining a strong, cohesive and compassionate society' (ibid., 1). She continued: 'While it is not an appropriate role for government to make choices on behalf of families, it does have an obligation to pursue policies that enable families to choose how they balance their work and child raising responsibilities. The Coalition is committed to ensuring that families with young children are given greater freedom to choose whether one parent cares full-time for their children at home or whether both are in the paid workforce' (ibid., 1). The minister noted that, after thirteen years of Labor governments, her government (National-Liberal) was in debt. Nevertheless, she announced the Family Tax Initiative, which increases the tax-free threshold especially for single-earner families with a child under five and provides more money for special-needs children. This speech contained a strong emphasis on 'choice,' but what influences choice in this realm? Entering the labour force or staying at home with children is not just a matter of personal whim. Decisions involve economic, cultural, social, and policy constraints such as the earning capacity and income of one's partner, the availability and affordability of childcare within the community, and access to transportation. Decisions are also influenced by social expectations and values, and are shaped by past experiences and the range of opportunities people perceive to exist (Bradbury 1996).

In 1996 the Department of Social Security commissioned an evaluation of the Parenting Allowance, comparing 1,003 clients to 322 nonbeneficiaries. Wilson (1996) has reported on the initial stages of this longitudinal survey. Parenting Allowance recipients decided to stay at home and accept the government benefit because they felt that their children needed their full-time care, because of health problems of their own or their children's, or because their partners earned an adequate income to support the entire family. Particularly mothers with pre-school children preferred to remain at home. Among the non-clients, women already in the labour force were reluctant to leave their jobs for fear of losing income, losing or waiting longer for workplace benefits (such as long-service leave), being discriminated against after maternity leave, and being 'left behind by technology' if they left the workforce temporarily. Mothers who returned to work shortly after their children were born (also non-recipients of the Parenting Allowance) did so for many reasons. Home-ownership costs were too high to be covered by one family income, their family income was insecure, they wanted the 'little extras,' and they needed intellectual stimulation and social contact. These preliminary results certainly indicate that women's perceptions and choices are socially constructed (Wilson 1996).

One factor shaping lifestyle choice is the availability of adequate income. Mothers who want to care for their own children at home are usually dependent on their partner's income or on government benefits. When mothers are forced to raise their children on a subsistence income, including low wages, they may be restricting the future choices of their children. In 1987 the prime minister (Bob Hawke) stated that by 1990 no child should be living in poverty in Australia. In 1990 the Life Chances of Children Study commenced in Melbourne, sponsored by the Brotherhood of St Laurence (Taylor 1996). The sample included 167 children born in that year in inner Melbourne, comparing those living in a high-income area with those living in a low-income area. This longitudinal study found that low income is associated with poor health, high stress, marital problems, and less informal support and assistance from family and friends. Furthermore, after five years, more families were in the low-income category and many experienced high residential mobility. Some children lacked access to pre-school because of fee requirements, even though their parents valued education. This research suggests that, despite government rhetoric about reducing poverty, income discrepancies continue that reduce the opportunities of poor children (ibid.).

Labour-force participation rates remain low in Australia compared to Canada, the United States, and Sweden, especially for lone mothers. Although 51 per cent of mothers in two-parent families and 43 per cent of lone mothers were in the labour force in 1994–5, only about 27 per cent of partnered mothers and 22 per cent of sole mothers were employed full-time. (See Table 1.4 in chapter 1.) In Canada, the comparable figures for full-time employment are 41 and 32 (Baker and Tippin 1997). Nevertheless, more Australian mothers have been entering the labour force in recent decades.

Despite increases in women's employment rates, their poverty rates have not diminished. Poverty rates for lone parents actually increased from 40.8 per cent in 1981–2 to 47.9 per cent in 1989–90 (Mitchell 1995, 91). This is consistent with other observed increases in overall income inequality in Australia during the last two decades (Castles and Shirley 1996, 100). Women workers tend to occupy low-paid jobs that are more vulnerable to economic recession and they also tend to receive fewer occupational benefits. This persistent gender segregation and inequality suggests that employability programs need to be rethought for lone mothers, since they require more than jobs. They would also benefit from long-term educational training leading to higher-paid positions, inexpensive but reliable childcare, and the reduction of tax-back rates when they leave social benefits (Vrielink 1996). In addition, women's employment status cannot improve without changes in cultural values about women's role, which is still seen as primarily domestic in Australia.

The increase in women's employment has also led to little change in men's participation in housework and childcare (Bittman 1991). Research on the division of labour in Australian homes has led to concern among conservatives as well as social democrats. Conservative groups, such as the Australian Family Association, have campaigned hard for a homemakers' allowance to recognize fully such activities (Bradbury 1996). Researchers such as Shaver and Fine (1995) have recommended the 'co-production of care' as a shared responsibility between families and communities, by providing either payment for care or in-kind support for caregiving.

Considerable concern is expressed from both the political left and the right about who will care for children, persons with disabilities, and the frail elderly if women's employment begins to mirror men's. Furthermore, the political left is concerned about the lack of social justice in a society where caring activities are not valued equally with paid employment.

Conclusion

We have shown in this chapter that the restructuring of Australian social-welfare programs affecting low-income mothers has proceeded on a wide range of fronts in the past decade and a half. Successive governments have addressed the 'crisis of the welfare state' and demands for smaller government in several ways. A focus on cost effectiveness and efficiency has led to extensive administrative reforms and restructuring of government, welfare measures have been tightened through targeting and narrowing eligibility, and more services have been privatized (Baldock 1994).

The effects on low-income mothers have been mixed. Policies such as the introduction of the Family Allowance Supplement and increased efforts to move lone parents into the workforce have led to a 12 per cent increase in the incomes of lone-parent families between 1982 and 1990 (ibid.). Yet other changes have led to considerable hardship. The deinstitutionalization of mentally disabled people, for example, has created homelessness, poverty, and family stress. The means-tested Family Allowance took away one of the few benefits available to all mothers. Governments have shifted many lone parents from public dependency to private dependency, expecting greater reliance on paternal child support and the vagaries of the lower end of the labour market. This has been accomplished through policies such as the curtailing of the Sole Parent Pension when the youngest child is sixteen, enforcing paternal child-support after marriage dissolution, and introducing the JET scheme in 1987. Yet 40 per cent of female Sole Parent Pensioners who moved into employment actually experienced a drop in income (Baldock 1994). Some who were unable to find jobs moved to unemployment benefits, which are more stigmatized than SPP (Shaver 1993b). In addition, the abolition of unemployment benefits for sixteen and seventeen year olds placed greater financial hardships and stresses on parents.

Changes to eligibility requirements and benefit levels have occurred within a complex social, political, and ideological environment. The state's encouragement – but not direct compulsion – of more women to see themselves as actual or potential paid workers outside the home is mediated by ambiguous and contradictory attitudes about women's appropriate roles and responsibilities. As in Canada, state initiatives in employability and related areas are attempting to reconstruct and rebalance the multiple identities of low-income women – including those of mother, paid worker, unpaid carer, and more frequently head of household. Different from Canada, however, is the pronounced social and political unease in Australia about accepting non-family childcare, especially when children are young, as a critical component of the restructuring package. Indeed, one striking aspect of Australian restructuring is the increasing social emphasis on the concept of 'care' and 'carers.' Nevertheless, the issue is framed within traditional assumptions of gender segregation and responsibilities of women for providing this care.

Gender segregation in Australia is reinforced by three important factors. First, the greater presence of part-time work in the lives of women leaves more time for caring activities. Second, official discourse and policy offers the 'choice' of paid work and family activities only to women. Third, there is continuing ambivalence on the part of the Australian feminist movement over women's caring and labour-market roles when children are young. The unstated objective of Canadian employability programs seems to be to create the 'worker-mother' as a new citizenship image and ideal for low-income women early in their childraising period, but in Australia the mixture is decidedly different. The 'mother-worker' will continue to focus on unpaid caring work within the household while she has young children, with moderate incentives to move into paid work when all her children are grown.

In comparison to some other countries, Australian reforms seem moderate. In the next chapter, we will examine the case of New Zealand, which has been viewed by the political right as the 'great experiment' in economic restructuring and by the left as a great failure leading to a growing gap between the rich and the poor.

5

The 'Great Experiment': Restructuring New Zealand's Social Programs

Introduction

Historically, Labour governments in both Australia and New Zealand relied on the wage-earner's welfare state for social well-being, although some national variations were always apparent. In the 1980s, restructuring was initiated and led in both countries by Labour governments, and it was continued in the 1990s by more overtly conservative regimes. Yet, as we will see in this chapter, the process and outcomes of New Zealand's reforms differentiate it from similar attempts at reform in Australia and Canada. New Zealand's unique brand of economic rationalism has exposed more of its social structures to the governance and vagaries of deregulation, which has increased poverty and inequality. At the same time, however, many low-income mothers continue to be insulated from full exposure to the labour market.

This chapter will show that the restructuring of New Zealand's welfare state looks both forward and backward, in an uncomfortable and contingent relationship with changes in labour markets and family structures. In the 1930s, when many of the programs were created, the primary source of family income derived from the full-time work of male wage earners (NZ, Department of Social Welfare [DSW] 1996, 18). Women were not significant earners, and part-time employment was seldom utilized. Most families had two parents in the household, but both married mothers and children were considered to be the dependants of the husband/father.

As restructuring entered its second decade in the 1990s, over half of two-parent families had two incomes, with 57 per cent of women of working age in the labour force (ibid., 18). In addition, part-time work has grown faster than full-time work and now comprises about 29 per cent of all jobs. Furthermore, lone-parent families now make up one-quarter of all families with dependent children.[1] New Zealand's restructuring is a fascinating case to study because of its sweeping changes to state institutions, changing employment laws and conditions, and gendered assumptions in social benefits.

The Development of Social Security in New Zealand

Beginning in the late nineteenth century, New Zealand established one of the most comprehensive social-security systems in the world and by the 1950s was considered to be a model welfare state (International Labour Office 1949). The development of social provision occurred against a particular historical backdrop of European settlement and demography, which must be outlined to understand the principles of the welfare state and its restructuring choices.

In 1996 the population of New Zealand was about 3.6 million, of which 80 per cent were 'Pakeha,' meaning of European descent (mainly British). The remaining fifth of the population is about 14 per cent Maori and 5 per cent Pacific Islanders, with most of the rest being of Asian descent (NZ, Statistics NZ 1997). In 1840 New Zealand effectively was ceded by Maori to the British crown under the Treaty of Waitangi, which promised (but failed to deliver) a balance between European colonization and indigenous rights to the land (Cheyne, O'Brien, and Belgrave 1997). Unlike in other colonies, however, the British granted full citizenship rights to the Maori people early in the colonial period. Maori men were granted the vote in 1867 while both Maori and Pakeha women were given the vote in 1893, earlier than in all other British colonies. In 1877 the Education Act offered primary and secondary education for both for Maori and Pakeha children (Shirley et al. 1997, 213).

New Zealand is the one country among the four examined in this study where indigenous and non-white populations have played important historical and political roles. Maori influence has been paramount. Political consciousness, nationalist sentiments, and militancy have grown among them, and the issues of Maori sovereignty and government adherence to the spirit of the Treaty of Waitangi are constants in New Zealand politics. The New Zealand First Party, with significant Maori representation, was the junior partner in a centre-right coalition government with the conservative National Party from early 1997 until mid-1998, when the coalition dissolved. Maori social structures are collectivist and group-oriented, and children are viewed as a means of supporting and sustaining extended families and lineage groups (Shirley et al. 1997, 218; Cheyne, O'Brien, and Belgrave 1997, 22).

State attempts to integrate Maori into values of capitalist enterprise have had mixed results, and some individualistic aspects of the welfare state are viewed as assimilationist and contradictory to Maori value systems (Spoonley 1994). Although some Maori are upwardly mobile and visible in New Zealand social, economic, and political life, most are found in lower socio-economic categories. There is now a large, growing, and visible non-white underclass in New Zealand of Maori and Pacific Islanders, especially in urban areas of the North Island. According to the 1996 census, unemployment is about three times higher among Maori than for non-Maori,[2] and the gap appears to be growing as Maori are under-represented in areas of new job formation (such as service industries) and over-represented in primary industries damaged by economic restructuring. Maori and Pacific Island women form a significant pool of unskilled and semi-skilled labour.

Historically, Maori women have had higher fertility rates and a higher percentage of lone-parent families than Pakeha women.[3] In addition, nearly 50 per cent of all Maori families are on government benefits. In 1992 about 40 percent of the income of Maori women came from government income-support programs, compared to 9 per cent for non-Maori women (NZ, Statistics NZ 1993, 227). These statistics have provided fertile ground for restructuring advocates concerned about reducing 'welfare dependency.' As in the United States, the poor, low-income, non-white women with children have been targets for new right rhetoric (Baker 1997d; Cheyne, O'Brien, and Belgrave 1997, 120; Kelsey 1995).

Initially, the state controlled land acquisition and invested heavily in infrastructure to enhance returns on private capital, facilitate immigration, and develop the country. Labour was scarce and agricultural productivity was high. State provision for the poor and indigent was minimal as the British poor laws were not transferred to the new colony. Instead, New Zealand relied on employment-based welfare for men and a female-dominated formal and informal caring sector, as did Australia (Cheyne, O'Brien, and Belgrave 1997, 24–6; Castles and Shirley 1996, 90–1; Jones 1997, ch. 3).

Income security in New Zealand was embodied in the male wage-earner's welfare state, characterized by wage regulation and full employment (Bryson 1992; Castles 1996; Rudd 1997). After regulating wages during the 1880s depression, the New Zealand government created an industrial arbitration court in 1894 to settle disputes between employers and employees, to set a minimum wage, and to make compulsory awards for wages and working conditions (Shirley et al. 1997). There were strong parallels with the Australian system. A 'fair wage' provided a decent living for a male breadwinner to maintain his home-maker wife and children (two at first, and later three) in a 'fair' and 'reasonable' standard of comfort (Woods 1963; Rudd 1997). The family wage established a minimum income for the majority of households but also protected working conditions and included provisions for sickness leave and overtime (Shirley et al. 1997).

By the early twentieth century, New Zealand had developed a reputation as a 'social laboratory,' creatively integrating economic and social policy (Shirley et al. 1997, 213). A means-tested Old Age Pension had been implemented in 1898 and the Public Health Act set down a comprehensive health system that lasted until the restructuring of the 1980s. Child-welfare legislation was enacted in 1925 to provide a framework for the care of children, and a means-tested Family Allowance was given to mothers with three or more children in 1926 to bolster the family wage and to encourage women to have more children (Cheyne, O'Brien, and Belgrave 1997, 33; McClure 1998).

The election of the first Labour government in the midst of the mass unemployment and destitution of the 1930s and the passage of the Social Security Act (1938) were major turning points for New Zealand social policy. The act established the concept of the 'social wage': a low-level means-tested benefit for those in financial need who were unattached to the labour force or to a breadwinner. All families and individuals were thus protected at a minimum level by the state (Shirley et al. 1997). In 1946 the means-tested child allowance was converted into a universal benefit, effectively giving mothers a social wage for domestic work (Cheyne, O'Brien, and Belgrave 1997, 36).

The family wage, which provided a minimum income for family households, was enshrined in legislation in 1935. In addition, the state offered free primary and secondary education, a community-based preventive health-care scheme, a salaried medical service, a free public hospital system, and a state housing program for those who could not afford a home of their own. In the post-war period, New Zealand experienced an unparalleled record of full employment for men, and breadwinner families enjoyed one of highest living standards in the industrialized world (Shirley et al. 1997). Rates of home ownership were high compared to those of European countries and were assisted by such legislation as the 1958 and 1964 Family Benefits (Home Owner-ship) Acts which allowed family allowances to be capitalized and paid in advance to allow parents to purchase a home. In the 1970s, the wel-fare state was further expanded. The concept of illegitimacy was elimi-nated, which expanded the rights of children born outside marriage. The Equal Pay Act (1972), the Matrimonial Property Act (1976), and the Human Rights Commission Act (1977) were also passed (Shirley et al. 1997), along with several income-support programs that we will discuss later in this chapter.

Through these measures, New Zealand avoided the European pattern of social insurance or expensive universal programs, with the taxation system as the primary means of income redistribution. Contributory social-insurance schemes were discussed but were not popular as a means of ensuring social integration and solidarity (Jones 1997, 36; McClure 1998). Those outside the wage system (or with special needs) had access to a selective benefit system that distinguished between the 'deserving' and 'undeserving' poor. Yet the exceptional record of full employment meant that few so-called undeserving beneficiaries existed before the 1960s. Benefits were flat-rate rather than earnings-related because the minimum wage protected most breadwinners and their dependants. The combination of the family wage and full employment dominated New Zealand for almost fifty years and high levels of home ownership served as retirement security (ibid.). This was buttressed by a universal old age pension (National Superannuation) paid to individu-als at age sixty on the basis of residency and financed through general revenue (St John 1994). The taxation system, central to the viability of the social wage, has been a means to fund income-maintenance pro-grams but also to subsidize the routine costs of family life for employ-ees, including tax rebates for low-income families.

Disparities between the rich and the poor were small in New Zealand, but income disparities between men and women led to demands on government during the 1960s to protect the incomes of the rising num-bers of lone parents (mainly mothers). In 1973 the government reluc-tantly created a statutory benefit to allow low-income lone mothers to care for their children at home (the Domestic Purposes Benefit). The government hoped to inhibit women from competing with male bread-winners in the workforce, but it was also concerned that such a benefit would encourage married women to leave their husbands. In the 1970s, labour unions sought compensation for the relative decline of the social wage as inflation rose, while employers agitated for greater profitability and an end to 'over full employment' (ibid.). The government attempted to control prices and wages, but production slowed considerably as a result.

Although cracks and dissent appeared in the 1960s and 1970s, especially as more women moved into the labour force, the New Zealand system of social provision was still well entrenched by the early 1980s and had shown itself capable of gradual evolution and modification to meet new demands. But a far greater economic and social cataclysm was on the immediate horizon. Long-standing assumptions about many of the foundations of New Zealand society and its welfare state were about to be put to a stringent restructuring test, and the consequences for low-income mothers would be particularly severe.

Restructuring the New Zealand Political Economy

The origins and consequences of the restructuring of New Zealand's economy and society since 1984 have been well documented (Sharp 1994a; Kelsey 1995; Castles, Gerritsen, and Vowles 1996; Larner 1996; Rudd and Roper 1997). Our discussion is devoted to understanding the implications for the economic situations of low-income mothers, and how economic-rationalist reforms paralleled and helped contextualize the employability debate.

The economic crisis in New Zealand built up through the 1970s and revealed the structural untenability of the earlier periods of prosperity. In the 1960s and 1970s, the economy that was built on production and export of agricultural commodities and resource extraction, protective tariffs for secondary industries, and preferred access to the United Kingdom market gradually disintegrated. Higher oil prices, lower returns on exports of wool, meat, and dairy products, and the United Kingdom's entry into the European Community's common market in 1973 placed great pressure on the economy. Declining terms of trade, the loosening of import controls, rampant inflation, lower productivity, and capital-intensive public investments were accompanied by rapidly rising levels of external public debt and unemployment. As early as 1972, the Royal Commission on Social Security outlined how these global changes were beginning to have negative repercussions for the well-being of individual social beneficiaries and families (Cheyne, O'Brien, and Belgrave 1997, 39; Larner 1996; Shirley et al. 1997).

The necessary reorganization and revitalization of New Zealand's economy coincided with a domestic loss of faith in Keynesian principles and the popularization of economic rationalism among political, economic, and bureaucratic elites (Kelsey 1995). Implementation of this agenda proceeded rapidly, aided by a currency crisis that overlapped with the election of the Labour government in 1984. The currency was devalued by 20 per cent but, by early 1985, the dollar was floated and relaxation of regulatory structures began. The government removed interest-rate controls and lifted restrictions on the flow of money in and out of the country.

In 1986 the government initiated a Goods and Services Tax (GST)[4] and personal income taxes were flattened. Foreign companies were granted greater access to New Zealand markets, agricultural subsidies were phased out, government departments were reorganized along commercial lines, and monetary and fiscal policies were tightened to reduce inflation (Kelsey 1995). Fifteen years later, the major macro-economic achievements of economic rationalism have been diversification into new markets, more flexible production, greater economic domination by large international investors, trade liberalization, and the substantial growth of service industries.

The fourth Labour government (1984–7 and 1987–90) was ostensibly social democratic. Yet it transformed New Zealand from the most regulated to the most deregulated economy within the OECD countries, a process that has been continued and consolidated since 1990 by the conservative National Party and its coalition partners (Sharp 1994b; Castles et al. 1996). This has substantially changed the labour markets that typically employ low-income mothers, as well as conditions of entry and exit, as we shall later show.

The breathtaking rapidity and sweeping nature of New Zealand restructuring was facilitated by the nature of its political system, reforms made to its underlying political economy, and the relative balance of interest groups. At the national level, the New Zealand political system is characterized by a lack of checks and balances. It shares with the United Kingdom a unitary non-federal system. Its legal controls over other levels of government (such as regions and municipalities) and the absence of an upper house of parliament combine to make New Zealand governments more powerful than others in the Westminster tradition (Mulgan 1997, 63).[5] This was further supported prior to 1996 by the first-past-the-post electoral system that accentuated the power of the governing party and Cabinet. While the structural conditions might have been in place for a directive government to override opposition to a broad and radical program of reform, this possibility was mitigated by a tradition of consultative governments acting as consensus-builders and as brokers and mediators of interest groups (ibid.).

The policy-making process changed substantially in the mid-1980s under relentless pressure from forces sympathetic to economic-rationalist ideas. Externally, most of the New Zealand business class had gradually rallied around the banner of economic rationalism by the late 1970s and early 1980s. In this small society, the business community historically has played a strong role in politics, but this was further enhanced by the increasing dominance of international capital and the new links forged between it and the domestic business elite (Kelsey 1995; Mulgan 1997, 222). The fiercely pro-market Business Roundtable – strongly policy-oriented and with a small invited membership – was the leading ideological vehicle of economic rationalism within the business elite. Other business organizations, such as Chambers of Commerce, the Employers Federation, and associations of manufacturers and bankers gradually adopted similar perspectives. The leadership of Federated Farmers, the major agricultural lobby, was also an enthusiastic free-market advocate, even though the removal of state subsidies damaged its membership considerably in the 1980s (Mulgan, 223; Kelsey 1995, 78).

Consensus within the business community was complemented by growing sympathy for economic rationalism within the bureaucracy. The government reformed its own decision-making and administrative structures along private-sector and managerial lines, with enhanced powers for ideological purists within the Treasury. Major reforms such as the State-Owned Enterprises Act (1986), the State Sector Act (1988), and the Public Finance Act (1989) combined to enhance the private-sector outlook, as did further initiatives in contracting out, user fees, and privatization (Mulgan 1997, 140–1). The Department of Social Welfare was reorganized into a series of 'business' units in 1992. Business lobbies made effective use of formal and informal contacts within the state and Cabinet ministers more frequently used outside policy advice in the form of ad hoc expert panels, committees of inquiry, and consultants (Boston and Uhr 1996; Mulgan 1997, 224–5; Cheyne, O'Brien, and Belgrave 1997, 87).

Coupled with the personal power and pro-market convictions of the minister of finance in the Labour government (Roger Douglas), the state became less a mediator of interests in the 1980s and much more an eager advocate of radical economic restructuring, known as 'Rogernomics.' Both the Labour and subsequent National governments, supported by the upper levels of the civil service, pushed economic restructuring agendas through Parliament with limited consultation. Cabinet dominated the government, party caucuses played limited and sharply circumscribed roles, and policy development increasingly was removed from Parliament and its committees (Easton 1997; Mulgan 1997). In the early stages of restructuring, the lack of public consultation on economic policy was mollifed by Labour's considerable consultation on non-economic issues.

Restructuring also included significant changes to the underlying rules of the game governing the political economy and social policy. The goal of full employment was formally abandoned by the Labour government in 1987, and the Reserve Bank Act of 1989 made the objective of monetary policy solely one of price stability and control of inflation. The regressive indirect taxation of the GST and reductions in personal income-tax rates meant that revenues for future initiatives in social programs would come increasingly from the poor themselves. The passage of the Fiscal Responsibility Act (1994) was an additional impediment to restoration of social provision and future welfare spending. A government wishing to raise spending by using previous budget surpluses, increasing the public debt, or raising taxes would have to repeal the act or clearly justify any departure from it. The politics of coalition-making inspired by the new electoral system make this highly unlikely (Rudd 1997).

While restructuring did not occur seamlessly or without opposition, the forces critical of it were weak. The New Zealand labour movement, unlike its Australian counterpart, played a marginal role in policy making in the 1980s and 1990s. Historically, New Zealand unions have been comparatively feeble, partially because of the dispersed nature of economic production (Shirley 1994). Wage setting under judicial management had existed since 1894 and the export of farm products was heavily controlled by the state, but these elements of historical corporatism were not supported during the restructuring by a formal accord with the governing party as occurred in Australia. The New Zealand unions were fragmented at the national organizational level between the Council of Trade Unions and the Trade Union Federation. They were not dominated by those sympathetic to economic reforms, but neither had they played important roles within the Labour Party. Without an institutional base within the state from which to negotiate, the unions were marginalized in restructuring. Even their limited influence and involvement in formal consultations ended with the demise of centralized wage-fixing, and their vigorous opposition to the Employment Contracts Act (1991) was largely ineffective (Castles and Pierson 1995; Easton and Gerritson 1996; Bray and Neilson 1996).

The New Zealand women's movement, as in Australia and the United Kingdom, was also fragmented and only sporadically effective. Women have always been a heterogeneous category, divided by class, race, culture, and urban-rural residence, but this is especially the case in New Zealand. The experience of restructuring for women has been uneven, with Maori and Pacific Island women affected more severely (Larner 1996). However, white middle-class women have been reasonably well organized at the national level in New Zealand, unlike their Australian counterparts. A women's electoral lobby was created in 1975, quickly superceded by the long-standing but conservative National Council of Women with its national system of organizational affiliates. Women have also been relatively strong participants in the Labour Party. Single-issue campaigns posed diverse and fragmented demands upon the national government, with mixed success. For example, an umbrella group exists for private and community-based providers of childcare (the New Zealand Childcare Association), but the level of services in New Zealand remains weak (Curtin and Sawer 1996), as we will show later in this chapter.

Feminist groups, although wary of the dependency-enhancement tendencies of social programs, were instrumental in increasing the generosity of the welfare state in the 1970s. They lobbied for the Domestic Purposes Benefit (DPB), which gave low-income women without partners an income independent of their families. The 'no-fault' Accident Compensation Commission was made to acknowledge in its payment schemes the costs of unpaid caring work, and payments from the universal retirement system were made to be gender-neutral (Rudd 1997). Working within the Labour Party's social-democratic traditions, women were able to obtain some victories in the area of parental leave and pay and employment equity as restructuring went forward.[6] Yet they were powerless to halt or modify significantly the economic effects of the reform package, especially as these affected low-income women in the labour market (Du Plessis 1992, 214).

Within the government, the Department of Women's Affairs has had a relatively minor impact upon policy development (Mulgan 1997, 145). Prior to 1991 there were no formal requirements for other government departments to consult it. Renewed attempts were made in 1996 to incorporate more gender analysis into policy formulation and service delivery (Curtin and Sawer 1996), yet the department was not consulted in the preparation of the coalition government's major social-policy initiative in 1998, the proposed Code of Social and Family Responsibility, to be discussed in more detail later.

As New Zealand approaches the millennium, a striking feature of its politics is the degree of consensus among the two major political parties (National and Labour) on the necessity and general thrust of restructuring. Both parties are deeply implicated in this process, and, while there are growing differences on the necessity and means of addressing the 'social deficit' arising from restructuring, there is little indication that substantial policy reversals would occur if the government changed. Yet, among the public, there is considerably more dissent. The public responded to the perceived betrayals and lack of consultation by both parties during the 1987–93 reforms by voting for a Mixed Member Proportional (MMP) electoral system, which was implemented in 1996. This procedural reform was intended to make politics more responsible and representative. When the coalition government proposed a new contributory superannuation scheme (similar to the Canada Pension Plan but with private administration) in 1997, 94 per cent of the public voted against it in a national referendum.

The political processes underlying restructuring marginalized many women, who historically have been insulated from the labour market. High male wages enabled and encouraged many partnered women to stay out of paid work entirely or to work part-time. Historically, women had been the objects of structural discrimination in the labour market, through lower minimum wages, exclusion from certain occupations, and restricted working hours in some industries (Davies 1993). These impediments to paid work interacted with models of motherhood emphasizing the full-time care of children at home, especially when children are young. The New Zealand 'cult of domesticity' (Shirley et al. 1997, 290) was supported by men and women for different reasons; male breadwinners were provided with comfortable homes, while the glorification of motherhood and homemaking gave meaning to women's lives in the face of limited opportunities elsewhere. Women's resistance to childcare outside the home was considerable (ibid., 290). As will be seen in the next section, social-assistance policies further cemented women's exclusion from the paid labour market.

Especially since 1945, women's participation in the labour force[7] grew with the expanding economy and the deteriorating effects of inflation upon male wages (Easton 1997). Table 5.1 shows these rates from 1951 to 1996. Yet women's full-time labour-force patterns still look much like

TABLE 5.1
Labour-force participation rates by gender, 1951–96
(% of population aged fifteen years and over)

Year	Men	Women
1951	83.3	25.0
1961	83.3	27.7
1971	81.2	33.8
1981	76.5	38.6
1991	68.6	44.7
1996	73.5	57.9

Source: NZ Census.

Canada's did years ago. After childbirth, for example, many women withdraw completely from the labour force although there is a decreasing tendency to do so (Davies 1993, 72). In the 1990s, New Zealand women's labour-force participation is characterized by multiple entries, an over-reliance on part-time work, concentration in lower-paid and lower-status occupations, and a lower annual income than men. Pakeha women are relatively advantaged compared to Maori and Pacific Islanders. Gender inequalities in domestic and unpaid caring work further exacerbate women's disadvantages (Davies 1993; DuPlessis 1994).

The changes in New Zealand political economy resulting from economic restructuring were felt most strongly by low-income men and women, who are disproportionately of Maori and Pacific Island background. Gender, ethnic, and racial segregation are characteristic of portions of the New Zealand employment market (Larner 1993). Both male and female Maori workers have long been concentrated in the primary sector and seasonal agricultural jobs. With more recent migration to urban centres, they have moved into unskilled or semi-skilled manufacturing work where they have been joined recently by Pacific Islanders. Restructuring affected these industries greatly, since the growth in jobs has been concentrated in the service sector, which now employs about 80 per cent of women workers. Redundant unskilled workers with poor education encounter difficulties in transferring to other jobs, which has been a particular problem for Maori women trying to enter the rapidly expanding finance, insurance, and business-services industries (Davies 1993).

By the early 1990s, as noted earlier, unemployment rates for Maori and Pacific Islanders were about three times higher than for Pakehas, which indicates an ethnically segregated underclass, lacking job skills in an increasingly fragmented and 'flexible' labour market (DuPlessis 1992; Larner 1993). Full-time employment declined between 1981 and 1991, and overall unemployment rates rose, peaking at 10.9 per cent in September 1991, as the economy oscillated between expansion and recession.

Between 1986 and 1991, restructuring as well as the recession slowed the growth of women's participation in employment, but this was almost exclusively due to a decline in full-time employment by Maori and Pacific Islander women to levels at or below those of 1976. Maori and Pacific Island women have worked full-time because of lower levels of household income, the need to support large extended families, and the tendency of unskilled manufacturing jobs to be full-time (Davies 1993, 57).

From 1986 to 1996, the number of full-time jobs grew by 1.3 per cent while part-time jobs increased by 52.1 per cent (Maré 1996). For women, part-time work increased by 9 per cent during these years, and about 73 per cent of part-timers are women. The percentage of women in full-time work declined by 5 per cent in the same period, down to 36 per cent (Davies 1993, 88). In 1996, only 4 per cent of female part-timers expressed a desire to work full-time but one in four wanted to increase their working hours (NZ Government, *Household Labour Force Survey 1996*).

The emerging picture for the labour-market situation of low-income mothers is one of intensified marginalization and growing poverty, especially for Maori and Pacific Island women. Wage and income inequality has widened in New Zealand to levels greater than in any other OECD country, and indirect measures of poverty suggest that it too is growing (Cheyne, O'Brien and Belgrave 1997, 184–5; Kelsey and O'Brien, 1995, 14–5). From 1981 to 1991, incomes declined for lone-parent families and two-parent families with parents or partners who are unemployed or not participating in paid work (Shirley et al. 1997, 242; Cheyne, O'Brien, and Belgrave 1997, 186). In 1991 women's median total annual income was only 59 per cent of men's (Briar and Cheyne 1997). Yet employment growth is in low-paid, insecure, and increasingly part-time service-sector work, which is not always covered by minimum-wage legislation (Kelsey and O'Brien 1995, 45). Competition among women for part-time and casual employment is growing as more women seek paid work.

The low rates of full-time employment for New Zealand mothers, especially lone parents, are particularly striking. In the early 1990s, about 27 per cent of lone mothers were employed, compared to 43 per cent in Australia and 57 per cent in Canada. Among employed lone mothers, less than 40 per cent worked full time in New Zealand; the comparable figures in Australia and Canada are 50 per cent and 80 per cent respectively (Rochford 1993, 48; Bradshaw et al. 1996, 8; Canada, Statistics Canada 1996). Throughout the 1980s, there was a significant decline in both full- and part-time labour-force participation among lone mothers (Shirley et al. 1997, 245), and recent reforms have resulted in increased economic vulnerability for many employed mothers with low income. Yet the political right has continued the push for greater individual responsibility and employability of beneficiaries. It is to this restructuring of social programs and their gendered and racial nature that we now turn our attention.

Social-Program Restructuring: Redefining Dependency

The first policy moves towards restructuring social programs along economic-rationalist lines were initiated by a Labour government. The Lange government elected in 1984 held within it the contradictory combination of neo-liberal economic policy and social-democratic tendencies (Cheyne, O'Brien, and Belgrave 1997, 41). The initial concentration on economic problems in the mid-1980s temporarily postponed attention to social programs. Labour's re-election in 1987, however, opened the door for those within the government, led by Treasury Minister Roger Douglas, to apply new right principles to the welfare state's eligibility and entitlement provisions. The Treasury briefing papers to the incoming government in 1987 (one of the important initial statements of economic-rationalist social policy) rejected an activist role for the state. These documents stressed the need for greater market activity and a healthy economy as prerequisites for social well-being and asserted that, although paid work was crucial for both income and social identity, unpaid caring work also contributed to the economy (Cheyne, O'Brien, and Belgrave 1997, 11; Kelsey 1995, 57–62). The assumptions about gender within new right ideology remained traditional: women were still expected to be carers while men had responsibilities in the workforce (Else 1992).

The new right's assault on social provision was encouraged by the growth of welfare expenditures from rising unemployment and declining capital investment. Nevertheless, the neo-liberals were able to phrase public discussion in terms of the need to control 'overspending.' Social welfare expenditure as a percentage of GDP had risen from 11.27 per cent in 1984–5 to 13.73 per cent in 1988–9, and benefits as a percentage of total net government expenditures had increased in the same period from 29.1 per cent to 38.42 per cent (Rudd 1997, 258). From 1981 to 1992, the number of people receiving a welfare benefit (excluding the universal superannuation and Family Allowance benefit) had trebled, and one-quarter of dependent children were in households receiving a government benefit in 1993 (Shirley et al. 1997, 294). Conservative researchers, such as Jones (1997, 47) note that, by mid-1996, about 30 per cent of the population was on 'income support schemes' of various sorts, but the number drops to under 15 per cent if the universal old age benefit is excluded.

Neo-liberals conveniently ignored the fact that rising unemployment claims and lower disposable incomes, which are a direct result of government economic policies, were responsible for much of the increase in 'welfare dependency.' Despite the moderate social liberalism of the 1988 Royal Commission on Social Policy, the Labour government, by the time of its defeat in 1990, had begun to roll back the welfare state in areas as diverse as unemployment benefits, housing, and superannuation (ibid., 261).

The election of the conservative National Party, which has held power alone or in coalition arrangements throughout the 1990s, accelerated social-program restructuring and gave it a more overtly libertarian and 'moral' emphasis (Boston 1991). National, like Labour before it, spent little time during election campaigns discussing plans for drastic social reform. Nevertheless, the National government launched an assault upon 'the crushing burden of government spending' and 'welfare dependency,' with little public consultation (Kelsey 1995). It sought to reduce permanently the size of the welfare state to the level of a minimal safety net, emphasizing effectiveness, efficiency, and managerial considerations more than equity or quality of life. Citizens began to be described as 'clients' and 'consumers,' and the public discourse focus gradually shifted away from discussions of 'rights' to those of 'obligations.' Greater application of commercial principles was essential in emphasizing that benefit recipients need to consider their duty to get off welfare dependency and into the job market.

The cornerstones of National's policies were cuts to real benefit levels (for the first time in New Zealand's history), targeting benefits to low-income people, employability programs, tax cuts, greater reliance on user fees, and cost shifting from the state to individuals (Castles and Shirley 1996, 104). Cuts were predicated on a simple proposition: growing state expenditure and beneficiary dependency could be reduced by negative incentives, thereby increasing, as Treasury Minister Ruth Richardson said, 'the rewards for moving from welfare to work' (Kelsey 1995, 230). The assumption was that New Zealanders would be more self-reliant and that work would be available for those deemed employable (Cheyne, O'Brien, and Belgrave 1997, 54).

The initial reforms were set out in an economic statement in late 1990 and in the document symbolically entitled *Social Assistance: Welfare That Works* (Shipley 1991) in mid-1991. These were buttressed by the publication of the 'Porter Report' on New Zealand competitiveness that asserted the negative effects of social provision on work incentives and independence (Rudd 1997, 260). The government stated that the social-safety net should be modest and contingent: 'Assistance will be closely targeted on genuine need and people will be expected to support themselves when they have the ability to do so' (Shipley 1991, 13). Support would be available both through the paid labour market (at a time of historically high unemployment) and through greater responsibility exercised within families. By attempting to break dependency on government welfare, greater dependence on the family was expected (Du Plessis 1992, 216; Shirley et al. 1997, 235).

Social benefits were cut at different rates for different categories of recipients and were based on a minimum subsistence budget (Shirley et al. 1997, 297). The unemployment benefit for young single people was cut by 24.7 per cent. Those under eighteen were no longer entitled to it, and those under twenty-five received lower benefits than older unemployed people. Sickness benefits for single people aged eighteen to twenty-four were cut by one-fifth. The Domestic Purposes Benefit (overwhelmingly received by women) was cut by 16.7 per cent for single people[8] and by 8.9 per cent for people with two children (Kelsey 1995, 276). Rather than preventing poverty, the reforms require people to be poor in order to receive anything from the government (St John 1994). Furthermore, the government proposed, and later abandoned, the nostalgic notion of the 'core family' (which essentially means the nuclear family) as the unit of most social benefits, rather than the individual or family household (Shirley et al. 1997, 297). Many low-income New Zealanders were also subject to sharp rent increases as state housing was raised to market levels, which particularly affected Maori and Pacific Island women. These increases were not related to ability to pay and compelled beneficiaries to act as 'consumers' who would judge how much they could afford to pay in the housing market (Cheyne, O'Brien, and Belgrave 1997, 181).

In the early 1990s, the balance between universal and targeted programs moved sharply in favour of more targeting, and the family household was retained as the unit of assessment for most benefits. Social programs were made 'residual,' meaning, mainly for those with no other means of economic support. The universal Family Benefit was amalgamated with Family Support (social assistance) to create a benefit targeted to low-income families (St John 1994). Although its value had been low, it was the only source of direct income for some mothers. The Department of Inland Revenue took over the function of subsidizing low-income families from the Department of Social Security, and housing from the Housing Corporation (Sharp 1994b). The government also tightened eligibility criteria for social programs, reduced funding to education, housing, and health, and tightened up child-support enforcement. After 1992, families with earnings above NZ$17,000 faced increased user fees for visits to family physicians and for pharmaceutical drugs (Briar and Cheyne 1997).

In the labour market, low-income women were further disadvantaged by three National government actions. First, the Employment Equity Act, passed by Labour through effective coalition-building in 1990, was quickly repealed as an unnecessary interference in market functioning (Curtin and Sawer 1996, 167). Second, the Employment Contracts Act (ECA) of the following year removed union bargaining rights and effectively dismantled the national award system for wages and working conditions by decentralizing collective bargaining. Contracts were negotiated with individual employers through 'enterprise bargaining' (Sharp 1994b). The ECA rapidly diminished union membership and protection, and its emphasis upon labour-market flexibility reinforced structural inequalities between employers and employees, especially for workers in marginal and low-paid jobs. Moreover, the effectiveness of the 1972 Equal Pay Act was compromised; once national awards and agreements were replaced by individual contracts, it was more difficult to compare the wages of men and women, as well as wage rates in occupations that were typically dominated by males or females (Hyman 1995; Dannin 1997, 188).

The state withdrew from labour-market regulation, which caused the final demise of the 'family wage' (Shirley et al. 1997). Since 1990, the gap between the hourly and weekly wages of men and women has declined

slightly, but, because of women's irregular and discontinuous employment, the gender gap in annual incomes has become much wider (NZ,
Statistics New Zealand 1996b; Briar and Cheyne 1997). The impact of
these changes has been to create a larger gap between the wealthy and
the poor and to increase economic and social insecurity (Shirley et al.
1997). Restructuring social programs has reduced income for some low-
wage workers at a time when full-time permanent jobs are disappearing.

Between 1989 and 1992, poverty levels increased by 40 per cent
(Easton 1993, 11). Although there is no absolute and official poverty line
in New Zealand, various studies indicate that the level of structural
poverty is growing, meaning that the economic system is unable to provide adequate incomes. This is especially the case with lone mothers
(Kelsey 1995, 273–5). Increasingly, the only paid work available to many
middle-aged women is part-time, insecure, and low paid (Davidson and
Bray 1994).

Prior to National's 1991 cuts, disposable income of beneficiary households was 72 per cent of the level of all households; by 1994 it had fallen
to 58 per cent (Rudd 1997). Government assistance to families (in real
dollars) has fallen from 1986 to 1994 by about 46 per cent depending on
the type of benefit (Shirley et al. 1997). This can be explained by lost
entitlements to Family Support as wages increased, the effects of inflation on partially indexed assistance payments, the impact of user fees,
and market-driven costs. Although the government is emphasizing family responsibility, some families have been torn apart as a result of these
policies. In addition, the pressures of supporting adolescents in school
have become more difficult (St John 1994).

Overall levels of social protection have declined more markedly in
New Zealand than in Australia (Castles and Shirley 1996). Between 1991
and 1997, social-welfare expenditure (excluding superannuation) as a
percentage of GDP fell from 6.0 per cent to 5.4 per cent (NZ, Department
of Social Welfare 1997, 3). The Department of Social Welfare prepared a
ministerial briefing paper for distribution after the 1996 election. It
noted that, in past decades (and especially since the mid-1980s), the
country had 'been through a period where the combined impact of
interrelated social and economic pressures have [sic] resulted in a significant and growing proportion of the population suffering severe and
persistent disadvantage' (NZ, Department of Social Welfare 1996, 5).
Although the unemployment rate had declined by about 40 per cent
since its 1991 peak, the percentage of unemployment beneficiaries fell at
a slower rate (12 per cent). At same time, the number of other beneficia-

ries rose substantially. For example, recipients of the Domestic Purposes Benefit (for lone parents and older women) rose by 11 per cent, recipients of the sickness benefit rose by 68 per cent, and recipients of the invalids benefit rose by 44 per cent. This suggests that fewer people are reporting themselves as 'unemployed' but they are definitely in need of some form of government assistance. The government reports that people of working age who are 'benefit dependant' increased from 8 per cent in 1985 to 21 per cent in 1996 (ibid., 5). Furthermore, 54 per cent of beneficiaries remained on government assistance for longer than one year in 1996.

The DSW has especially expressed concern about the welfare of children, since 30 per cent now live in benefit-dependant families compared to 12 per cent in 1985 (ibid., 5). Most of these 'beneficiary children' (76 per cent) live with a lone parent and 25 per cent live in families where no parent holds a paid job. The disproportionately bleak position of non-white groups is evident: 48 per cent of Maori children and 45 per cent of Pacific Islander children (compared to 16 per cent of Pakeha children) live in households where neither parent has a paid job (ibid., 5). By 1990, (prior to National's benefit cuts) 45 per cent of all Maori families and 40 per cent of all dependent Maori children relied on government support (Larner 1996, 43). The DSW acknowledges that the rapidly growing population (especially in Auckland) will increase pressure on public resources for services for families and children. This is a well-founded concern, for child beneficiaries are twice as likely to require public care and protection services and more than twice as likely to require youth-justice services (NZ, DSW 1996, 6).

Economic restructuring and cutbacks in social programs have been consequential for the social circumstances of families and children. From 1990 to 1994, apprehensions for violent offences committed by fourteen to sixteen year olds rose by 50 per cent. School suspensions doubled between 1991 and 1995. Among all OECD countries, New Zealand had the highest rate of suicide in the fifteen- to twenty-four-year age group in 1993. From 1984 to 1990 non-Maori suicides doubled and Maori suicides trebled. In addition, compared with similar countries, New Zealand has relatively high rates of teenage ex-nuptial births (30.4 per 1000 teenage females in 1994). From 1988 to 1993, 40 per cent of homicides resulted from domestic disputes and a further 4 per cent from child abuse. The economic cost of family violence was estimated at between $1.187 billion and $5.302 billion in 1993–4 (ibid., 6). All these issues were noted as areas of concern, yet neo-liberal policies continue.

Restructuring in New Zealand has affected not only programs for the poor but also programs for middle- and higher-income people. The government medical scheme was largely privatized, bargaining rights were removed from employees, and families were asked to pay tuition fees or borrow the money for their children's tertiary education. The student loan system has meant disproportionate hardships for women, since their ability to repay loans is typically lower than men's as a result of their lower-paid jobs and work absences for childrearing (Briar and Cheyne 1997).

Restructuring Social Programs: Towards Employability?

New Zealand's reputation for work-related benefits and means-tested social assistance paid without time limits does not mean that discussions about the relationship between paid work and benefit provision have appeared only recently. The debate over the old age pension at the end of the nineteenth century and the family allowance in the 1920s was marked by disagreements over its potential impact on male self-reliance, hard work, and independence, as well as who 'deserved' it and under what conditions (McClure 1998). Moreover, a strong residual sense of the 'social' is evident in the New Zealand public consciousness which economic rationalism has had to struggle against and attempt to overcome in the restructuring process (Larner 1997). This is seen most clearly in the retention of a universal superannuation scheme. New Zealand remains the sole Western industrialized country without a compulsory contributory retirement scheme (Jones 1997, 49), and a referendum to introduce one was defeated massively in 1997. In April 1998 the superannuation surtax for high-income New Zealanders was removed in response to political pressure from the seniors' lobby (Grey Power), returning the state pension to full universality (Laugesen 1998). Yet discussions about the 'high' cost of superannuation continue.

Since restructuring commenced, the employability theme in New Zealand social policy has been linked closely to neo-liberal arguments concerning 'welfare dependency,' incentives, and personal responsibility. Following the 1993 election, the Alliance, Labour, and National parties collaborated on proposals to improve employment prospects. Two years later, the National government's public response laid out three guiding principles: 'strengthening the incentives for those currently on benefits to actively involve themselves in the growing work opportunities available, or education and training activities that will improve their work skills; encouraging those currently on benefits to accept responsibility for taking advantage of the opportunities on offer; [and] providing additional opportunities for people to move into paid work' (NZ Government 1995, 6). Initiatives in 'income support that encourages work' included relaxing tax back rates on benefits when beneficiaries had employment income, and requiring spouses of employment beneficiaries and Domestic Purposes or Widows benefit recipients to seek work under certain circumstances (ibid., 8–9). These are discussed later in this chapter.

The employability discourse reflects contradictions inherent in neoliberal thought between expenditure restraint and concern about moral laxness. These contradictions predate the new right's rise in New Zealand, originating with women's increasing employment after the Second World War and its reconciliation with traditional views of the domestic responsibilities of women. For example, the objectives of the National Advisory Council for the Employment of Women, created in 1967, were 'to create the conditions for women to make their full contribution to the national economy consistent with their individual freedom, and their responsibility as wives and mothers' (Goodger 1998).

The DSW's Strategic Directions report (1996) acknowledges that the traditional approach to benefit design has produced disincentives to self-reliance and argues that recent changes have improved incentives only to a limited extent. Despite the growth in employment, an increasing percentage of the population is dependent on social benefits, which, according to the government, indicates that fundamental changes are necessary to the benefit system (ibid., 17). The report notes that much of the discussion on long-term or intergenerational dependency is focused on the advantages of maximizing the employment potential of those on benefits, but it adds that 'an important and related emphasis should be placed on supporting people to contribute to a strong society even when employment is not realistic. Incentives should encourage participation in a broader range of activities than just employment. Participation and contribution can include caring for children, being a good citizen, and developing personal and homemaking skills' (ibid., 18). This emphasis on activities other than employment is somewhat different from the orientation of other departments in the New Zealand government and from the focus on 'employability' in Canada. The historical ambivalence of messages to women regarding caring work and paid employment, and the social programs that support these two areas, persists and is embodied in the restructuring process. But it is for low-income mothers that the contradictions and consequences become most apparent, as we shall now show.

New Zealand's restructuring of social programs has yet to resolve the tensions embedded within traditional models of motherhood and 'the pro-natalist, child-oriented values of Pakeha society' (Shirley et al. 1997, 211). Sustained full employment for men and strong political pressure for a high birth rate to populate the European settler colony combined to keep many women in the household through the nineteenth and much of the twentieth century. This was further cemented by a dominant male culture expressed in government policy that regarded childrearing and domestic work as women's responsibility and by a persistent lack of affordable childcare. The grip of the home and caring activities on New Zealand women was reinforced by institutions such as community drop-in centres for parents (Plunket Rooms) and the Plunket Society (Kedgeley 1996, 303). Plunket and its network of pre- and post-natal care institutions and nurses were established throughout the country in the early 1900s and supported partially by government funding. They advocated 'scientific' mothering but also emphasized the importance of mother-child bonding. Generations of New Zealand Pakeha women regarded the Plunket Society as a major source of advice, support, and social networking and its influence persists. Plunket's elevation of the status of mothering to a vocation was accompanied by strong messages about the damage that women working outside the home could do to their child's development (ibid., 43–54). This emphasis complemented male labour-market dominance.

The neo-liberal themes of choice and responsibility mean that for all women there is an emphasis on the continued social importance of caring work and the possibility of choosing to remain at home with children or entering paid work. Low-income mothers in New Zealand face more complex messages. Choice for them is contextualized in part by paid work opportunities, the availability of affordable childcare, social-benefit levels, partner support, and government pressures to become 'employable' in the face of societal ideas about what constitutes appropriate motherhood. Choice is also structured by the taxation system's penalties on earned income for beneficiaries. Benefits are reduced substantially as employment income rises. These abatement rates[9] were relaxed in 1996, allowing unemployment beneficiaries to earn NZ$80 weekly (about $68 Can.) before reductions set in. Domestic Purposes recipients were allowed to earn NZ$180 or $153 Can. (up from $80) before a 70 per cent abatement rate was applied (NZ Government 1995,

17–18). Nevertheless, the cumulative impact of abatements, taxes, accommodation supplements, repayment of student loans, and who earns the extra income in a two-adult household could still mean prohibitively high penalties on earned income (Shirley et al. 1997, 268). An interview-based study of the obstacles to paid employment faced by 95 lone mothers on benefits showed that the tax structure was a clear disincentive to part-time work. The study also indicated the importance given to affordable childcare, especially prior to and after school hours, and the limitations of a childcare-subsidy scheme confined to preschoolers and registered caregivers (Levine, Wyn, and Asiasiga 1993).

Let us now consider briefly the major social programs of relevance to low-income parents.

Unemployment Benefit

Eligibility for unemployment benefits is still calculated on the basis of family household income rather than individual income. This means that unemployed people may not be entitled to benefits if their partner's income is too high, and this is frequently the case for partnered women (Davies 1993, 59). Historically, unemployment policy in New Zealand has considered partnered women to be the dependants of unemployed men, who are caring for the household or children rather than seeking paid work (Shirley et al. 1997, 258–60). Unemployed people (mainly men) receive additional benefits if they support a spouse and children. Women earners are usually considered as secondary earners if they are in a couple relationship, and using the family as the unit of income-testing for social benefits has discouraged low-income partnered women from seeking paid work (ibid., 268). Yet the National government cut unemployment benefit rates in 1991 to encourage more beneficiaries into paid work rather than treating unemployed married women as 'unemployed.'

Portions of this long-standing unemployment policy have changed. In 1997 spouses of unemployment beneficiaries who are childless or whose youngest child is fourteen years old or older were required to look for full-time work or to improve their job prospects through an organized activity, in order for their partner to continue to receive full benefit. Spouses with a youngest child between seven and fourteen must now be interviewed annually by Income Support employees to discuss their future job plans (NZ Government 1995, 8–9). Seeking or preparing for paid work is more important than actually finding a job, which means that the dependency relationship within the household may persist but links to the labour market are expected to be strengthened.

Effective October 1998, unemployment benefits were further tightened as 'work for the dole,' or workfare, was introduced. All unemployment beneficiaries (of whom 29 per cent were female in 1997) (NZ, Department of Social Welfare 1997, 20) are now compelled to accept community work or training for up to twenty hours per week or their benefits will be withdrawn for up to thirteen weeks. Those deemed able to work only part-time are required to perform up to ten hours weekly. Beneficiaries receive an extra $20 per week when they work for community organizations. If an unemployed person refuses work, his or her benefits will be cut, but households with dependent spouses and children will continue to receive a partial benefit (about half the normal benefit rate). The employment minister referred to this as a 'bottom-line safety net.' Unsatisfactory performance in community work or training could also result in a 40 per cent benefit reduction (Herbert 1998, 1).

Under the new scheme, a maximum of $21 may be paid for travel and work-related expenses, but no childcare assistance has been announced for parents engaging in community work. There are also no articulated links between this compulsory work and future employment outside community-related tasks. In sum, employability requirements have been extended to all unemployment-benefit recipients (mainly men), and the renaming of the benefit as the 'community wage' further links this social-welfare provision to work discipline and labour market demands. As of December 1998, however, mothers on the Domestic Purposes Benefit with children under fourteen were not included in this scheme.

Domestic Purposes Benefit

The Domestic Purposes Benefit is a means-tested benefit[10] to provide a stabilized income for various categories of women who had lost the support of their husbands and for lone-parent families. The benefit was first paid in 1964 under emergency provisions of section 61 of the Social Security Act (although deserted wives had been eligible for the Widows Benefit since 1936). As a result of a recommendation in the 1972 Royal Commission on Social Security, the DPB became a statutory benefit in 1973. Conservatives reluctantly implemented the benefit, fearful that it would encourage nuclear family breakdown and increase job competition for men (Kedgley 1996, 273; Shirley et al. 1997, 291).

The DPB is now available to recipients in several social circumstances.

Both male and female lone parents (over the age of sixteen) with dependent children (under the age of nineteen) living with them may be eligible for DPB if their income and assets are below a certain level. Unsupported women over the age of fifty may also be eligible if they are living alone and had been homemakers for a number of years in the past.[11] The DPB is also paid to people caring for the sick and frail at home (but not their own partner or child) (NZ Government 1996a). Lone parents are expected to make a reasonable attempt to obtain child support from the absent parent. About 91 per cent of DPB recipients are women with small families (about one-half have one child only), and Maori and Pacific Islanders comprise about 47 per cent of all recipients (NZ, Department of Social Welfare 1997, 11). About 89 per cent of all New Zealand lone mothers receive the DPB. As we indicated in chapter 1, this percentage is similar to the percentage of lone mothers on social assistance in Australia and the United Kingdom but much higher than the percentage in Canada (Bradshaw et al. 1996, 52). The DPB provides a social wage for low-income lone mothers, recognizing their statutory rights to income support (Rudd 1997).

The amount received by women under DPB has been raised over the years and depends on her income and the number of children living with her, but the maximum weekly payment is NZ$204 for one child. Beneficiaries are permitted to work part-time and earn up to $4,160 per year and retain full benefits (NZ, DSW 1996, 13). Even though abatement rates have been changed to permit more earned income to be retained, DPB could be seen as a poverty trap for low-income mothers. Linking benefits to labour-force participation began in 1986 when the Transition to Work Allowance was added to DPB to encourage beneficiaries to search for full-time employment, but participation in this program is voluntary and monetary incentives are small.

In 1989 the basic benefit for lone parents with one child was increased by a smaller amount than the benefit for those with two or more children. This had been recommended by the 1987 Report of the Ministerial Taskforce on Income Maintenance, on the basis of a study of relative benefits using an equivalence scale (NZ Government, undated). In 1990 lower benefits were paid to lone parents who failed to identify the other parent and a two-week waiting period was initiated. In 1991 the telephone-rental allowance was abolished, the residence test was tightened,[12] rates were reduced for different classes of beneficiaries from about 9 per cent to 17 per cent,[13] and the age of eligibility was increased to eighteen,[14] making the parents of those under eighteen responsible for emergency support in some cases. In the same year, the previous policy of cutting benefits for the DPB recipient who failed to identify the other parent was rescinded when the process of identification would 'jeopardise a stable family relationship' (ibid.). In 1995 the government stated that the DPB 'is paid to sole parents, in the recognition that while their children are young, they are their first responsibility. As the children grow older, and the parent's childcare responsibilities diminish, the government believes that a move should be made towards self-reliance' (NZ Government 1995, 19). Between 1987 and 1997, the numbers of recipients increased by about 63 per cent and expenditures more than doubled. This was caused by increases in the number of women of childbearing age in the population, as well as the difficulties of finding secure well-paid work. These trends helped push policy initiatives towards greater self-reliance (NZ, DSW 1997, 8–9; Cheyne, O'Brien, and Belgrave 1997, 178).

In 1997 eligibility and labour-market links were accordingly tightened. For the first time, DPB recipients whose youngest child was at least fourteen years old had to undergo a mandatory 'activity test' to prove that they were searching for part-time (but not full-time) employment, training, or education. Moreover, recipients with children aged seven to thirteen had to report to the government employment office for an annual interview to discuss their work plans for the future. This gave the clear message that mothers should be viewing themselves as potential employees well before they are legally expected to seek paid work. There is still no compulsory requirement for recipients to enrol in a job-readiness program or to find paid work. Furthermore, a lone mother with two children spaced six years apart could receive the full benefit for twenty years without being required to search actively for even part-time paid work. This prolonged absence from the labour force would certainly inhibit her chances of finding a job after the period of childrearing. After more than a dozen years of restructuring in New Zealand, the model of mothering at home still remains culturally imbedded, although the government attempted to change this in 1998, as we will discuss later.

The low employment rates for low-income mothers form an important part of the ideological background for recent policy reform. One of the first available analyses of 1996 census data (Goodger 1998) suggests that low-income mothers without partners have already entered the labour market in greater numbers in recent years without direct state compulsion, in response to benefit cuts and an expanding low-wage job

TABLE 5.2
Proportion of sole mothers employed, 1976–96

	1976 %	1981 %	1986 %	1991 %	1996 %
All Sole Mothers					
Full-time	25	22	22	17	20
Part-time	15	13	11	11	16
Total	40	35	33	28	36
Maori Sole Mothers					
Full-time			13	9	14
Part-time			5	5	11
Total	n.a.	n.a.	19	15	25
Non-Maori Sole Mothers					
Full-time			26	20	23
Part-time			12	13	18
Total	n.a.	n.a.	38	33	41

Source: Goodger 1998 (from census data).

market. As Table 5.2 indicates, labour-force participation of lone mothers has risen between 1991 and 1996 from 28 per cent to 36 per cent, but most of the gain is in part-time work. This trend applies to both Pakeha and Maori women, although the lower level of Maori employment persists.

In mid-1997, about 22 per cent of DPB recipients reported additional income, mostly from part-time employment since it does not disqualify a low-income mother from receiving social benefits (NZ, DSW 1997, 33). Non-Maori lone mothers in their twenties and late forties are responsible for much of the increase in employment, while the rise for Maori mothers has been in all age categories. A marked increase has also been apparent in the employment of mothers with young children: about one in five lone mothers with pre-school children had a paid job in 1996, compared with one in eight in 1991. Lone mothers tend to work full-time when their youngest child becomes older, especially after the age of nine (Goodger 1998). Despite these trends, only about 17 per cent of DPB recipients leaving the benefit went into paid work since 1991. The rest found new partners, transferred to another government benefit, or no longer had dependent children at home (Kelsey 1995, 279).

In the May 1998 budget, the government announced that work

requirements would be tightened further. Women on the DPB whose youngest child is aged six to thirteen were told that they would be expected to look for part-time work, and those whose youngest child is aged fourteen and over would have to look for full-time work. The details of this budget and its outcomes are discussed later in this chapter.

Widows Benefit

This gender-specific benefit complements the DPB and is designed to support low-income widows living with their dependent children or older widows whose children have left home. If women are now fifty years old, were married for ten years, and widowed after the age of forty, they may receive the benefit even if they have not had children. The maximum Widows Benefit is about NZ$222 per week for those with two or more children. Widows may also be eligible for a Funeral Grant to help with funeral costs (NZ Government 1996b & c).

Prior to 1997, Widows Benefit recipients were untouched by restructuring and employability requirements, but they have now been brought under the same employability and earnings-abatement regimes as DPB recipients (NZ Government 1995, 19). About 71 per cent of recipients have no children at home, but 86 per cent are forty-five years old and over, when re-entry into paid work becomes more problematic (NZ, DSW 1997, 43). Those aged fifty-five years and older were exempt from the 1997 work tests. The policy message to low-income widows was conditional responsibility – modest encouragement to find paid employment, but without penalty. In the May 1998 budget, however, the government attempted (but failed) to strengthen the work test for Domestic Purposes and Widows beneficiaries.

Family Support

New Zealand introduced a targeted family allowance in 1926 for married mothers with three or more children, but it made this benefit universal and non-taxable in 1946 at about the same time that the other three countries in this study introduced their universal family allowances. Tax benefits were also paid to the main income earner in the late 1970s to assist low-income families with children and to combat child poverty and inadequate incomes (Shirley et al. 1997, 255). In 1987 attempts to transform the Family Allowance into a targeted benefit were defeated by the combined lobbying efforts of several groups, including the National Council of Women, the Committee for Children, the Federation of New Zealand Parents' Centres, and the Ministry of Women's Affairs. This lobby effort was supported by an opinion poll from the readers of a major women's magazine. Although the universal family allowance was worth only NZ$6 a week for each dependent child, many mothers had no other income to call their own. While another attempt at targeting was defeated in 1990, the National government eventually succeeded in eliminating universality in this benefit in 1991 (Curtin and Sawer 1996). This policy decision is similar to the ones made in Australia and Canada. Of the four countries in this study, only the United Kingdom has retained a universal child benefit.

In 1986 a refundable tax credit called Family Support was introduced to replace family tax rebates and other related benefits, and it is now targeted to low-income families with dependent children up to age eighteen, if they are still in school (NZ Government 1996a). Support is paid on the basis of household income and the number of children, and the benefit is an important supplement for large low-income families. In 1989 the abatement threshold was increased to $17,500, although tax rates on earned income mean that the benefit still constitutes a poverty trap (Cheyne, O'Brien, and Belgrave 1997, 192). In 1990 the government began to pay Family Support to the principal carer of the children (usually the mother), rather than splitting it between partners for couples with children, to increase the chances that the money would be spent on the children. The reliance on joint-household income as the unit of assessment for two-parent families and the reduction in eligibility as earned income rises limits the incentive for the lower-income partner (usually the woman) to seek paid work.

Child Support

A new system enforcing child support was implemented in 1992. As with the Australian scheme, child-support assessment was taken out of the courts and placed in the hands of a new Child Support Agency, which is part of the Inland Revenue Department. Any custodian of a child or children may apply for support from the non-custodial parent, but those receiving social benefits must do so. Voluntary agreements are permitted as long as the amount agreed to is at least equivalent to the formula assessment. Child-support payments received on behalf of parents who are social-security beneficiaries are used to offset the cost of the benefits, and, unlike in Australia, beneficiary parents receive only the child-support money in excess of the benefit. Custodial parents receiving social-security benefits must identify the other parent or risk losing benefits (NZ Government, undated).

Childcare

The post-war baby boom, which was more pronounced in New Zealand than in other countries, lasted thirty years. During that time, marriages typically occurred earlier, which may help to explain high divorce rates (NZ, Statistics New Zealand 1995), but high levels of teen pregnancy peaked in 1971. In recent years, total fertility rates have dropped below replacement levels. About 41 per cent of all live births in 1995 were out-side legal marriage but half of these are estimated to be from cohabiting couples (ibid.). In the early 1990s, total fertility rates still remained higher than in many industrialized countries, at 2.1 live births per woman compared to 1.7 in Canada and 1.9 in both Australia and the United Kingdom (UN 1992). This high birth rate has impeded women's labour-force participation and encouraged policies supporting mother-ing at home. Nevertheless, the historical underdevelopment of public childcare could not withstand the incessant pressure from the growing labour-force participation of mothers.

In New Zealand as in Australia, the Labour Party increased childcare funding in the first year that it returned to government in the 1980s (Curtin and Sawer 1996). In 1985 Labour created the Ministry for Women's Affairs, which, along with feminist groups, trade unions, and (female) Labour MPs, served as a strong lobby for improved childcare services. Jurisdiction for childcare was moved from the Ministry of Social Welfare to the Ministry of Education, as a result of the efforts of the two women Cabinet ministers of those departments. Funding increased by 125 per cent from 1989 to 1994, when childcare was 'sold' as an educational issue. In contrast, the Australian Labor government increased childcare funding by arguing that it was a necessity for moth-ers to enter the labour force (Curtin and Sawer 1996).

There is now a well-developed system in New Zealand for commu-nity pre-school childcare in such forms as childcare centres, kindergar-tens, play centres, Maori pre-school (Te Kohanga Reo), and Pacific Island Language Groups. Over 93 per cent of four year olds and about 83 per cent of three year olds participated in some form of early child-hood service in 1996. These services, however, usually operate only a few hours a week. Licensed childcare centres (both for profit and not-for-profit) comprise about 40 per cent of available spaces for pre-school children, yet children attend for only fifteen hours per week on average (NZ, Ministry of Education 1997). After-school care has not been developed since most mothers are at home during the day. In the May 1998 budget, however, the government attempted to tighten work requirements for all beneficiaries and new childcare initiatives were introduced. The government promised NZ$3.15 million over three years for out-of-school childcare, and the childcare subsidy for low-income families was extended to children aged five to thirteen (NZ Government 1998). Yet the subsidy was not extended to full-time work.

The cultural messages in favour of stay-at-home motherhood reinforce the government's reluctance to acknowledge the links between childcare and employment. Shortly after assuming office in 1990, National rolled back childcare support. Childcare subsidies for children under two were reduced substantially and proposed increases in overall childcare funding were abandoned. The initiative called 'Parents as First Teachers' was introduced to encourage parents to take primary responsibility for early childhood education (Kedgley 1996, 304). Given the prevailing division of labour within households (Habgood 1992), this meant additional responsibilities for mothers and a further disincentive to seek paid work outside the home.

Affordable childcare remains an obstacle to paid work for low-income mothers, particularly as user fees rise with neo-liberal reforms. The existing Childcare Subsidy helps to fund childcare services for children under five from low-income families who are citizens or permanent residents. To qualify, the child must attend licensed care for at least three hours a week. If the parents are unemployed, they may be entitled to only nine hours of childcare subsidy; if they are employed, studying, in a training program, ill, or disabled, they may qualify for up to thirty hours a week. The subsidy does not support full-time work, especially when workplace travel times are taken into account.

The value of the childcare subsidy varies with the parents' income and the number of children in the family. The maximum rate noted in the May 1998 budget is about NZ$70 a week if the parents work thirty or more hours a week, earn up to NZ$520 a week, and have one child (NZ Government 1998). The subsidy is paid directly to the early childhood service rather than to the family and can only be claimed for only twelve months at a time. If the child's care centre is changed, the parent has to reapply for the subsidy (NZ Government 1996a).

The structure of childcare subsidies reflects the ambivalent messages about unpaid caring and paid work in New Zealand. Despite the government's ostensible emphasis on low-income people's self sufficiency and work incentives, the subsidies do not support full-time work. Their partial nature and the relative lack of after-school care for older children reinforce the low-income mothers' status as part-time workers who must still take responsibility for dependent care. Full-time work is seen as interfering with mothering in a society that offers weak public support for childcare. The absence of statutory parental benefits and the relative underdevelopment of flexible employment policies augment the problems of employment for mothers (Baker 1997d). Childbirth means withdrawal from the labour market for many women, with no pay, benefits, or even guarantee of a return to their previous job.

The political parties of the left (Labour and the Alliance) support state-funded parental benefits. Right-wing parties and interest groups either support an allowance and tax incentives for full-time parental childcare (the Christian Coalition) or regard children as the product of parental choice and therefore their exclusive responsibility (Association of Consumers and Taxpayers). The ruling National/New Zealand First coalition preferred the status quo, although there was recurring pressure from the Treasury to reduce childcare expenditures further (Kedgley 1996, 335). The lack of political consensus on public childcare reflects concern that women's greater participation in the workforce might increase unemployment rates, that public childcare will be too expensive, and that it will harm children.

New Zealand governments have encouraged low-income mothers to search for paid employment but have neither compelled them to do so nor offered employed mothers much public support. The preferred policy option is part-time work while receiving the Domestic Purposes Benefit, which reinforces the image that low-income women remain primarily responsible for unpaid caring and domestic duties. Increased pressure to engage in paid work coincides with a decline in full-time jobs, which contributes to guilt and economic insecurity for low-income mothers.

Consolidating New Directions: Well-Being and Responsibility

In the first ten years of welfare-state restructuring, New Zealand moved in a gradual yet limited way towards a greater emphasis upon the employability of low-income mothers. The 1995–8 period marked a subtle ideological watershed in the 'dependency' debate, followed by several policy initiatives that culminated in extensive welfare reforms attempted in the May 1998 budget. Taken together, these reforms have moved New Zealand a little closer to Canadian policies and farther away from some of those in Australia and the United Kingdom.

Despite a modest economic recovery in the early 1990s, New Zealand's social problems appear to be persistent and intractable. The government acknowledged this in a Department of Social Welfare (DSW) report which declared that 'resolution of these problems will require reexamination of the issues and may necessitate the adoption of radical shifts in approach rather than incremental development of current approaches' (NZ, DSW 1996, 4). Moreover, the pressure on state funding will grow after 2006 as the health and welfare costs of the baby-boom generation make themselves evident (NZ, DSW 1995, 14). These structural factors combine with the necessity to maintain right-wing political alliances in order to win the 1999 election under the proportional representation voting system.

Considerable concern is also apparent in New Zealand about future social cohesion. Greater emphasis upon achieving social integration through paid employment is becoming a politically acceptable solution to this problem. The political right is focusing on the divisive effects of high rates of welfare dependency, the moral significance of work discipline, and the socio-economic benefits of paid work over other forms of work. Yet traditional models of motherhood are not being denied, especially for the middle classes.

An important discourse change was evident in such documents as the DSW's strategic directions for income support for the decade of 1995–2005 (NZ, Department of Social Welfare 1995). The vision of an income-support system for the millenium is based upon 'rights and reciprocal obligations,' 'empowering individuals to take greater control and responsibility for themselves in order to reduce dependency,' 'and is focused mainly on the working-age population' (ibid., 1). The government believes that problems with the welfare state include 'a weakened sense of responsibility for oneself and others,' 'disincentives to work' inherent in benefit rules, lack of flexibility in responding to labour-market changes, 'long-term benefit dependence and inter-generational cycles of dependency' which cannot be resolved solely by economic growth, and negative effects on self-esteem and self-confidence (ibid., 8–9). The welfare system requires restructuring, just as had been done with the economy. The government argues that reform is needed to integrate welfare provision with the needs of an increasingly globalized and competitive economy, in which part-time work is playing a greater role (ibid., 6–7). This assertion ignores the evidence that 'labour market flexibility' has led to a reduction in wages and deterioration of working conditions in New Zealand, disproportionately affecting women workers (NZ, Statistics New Zealand 1996a).

The promotion by the government bureaucracy of a more aggressive work-oriented approach was a departure from earlier policy. Although compulsory workfare was rejected, the DSW promoted changing 'passive' benefits into 'incentive-oriented entitlements' and providing more customized services to help beneficiaries obtain more income from paid employment (ibid., 17). Special services for Maori would be required, it noted. In return for more active assistance from the state, benefit recipients 'should have opportunities to give, within their capacities, some return for their income in the form of a contribution to their community, either personally or indirectly' (ibid., 21). A minimum social-safety net would be reserved to 'ensure that people do not suffer material hardship which cannot be avoided through their own efforts or the efforts of others with an obligation to help' (ibid., 24). In other words, employability through local community-based initiatives is directly linked to greater self-reliance, reduced dependency, and a reduction in benefits.

This 1996 strategy was called 'From Welfare to Well-Being.' The intention is to move away from the negative connotation of the word welfare by focusing on well-being, defined as 'the things which people commonly strive to achieve – material adequacy, good future prospects, good health, good family relations, happiness, self-esteem, and respect for others' (NZ, Department of Social Welfare 1996, 7). The reassertion of 'the family' at the centre of welfare reform is paramount. Efforts have been concentrated on 'strengthening families' and their capacity to raise children and reducing the 'incidence of disfunction in families and its negative impact on the development of children and young people' (ibid., 12). The rationale for this concern is that 'stronger families are less likely to find themselves requiring crisis help from government agencies' (ibid., 12).

Some of this discourse found expression in the tightened work-tests for beneficiaries implemented in 1997 and in the transformation of the unemployment benefit into the 'community wage' in early 1998. In 1998 the government also merged Income Support offices with Employment Benefit offices, renaming them 'Work and Income' and giving the strong message that recipients of social benefits are expected to be searching for employment or engaged in job training. The Canadian Liberal government made a similar structural change in 1993 when it created Human Resources Development Canada.

Although the ruling National Party has been heavily penetrated by new right ideology, a vigorous lobby outside the government advocates even greater reductions to the welfare state by withdrawing funding and further targeting benefits. The far-right Association of Consumers and Taxpayers (ACT) Party, which wants to privatize social welfare, retains significant political support and is a potential coalition partner with future National governments. The influential Business Roundtable publishes works emphasizing voluntary action, mutual aid and personal responsibility, and a non-political welfare system (Green 1997). In mid-1997 the government-owned television network presented a documentary entitled 'Time Bomb,' which emphasized the growing problem of welfare dependency and raised the possibility of future social unrest if further restructuring of the welfare state was not undertaken (Campbell 1997). The government itself convened and hosted a conference in 1997 entitled 'Beyond Dependency,' at which international new right social policy experts decried long-term benefit provision and advocated compulsory workfare for low-income mothers (Goodger 1998, 92).

The employability discourse culminated in the government's distribution in February 1998 of a public-discussion document entitled 'Towards a Code of Social and Family Responsibility' (NZ, Department of Social Welfare 1998). As has been shown, a strong sense of moral rectitude and blaming the disadvantaged has characterized the history of benefits for New Zealand's deserving poor, including the cuts of 1991. This has been accompanied throughout the restructuring process by an emphasis on personal and family responsibility, choice, and self-determination (Rudd 1997; Kelsey and O'Brien 1995; Cheyne, O'Brien, and Belgrave 1997, 182; Shirley et al. 1997, 214–15). These neo-liberal themes find strong expression in the Code.

The proposed Code was a unique document. Although all four countries have used public consultation mechanisms at various points in the restructuring process, the Code was the only document to be distributed to all households and to which all citizens were encouraged to respond. Most public consultation, where it exists, involves initiatives taken by the public to respond to a government report. The proposed Code consisted of eleven issues pertaining to social and family responsibility and attached to each issue was an attitudinal or behavioral expectation. The issue of 'work obligations and income support,' for example, contained the expectation that 'people receiving income support will seek full-time or part-time work (where appropriate) or take steps to improve their chances of getting a job.' The public was then asked to respond to specific questions pertaining to each issue.

The Code was presented to New Zealanders as a proposal to integrate legal obligations and social expectations. Its final form was left purposely uncertain, ranging possibly from legal codification to policy guidelines, and pending responses to the discussion document itself. A mixed reception greeted the document: enthusiasm from some employers' groups, denouncement by the New Zealand Council of Social Services, criticism of its unbalanced questions by methodologists, derision from many parents at the prospect of being told how to raise their children, and lukewarm support in public opinion polls.

Late in 1998, the New Zealand government announced that, as a result of the public consultations, it would not develop a formal Code of Social and Family Responsibility. Despite the lack of formalization, however, the publication and distribution of the proposed Code was important for several reasons. First, it was a device designed to lower the expectations of citizens about state social provision, since 'social' responsibility focuses on individuals, their families, and friendship networks rather than the state. The individualistic and local community conception of 'the social' follows in the tradition of more than a decade-long redefinition of citizenship in New Zealand society (Larner 1997). Absent from the code were unifying ideas of the advantages of collective provision and support, as well as any mention of obligations to strangers as a consequence of citizenship. Instead, the document was filled with references to 'the taxpayer' and the costs of social provision. Economic rationalism and individualism were being applied vigorously to social policy.

Second, the document was ridden with implicit messages concerning social class, race, and gender. Discussions of best practices for childcare, parenthood, health, and personal-money management, and emphasis on moving beneficiaries off the social-welfare rolls, were all pointedly targeted at low-income people. Demographically in New Zealand this means low-income women with children, who are disproportionately non-white. The values and behaviour of the poor were the targets, with the implication that the 'responsible' may be deserving of limited public support while the 'irresponsible' poor are to be left to their own private means. Moreover, the Code's notion of responsibility did not acknowledge unpaid work by women in the family and community, nor did it offer alternative ways of doing this work.

Third, the document extended and clarified the government's previous income-support strategy concerning employability. It posed such questions as what the taxpayer should expect in return for funding education and training, what groups of beneficiaries should be required to accept job-related training, and what else the government could do to encourage beneficiaries to move into paid work or community service. Parts of the Code were, therefore, attempts to reshape public discourse and social identities into closer integration with labour-market expectations.

Complementing the Code was a government strategy in 1998 to reduce public expenditures by encouraging the general public to report cases of welfare fraud by their neighbours and associates, or, in the local slang – 'to dob in a fraudster.' Expensive television and newspaper advertisements suggest that beneficiaries do not really need the benefit they are drawing and therefore are cheating both the government and the taxpayer. This welfare-fraud campaign was powerful in its implications that the viewer is being 'ripped off,' but it also created a backlash against the government among social-democratic groups.

The government itself described its May 1998 budget as 'a radical change in welfare direction,' based on its belief that 'paid work is the key to achieving personal economic and social independence' (NZ Government 1998). The budget announced that, from 1 February 1999, the value of the Sickness Benefit would be reduced to coincide with the Unemployment Benefit and that new work-testing obligations would apply to Domestic Purposes and Widows beneficiaries. If the youngest child is aged fourteen and over, the beneficiary is expected to look for full-time work (previously they were required to look for part-time work). If the youngest child is aged six to thirteen, the beneficiary is expected to look for part-time work (previously they were asked to come into the Income Support office for an interview). If the youngest child is under six, the beneficiary is expected to have an annual interview with Income Support. To enable parents to enter the labour force, more out-of-school childcare services will be developed with additional funding and the childcare subsidy has been expanded for low-income families with children aged five to thirteen. The government also promised to extend financial assistance in the near future to parents who need to take time off work to care for sick children but are not eligible for sick leave from their employers. New work-testing obligations also apply to the spouses of recipients of all benefits (previously they applied only to the spouses of unemployment beneficiaries). These changes place greater pressure on low-income mothers to leave their school-aged children in out-of-school care in order to seek (low) paid employment. These budget reforms were treated as 'urgent' and pushed through Parliament, giving the New Zealand public little opportunity to discuss them.

The 1998 budget reforms were applauded by most business groups, and the Reserve Bank governor (Dr Don Brash) told a parliamentary committee that he expected that the community-wage scheme would depress wages and reduce inflation (NZ *Herald*, 28 May 1998, A3). The political left strongly opposed the reforms. The Council of Trade Unions said that Brash's comments had exposed the community wage as a 'farce.' The leader of the left-wing Alliance Party proclaimed that 'solo mothers, on the DPB, are being told to abandon their children. What sort of a government attacks solo mothers!' (Anderton 1998).

The budget proposals related to low-income mothers also encountered vigorous opposition within the ruling National Party. In June 1998 a National Party MP (Christine Fletcher) spoke out against including DPB recipients (mothers with dependent children) in the community-wage scheme, arguing that they are 'working' raising their children at home. In her June 1998 newsletter to constituents, Fletcher noted: 'Many women find the time required to be a good parent is a full time responsibility. I believe that we should be encouraging choices for women. If women choose to be in the paid work force full time that is fine ... I believe that quality parenting is work in itself and too often its importance is overlooked until children are teenagers and society is forced to pick up the cost.' Considering the strong historical emphasis placed on mothering at home in New Zealand, asking mothers with school-aged children to work part-time is seen by some as a 'radical' reform. Faced with both internal and external opposition, the government quietly withdrew the portion of the proposals related to mothers with children under fourteen years (NZ *Herald*, 23 July 1998).

Conclusion

Castles and Shirley's (1996) argument that successive Labour governments in New Zealand acted as 'gravediggers' for the welfare state (in contrast to 'refurbishers' in Australia) requires important qualifications in reference specifically to low-income mothers. During the period of

Labour Party restructuring (1984–90), the principle of paying low-income mothers a social wage to care for their children at home remained untouched. The public ideal of mothering, the weak political mobilization of pro-childcare forces, and rising unemployment in the late 1980s further insulated these mothers from the labour market.

Under the conservative National Party and its coalition partners, the 1990s have been characterized by the gradual ascendance of economic-rationalist principles in social policy. This has culminated in an ever-expanding net of work-related tests for beneficiaries. Further pressure on low-income mothers to enter the workforce will not necessarily improve their incomes or raise them out of poverty. Full employment is no longer a government goal since the economy is unable to create sufficient full-time jobs for all those who need them.

The evolution of employability in New Zealand is a highly gendered and racialized process. For low-income mothers on social benefits, restructuring policies attempt to promote the new identity of 'mother/part-time worker,' whose economic self-sufficiency can be assured neither by the contracting social welfare system nor by marginal paid employment. The contradictions are evident in imposing paid-work requirements as a method of alleviating poverty and creating more 'independent, responsible and self-sufficient' lower-income groups. The new right formula for relations among the state, markets, and family is a globalized and structurally vulnerable export economy, greater emphasis on employability, declining real social benefits, and continued glorification of motherhood and women as the primary unpaid carers in households. This is likely a recipe for continued poverty and, ironically, a deficit in social well-being.

6

The United Kingdom: Restructuring the 'Nanny State'

Introduction

Among the more vivid phrases introduced by Margaret Thatcher into the British political lexicon of the 1980s was the 'nanny state culture of dependency' (Maclean 1997b). Conservative government rule from 1979 to 1997, under Thatcher and later under John Major, was filled with political rhetoric about the need to reduce social-welfare expenditures, the necessity of self-discipline and individual responsibility, the moral deficiencies of the poor, and the benefits of privatization. Low-income mothers, especially lone mothers dependent on social provision, quickly emerged as both a policy and a moral-reform target. Yet the Thatcher revolution remained curiously unsuccessful in its attempts to reform major elements of the social-welfare system (Pierson 1994).

This chapter will show that reducing welfare dependency through greater employability proved to be a highly problematic policy for the Tory new right to implement. While increased labour-force participation by the 'dependent' was viewed as the preferred path from poverty, in practice Thatcherism's halting reforms in this field were intended to confront and overcome the widespread belief in British society that children need their mothers at home when they are young. It has been left to New Labour's post-1997 regime to attempt to 'modernize' the British system of social welfare along the lines envisioned by employability advocates. Labour has raised the policy and discourse stakes in this area profoundly.

As shall be seen, the centre-right Conservatives and the centre-left Labour share a profoundly gendered approach to restructuring programs affecting low-income mothers. For the Conservatives, images of women's caring roles outside the paid labour market predominated; for Labour, greater exposure to the gendered inequalities of paid work is emphasized. The result is that the organizing principles of British society are moving away from core values and rights associated with social citizenship and redistribution, as Raymond Plant (1997) and Will Hutton (1997) have observed in other contexts. These are being replaced by the individual's responsibility to engage in paid work, enabled by the state and supported by a residual safety net. The benefits of this safety net will be increasingly linked to claimants' relationships with the employment market.

The Questioning of Collectivism and Social Citizenship

The inequalities and miserable social conditions of capitalist industrialization and urbanization in Britain formed the backdrop for development of its welfare state. Laissez-faire ideologies allocated a marginal role for government in the nineteenth- and early-twentieth-century economies (Bolderson and Mabbett 1991, 55). Before 1908, the only government social security was provided by the 1834 Poor Law, which differentiated between the deserving and undeserving poor, obligated employed persons to support other family members, and, as a last resort, provided a place in 'workhouses' for the destitute. 'Paupers' were given accommodation, but they were also forced to give up their citizenship rights, which meant the right to vote as well as the right to raise their children and live as a family unit (Baker 1995). Families and charitable organizations provided most assistance to the poor, as they did in Canada, Australia, and New Zealand.

An old age pension was introduced in the United Kingdom in 1908, ten years after New Zealand, partly in response to the growing political strength of the organized working class, followed three years later by a national insurance scheme for unemployment and sickness. After the First World War, the government expanded unemployment insurance and increased spending on social housing. In 1934 a means-tested unemployment-assistance scheme was established, funded through general taxation. The Beveridge Report of 1942, a landmark of British social policy, recommended an expansion of the scope and coverage of the existing social-insurance programs, the introduction of universal family allowances, and the creation of a national social-assistance program. The government implemented these recommendations, which greatly influenced the development of the Canadian welfare state, by

1948. One impact of the post-war Beveridge scheme was to differentiate workers from non-workers, with social-insurance benefits paid only to those who had 'lost' their wages through sickness, unemployment, or retirement (Webb, Kemp, and Millar 1996).

In a class-ridden, highly unequal society with comparatively low social mobility, British social programs affirmed principles of collectivism, social solidarity, and integration. State-run social insurance was available for all waged employees and their dependants. An exception was the Family Allowance, which was the sole cash benefit (paid initially to families with two or more children). For those not eligible for social insurance, means-tested benefits were provided that were not to be below subsistence (Bolderson and Mabbett 1991, 67). Throughout the 1960s and 1970s, social-security programs were expanded under the influences of economic prosperity, social-democratic ideologies, and changing demographics. In 1966 national assistance became a two-tiered system with the introduction of the Supplementary Benefit for long-term recipients (later renamed Income Support), but the able-bodied unemployed were paid at a lower rate. In 1970 equal-pay legislation was introduced (Webb, Kemp, and Millar 1996).

Despite Britain's development of social insurance, earnings-related benefits occupied a modest position in income-maintenance programs compared to other welfare states such as Australia and New Zealand. Furthermore, Beveridge's brand of universalism did not leave much room for generous benefits whose entitlement is based on citizenship or residence, as in Scandinavian countries. British social policy also placed a heavier emphasis on a typical male-breadwinner family as the unit of social benefit than did countries such as Sweden, which based entitlement on the individual (Sainsbury 1996, 31).

Partnered women, when they were in the paid labour force, were regarded in policy terms as second earners at best. Their waged work was limited by a chronic lack of publicly funded and affordable child-care, low educational attainment, poor training opportunities, and inflexible employer policies regarding leave for caring responsibilities. Low-income unpartnered mothers also faced these conditions. As in Canada, Britain has a smaller percentage of lone mothers than partnered mothers in the workforce, since social-assistance rules have tended to discourage part-time work (Ermisch 1991). Labour-force participation rates, however, are significantly lower in the United Kingdom than in Canada. Only 41 per cent of British lone mothers are employed (Ford and Millar 1997) compared to 57 per cent of Canadian lone mothers, and more Canadian mothers are employed full-time: 32 per cent compared to 17 per cent (see Table 1.4 in chapter 1). Of all employed women in the United Kingdom in 1997, about 45 per cent work part-time, as compared to 7 per cent of male workers (UK, HM Treasury 1998a).

As in the other countries in this study, UK policy makers have been concerned for a long time that generous social provision could discourage beneficiaries from seeking low wage work, thereby increasing dependency on a welfare system that already promotes dependence. Yet historically the United Kingdom has done little to encourage low-income mothers to enter the workforce. Instead, policy has concentrated upon enforcing child-support payments, as will be shown later in this chapter. These payments by themselves are woefully insufficient in reducing the poverty of lone mothers.

Lone mothers and their children now comprise about 20 per cent of all families with dependent children in the United Kingdom, higher than other European countries[1] but lower than New Zealand, and their numbers have nearly trebled since 1970 (Silva 1996). Women head over 90 per cent of these families. About 72 per cent of lone mothers rely on social benefits of some sort, and the percentage in the labour market actually decreased in the early 1990s (Bradshaw and Millar 1991). In the 1980s, total benefit expenditure on lone parents started to grow faster than their numbers: from £1.8 billion in 1979 to £9.9 billion in 1996–7 (Finlayson and Marsh 1997). Part of this growth reflected the policy change from housing subsidy to Housing Benefit, but by 1996, 63 per cent of lone parents were receiving Income Support compared to 40 per cent in 1979. The average length of current spells on Income Support is four years (longer than in Canada) but a quarter of recipients have received benefits for more than seven years (Finlayson and Marsh 1997).

At the end of the 1980s, only 40 per cent of lone parents in Bradshaw and Millar's (1991) study were receiving any earned income at all. Furthermore, there was little difference in disposable income between employed lone parents and those receiving only welfare, a fact attributable to benefit losses, the extra costs of working, low-wage jobs, and part-time working hours. One-half had no educational qualifications and 63 per cent had no vocational training. Bradshaw and Millar also found that lone parents in their sample lacked knowledge about the benefits to which they were entitled. As with Canadian lone mothers (Dooley 1995), the British women most likely to be economically active were divorced and older, had school-age children, and had some educational or vocation qualifications.

The 1979–97 Conservative attempt to remake British society in a less collectivist and more private sector-oriented mould met with mixed success as far as the welfare state was concerned. The growth of social inequality under Tory rule is well documented. By the late 1980s, as we indicated in chapter 1, poverty rates within lone-parent families were higher in the United Kingdom than in Canada or New Zealand but comparable to those of Australia. In 1998 one in five UK citizens lived below the poverty line (that is, on less than one-half the average national net income), compared to one in ten in 1979. In comparative terms, the 1993 poverty rate of British households (23 per cent) was third-worst in the European Union (EU) and well above the EU average of 17 per cent (Child Poverty Action Group 1997). The poorest 20 per cent of British citizens receive a lower share of social benefits than they did two decades earlier. In 1998 an estimated 4 million children lived in poverty, and the number of adults claiming incapacity benefits had tripled to 1.75 million compared to 1979. Nearly two-thirds of the lowest decile of wage earners are women (UK, HM Treasury 1998a).

Successive Conservative governments were reluctant to accept that poverty was a significant problem, even though more lone mothers and their children lived in poverty. Nor did Tories accept that benefit levels were precariously low for families with children (Millar 1996). Instead, the Conservative agenda was to reduce public expenditure by moving social policy away from state welfare towards increased individual and family responsibility.

Neither the feminist movement nor the labour movement successfully challenged the policy direction. As Pierson (1994, 158–9) has shown, Conservative strategy was to portray interest groups as selfish and inward-looking and/or to ignore them. Tory governments' animosity towards trade unions is well documented, and the restrictions on their activities in the 1980s and the celebrated wars with individual unions reduced the policy influence of the movement as a whole.

From 1983 to 1988, unemployment benefits fell relative to wages, child benefits were frozen, and the government unsuccessfully tried to eliminate the state earnings-related pension (SERPS) and make it a flat-rate retirement benefit. Despite public support for universality, some British benefits became more targeted, as they have in the other liberal welfare states, yet the principle of social insurance was not dislodged (Bolderson and Mabbett 1991, 179). Public expenditure under the Tories continued to rise and support for state involvement in social policy remained strong. The Thatcherite revolution, however, was able to open the door slightly towards a more active employability model for low-income mothers, which has been enthusiastically taken up by the Labour Party since 1997. The achievements of the 1980s were to entrench a discourse of individual responsibility and anti-welfare dependency and to move towards modest work incentives for low-income mothers. The next section will show how this laid the ideological and policy basis for Labour's further acceleration towards employability.

Restructuring British Social Programs for Low-Income Mothers

The 1986 Social Security Act

The reforms in the 1986 Social Security Act created three new benefits: Income Support, Family Credit, and the Housing Benefit, all based upon similar principles. The act nudged the social-security system in the direction of a negative income tax and placed means-testing at the centre of its overall design. A new structure was introduced which discriminated less between different categories of claimants, such as persons with disabilities, old age pensioners, and lone parents (Baker 1995, 107). The act also created a dual system of means-tested support: Income Support for those not employed or working less than twenty-four hours a week, and Family Credit for parents employed for twenty-four hours or more per week (later reduced to sixteen hours a week). Lone mothers with dependent children under sixteen, however, were not subject to a work test and could receive social assistance as well as the universal Child Benefit and/or the One Parent Benefit (to be discussed later in this chapter). Partnered mothers living on low incomes were eligible for social assistance only indirectly through their husband's unemployment benefits, but they continued to receive the universal Child Benefit in their own name.

Income Support (IS)

Income Support was introduced in 1988, replacing the former Supplementary Benefit. Income Support is a benefit for people aged sixteen or over whose income is below a certain level and who are not working sixteen or more hours per week (and do not have a partner who works twenty-four hours or more hours a week). Persons eligible for IS are also not required to be available for paid work because this benefit is paid only to people who are sick or disabled, to lone parents or foster parents, aged sixty or over, or those receiving the Invalid Care Allowance for looking after someone. The amount received depends on age,[2] living arrangements, presence and age of children, and income and savings of recipient and partner.[3] In families receiving IS, pregnant women and children under five are entitled to free milk and vitamins (UK, Department of Social Security [DSS] 1996) and families are paid higher rates for adolescents than for school-aged children. Middleton and Ashworth (1997) argue that paying substantially larger amounts for older children in IS is not justified by their research on family spending. Allocating more for younger children and less for older would more accurately reflect what parents actually spend on children in different age groups.

A premium for lone parents has been paid above the basic personal allowance in Income Support that is slightly higher than the premium for two-parent families (£15.75 per week for a lone parent in 1997 compared to £10.80 for two-parent families).[4] Recipients of Income Support are also entitled to a Housing Benefit covering all eligible rent and other housing expenses, and a Council Tax Benefit covering the entire municipal tax bill[5] (UK, DSS 1997).

The unit of assessment for means-testing is the (nuclear) family household, and cohabiting partners of the opposite sex are treated as married spouses. Most income, including insurance benefits, child benefit, severe-disablement allowance, and invalid-care allowance, is taken into account against IS entitlement. Although a portion of family income is disregarded, recipients of IS in 1994 could typically work only a few hours per week before they began to lose the benefit, which was much stricter than in New Zealand, especially for lone parents (Eardley et al. 1996a). In addition, eligible claimants and their partners or dependants are allowed only limited assets in addition to their home.

The Tory ideological attack on welfare dependency significantly stopped short of requiring lone parents with dependent children (the vast majority of whom are female) to submit to a work test or register in a job-readiness program in order to receive IS. The solution to the poverty of low-income mothers was not active government assistance in moving into paid employment. Instead, the Thatcherite agenda was to promote individual and family responsibiity for dependant care and the family unit as the social-safety net (Pascall 1997, 68). About 57 per cent of those on IS used it as short-term emergency support when first becoming a lone parent. In addition, over half of those on IS said that they wanted to work or would enter the workforce if they had access to childcare, and their preferred employment rates – meaning, the amount of work they would like to do if they did not have childcare or other problems – were similar to the actual rate for married mothers. Most employed lone mothers worked in the service sector, but those working full-time typically earned below-average wages for full-time female employees. Finding a job or increasing working hours was the main route off social assistance for these women (Bradshaw and Millar 1991).

In 1996 the Conservative government announced its intention (effective in 1998) to discontinue the payment to new lone parents of the lone-parent premium on Income Support and the Child Benefit (Ford and Millar 1997). This decision was upheld by the Labour government following its election in 1997 despite the fact that UK lone mothers tend to have higher poverty rates than their counterparts in many other European nations and government benefits are relatively low (Bradshaw 1997). The Tory government argued that it was necessary to redress the balance between lone parents and couples by removing 'additional' support for lone parents (Ford and Millar 1997). Yet the economic plight of these parents, overwhelmingly women, remains bleak. By the end of the century, researchers project that one-quarter of British families will be headed by a lone parent. Furthermore, the proportion of children likely to experience lone parenthood by the end of their dependency is one-third to one-half (Clarke 1996). The repartnering rates of lone parents are relatively low in the United Kingdom; in an eighteen-month period, only one in ten lone parents repartnered although half said that they would be happy with such an outcome (Ford et al. 1997; Marsh et al. 1997).

Bradshaw (1997) notes that removing the lone-parent premium is not justified through comparative (or any) research, since other European nations (such as Belgium, Germany, France, the Netherlands, and Portugal) already pay lone mothers higher benefits than the United Kingdom. He describes this policy reform as simply 'mean-spirited' because it will deepen the poverty of lone-parent families, particularly affecting their children. Middleton and Ashworth (1997) argue that removal of the lone-parent premium for IS may lead to a situation in which lone parents are forced either to reduce spending on their children or to make even greater sacrifices in their own consumption. As we shall, see, however, this policy change complements other recent initiatives to induce more female beneficiaries into paid employment.

Family Credit and the Working Family Tax Credit

The Conservatives' Family Income Support legislation of 1971 treated one-parent and two-parent families identically (Land and Lewis 1997). This was replaced by Family Credit (FC) in 1988, a means-tested benefit that tops up the wages of low-waged parents who work more than twenty-four hours per week, later reduced to sixteen hours.[6] Since many mothers (especially lone mothers) wish to work less than full-time and are often in low-paid employment, FC was expected to be of particular value in assisting them back to work (Middleton and Ashworth 1997). Eligibility rules are similar to IS, but the maximum credit ensures that most families, where there is a full-time breadwinner, are better off than comparable families on IS. The same amount is paid to two-parent and one-parent families, depending on the number of children and their ages, the net family income, savings,[7] childcare payments, and the number of hours worked. Also, under this program, parents with a child under the age of one who is not being breast-fed can buy reduced-priced dried baby formula from a maternity or child-health clinic (UK, DSS 1996).

The reduction in the minimum number of hours worked each week to qualify for FC, from twenty-four to sixteen, occurred in 1992. This change is considered responsible for a small rise in the employment rates of lone mothers working between sixteen and twenty-three hours per week between 1991 and 1993 but also for a decline in those working from twenty-five to thirty hours (Finlayson and Marsh 1997). In 1992 the government also added a child-support (maintenance) 'disregard' (tax exemption) of £15 of earned income per week to FC for lone parents, as an intended work incentive. A bonus payment for FC recipients working thirty hours or more each week was added in 1995, to encourage more employment hours (Ford and Millar 1997).

In 1995 recipients of FC using registered childcare became eligible for a disregard of £40 per week on their earnings if they used government-regulated services. This reform was instituted after research indicated that it was hardly worth entering the labour force if low-income mothers had to pay for childcare expenses. Finlayson and Marsh (1997) found that, in 1994, lone parents on FC who had to pay for childcare (one-quarter of their sample) came uncomfortably close to losing money from working for pay. They cleared £10 above the income they would have received if they had been out of work. Yet Finlayson and Marsh also found that only 9 per cent of lone parents on FC actually use the kind of formal registered childcare that would enable them to qualify for the disregard.

As with other wage-subsidy schemes, Family Credit was criticized for discouraging employers from raising wages over time if they know that workers are unlikely to gain from it. In addition, FC could be perceived as a 'poverty trap' if it increases recipients' preparedness to accept low-wage work while discouraging them from increasing their working hours or investing in their earning potential. Unless recipients can achieve high enough earnings to push themselves off social benefits, there is little motivation to work full-time (Bryson 1997).

Family Credit under the Conservatives can be considered, then, as a tentative step towards inducing low-income mothers into the labour force. Between 1993 and 1996, the number of families receiving FC benefits at any one time rose by about 51 per cent (Child Poverty Action Group 1997), reflecting the success of this policy and the growth in numbers of low-paid jobs in a period of economic expansion. At the same time, FC's structure discouraged women from accepting low-wage work, even part-time, thus implicitly reinforcing the idea that it is acceptable for low-income mothers to remain on benefits.

New Labour's first full budget, in May 1998, marked an aggressive policy shift towards employability. A major tool was the replacement of Family Credit by the Working Family Tax Credit (WFTC), effective October 1999. The WFTC is a Canadian-style tax benefit, explicitly portrayed as an effort to boost income of poor families with at least one adult in paid work and to encourage adults in 'workless households' to move into the job market. Indeed, the introduction of WFTC was prominently accompanied by data from the Treasury highlighting the fact that one in five working-age households in the United Kingdom (about 3.5 million households) had no one in paid work in 1997, double the figure from 1979 (UK, HM Treasury 1998a). The tax credit will further integrate the tax and benefit systems.

The WFTC is projected to expand subsidies for low wages for 1.5 million families, more than double the number under Family Credit. A basic weekly credit consists of £48.80, with additional amounts that increase with the age of the child, peaking at £25.40 per week for sixteen to eighteen year olds. Claimants must work a minimum of sixteen hours weekly, but those working a full-time equivalent (over thirty hours) receive an extra £10.80 credit. A full credit begins to be reduced as income rises over £90 per week, as opposed to £79 weekly under Family Credit. The government estimated that, compared to the FC scheme, a working family with two children earning £200 per week would have an additional £23 week, and it pledged that no tax would be deducted until earned income exceeded £220 week (ibid.).

The targets of the WFTC initiative are low-income families where one or both adults is unemployed. Family Credit was paid primarily to women (50 per cent of FC recipients were lone parents, mostly women), whereas the WFTC will be paid to the 'household,' which can then decide, in the case of a two-partner family, who shall receive the benefit. This raises the possibility that the transition from FC to WFTC will promote income transfers from women to men, who will be the principle wage earners in about half of eligible households (Walker 1998a). The WFTC is a more explicit attempt to change beneficiary behaviour through financial incentives. It is accompanied by a childcare tax credit, discussed shortly, also aimed at improving paid-work incentives for low-income mothers.

In June 1998 the British government introduced a minimum wage of £3.60 per hour for the first time in its history, and two million people are expected to be removed from the worst of poverty wages (*Guardian* 1998). A lone parent with one child working thirty-five hours a week would have an income equal to £6 an hour once the WFTC, housing benefit, and child benefit are added to basic pay (ibid.). In May 1997, 36 per cent of Family Credit recipients earned less than £3.50 per hour (UK, Department of Trade and Industry 1998, 71).

Housing and Council Tax Benefits

At the beginning of the 1990s, changes in labour and housing markets led to government concern about the rising costs of the Housing Benefit as well as other means-tested benefits (Land 1998a). The Housing Act 1988 had deregulated private-sector rents, with the result that rents increased significantly. Thus, despite the cuts to the Housing Benefit since 1988, it costs increased faster than the number of recipients. One of the major problems now facing low-income families in the United Kingdom is the inadequate supply of affordable housing (ibid.).

Beneficiaries may be eligible for means-tested[8] Housing and Council Tax Benefits if they are not already living in subsidized housing (Ringen et al. 1997, 68). These benefits, administered by local government but subsidized by the central government, provide assistance for housing costs and municipal taxes (including rates and poll taxes). They are designed to be compatible with the other two means-tested benefits (IS and FC/WFTC). Anyone at or below IS level is eligible for the full housing benefit, which is paid regardless of work status and covers full rent and 100 per cent of municipal taxes (UK, DSS 1996, 23). The cost of these benefits is rapidly increasing and in 1998 was approximately £12 billion (UK, HM Treasury 1998a).

Until an amendment in 1996, lone-parent families were able to obtain local authority-controlled housing because the 1985 Housing Act required local authorities to give priority to homeless households including pregnant women and parents with dependent children. Accusations that this policy was encouraging the formation of lone-parent households led to the 1996 amendment that gives priority to those already on the waiting list. Homeless households should now have their needs met through temporary housing (Ford and Millar 1997).

Additional Means-Tested Benefits

Recipients of IS and FC and their families are also entitled to free prescriptions, dental treatment, eye examinations and vouchers towards eyeglasses, and travel costs to hospital, but the National Health Service provides medical and health services to all UK residents. Female beneficiaries who become pregnant may be eligible for a Maternity Payment from the Social Fund. The Home Responsibilities Protection is designed for a person who is looking after a child or sick or disabled person and is therefore unable to work for pay or cannot earn enough to contribute to a retirement pension. This special arrangement helps to protect the basic Retirement Pension or to protect the wife of a recipient's right to a widow's pension.[9] In addition, beneficiaries may be eligible for a Funeral Payment (UK, Department of Social Security 1996).

Widow's Payment and Widowed Mother's Allowance

As in New Zealand, the UK government pays a tax-free lump-sum payment to widows (but not to widowers) under state pension age, and also to those over state pension age whose husband was not receiving Retirement Pension when he died. The payment was worth £1,000 in 1996. In addition, widows living with their dependent children under nineteen may be eligible for an allowance regardless of their employment status. The rate was £61.15 a week in 1996, plus an additional amount for each child (UK, Department of Social Security 1996). This benefit is paid only to women, thus reinforcing the male-breadwinner model of family. As another indicator of the residual power of male-breadwinner models of the family, a widower with two dependent children applied for the Widows Payment and the Widowed Mother's Allowance and was refused on the grounds that these benefits were for women only. The decision was upheld by the High Court in April 1997 but was appealed to the European Court of Human Rights.

Statutory Maternity Pay (SMP) and Maternity Allowance

Unlike Australia and New Zealand, low-income mothers in the United Kingdom receive some state support for moving in and out of paid employment as a consequence of childbirth. Women who have worked for the same employer for at least twenty-six weeks (including the fifth week before the baby is due) and with average weekly earnings above the rate for paying National Insurance (NI) contributions may receive eighteen weeks of maternity pay. Two rates are available for this taxable benefit: a higher rate of 90 per cent of average weekly earnings for the first six weeks, followed by a flat rate of £54.55 for the rest of the SMP period.

Those who do not qualify for SMP because they are self-employed or recently changed jobs may be eligible to receive eighteen weeks of the Maternity Allowance if they made NI contributions in a qualifying period. Yet this benefit was worth less than the government social insurance[10] (UK, Department of Social Security 1996).

The Universal Child Benefit and Income-Tax Benefits

In response to a recommendation in the Beveridge Report, a universal Family Allowance was created in the UK in 1945. The original idea of the Family Allowance was to assist families with some of the costs of childrearing and to bolster family income, since the average incomes of British households with children were and still are lower than the average income of childless households (Jenkins 1996). Over the years, the government has modified this benefit. The Conservatives added a supplement for low-income earners in 1970, which was the forerunner of Family Credit. In 1975 the Labour government combined the Family Allowance with child-tax benefits to create the existing Child Benefit. The amount of this benefit was frozen for three years from 1988 to 1991 by the Conservative government, and, without indexation, it did not recover its real value (Brown 1992). The Conservatives were, however, unsuccessful in their attempts to target this benefit, as was done in the other three countries.[11]

The Labour Party, women's groups, anti-poverty groups, and trade unions resisted any attempt to eliminate what was widely regarded as a basic citizenship right. In its 1998 budget, the new Labour government gave a strong message of its commitment to a universal, indexed, and enhanced Child Benefit. The benefit remains a weekly tax-free cash payment paid to the mother (or guardian) of a child under sixteen (or under nineteen if a full-time student) and was worth £11.05 per week for the oldest child and £9 for each other child in 1998. A further increase of £2.50 weekly for the first child will be paid effective 1999 (UK, HM Treasury Press Office 1998).

In 1996 the Conservative government announced that both the One Parent Benefit and the Income Support supplement would no longer be paid to *new* lone parents beginning in 1998. Instead, two-parent and one-parent families would receive the same amount, with the rationale that the government is treating them 'equally' (Ford and Millar 1997). The new Labour government's decision not to overturn this measure provoked considerable controversy. The 1998 budget paid lone parents who were still receiving the One Parent Benefit a Child Benefit of £17.10 per week (tax-free for their eldest child), regardless of their income. Lone parents receiving Income Support have the value of the Child Benefit deducted from IS.

Income-tax allowances (exemptions) are also available for married taxpayers, but exemptions for children, created in 1909, were eliminated in 1975 with the new Child Benefit[12] (Baker 1995, 150). Lone parents are entitled to claim the single person's allowance as well as an additional personal allowance, equalizing the tax benefits of one- and two-parent families. Married couples are now able to split between them the married person's allowance, a benefit previously available only to husbands (Land 1998c).

During the 1997 election, the male-breadwinner family was still portrayed as the typical family in policy discussions. For example, the Conservative Party proposed that legally married spouses who paid no income tax (homemaker wives) should be permitted to transfer their personal allowance (or tax exemption) to the working spouse (husband), who would gain up to £17.50 a week (UK, Conservative Party 1997). The Conservatives portrayed this as recognition for the caring activities of the homemaker, but, ironically, her husband would have received the tax advantage. Also, the proposal would have benefited only one in six couples because it excluded both 'common-law' couples and lone parents and would have been of greatest value to families with incomes of at least £15,000 per year (Jones 1997, 1). During the 1997 election campaign, Prime Minister John Major declared himself and his party to be in favour of 'marriage and the family' (White 1997, 11). One aspect of the Tory election manifesto was 'to support the family in providing security and stability' and 'to reform the tax system so that it gives substantially more help to families.' Underpinning the manifesto was the idea of 'choice,' accompanied by personal responsibility and risk-taking (Shrimsley 1997, 8). The proposal was partly intended to compensate for the reduction of £3 billion in the value of the married couple's allowance[13] since 1992. The Tory election manifesto also pledged to 'protect the value of Child Benefit and Family Credit which help with the cost of bringing up children. This is our Family Benefits Guarantee. We will bring the structure of benefits for lone parents into line with that for two-parent families. We will pilot our Parent Plus Scheme that gives special help to lone parents who want to work, and extend it as it proves successful' (*Guardian*, 3 April 1997, 12).

Significantly, the Labour Party's sole official response to the proposal was to denounce it for its fiscal shakiness: that it had not been properly costed and that the source of revenue for the initiative was unknown (White 1997, 11). The Liberal Democrats were the only party of the three major political parties to have a section in its manifesto devoted to women's issues. It declared that the Tories' proposals were premised on the assumption that women's status and significance was derived from being one-half of a married couple (Smithers 1997, 13).

The Conservative proposal was criticized by journalists, researchers, and advocacy groups on a number of grounds. Potentially eligible couples may already be receiving Housing Benefits, Family Credit, and other means-tested benefits which may be added to paid earnings; the tax concession may result in them losing these benefits (*Guardian*, 4 April 1997, 20). Furthermore, the benefits of the 1997 election proposal would have been counteracted by other changes to the tax and benefit system made by the Conservative government in the early 1990s, such as cuts to lone-parent benefits and the erosion by inflation of the married couple's allowance.

The Institute of Fiscal Studies concluded that the overall effect of Tory policies of the 1990s has been to redistribute tax burdens away from married couples with children and one earner to other family forms, such as employed lone parents. In contrast, the Child Poverty Action

Group declared that the Tory proposal would not assist those most in need. They were referring to children who live in households with no income earners and the one-third of households that are not headed by a married couple, most of whom are lone-parent families (Millar, Hencke, and Ryle 1997, 13). Although the Conservatives' proposals were abandoned with their defeat in the May 1997 election, the political discussion surrounding them illuminates British policy priorities.

Child Support

Child-support policy, and its calculation and enforcement, has assumed considerable importance in British welfare-state restructuring. The Thatcherite preoccupations with the moral underpinnings of the family, the family's capacity to act as a 'private' safety net, and public-expenditure reductions melded with broader concerns about government support for mothers caring for children at home. The significance of this combination of factors for low-income mothers and their relationships to paid work requires some detailed elaboration.

Historically, British policy allowed the absent parent to support his current family while the first family was supported by the state through social security (Maclean 1997b). A new law in 1969 permitted 'no fault' divorce, but concern grew throughout the 1970s and 1980s over the rising rates of divorce and births outside marriage, the lack of paternal child support when couples do not live together, and the high rates of welfare dependency within lone-parent families.

Throughout the 1980s, the Thatcher government oversaw a major revision and codification of family law. The objectives were to reduce legal intervention into family life except in extreme circumstances, and to change the emphasis from partnering to parenting, towards concern for the protection of children rather than individual decisions of adults about their choice of partner. Beneath these goals was a desire to reduce the costs of the state's provision of a publicly funded legal aid system as well as the burden of private quarrels upon public budgets (Maclean 1997a). The Matrimonial and Family Proceedings Act (1984) reduced the long-term commitment of spouses (husbands) to support their former partners (wives) and the Children Act (1989) differentiated between 'good enough' parents and those who fail to meet this criteria. The two more recent developments in family law, the Child Support Act 1991 and the policy document on divorce reform 'Looking to the Future' (1993), both follow this policy direction (ibid.)

In 1989 the Conservatives created an inter-departmental committee to examine childcare arrangements. This can be seen as another attempt to address the policy vascillation between the ideals of facilitating labour-force participation for low-income mothers and supporting them at home as the preferable means of childcare. The work of this committee formed the basis of a Department of Social Security (DSS) white paper entitled *Children Come First*, released in October 1990.

The British Social Attitudes Survey had asked respondents whether they thought a father should make maintenance payments for his children after divorce: 90 per cent of men and 95 per cent of women said that he should (Kiernan 1992). Encouraged by public support for stricter enforcement procedures, the DSS white paper, and all-party support in the House of Commons (Millar 1996), Parliament passed the Child Support Act in 1991. The speed and magnitude of the change is without precedent in British social policy (Maclean 1997a).

The Child Support Act, effective 1993, made sweeping changes both in the enforcement of child support and their relation between families and the state. It removed the assessment and enforcement of child support from the courts (and in some cases from voluntary arrangements) and placed both in the hands of a new Child Support Agency (CSA) located within the DSS (Millar and Whiteford 1993). The act established that children, regardless of their parents' marital status, have a legal right to financial support from both parents, and it legally divided the concept of child support from spousal maintenance. The act also contained a clear moral agenda for 'absent parents,'[14] namely, that biological parenthood (and paternity in particular) is always accompanied by a financial obligation (Clarke et al. 1997).

Both the Child Support Act and the white paper viewed the responsibility of absent parents as purely financial, with little regard for their social and emotional responsibilities. Furthermore, they both concentrated on the financial problem that welfare dependency among lone parents creates for the Treasury or public expenditure, rather than attempting to resolve their poverty (ibid.). The act also changed the traditional balance between the entitlement of first and second families, giving first families greater claims on the absent parent's resources and thereby causing considerable controversy (Maclean 1997b).

The new CSA was made responsible for tracing absent parents and for the assessment, collection, and enforcement of child-support payments. It assesses the levels of support for all families where child support is an issue, including those who made their own arrangements years ago. Parents on social assistance are obliged to use the CSA and identify the absent parent, while those not on benefit may choose whether or not to use it. Parents may still make their own private arrangements although these can be reassessed by the agency on the request of only one parent.

The UK formula starts with a calculation of a 'maintenance bill' to establish the required level of child support, using social assistance (Income Support) rates which Parliament has established as minimum living requirements. The formula also includes a personal allowance for the lone parent on the grounds that this is the cost of the 'parent as carer.' The net income of the absent parent is calculated (after tax and national-insurance payments) and his/her living expenses are then deducted (calculated by the level of Income Support and 'reasonable' housing costs). Living expenses include allowances for natural or adopted children in second families, but not the children of a new partner. The formula then takes 50 per cent of the remaining income, up to the level of the 'maintenance bill,' and if the parent can meet this amount with less than half of his remaining income, then a further 25 per cent is required. The income of the lone parent is taken into account and may reduce the amount of child support required. Modifications are also made for split (or shared) custody (Millar and Whiteford 1993).

The Child Support Act requires that all 'parents with care' who live on social benefits must have their previous child-support agreements reassessed. Some low-income mothers had chosen not to ask for child support. Others had made private arrangements, trading a lump-sum financial settlement for regular support, or voluntarily accepting a lower amount in return for occasional gifts for the children or because of recognition that the father could not or would not pay more. The possibility that reassessment could lead to overturning these agreements has caused considerable dissatisfaction. In some cases, parents with care now receive less for their children than before reassessment because the absent parent, angry that the voluntary agreement has been overturned, has withdrawn his occasional gifts of clothing, holidays, or treats for the children. In other cases, the receipt of child support has been delayed months after the application despite the lone parent's financial need. In addition, fathers who have been paying regularly feel that they should not be targeted by the government through reassessment or asked to pay more.

Clarke et al. (1997) have undertaken a detailed analysis of the substantial inconsistencies that are apparent between the 1993 child-support legislation and the 1996 Family Law Act which focuses on children in need of protection, assistance, or care. Although the Family Law Act introduced a compulsory eighteen-month conciliation period, the Child Support Act significantly reduces the scope of conciliation by 'inflexible specification of child support obligations' (ibid.). Furthermore, the two acts have quite different definitions of 'support.' While the Family Law Act includes various services and financial assistance available to children and families in order to serve the interests of children, the Child Support Act focuses solely on private financial obligations.

Low-income mothers on Income Support (but not Family Credit) have their payments guaranteed by the CSA, but this only means that non-payment of child support does not reduce their income. They do not receive any of the money paid by the absent parent to the agency, which is retained by the government to help defray the cost of their social benefits. They can only gain financially from moving off Income Support, but if they do this they may lose some of the accompanying 'passported' benefits associated with being on social assistance. Mothers on Family Credit can keep the first £15 a week of child support before losing any of their FC benefits, but if child support is not paid by the absent parent, the agency does not guarantee it to the parent with care.

Since October 1996, a benefit penalty of over £20 per week has been in force for mothers on Income Support who refuse to complete the necessary forms or who fail to name the father of the child (Clarke et al. 1997). The assumption is that refusal to cooperate with the CSA is an indication of 'fraud,' although some acknowledgment is made that previous abuse and fear of renewed violence might be legitimate reasons for non-compliance.

Despite the fact that the CSA can deduct child support from the absent parent's earnings, the amount of unpaid support remains substantial. By December 1996, £438 million was outstanding on full maintenance assessments, of which £271 million was being paid in instalments, leaving £167 million to be collected (ibid.). The principal group where enforcement becomes a problem is the self-employed, as in Australia.

Opposition to the Child Support Act has been intense and prolonged, through protests, demonstrations, and critical evaluations of the legislation ranging from fathers' rights to feminist perspectives. Interest-group mobilization against the act covers such disparate interest groups as the Network Against the Child Support Act, Families Need Fathers, the Child Poverty Action Group, and the National Council for One-Parent

Families (Millar 1996; Bashevkin 1998; Land 1998c). The act has been criticized for its unrealistic benefit-savings targets, given the costs of pursuing absent fathers, and for the lack of incentives for lone mothers to cooperate or for fathers to pay. It also encourages social divisions between mothers and fathers, first and second families, and two-parent and one-parent families.

The scheme's impact has been one of small gains and losses (Maclean 1997b). Preliminary findings indicated that 8 per cent of women were worse off and 20 per cent better off under the scheme, with the rest unaffected. Among the men, 38 per cent were worse off and 15 per cent better off. From the point of view of the Treasury, the scheme has been beneficial: in 37 per cent of cases it saved money, as opposed to 12 per cent of cases that cost more (ibid).

Comparing the UK Child-Support Scheme

A comparison with the Australian system[15] established in the late 1980s, on which the British one is modelled, is instructive. In the United Kingdom, the CSA is part of the Department of Social Security. In Australia it part of the Taxation Office, with child support collected through the income-tax system but paid through Social Security. Australia's formula for calculating child-support levels allows more flexibility and applies only to parents separating after the scheme was put in place in 1989. In the United Kingdom, all existing maintenance orders will eventually be reassessed according to the formula, which is seen as unfair by those couples who had already come to agreement to trade property[16] for child support (Millar and Whiteford 1993). Both treat second families in the same way and both set aside living expenses for the absent parent. The Australian scheme uses gross income and relates payments directly to the number of children, while the UK scheme uses net income and social-assistance levels to set the amount, relating payment only indirectly to the number of children in the family.

Lone parents in the United Kingdom receiving Income Support lose all child-support money received, but the first £15 a week is disregarded for Family Credit recipients. Absent parents may be even less willing to pay when they realize that their children were not receiving the support money but instead it was returned to the government (ibid.). In contrast, Australia never considered the receipt of maintenance payments as a major reason to withdraw social assistance, and lone parents keep three-quarters of child support when the father has low earnings and half when earnings increase. In the United Kingdom, the parent on income support gains little until maintenance paid takes the family off social assistance (Ford and Millar 1997).

The Australian income-tax system and the child-support scheme are more progressive than those of the United Kingdom. At average incomes, the Australian formula produces a somewhat lower child-support payment than the British scheme, but, at higher income levels, Australian fathers are expected to pay more. Also, the UK scheme is not related to family size, which may have affected its perceived fairness and acceptability (Millar and Whiteford 1993).

Before the introduction of the British child-support scheme, less than a third of lone parents received child support from a former partner. By 1994, this rate had not improved although not all lone parents were included in the scheme by that date. Yet the average payment was higher in 1994 than in 1993 (£39 a week versus £32). This was due partially to higher assessments by the Child Support Agency in comparison to those of the courts or voluntary agreements (Ford and Millar 1997), although higher CSA assessments are less likely to be paid (Marsh et al. 1997). Consequently, the Child Support Act has done little to reduce the vulnerability to poverty of lone mothers and their children or to facilitate contact and good relationships between the various parties concerned (Clarke et al. 1997).

In the United Kingdom, about 94 per cent of the children of separating couples live with their mother (Jarvis and Jenkins 1997). Research from the United Kingdom, Canada, Germany, and other countries confirms that marital dissolution is associated with significant decreases in real income for separating wives and the children of separating couples, but that separating husbands do not fare as badly. Although the tax-transfer system mitigates the income differentials between ex-wives living with their children and ex-husbands, significant differentials remain. After housing costs, the net income of husbands declines somewhat but almost as many wives as husbands move after a marital split and the general trend in income differentials remains. Despite diversity in labour markets and welfare states, these cross-national similarities in income after marital separation suggests that gender-related differences are common across countries (ibid.).

Lone mothers in the UK have a relatively high reliance on social-assistance benefits (79 per cent) and low labour-force participation rates (41 per cent), as we showed in the tables of chapter 1. British governments have attempted to reduce poverty by raising the generosity of in-work benefits (such as Family Credit) relative to social-assistance benefits and by introducing a mandatory child-support payment scheme. In the view of some researchers (Bradshaw 1997; Clarke et al. 1997), these initiatives have not yet proven to be successful. A more effective measure would be to raise substantially the labour-market participation rates and earnings of lone parents, in part by providing more affordable childcare (Jarvis and Jenkins 1997). In March 1998 the Labour government announced another review of the CSA in the Labour welfare-reform green paper (UK, Department of Social Security 1998).

In sum, the policy preoccupation with child support reflects concerns over high welfare expenditure and child poverty, as well as an attempt to enforce private financial responsibility after marriage breakdown. Yet it also reinforces historical biases towards ensuring that mothers have the financial capacity to care for their young children at home. While regular maintenance payments may enable low-income mothers to consider entering the labour force (McKay and Marsh 1994), the child-support system, as currently constituted, is not a major inducement for entry into the paid labour force, especially for low-income lone mothers.

Childcare

The persistent power of the male-breadwinner model of the family in British policy and the lack of incentives for low-income women to enter paid work are well illustrated in the United Kingdom's childcare policies. The affordability and availability of childcare is an important factor in enabling mothers to combine paid work and family life. The 1991 British Social Attitudes Survey estimated that 69 percent of mothers working full-time, 51 per cent of mothers working part-time, and 42 per cent of those not in paid work felt that a paid job was the best way for a woman to be independent (Ward, Dale, and Joshi 1996).

The need for childcare is not met by state provision in the United Kingdom. Britain has one of the lowest levels of publicly funded childcare in the European Union: publicly funded childcare places are available for only 2 per cent of children under three (ibid.). In 1998 there was one registered childcare place for every eight children under the age of nine, and places were available for less than two per cent of five- to twelve-year olds. The social-welfare system, excluding the universal Child Benefit, helped only about 30,000 families with childcare costs (Buckingham and Finch 1998). Prior to 1998 there was no tax deduction for childcare expenses (as in Canada), and only since 1994 was a 'disregard' added to Family Credit for childcare expenses.

Lone mothers with access to childcare (especially from their own mothers) report higher levels of satisfaction on a wide range of life concerns compared to those with childcare problems (McKendrick 1997). Lack of childcare not only makes employment difficult but places lone parents at risk of social exclusion from the wider society. Between one-third and one-half of British lone parents who are not employed say that the cost or availability of childcare keeps them from paid work. Others give reasons that are associated directly with the affordability or acceptability of childcare: their child is 'too young' or they are 'better off' not working for money (Ford and Millar 1997; Ford 1997). The childcare issue is exacerbated by other barriers keeping lone parents outside the employment market, including poor health, problems adjusting to separation, resistance to formal childcare, low wages, and poor employment prospects (ibid.).

Since 1994, up to £40 worth of earnings spent each week on formal or registered childcare services could be disregarded from income assessable for means-tested benefits (such as Family Credit, Housing Benefit, and Council Tax Benefit). This allows beneficiaries to increase their earnings before losing entitlement to social benefits. The childcare disregard was increased to £60 in 1996 and £100 in 1997. Intended to provide parents with a financial incentive to enter the labour force, it is available to parents with children under eleven years old who work sixteen or more hours each week and who pay for formal childcare with professional sources (registered childminders and nurseries) (Ford 1997). This disregard is not widely used, however, because of a lack of knowledge about it, parents' preference for informal childcare, and the fact that shift workers and those working irregular hours can seldom find formal childcare services (Ford and Miller 1997). The average cost of registered care is higher than informal care (£37.76 per week for one child and £42.86 for two children in registered care) and the disregard meets the cost of only 74 per cent for one child and 65 per cent for two children (Middleton and Ashworth 1997).

The inadequacies of the current system in addressing the multiple responsibilities of workplace and household for many women were acknowledged in Labour's 1998 budget. The new Working Family Tax Credit, discussed previously in this chapter, included a childcare tax credit as an explicit incentive for low-income women to enter paid work or to increase their weekly work hours. This credit, which replaces the disregard in Family Credit, will meet up to 70 per cent of childcare costs (to a maximum payment of £100 per week for one child and £150 per week for two or more children) (UK, HM Treasury 1998b). Families with incomes up to £14,000 (with one child) and £17,000 (with two or more children) can claim the maximum credits.

The WFTC childcare tax credit is the first new initiative to help working parents with the cost of childcare since 1990 and received initial support from a broad range of childcare-interest groups. Its impact on increasing workforce involvement of low-income mothers will not be determined for several years, but the policy does have some clear limitations. The credit will cease when a child reaches the age of eleven and eligible expenses include only those of registered caregivers, ignoring half of working women whose children are cared for informally. This is especially applicable in poorer families. The closing times of after-school clubs, on which the Labour government relies increasingly as a source for organized short-term daily childcare, do not necessarily coincide with the part-time irregular working hours of many mothers. Lack of flexible workplace policies by UK employers, who, according to anecdotal evidence, often penalize women who take time off for caring responsibilities, remains an important obstacle. Revealingly, one of the initial concerns expressed about the new tax credit was that it would force mothers with pre-school children into paid work (Buckingham 1998).

Welfare to Paid Work: 'New Deals' for the Unemployable

Background to Employment Benefits

An unemployment-insurance program was created in the United Kingdom in 1911, and the current law dates from 1975. The insurance, which is financed through contributions from employers, employees, and government, pays a flat-rate benefit to employees who have contributed for a specified length of time, with an additional amount for a dependent spouse (U.S., Dept. of Health and Human Services 1992). The UK insurance scheme differs from similar programs in Australia and New Zealand, where unemployment benefits are financed through general revenue. The UK program also differs from the Canadian Employment Insurance, where the unit of assessment is the individual rather than the family and the benefit depends on previous earnings rather than being the same for everyone.

Unemployed youth have been the target of recent employability policy in the United Kingdom. By 1988, two main employment and training programs had emerged: the Youth Training Scheme (YTS) for young people under eighteen and the Employment Training Scheme (ETS) for people over that age. The government deemed that young single people under eighteen should normally receive a government allowance only if they participated in a training scheme. Exceptions were allowed for certain groups of vulnerable youth without parental support, but the majority of young people who refused to participate in training forfeited income maintenance.

The Employment Training Scheme was introduced in 1988 as a twelve-month training program targeted to the long-term unemployed, particularly those between the ages of eighteen and twenty-five. ETS involved a combination of training and private-sector employment. Each participant was offered advice and information about job training and the aim was to agree on a course of practical action to help the person get back to work. Participants received basic income support with a supplement each week, and lone parents could obtain an additional amount for childcare costs. Travelling, accommodation, and equipment expenses could be met and bonuses were payable upon completion (Hill 1990). After 1991, unemployed people who previously refused training had to attend courses or suffer a financial penalty (International Social Security Association 1992).

Low-income mothers (especially lone mothers) were targeted for an employability-enhancement pilot project called Parent Plus. This program emphasized one-to-one counselling to plan their employment strategies, upgrade their skills, and find work. Yet this program, and similar ones in other countries, have not been successful in reducing beneficiary levels among lone mothers because their bargaining position in the labour market is weak and entry-level wages have fallen in real terms (Finlayson and Marsh 1997). Despite receiving mainly low-wage dead-end jobs, employed lone mothers typically express much more satisfaction across a wide range of life concerns than those without paid work (McKendrick 1997).

Employability Policy and Ideology

The Conservatives' employability policy lacked coherence and was ambivalent about taking concerted activist measures to require more low-income mothers to enter the labour force. In 1992 a Cabinet briefing paper on lone parents floated some ideas for policies 'directed towards discouraging lone parenthood and other ways of reducing public expenditure which do not harm the interests of the children of lone parents.' The mere existence of a document raising these ideas proved to be controversial (Ford and Millar 1997). During the International Year of the Family, the then minister for the family (Virginia Bottomley) argued that governments should acknowledge the privacy of the family and recognize the importance of keeping the state out of private family matters (Jones and Millar 1996). The 1995 *Social Security Report* was more activist. It noted, under the heading of 'Family Policy,' that 'the Government believes the best way to help parents with children improve their standard of living is through measures which assist their attempts to help themselves through taking full or part-time work' (UK, Department of Social Security 1995a). The government wanted social-welfare change but was unwilling to intervene in family relationships.

Employability initiatives, however, are being introduced at a time when labour markets are rapidly changing. Webb, Kemp, and Millar (1996) show that in Britain approximately 4.6 million employees received 'low pay' in 1994–5 (about 22 per cent of the workforce and two-thirds of women workers). Low pay is defined as a figure falling below two-thirds of median hourly wages. For women, the incidence of low pay fell sharply between 1968 and 1977 from around 48 per cent to 30 per cent, before stabilizing at around 32 to 34 percent for most of the 1980s and early 1990s (ibid., 261). The gender gap in the percentage of low-paid employees has narrowed by about half during the 1968–94 period, but women are still three times more likely to be low paid than men (ibid.).

The average age of low-paid workers in the 1990s has increased from the 1960s, with a higher percentage between the ages of twenty-five and forty-nine and a lower percentage under twenty-five. This trend has been particularly apparent among men, however; the age of low-paid women has been relatively stable over the years. Many traditional male jobs in industry have disappeared, and married men are increasingly finding themselves among low-paid employees (McKendrick 1997). Furthermore, paid employment today is less often an escape route from poverty than it was in the past, for growing numbers of low-paid employees fail to reach an income of half the national average.

These labour-market trends prompted debate over a minimum wage. The Blair Labour Party was elected on a platform that included introduction of a minimum wage, and in June 1998 the government

announced that adults over the age of twenty-one must be paid at least
£3.60 an hour beginning in the spring of 1999. Part-time female employees are expected to be major beneficiaries of the minimum wage (Milne
and White 1998). When the Tories were in power, the Department of
Social Security had dismissed a minimum wage on the ground that most
low-wage earners are 'second earners in the family' (UK, Department
of Social Security 1995a). Yet women now comprise almost half of the
British labour force, many families rely on two earners to achieve an
adequate income, and more women are sole earners for their families.
Characterization of women's wages as 'secondary' is increasingly unjus-
tified, yet it reflects the ways in which women workers are still viewed
within part of the UK political culture (Webb, Kemp, and Millar 1996).
In fact, they were still portrayed as second earners in the 1998 Labour
budget (UK, HM Treasury 1998a, 16).

Although Conservative policy was designed to contain social-security
costs and 'reduce dependency' throughout the 1980s and 1990s, there is
little evidence that these two objectives were achieved. Welfare spending was higher in real terms in 1993 than it was in 1979 (Castles and
Pierson 1995). Between 1990 and 1993, welfare spending as a percentage
of GDP rose by 5 per cent, while the replacement rate of benefits fell
between 1979 and 1993 for both the unemployed and pensioners.
Income inequality grew, with the poorest tenth of the population more
than 10 per cent worse off in 1994 than in 1979. Furthermore, taxes were
higher under the Conservatives than under the previous Labour government (Hills 1994; Castle and Pierson 1995).

By the mid-1990s, the political discourse concerning social beneficiaries and paid work contained greater emphasis on employability
schemes for a larger group of beneficiaries. Indeed, the 1997 election
campaign and its aftermath were a watershed in two ways. The restructuring baton passed from the right wing to the centre-left political party.
But, more important, the ideological and policy thrust was altered
substantially.

Employability and the 1997 Election

During the election campaign, each of the three major parties offered
supply-side plans, with little government outlay, to encourage the 'hard
core jobless' back into the labour force. The Liberal Democrats' scheme
would have allowed the long-term unemployed to turn their unemployment benefits into 'working benefits' which would be paid to an
employer willing to recruit and train them. The Conservatives, desper-

ately seeking to solidify electoral support among their anti-welfare constituencies, moved directly towards compulsory workfare for the long-term unemployed. 'Project Work' required these beneficiaries to upgrade their job-seeking skills and to take part in work experience for up to six months or lose benefits. Directly coercive and punitive measures were thought by Tory ministers to be the best way of reducing the number of people 'on the dole,' regardless of gender and family status. The Tories declared their intention to create a 'lean welfare machine,' which would have also included tough action against 'benefit cheats' (Wastell 1997).

Pilot employability schemes for the unemployed had already been initiated during the Conservatives' last electoral term in several regions of Britain. These programs offered thirteen weeks of intensive training in job seeking, including in some cases basic literacy and numeracy, followed by thirteen weeks on community programs. Full benefits plus an extra £10 per week were paid in return. The Department of Education and Employment calculated that the number of long-term unemployed returning to work since the scheme began in 1996 rose by more than 20 per cent and a further 2,000 voluntarily stopped claiming benefits. If the Conservatives had won the election, the pilot project would have been expanded since the House of Commons had already approved a new 'work skills' scheme which would have allowed the unemployed to study for vocational qualifications while receiving a jobseekers' allowance. The Treasury expressed doubts about whether the employability scheme represented 'value for money.' Nevertheless, the Tory Chancellor (Kenneth Clarke) favoured expanding it Britain-wide following the election if the number of people leaving the unemployment register as a result of Project Work continued to make it self-financing.

New Labour, led by Tony Blair, was elected in May 1997 on a platform that included targeting employability measures at specific groups. Prime Minister Blair's first speech on welfare after the general election stressed the personal responsibilities of beneficiaries to find paid work and advocated 'empowerment, not punishment' (Smithers 1997b). In fact, Labour's plan was to constrain some beneficiaries' options in order to persuade them of the attractiveness of low-paid work, while offering some financial incentives to find work. This focus accelerated and broadened existing Tory policies.

Labour's 'Welfare to Work' Scheme

Ironically, Labour's 'Welfare to Work' scheme is funded from a one-time windfall tax imposed on electricity and water companies previously privatized by the Tories. This work or training program, symbolically presented as a 'New Deal' and a 'ladder of opportunity' into paid work for beneficiaries, bears some resemblance to the workfare program in Wisconsin, USA (Wintour 1997). It targets specific groups: long-term beneficiaries among those traditionally defined as 'employable,' along with new categories of employables such as lone mothers with school-age children. The long-term employables include those under twenty-five who have been out of work for at least six months (and are therefore seen as being at risk for crime, drugs, and long-term social benefits), as well as adults who have received unemployment benefits for more than two years. The younger (eighteen to twenty-four) group were given four options: a job in the private sector for which the employer receives a six-month wage subsidy, work with a voluntary organization with a wage slightly above benefit levels for six months, full-time study in approved courses for those without qualifications, or a job with a new environmental task force. The system was designed to be coercive and punitive. Refusal to accept any option results in a heavy benefit penalty. Employers also receive a tax rebate of £75 a week in return for hiring any adult over twenty-five who has been unemployed for over two years.

In 1997 Labour confidently asserted that 'the aim of the New Deal is both to cut unemployment and increase the employability of dole claimants shut out of the labour market' (*Guardian*, 3 July 1997, 17). No mention was made of the potentially depressing effect that subsidies could have on general wage rates. Neither was the possibility raised that the New Deal might pay companies to hire workers that they may have taken on in any event, or that benefit cuts for those who refused to participate in or complete the program might have serious social consequences (Thomas 1997).

Employability and the 1998 Budget

Incentives for entry into low-paid work were further expanded in the 1998 budget. On the demand side, unemployment-insurance premiums were reshaped to make low-paid workers more financially attractive to employers. On the supply side, employers who hire unemployment beneficiaries over twenty-five who have been receiving a benefit for more than two years will receive a weekly subsidy, and one-third of these beneficiaries will be given intensive job counselling. A special program was also established to aid beneficiaries over the age of fifty to find paid work. The concept of employability was expanded further by incorporating partners (over age twenty-five) of unemployment-benefit claimants (95 per cent of whom are women) into the New Deal with personalized job-finding aid. Lone parents are permitted to take short-term jobs without penalty to benefit levels. Families with one parent in full-time work, paying £100 per week for childcare, will be guaranteed an income of at least £180 weekly and will pay no tax until they earn at least £220 per week. The number of low-paid earners facing marginal tax rates of more than 70 per cent will be cut from 740,000 to 260,000. More stringent work tests were instituted for persons with disabilities, turning the definitional criteria on their head: focus would be on what the disabled could do in terms of work, not what they were incapable of doing (UK, HM Treasury 1998a; Elliott and White 1998).

Significantly, the Welfare-to-Work program displayed none of the Conservatives' reluctance to incorporate low-income mothers into voluntary employability schemes. The program contained a 'New Deal for Lone Parents,' implicitly seeking to confront the scourge of Tory moral concern, the poor lone mother without a paid job. The program was predicated on the unsubstantiated assertion in the 1997 budget that 90 per cent of lone parents wanted to engage in paid work of some sort. Harriet Harman, the secretary of state for social security, declared that 'this Government will not leave lone mothers dependent on benefit when they want to work, and then stigmatise and blame them for society's ills. Our approach is different' (quoted in *Guardian*, 3 July 1997, 17). The 'carrot' approach also included a 'stick,' as discussed earlier: Labour retained the lone-parent benefit cut for new lone parents previously announced by the Tories.

Initially, eight pilot projects were created, involving volunteer beneficiaries who would be given individual help with job readiness, employment applications, and childcare assistance. The rule that beneficiaries could study only sixteen hours a week and retain full benefits was relaxed. The program was made available to all lone parents making new Income Support claims effective April 1998, which was extended in the March 1998 budget to all lone parents receiving Income Support. In mid-1998 the Labour government launched an extensive media campaign, called 'Working Benefits,' which was followed up by letters from the Department of Social Security informing lone mothers with children over the age of five about how much better off they would be in paid work. The campaign was predicated on the belief that low-income mothers on benefit were imbued with a sense of rational economic calculation equivalent to that of other potential workers. It assumed that, if these mothers had better knowledge of the income advantages of paid work, including the supplementary income available through Family Credit for low-paid jobs, then more would move into paid employment (Walker 1998b).

As of mid-1998, there is no coercion or benefit penalty for low-income mothers who do not participate in the program. Instead, they will be required to attend a job-search interview when their youngest child reaches the second term of full-time education (at the age of five). Clearly, there will be sustained messages and pressure from the government about the social necessity and desirability of paid work.

As a further inducement for beneficiaries to enter into paid work, the Labour government has taken some steps to address childcare obstacles, adding £200 million over five years and promising the training of 50,000 new childcare assistants through voluntary organizations by 2002. For beneficiaries, the childcare 'disregard' was raised from £60 to £100 a week for lone parents with two or more children, which means that, if they produce receipts for registered childcare services, their take-home earnings could be higher before benefits are reduced. Childcare costs for up to 500,000 parents may be affected (*Guardian*, 3 July 1997, 17). In the 1998 budget, Income Support was raised by £2.50 per week with an additional £2.50 per week increase above inflation for each child under eleven (UK, HM Treasury 1998b). This was designed to address both the high costs of the early years of child raising and the costs of childcare if the parent or parents are in paid work.

The childcare provisions associated with employability were greeted favourably by interest groups associated with low-income mothers. The director of the National Council for One Parent Families declared that 'the additional support with child care costs will help break down one of the greatest barriers to work, and combined with the new national employment scheme at last promises a route out of poverty for these families' (*Guardian*, 3 July 1997, 17). The chief executive of Gingerbread, a lone-parents group, was also pleased: 'at last a recognition that lone parents want to work and the guts to put money up front to ensure that they have the chance to do so' (ibid.). The Child Poverty Action Group welcomed the recognition of the links between childcare and movement into paid work but demanded additional state funding and an expansion of credits to include non-registered childminders, who are used extensively by low-income mothers (Cooper 1997).

New Labour's belief that paid work is the best mechanism to alleviate

poverty was clarified politically in early 1998 in two seminal government documents: the budget and a green paper on welfare reform. Neither of these documents was produced with any extensive consultation
with Labour's traditional political allies in the trade union movement.
The discourse of both is indicative of the ideological shifts associated
with employability initiatives: equality and redistribution of wealth are
replaced by emphases on paid-work opportunities, the state's role as an
enabler of equal entitlement to work, and the responsibility of individual citizens to take up paid employment. Labour's political objective
was to redefine and limit citizens' expectations of state assistance: 'The
Government's strategy is to provide employment opportunity for all –
the modern definition of full employment for the 21st century' (UK, HM
Treasury 1998a). The chancellor of the Exchequer, Gordon Brown,
declared to beneficiaries that 'this is our New Deal. Your responsibility
is to seek work. My guarantee is that if you work, work will pay'
(quoted in Elliott and White 1998). Treasury budget documents further
reinforced the social message: 'Because in the future work will pay,
those with an offer of work can have no excuse for staying at home on
benefits' (UK, HM Treasury 1998a). Modernization of the British welfare
state further ties the social-safety net to the labour market, while simultaneously equating an individual's sense of self-worth with economic
aspiration and achievement (ibid.).

The 1998 Green Paper

Modernization under the banner of employability was further reinforced shortly after the 1998 budget by the publication of New Labour's
green paper (or discussion paper), a major reconsideration of the principles of the welfare state (UK, Department of Social Security 1998). The
ten- to twenty-year vision presented in the document (*New Ambitions for
our Country: A New Contract for Welfare)* was presented as the most
sweeping review of social policy since the Beveridge Report over fifty
years ago. Comments were invited from the public, on their own initiative, but the document was not distributed directly to citizens, as New
Zealand did with its proposed Code of Social and Family Responsibility.
  The green paper's point of departure is the multiple failure of the
social-welfare system under Tory rule in the 1980s and 1990s. The
growth in social inequality, the changing demographics of an aging population, rising levels of marital dissolution and lone parenthood, and the
lack of social justice and economic prosperity for many citizens are pre-

sented as justification for reform. Dichotomous images abound in the document. The paper argues for the necessity to change the welfare state because 'too many people are trapped in passive dependency, rather than being helped toward independence.' Households are categorized on the basis of their relation to paid work: there are 'working' and 'workless' households. Greater public/private partnerships in social welfare are anticipated (ibid.).

The Labour government foresees a 'New Contract' between citizen and state, re-balancing the rights and responsibilities of both, in order to take advantage of opportunities afforded by more citizen involvement in paid employment. 'We will rebuild the welfare state around the work ethic: work for those who can; security for those who cannot' (ibid.). Paid work is portrayed as the route out of poverty and the best form of welfare – 'the surest route' for those who can perform in the workplace. Through assertions such as 'the new welfare state should help and encourage people of working age to work where they are capable of doing so,' the government is seeking to reshape and enlarge social definitions of who can and should be working for pay.

Through paid work, citizens will be 'empowered.' Empowerment for beneficiaries will include their responsibility to accept help offered by state, to become 'independent,' to support other family members, and to save for retirement. The state in the new millenium is increasingly an enabling institution, assisting (and occasionally coercing) the British citizenry into paid work and providing a social-safety net for the assumed diminishing numbers who are unable to work. The Department of Social Security will become a work-focused organization. It will deliver services to its 'customers' (and monitor them) through personal advice on training, work placements, and childcare. With the proper 'tools' thus supplied, the state has fulfilled its major obligations to beneficiaries to alleviate poverty. The rest of the task lies with individual responsibility.

The green paper's vision still includes images of universalism and collectivism, such as its endorsement of increases in the universal child benefit and its renewed commitment to attack 'child poverty,' yet its failure to identify gender-related issues in its vision is striking. Both the green paper and the budget document are remarkably gender-neutral, treating the socio-economic conditions of men and women similarly. No gender differences are acknowledged in the ease of assisting beneficiaries to move from welfare to work, or in the difficulties encountered by women in re-entering the paid workforce after prolonged absences for caring activities.

The Impact of the European Union

Following the end of the Second World War, the major nations of Western Europe united to share and plan future economic development. The European Union's membership has since expanded considerably, taking in most of the continent's countries including Britain. What started out as a community of nations sharing economic planning has become a single European market for goods and services, capital, and labour, with European-wide legislation supported by a massive bureaucratic apparatus. The pressure in the 1990s to develop a political union and the forthcoming creation of a single currency have potentially important implications for economic and social policy in individual member states (Alcock 1996, 173).

Substantial differences exist between social policy and family policy in the United Kingdom and its European neighbours, which have been discussed extensively in other volumes (Lewis 1993; Baker 1995; Hantrais and Letablier 1996; Sainsbury 1996). Each country has its own procedures for organizing social protection, procedures that are products of different cultural traditions, interest groups, and conceptions of welfare (Hantrais and Letablier 1996). Esping-Andersen (1990) classifies Britain as a liberal welfare state since it focuses on low-level means-tested benefits. Sainsbury (1996) bases her classification of welfare states on women's entitlement and notes that social provision in the United Kingdom is typically founded on the male-breadwinner family and low-income mothers have been encouraged to care for their children at home with low levels of income support. In contrast, Sweden developed social programs that guarantee a minimum level of income or services to everyone, based on citizenship or residence rather than financial need. The unit of benefit tends to be the individual rather than the family (ibid.). On the other hand, there are 'conservative' regimes such as Greece and Spain in which permanent full-time employees (and their dependants) are protected by social insurance. The extended family and voluntary organizations rather than the government provide many services and protections, and the patriarchal family forms the basis of entitlement. In short, the balance among state, family, and voluntary-sector provision varies considerably in Europe (Alcock 1996, 173).

Concern about social and economic trends continued with the creation of a single European market and the signing of the Maastricht Treaty on European Union in 1992. The British Conservative government expressed strong opposition to the creation of a federal superstate and opted out of the creation of a single European currency and the 'Social Chapter.' Britian feared that the Social Chapter would introduce more collectivist principles into British society since it contains a number of principles about working conditions and social rights, such as requiring member states to ensure 'fair remuneration' for employees (Webb, Kemp, and Millar 1996). The New Labour government expressed its intention to opt into the Social Chapter at some point in the future, as well as reconsider Britain's opposition to the single currency. Both intentions indicate that, in the future, Europe may have a greater influence on British social policy.

Alcock (1996, 178) argues that the former ideal of 'harmonizing' social programs appears unrealistic, considering the wider range of welfare regimes among countries included in the EU. The goal of harmonization has been replaced by a policy of 'concertation,' that is, a more limited commitment to standardizing practices to ensure fair competition between nations in a shared economic market while allowing other social-policy differences to remain intact (ibid.). Nevertheless, Britain has opposed many attempts in the past to upgrade its policies for low-income mothers and they remain less generous than similar policies in such countries as Sweden and France. As Britain becomes more 'Europe-friendly' under Labour, that concertation may facilitate better integration of paid work and family life for low-income mothers, and there may be pressure to provide more publicly funded childcare. This could improve low-income mothers' opportunities to engage in paid work while coping with gendered responsibilities outside the workplace.[17]

Conclusion

The British system of social provision was for many years predicated upon providing benefits for two distinct categories of citizens: those attached to the labour force received social-insurance benefits; those outside paid work received social assistance. Everyone was entitled to health care and education, and parents received received cash benefits for their children as well as social assistance if their incomes and assets were low. Low-income mothers were supported by the state to care for their children at home.

The Tory years of welfare-state restructuring changed this balance in two ways. Increasingly, citizens receiving benefits were portrayed as social problems, moral challenges, and burdens on the state and society.

The vehemence of the rhetorical assault was supported by less dramatic changes in social assistance for the poor. Yet Thatcherism never satisfactorily resolved its ambivalence concerning whether the state should encourage mothers – including those whose behaviour did not reach Tory moral standards – into paid work.

Incentive measures, without overt coercion, were taken in the 1980s and early 1990s to entice some low-income mothers into the labour force. These employability policies included the back-to-work bonus in Family Credit (for those working thirty hours a week or more), the childcare disregard in FC, and the reduction of working hours in order to qualify for FC (from twenty-four to sixteen). The child-maintenance bonus, expansion of holiday day care, the lone-parent case-worker scheme called Parent Plus (similar to Australia's JET program), and the decision to abolish the lone-parent premium on Income Support can also be considered as policy inducements to greater labour-force participation. Tighter moral regulation of the poor through control of benefit levels, tightened eligibility criteria, and intensified fraud detection were also part of the Tory plan. Total income increasingly comprised a combination of state benefits and earnings from paid work, with benefits focused on supplementing rather than replacing wages (Webb, Kemp, and Millar 1996; Millar 1996). There is little evidence, however, that these measures reduced the number of lone parents on Income Support, although some other categories of claimants have been declining since February 1994 (Bradshaw 1997). The 'nanny state' changed but basically remained intact.

The British Labour Party has further 'modernised' the relationship of social provision to paid employment, despite its traditional emphasis on social protection. The beginnings of this process were accomplished in the reforms of 1997–8, with only marginal involvement of interest groups such as the trade unions. These reforms mean that more citizens will find that their social rights and responsibilities revolve around paid work, and that earned income will be seen as the primary route out of poverty instead of state-income redistribution through social transfers.

Although low-income mothers are now directly targeted by widened employability schemes, these remain voluntary. Despite its greater aggressiveness, Labour government policy has yet to challenge through coercion the cultural approval in Britain of childcare at home by mothers. Employability initiatives have been complemented by increases in the independent incomes of low-income mothers through the Child Benefit increase, the Working Family Tax Credit, and cash assistance for childcare. Furthermore, the increased policy acknowledgement of the linkages between affordable, flexible, and convenient childcare and paid employment reinforces the gendered nature of employability policy.

Government reluctance to intervene on the demand side of the labour market, however, limits the effectiveness of employability initiatives sensitive to gender and social class. The inability of the economy to create sufficient new jobs and employers' extensive controls over conditions of entry and exit from the workforce continue to restrict the capacity of paid work to be a route out of poverty for low-income mothers. These deficiencies are shared in some manner by all four countries in this study. The neo-liberal origin of these contradictory tendencies in policies addressing poverty, social assistance, and the employability of low-income mothers is one of the issues that we turn to in the concluding chapter.

7

Welfare-State Restructuring:
The Poverty of Employability

Introduction

For nearly two decades, governments in many OECD countries have restructured elements of their welfare states in response to rising program costs, increased numbers of claimants, structural changes in labour markets and families, and political-ideological agendas asserting the primacy of markets over the state. We have shown throughout this book that Canada, Australia, New Zealand, and the United Kingdom are all shifting towards a more residual and moralistic state that focuses on need, individual responsibility, and work incentives.

Social-policy discourse in these countries used to place greater emphasis on social citizenship and universality, especially in the 1970s. Now, the targeting of benefits and a more punitive approach to beneficiaries coincides with greater economic globalization, the predominance of market capitalism and labour-market flexibility, and the international spread of neo-liberalism as a major organizing theme of state policy. In justifying recent restructuring, government officials have often said that they are modernizing social programs and promoting program effectiveness. Yet many researchers agree that restructuring has been designed mainly to reduce public expenditures, to stimulate international investment, to limit government deficits, and to offer voters lower taxes (Mishra 1990; Pusey 1991; Pierson 1994; Saunders 1994; Kelsey 1995; Castles 1996; Esping-Andersen 1996; Myles 1996; Boston, Dalziel, and St John 1999). What is unstated or downplayed in many official and critical discussions of restructuring, however, is the impact upon poverty and the poor.

We have shown that, throughout the 1980s and 1990s, reforms in all

230 Poverty, Social Assistance, and the Employability of Mothers

four countries made a greater impact on monetary and fiscal policies than on social policies (Castles and Pierson 1994). Indeed, in three of the four countries – Australia, New Zealand, and the United Kingdom – the initial concentration on getting the economy in order meant an increasing separation of economic from social policy. Social policy became a secondary consideration. Governments in all four countries dismantled controls on their economies, deregulated huge areas of industry, transportation, and finance, reduced the progressive elements in their tax systems, attempted to control public expenditures, and moved towards decentralization of labour-market policy. Yet restructuring efforts involved more than just cutbacks. In some cases, these governments actually improved social benefits for certain segments of the population while they were cutting in other areas. In other words, the restructuring record is highly variable cross-nationally and contains elements of uncertainty and contradiction. The focus of restructuring, the paths that it takes, its pace, and its outcomes show some uniformity but also important variations in national patterns.

When we examine policies directly affecting low-income mothers, we see a strong tendency to 'marketize' systems of social provision. The four countries tightened the enforcement of child support, emphasizing greater privatization or 'making fathers pay,' designed to reduce social spending and enforce parental responsibility. They added user fees for health services and post-secondary education and tightened eligibility for social assistance. They linked social assistance as well as unemployment benefits to work incentives, skills training, and work tests.

Despite these similarities, the British government was unable to target child benefits when Canada, Australia, and New Zealand transformed their universal child allowances into means-tested benefits. While some Canadian provinces and New Zealand were able to cut the absolute levels of social assistance, Australia was still raising welfare levels and adding new social benefits. Canada, in comparison to the other three countries, encouraged the movement of low-income mothers into the workforce much earlier, both in terms of the date of legislative change and in terms of the age of the youngest child. Furthermore, Australian politicians still emphasize the importance of women's caring work at home while this is rarely mentioned in Canada. These are only a few examples of the variations we discussed in the preceding chapters which now need to be explained.

In chapter 2, we outlined two broad paradigms concerning the analysis and explanation of welfare-state variations. Mainstream, or 'malestream,' approaches have concentrated on state provision for those in the labour force (mainly men) and emphasized power-resource theories that focus on the importance of social structure, class relations, political choices, and political alliances in explaining the uneven development of welfare states. In contrast, feminist approaches have studied both family welfare and state provision and concentrated mainly on women as mothers, carers, and employees. They highlight the gendered nature of work and family that underlies many social programs and keeps women in domestic and dependent roles.

Feminist researchers have demonstrated that restructuring efforts in recent years have disproportionately affected low-income women and other categories of economically disadvantaged people (St John 1994; Armstrong 1996). In some cases, benefits have been cut that were assisting women to become more independent from both their family and the state and were enabling mothers to compete more equitably in the labour force. Feminists argue that policy researchers and welfare-state theorists must ask what welfare states have done to reduce both gender and class inequality. They must also ask how welfare states have assisted women to maintain autonomous households, if they so desire (Orloff 1993).

A major concern of this cross-national study has been to move towards more precision and specificity in explaining the process and outcomes of social-program restructuring as it affects low-income mothers. To do so, we have integrated the two approaches mentioned above. We have elevated both gender and maternal status into central elements in our analysis but without excluding social class and the political and institutional factors considered important by mainstream theorists. Since we based our analysis on four national case studies, we have been able to draw some broad conclusions about the impact of restructuring on low-income mothers in liberal welfare states. Before we discuss these conclusions, we will summarize the relevant differences among the four nations. Then we will focus on the main reasons for variations in restructuring programs affecting low-income mothers.

Cross-National Variations in Welfare States

Although Esping-Andersen (1990) classifies all four countries in this study as liberal welfare regimes, other researchers have noted substantial variations in their social programs (Mitchell 1991 and 1992; Baker 1995; Castles 1996). These differences essentially relate to the use of social insurance in Canada and the United Kingdom, and the heavy reliance on the male-wage-earner's welfare state in New Zealand and especially Australia.

When the Canadian welfare state was designed in the 1940s, Leonard Marsh, who prepared the Marsh Report (1943) for the Canadian government, relied heavily on the British Beveridge Report, published in the previous year. He recommended a social-security system for Canada that was similar to Britain's, with social insurance for sickness, old age, disability, and unemployment and means-tested benefits for those outside paid work. In the 1940s, Canada's Parliament developed a national social-insurance program to deal with involuntary and temporary unemployment. Over the years, unemployment insurance (UI) has been restructured and cut back, and in 1996 was symbolically renamed Employment Insurance, reflecting a government-wide shift to more market-based terminology. This benefit, however, has always been social insurance, financed through contributions, paid as a percentage of previous earnings, and based on individual rather than family entitlement. Unemployed men receive no supplement for their 'dependants' and both men and women are considered to be potential earners. Maternity and parental benefits are also paid under this program. For those ineligible for federal Employment Insurance, the provinces offer less-generous and means-tested social-assistance programs financed through general taxes. This illustrates that Canada offers a mixture of social-insurance and social-assistance programs, leading to what Diane Sainsbury (1993) has called a two-tiered welfare state. Male earners can more often rely on social insurance while female carers typically must depend on less generous and stigmatized social-assistance benefits.

Canada also developed a universal Family Allowance in 1945 which lasted until 1993, and public medical insurance in the 1960s which still offers basic medical, diagnostic, and hospital services funded through taxes. The universal old age pension, established in 1951, was to be targeted in the year 2001 to those with low family incomes, but this proposal was rescinded in 1998. Since 1984, the Canadian government has eliminated universality from family benefits but has not been entirely successful in eliminating universality from old age pensions. Medicare has been eroded but basic services remain. The federal government has also 'downsized' the public service, privatized large segments of government infrastructure, and made major cuts in federal transfers to the provinces for health, tertiary education, and social services. The focus on 'employability' has pushed mothers with both school-aged and pre-school children into low-paying temporary jobs and coincided with a widened gap between rich and poor. Some benefits, such as tax deductions for childcare expenses, have been increased and considerable efforts have been made to improve gender equity in family law, labour legislation, and the constitution. Despite these efforts, however, the economic status of males and females remains discrepant, and poverty rates are particularly high among mother-led families, as we showed in chapter 1.

Britain's welfare state was developed much earlier than Canada's, with a combination of social insurance, social assistance, and universal programs. The unemployment-insurance program, established in 1911, was based on the male-breadwinner family and paid a flat-rate benefit to the unemployed, with a supplementary payment for a dependent spouse and children. Lone mothers with children under sixteen are still paid a means-tested 'social wage' (Income Support and Family Credit) to care for their children at home since they are considered to be engaged in the socially important but unpaid work of mothering. Britain also developed a universal child benefit (which remained as of December 1998), social housing for low-income families, and public health insurance.

The British Conservative Party's verbal assault on the cradle-to-grave 'nanny state' failed to destroy its social foundations (Castles and Pierson 1995). While Thatcher and subsequent Conservative governments privatized large segments of state infrastructure, they were not as successful in abolishing or reducing social benefits (Pierson 1994). Universal child allowances, Income Support, Family Credit, and tuition-free tertiary education for citizens were retained, although in 1997 the Conservatives abolished the special benefits for lone parents (for new applicants).[1] The basic National Health Service has been modified but still remains in place. When Tony Blair's New Labour government was elected in 1997, it did not restore the lone-parent benefit and also announced the end of free tuition for tertiary education. Yet these are minor changes considering that Canadian provinces have never offered free tuition for post-secondary students or a special benefit for lone mothers, nor permitted low-income mothers to stay on benefit until their youngest child is sixteen.

Australia and New Zealand were the only OECD countries that had not developed state-run social-insurance programs by the 1960s but instead relied on a centralized system of wage arbitration, high wages, and full employment for men in order to provide income security. For those outside the labour force, low-level means-tested benefits were paid. Both countries also developed universal child allowances in the 1940s and public health schemes, although there were substantial differences in the design of their retirement benefits and public health systems (Castles and Shirley 1996). The income-security system of Australia and New Zealand has been called the 'wage-earner's welfare state' by mainstream theorists (Castles 1985) but further specified as 'the *male*-wage-earner's welfare state' by feminists (Bryson 1992). Women in both countries have been entitled to social benefits mainly through their wage-earning (or unemployed) husbands, and unemployed men have been offered additional means-tested benefits for their 'dependent' wives and children. Mothers who are unattached to male breadwinners (and who therefore typically have low incomes) have not been expected to enter paid work but instead are entitled to a state pension to care for their children at home.[2] In chapters 4 and 5 we argued that employability programs in Australia and New Zealand have attempted to combine the role of unpaid carer with that of paid worker, but mothers are still seen as primary carers and secondary workers.

In New Zealand, major restructuring by both Labour and National governments included widespread privatization, the demise of centralized bargaining and trade union privileges, the introduction of tuition fees for post-secondary education, electoral reform, and severe cuts to social benefits. The universal child allowance was abolished in 1991. The National-dominated coalition government tried unsuccessfully in 1997 to target the universal old age pension (which was still under attack in 1998), while retaining a pharmaceutical plan that is generous by Canadian standards. In addition, state support has remained for low-income mothers to care for their children at home (the Domestic Purposes Benefit), which is set at a low level but is paid for much longer than welfare benefits in any Canadian province. Only in 1998 did New Zealand develop a workfare scheme (Community Wage), targeted initially at long-term unemployed males, but it was unsuccessful in its attempt to require beneficiary mothers with school-aged children to look for paid work.

Australia experienced some of the same economic problems as New Zealand but with a noticeably lower public debt. Yet the Australian Labor government chose to resolve these problems differently by negotiating with the trade unions in a quasi-corporatist way during the 1980s, which offered some protection for jobs and wages. Furthermore, Labor actually expanded the public health system during the same period and raised the old age pension, rent assistance, and subsidies for childcare. Even under the fiscal austerities of the 1990s, beneficiary mothers in Australia have remained comparatively insulated from the labour market. Some 'mother-workers' are being encouraged into paid work by job-readiness and training programs, but these employability programs still allow beneficiaries with young children to remain outside paid employment. There are, then, areas of convergence and divergence in the social-welfare restructuring process, pace of change, and outcomes among these four countries. When the focus turns specifically to the interrelationships among employability programs, social assistance, and poverty, as these pertain to low-income mothers, we see the same elements of convergence and divergence. But there is a unifying theme underneath.

The Unifying Banner of Paid Work

Within each country, entitlement to social programs has become increasingly conditional on the recipient's willingness to retrain, to search for paid work, to participate in a job-placement scheme, and to enter or re-enter the labour force. Paid work, governed by the rules and discipline of the capitalist labour market, is regarded in varying degrees in the four countries as superior – both morally and practically – to receiving entitlements through social programs. Moving people off these programs has become a more important policy priority than reducing poverty or assisting parents to combine paid work and family life in ways that do not discriminate by gender. Consequently, the rhetoric of social-program eligibility has shifted away from citizenship rights that imply some degree of permanent entitlement towards viewing social benefits as temporary and contingent, based on need, and designed to encourage self-sufficiency and labour-market attachment.

Links between citizenship status and paid work are not new. Work tests for unemployment benefits have been an acceptable part of the welfare state for decades, but with the advent of employability policies, paid work is now becoming a part of the eligibility criteria for an increasing number of beneficiaries. The question of who is considered as employable and under what circumstances is being redefined to draw more beneficiaries into wage work. Beneficiaries are now divided between potential workers and 'the workless.' This is seen most formally in 1998 policy pronouncements from the New Labour government in the United Kingdom, but it is also present in official discourses in Canada and increasingly in New Zealand.

The parameters of the policy debate and the criteria for assessing what is socially valid activity create a dichotomy between paid work and social welfare, and social-safety nets are being redesigned to revolve around a fulcrum of preparing for, searching for, and engaging in paid work. Citizen involvement in the paid labour market is becoming a new theme of both individual and societal governance. Paid work equals independence and worthy citizenship, and benefits are linked to whether one is or should be working or seeking work (Lister 1996). The most disadvantaged beneficiaries are those who are not fulfilling their job-seeking duties. Moreover, in discussions of unemployment and the need for greater personal and family responsibility for income security and welfare provision, an increasing emphasis is placed upon the negative attributes of individuals. Structural barriers to unemployment and social rights to benefits are no longer predominant parts of government discourse in any of the four countries. A positive orientation by an individual towards paid work is seen as a means of social integration and inclusion. Social exclusion and sanction are increasingly directed at those who ignore the labour market. The contradiction of greater emphasis on paid work at a time of elevated structural unemployment can partly be understood by the component of preparation and search for work. The application of labour-market discipline to social beneficiaries becomes more important than actually finding a job or overcoming poverty.

Although the overt degree of coercion to seek work in return for social assistance remains small, the options are narrowing. Each of the four countries is engaging in more surveillance of beneficiaries, usually under the guise of personal counseling. This is further intensified by well-publicized campaigns, particularly intense in New Zealand, to combat benefit fraud. The job-search activities of beneficiaries are trusted less and monitored more by the state. Beneficiaries are no longer free to wait for a desirable position but must accept the first one offered. This means that the conditions under which workers can sell their labour, as well as collectively control entry to the employment market, are increasingly circumvented by the state (Pixley 1993, 213).

These common features of employability policy must not be allowed to obscure important cross-national differences. The ascendance of neo-liberal organizing themes does not follow a uniform path. In the four countries, the elevation of paid work and labour markets has been interpreted somewhat differently and has had varying policy consequences, especially when applied to low-income mothers. These variations require explanation. A substantial part of this explanation lies in the different concepts of family inherent within social programs, national variations in economic and labour-market trends, the varying strength of interest groups and their alignment with government, and variations in the politics and structure of decision making. Each of these factors is addressed in the next section.

Factors Affecting Restructuring

The Models of 'Family' Inherent within Social Programs

This study has shown the variable tensions in these four countries between neo-liberal pro-market themes and cultural beliefs about mothering and the needs of children. Culturally-specific models of family, motherhood, gender roles, and ideas about the role of the state in family life underlie laws and social programs (Eichler 1997). When the British established their colonies in Canada, Australia, and New Zealand, they brought with them British common law and the idea that the state should intervene in family life only as a last resort. Not all the colonies accepted these British precedents in the same way and to the same extent, since they had to consider local interests and pressure groups. Yet, even after independence was achieved by each colony, the tenor of social and economic policy debates remained heavily influenced by Britain.

At the turn of the century, British social programs were founded on the male-breadwinner family and the family wage. Basing social provision on the family wage preserved male work rights and kept most married women out of the labour force by weakening their right to work, especially in times of high unemployment (Land 1979; Baker and Robeson 1981). Furthermore, the male-breadwinner model encouraged a system of unemployment benefits that viewed wives as dependants rather than unemployed individuals and paid married men benefits at a higher rate than unmarried men or women.

The institutionalization of the male-breadwinner family model in British social policy continued to reinforce popular notions of women's place long after families and labour markets had changed. Men typically supported this model because it allowed them to devote their full attention to paid work with little concern about housework and childcare. Governments approved of the model because they were not obliged to provide expensive employment-equity programs, maternity benefits, leave for family responsibilities, or public childcare services. Both men and women felt that children needed their mothers at home and few alternative forms of childcare existed (Sainsbury 1996). Social programs and legislation began to be reformed after the Second World War and especially as more women entered post-secondary education and the labour force from the 1960s onwards. These changes eroded the family wage and also began to challenge the idea of complementary roles for men and women within marriage.

Recently, all four countries have made attempts to reduce dependency on government income support among most categories of working-age beneficiaries. Restructuring efforts have enjoyed less success in reducing women's economic dependency on men in Australia, New Zealand, and the United Kingdom, partly because the 'dependent wife and mother' has always been more ensconced in social programs in those three countries than in Canada. Although changing social reality challenges the gender-segregated notion of women's proper roles, the strong policy legacy cannot be easily cast aside.

Most policy reform involves incremental change rather than radical alterations to the basic assumptions behind social programs. Not surprisingly, restructuring from the 1980s to the late 1990s in Australia, New Zealand, and Britain involved only minor changes to eligibility rules relating to the length of time that the state would pay for mothering at home. In Australia, for example, the age of the youngest child was lowered in 1989 from eighteen to sixteen for a mother to be eligible for the Sole Parent Pension. In 1995 the wives of unemployed men were considered to be unemployed themselves if all their children were grown up and if these women were not considered to be too old to find a job. In New Zealand, the age of the youngest child was reduced in 1996 from sixteen to fourteen for a mother's eligibility for the Domestic Purposes Benefit. In Britain, the youngest child's age remains at sixteen even though the New Labour government is encouraging more mothers with school-aged children to enter the workforce with its new 'welfare-to-work' program. Moreover, in these three countries, low-income mothers are expected to seek only part-time work, allowing them to retain caring responsibilities.

Canada presents a contrasting case. Despite the cross-fertilization of policy ideas, the family wage was never institutionalized in Canada in the same way that it was embedded into union agreements in Australia[3] and New Zealand and social programs in the United Kingdom. The family wage's failure to become entrenched in Canadian social policy was probably due more to structural than to ideological variables, including the relatively low pay for men that resulted from the political weakness of labour unions, as we will discuss later in this chapter. Since the 1940s, Canadian Unemployment Insurance has been based on individual rather than family entitlement and the same has been true for the old age pension since 1951. Once individual entitlement became an accepted part of social programs, there was greater demand, especially by feminist groups after the 1960s, for employment equity and social programs that recognized women as individuals (and employees) as well as dependants (and mothers).

Since 1966, the Canadian government has provided subsidies to the provinces for childcare spaces for low-income families, and since 1971 it has offered relatively generous income-tax deductions for employed parents using non-family childcare services.[4] Provincial governments have been actively encouraging welfare mothers with school-aged children to enter full-time employment since the mid-1980s. Alberta (with a Conservative government) requires mothers on social assistance to make every effort to find work when their youngest child is six months old. In most other provinces, the age limit varies from two to six years (Freiler and Cerny 1998, 67). In addition, the equality clause of the Canadian Charter of Rights and Freedoms[5] has forced Canadian governments to make most family laws and government benefits gender neutral (except maternity benefits which remained gender-specific) (Baker 1997c).

The United Kingdom, New Zealand, and especially Australia have retained a strong tradition of social benefits for mothering at home based on the male-breadwinner model of family. In Australia, additional government assistance for carers of children and frail elderly persons at home was widely supported at a time when benefits were being cut in other jurisdictions (Shaver et al. 1994; Bradbury 1996). In New Zealand, new workfare programs were introduced in 1998 but the Domestic Purposes Benefit continues to be paid until the youngest child is fourteen.

In the United Kingdom, there seems to be a discrepancy in political views about lone mothers and partnered mothers, with lone mothers the target of discussion about welfare-to-work programs because of their lower participation rates in the labour force. Nevertheless, recent Labour government policy documents still make reference to 'second earners' when speaking of wives in two-earner families (UK, HM Treasury 1998a), an updated formulation of the male-breadwinner model of family. In contrast, Canadians have been questioning this model since the 1970s, when governments were pressured to place more resources into helping mothers combine paid work and childrearing. This was followed in the 1980s by more stringent employability programs and continued downplaying of the importance of mothering at home.

The intersection of employability programs and the needs of low-income mothers raises the issue of childcare provision. Low-income mothers' greater involvement in paid work requires policies promoting the affordability and availability of good quality childcare. The degree of government involvement in childcare is partly ideological, relating to appropriate state expenditure, the mix of public and private facilities, and models of motherhood to be supported. Canada, and more recently and modestly the United Kingdom, have recognized some of the links between childcare and paid work for women. Australia and New Zealand still support childcare as an educational issue but not as a support for parents with full-time jobs. This is ironic since New Zealand has proposed an increasingly aggressive employability policy.

Employability schemes expose the inadequacies in childcare provision, especially when beneficiaries are expected to move into full-time work. There are profound differences in requirements between a mother who works ten hours a week and one who works forty hours. Moreover, childcare needs to respond to the irregularities arising from the nature of modern employment, but to date there is little evidence that this issue has been addressed. After-school clubs in Britain, for example, have already been criticized for favouring the needs of workers in traditional nine-to-five weekday jobs. The fact remains that friends and neighbours disproportionately care for the children of low-income mothers because they can respond to needs for flexibility and affordability. Therefore, tying employability policy to government-regulated childcare will not fully address the problem.

One further element of the childcare issue requires attention. Employability schemes in the four countries purposely do not address the gendered division of labour within households. Women are expected to become more involved in the labour force but are not absolved of their caring responsibilities. Instead, they are encouraged to manage better a double burden of paid work and care. Governments do not want, as part of employability policy, to involve themselves in social change within families. This remains deliberately untouched as something for partnered couples to work out for themselves. Nevertheless, as women's groups have pointed out, until the gendered inequalities within the home are resolved, women will continue to be at a competitive disadvantage in paid employment.

Economic and Labour-Market Trends

Restructuring in all four countries has occurred within the context of increasingly globalized markets, concern about high government debt and deficits, rising social expenditures as a percentage of GDP, and high unemployment rates that contribute to social program costs (Kelsey 1995; Castles 1996; Myles 1996). These economic constraints, however, have not been interpreted in the same way by governments in the four countries and therefore have influenced social policy differently.

The relationship between debt levels, politics, and social programs is striking. As we showed in chapter 1 (Table 1.8), both Canada and New Zealand experienced much higher government debt relative to GDP than the other two countries, especially after 1985. Resolving the 'debt crisis' became a major political issue in these countries, creating opportunities for manipulative politics and selective budget cuts. Only those two countries cut actual benefit levels. Yet, despite these cuts, the overall level of social security paid by government in 1995 as a percentage of GDP remained higher in Canada and New Zealand than in the other two countries (see Table 1.9).

In the mid-1980s, the New Zealand (Labour) government was pressured by foreign lenders and employers' groups to refinance the debt, float the currency, open the country to foreign investment, and reduce government spending. The dramatic changes that followed were unanticipated by many New Zealanders who had voted for Labour and consequently led to considerable debate about the honesty of politicians and whether the 'Great Experiment' should be a model for other nations to follow or a path to avoid.

Similarly, concern over Canada's high public debt permeated the policies and discourse of all political parties by the early 1990s, and it continues to preoccupy Canadian politics today. Relative to the other countries, Canada's debt has been high but unemployment rates have also remained higher in than the other three countries, which has become a major concern for both the political left and the political right. While the right believes that unemployment rates will fall with more competitive business practices, further marketization, and lower taxes, the left typically believes that unemployment is a political issue that should be resolved by government. Nations that have lowered their income-tax rates, such as the United States and more recently New Zealand, have experienced relatively low unemployment rates compared to Canada. Our tables in chapter 1 cannot show a link between lowering taxes and unemployment in New Zealand because the data predates this policy. Yet, in the United States, most new jobs are part-time and do not allow people to support themselves above established poverty lines, as Tables 1.2 and 1.3 in chapter 1 indicate. The United States is not a good model from the viewpoint of social democrats or feminists because it pushes mothers into low-wage work with little state support for their family responsibilities. Consequently, more lone mothers live in poverty in the United States than in most other OECD nations (Baker 1995).

From the 1940s to the 1960s, neither Australia nor New Zealand developed expensive social programs but relied mainly on high wages and state protection of labour and markets for income security. Both countries experienced a low dispersion of male earnings at the beginning of the 1980s, compared to other OECD nations with more generous social programs and lower poverty rates (Bradbury 1993; Saunders 1994). Yet this dispersion increased throughout the 1980s as unemployment rose and as Labour governments in both countries decentralized wage bargaining and further targeted social programs. By the 1990s, their policies had become even more divergent. New Zealand, in response to a monetary crisis and much higher government debt, reduced the highest marginal tax rate to 33 per cent, while Australia kept its rate at 49 per cent. New Zealand removed or reduced many protective tariffs, introduced a goods and services tax, and reduced the actual level of social benefits, while Australia reduced some tariffs. Consequently, the gap between the rich and the poor widened faster in New Zealand than in Australia (Castles and Shirley 1996).

Both New Zealand and several Canadian provinces cut their welfare rates, especially for single unemployed persons, at a time when Australia was improving health-care coverage and increasing benefits for caregiving. Furthermore, Australia, New Zealand, and the United Kingdom retained a social benefit for low-income mothers caring for school-aged and pre-school children at home, while the Canadian provinces expect these mothers to enter the workforce when or before their youngest child first attends elementary school, as Table 7.1 indicates. Except in Canada, removal of the government benefit for mothering at home would have proven too contentious, despite substantial cutbacks in other areas of state provision.

Our research suggests that providing a social benefit for mothering at home inhibits the labour-force participation rates of mothers, but that other factors contribute as well. Australia, New Zealand, and the United

TABLE 7.1
Employability requirements for mothers
on social assistance by age of youngest child

Country	Age of youngest child
Canada	Alberta: 6 months
	Quebec, Yukon: 2 years
	Ontario: 3–6 years
	Manitoba: 6 years
	British Columbia: 7 years
Australia	16 years
New Zealand	14 years
United Kingdom	16 years

Sources: Freiler and Cerny 1998, 67; government documents from other three countries.

Kingdom offer low-income mothers the opportunity to care for their children at home with a low-level means-tested benefit, and so full-time labour-force participation rates of mothers in those countries have been much lower than in Canada. Canadian lone mothers (with no special program that encourages mothering at home) are over twice as likely as New Zealand and British lone mothers to be employed full-time (see Table 1.6 in chapter 1). In the absence of a social benefit, full-time employment offers the possibility (but not always the actuality) of self-support, but the chances of supporting oneself on part-time earnings are minimal without additional government or family funds. Until 1996, Canadian welfare rules discouraged part-time work by allowing only a small amount of earnings a week before social assistance was withdrawn. With the establishment of the Canada Health and Social Transfer, some provinces now encourage beneficiaries to work part-time while receiving partial benefits. Yet some provinces have also created workfare programs and reduced benefit levels since 1996.

Labour-force participation rates of mothers are not only influenced by social-program rules but also vary with rates of marriage dissolution, fertility trends, and legal requirements. Marriage dissolution leads to greater economic uncertainty for all family members, but especially for women. Canada has the highest divorce rates of the four countries, as Table 1.4 indicates in Chapter 1, and most Canadian women, with little state support for mothering at home and a culture emphasizing financial self-sufficiency, have deemed it necessary to earn their own living regardless of marital status. Furthermore, Canadian family law makes it clear that mothers as well as fathers are expected to support their children financially (Baker and Phipps 1997). Higher female employment rates are also more compatible with lower fertility, and, not surprisingly, Canadian women have the lowest fertility rates of the four countries, as Table 1.4 indicates.

Levels of 'welfare dependency' for lone mothers are the highest in Australia and the lowest in Canada, but the discourse emphasizing welfare dependency seems to be less pronounced in Australia than in the other nations. In Australia, the emphasis is on mothers' 'choice' to work outside the home and their caring responsibilities within it. Most lone mothers in Australia, New Zealand, and Britain depend entirely or partially on government benefits rather than working full-time for pay. About 94 per cent of Australian sole mothers, 89 per cent of New Zealanders, and 79 per cent of UK sole mothers rely on social assistance (Bradshaw et al. 1996, 52), compared to only 44 per cent of Canadian lone mothers (Dooley 1995). Despite the comparatively low rate in Canada, there is still widespread consensus that 'welfare dependency' is too high, welfare rules are outmoded, and more work incentives are needed (ibid.).

Benefit levels and the incidence of low pay must also be factored into this discussion. In chapter 1 we showed that benefit levels varied considerably among the four countries. As Table 1.13 indicates, net disposable monthly income (after housing costs) for both two-parent and one-parent families on benefits in 1992 was the highest in Australia and the lowest in New Zealand. Since 1992, benefits have been reduced in several Canadian provinces, which may bring net disposable income in Canada closer to New Zealand levels. Table 1.14 also showed how poorly Canada ranks in terms of the value of social assistance relative to wages. This is especially pronounced after housing costs are taken into account. The poverty rates of beneficiaries in Canada, and to a lesser extent in the United Kingdom, are below commonly accepted definitions of poverty (50 per cent of median disposable income adjusted for family size).

This study indicates that social assistance does not resolve poverty in all countries, especially those that have recently cut benefit levels (such as Canada and New Zealand), but is paid work the answer, as employability schemes assume? The available evidence suggests that economic security for low-income mothers on benefits is not guaranteed by paid employment. The Canadian case is quite revealing in this respect. Canada has the highest labour-force participation rates for women of the four countries, and significantly more Canadian women are employed full-time (see Table 1.1). Yet, as we indicated in Table 1.3, the incidence of low-paid employment in Canada, for both men and women, is greater than in the other three countries. Indeed, the high incidence of low-paid work for Canadian men is probably one reason for the relatively high labour-force participation of women. Canadian mothers are likely to work for pay because male wages fell with global trade and the movement of manufacturing jobs outside Canada, while the cost of living increased rapidly throughout the 1970s and 1980s. Yet unions seem to have been less effective in protecting wages in Canada than in the other three countries (Baker and Robeson 1981; White 1993; Pixley 1993). A second income in two-parent families has become essential to maintain living standards. Furthermore, some employability programs subsidize low wages in order to persuade employers to hire beneficiaries, and the pressure to keep wages down will therefore be reinforced. If paid work is the answer to poverty, a conclusive case has yet to be made in Canada.

Mothers in Australia, New Zealand, and the United Kingdom have been marginalized in the paid workforce by structural constraints. Both Australia and New Zealand lack statutory maternity benefits, although paid maternity leave is available to many unionized workers in those countries. Affordable and high-quality childcare is hard to find in Australia, New Zealand, and the United Kingdom because only a small amount is subsidized by government and labour costs are high in childcare centres. Day-care costs are particularly high in the United Kingdom and New Zealand (Bradshaw et al. 1996). Without statutory maternity benefits and public childcare, many Australian and New Zealand women are still forced to leave the labour force upon pregnancy and childbirth, and they usually find it difficult to return, especially in times of high unemployment. Full-time jobs are also becoming scarce at the very time that more women are expected by their governments to become self-supporting. Yet cultural values still encourage many women in these countries to view themselves primarily as homemakers and mothers and therefore to forego the job training or work experience necessary to find well-paying positions. Low-income mothers thus face variable opportunities and constraints to earning a living wage in the four countries.

Underlying the expansion of employability initiatives in the 1990s is an assumption about the nature of labour markets. The last recession of consequence occurred in 1990–1, and since then Canada, Britain, Australia, and New Zealand have experienced a period of modest economic expansion and employment growth. Economies have been able to create jobs, with impressive gains in such areas as technology and the service sector. The assumption behind policies emphasizing work incentives and individual responsibility is that these economies will continue to create jobs and that demand for wage labour will remain roughly at current levels or even increase. Of course, policy makers are well aware that capitalist economies experience periods of expansion and contraction. However, in order to make employability policy politically acceptable and appear workable, the assumption has to be that labour demand will not decline significantly. Part of the policy answer to this dilemma is to assert that demand for workers will come not only from traditional market sectors but also from community organizations and environmental projects. Funding to employ these workers may come from social-program budgets, but this is only a short-term solution. Furthermore, many new jobs available to low-income women are part-time, and a person's ability to support children and form an autonomous household on part-time work is doubtful.

In none of the four countries have politicians confronted the slowing demand for low-wage labour arising out of economic recession. Employability policies are designed to encourage beneficiaries with marginal labour-force attachment to enter and remain in paid work. Future recessions, if they follow past patterns, will heavily affect the insecure and unskilled at the bottom of the employment market. Beneficiaries will be pulled or pushed into the low-wage labour force, then flung back out onto a redesigned social-assistance system whose benefits increasingly are linked to employment. Low-income mothers induced into the labour force become yet another component of a reserve labour force. For at least some, their place in paid work is contingent upon a prosperous and vibrant economy.

The implicit reliance of employability schemes upon the participation of the voluntary sector in providing jobs for social-assistance recipients is also a problem. Historically, voluntary organizations have played a key role in the provision of social welfare in all four countries. Indeed, new programs such as the 'Community Wage' in New Zealand reflect governments' attempts to incorporate organizations outside the private sector into the paid-work nexus upon which employability is based. These organizations are diverse in objectives and orientation, but they tend to rely on volunteers and experience chronic resource pressures. Community organizations in the four countries have expressed mixed reactions to acting as hosts for social-assistance recipients. While there is some enthusiasm at the prospect of additional labour power, this is tempered by concerns about the lack of resources for supervision and administration, as well as the perceived lack of work discipline of some beneficiaries. In other words, the voluntary sector cannot provide job training and future employment without additional financial resources.

This problem highlights the fundamentally contradictory nature of employability policies, which are designed to increase the supply of low-wage labour as these schemes become more widespread. The state plays an active role in expanding this labour supply, but, at the same time, the neo-liberal state increasingly adopts a non-interventionist posture concerning the demand for labour. All four governments have now abandoned full employment as a policy goal and replaced it by reliance on 'the market' to provide jobs. The viability of supply-side employability schemes remains problematic when they are presided over by a state that is reluctant to involve itself in influencing the structural demand for labour.

By late 1998, the Asian economic crisis threatened to drag many countries around the Pacific rim into slower growth, and Japan, the leading economy in the region, officially entered recession in 1998. The political consequences for the position of low-income mothers may be considerable, especially in the vulnerable resource-based economies of New Zealand and Australia. New governments may use problems arising from currency devaluation and large current-account deficits as justification for more aggressive employability programs.

The Political Mobilization of Interest Groups

Half a century of welfare-state development has led to powerful constituencies of support for existing social programs. These constituencies include traditional class and partisan divisions but also move beyond them (Pierson 1994; Castles and Pierson 1995). The mobilization of interest groups has differed somewhat in the countries in this study. The country chapters suggest that three constellations of interest groups – trade unions, feminist organizations, and employers' groups – have, among many others, played particularly important roles in the development and restructuring of social programs affecting low-income women.

Interest groups interact with a state that is by no means a monolithic entity in any of the four countries. At any particular time, the state is a matrix of political and bureaucratic structures within which social actors with different interests and power function and interest groups make divergent and inconsistent demands for government action. In each country, elements of both consistency and contradiction occur in the dialogue concerning restructuring and employability. As Du Plessis (1992) notes, the policy outcomes for women can often be fragmented, advancing and retarding inequality at the same time.

Trade Unions
In all four countries, the labour movement has played a central role in the development of the welfare state. Historically, labour unions and the political parties with which they were allied fought for minimum wages, protective legislation, a shorter work week, old age pensions, family allowances, and unemployment benefits. Since the 1980s, the labour movement has been challenged by government attempts to restrict their rights, changes in technology leading to 'downsizing,' free-trade agreements that increase competition for labour, and a growing number of part-time and women workers who historically have been difficult to organize. Earlier in the century, labour unions were linked with policy legacies that favoured men in the paid labour force and consigned women to the status of men's dependants. More recently, however, labour unions have increased their efforts to organize part-time and women workers, and women members have challenged their unions to fight for pay equity, childcare, and parental benefits (Pupo 1997).

Australian trade unions and the political left were long able to exert considerable influence upon social policy to protect the interests of working men and the male-breadwinner family, without necessarily including greater economic autonomy for women. They ensured that men's wages remained high through union contracts and that labour shortages encouraged by restrictive immigration policies and high protective tariffs discouraged wives from entering the labour force (Castles 1996). At the turn of the century, the family wage became integrated into labour-market policy and social programs precisely because it was encouraged by trade unions to protect male wage earners (Land 1979). In Australia and New Zealand, labour shortages and the demand for more workers in primary industries strengthened the labour movement, and unionization rates were relatively high. Australian and New

Zealand unions were most successful in persuading governments to control prices and restrict foreign competition and labour in order to protect local jobs and wages, which enabled high rates of home ownership (Castles 1996; Shirley et al. 1997).

The family wage was institutionalized through the centralized system of wage fixing and arbitration in Australia, New Zealand, and United Kingdom. Canadian and American unions supported the family-wage concept early in the twentieth century because it maintained high male wages and excluded cheap (female and foreign) labour (White 1993, 24). Yet the weaker North American union movement, with no history of centralized bargaining, was unable to maintain this position for as long as unions in the other three countries. Consequently, social reform and women's groups pressed for equal wages for males and females, and they began to be legislated in Canada in the 1950s, with Australia, New Zealand, and the United Kingdom following suit in the 1960s and 1970s, as we noted in Table 1.11 in Chapter 1.

In Australia, trade unions remained strong and influential in social policy even after free-market ideologies began to prevail. Ironically, Labour governments in both Australia and New Zealand introduced social-security changes in the mid-1980s, creating a political and ideological climate that enabled further restructuring by conservative parties in the 1990s (Castles and Shirley 1996). As in Australia, the New Zealand unions had supported the family wage and other policies to reinforce women's status as carers rather than employees. In recent years, however, they have modified this position and supported pay equity and increased funding for childcare (Curtin and Sawer 1996).

Restructuring in Australia was jointly negotiated through quasi-corporatist agreements between the union movement and government during the 1980s, leading to more gradual and careful reforms that were less detrimental to earnings and the social wage. In New Zealand, reforms were pushed through quickly with little public discussion, which partially explains the more negative reaction from unions and social reformers. Yet centralized bargaining has been eroded in both countries. Enterprise bargaining was introduced in Australia. Individual and enterprise bargaining were institutionalized in New Zealand through the Employment Contracts Act in 1991, which also made union membership voluntary (Pusey 1991; Castles 1996). This means that trade union membership will likely decline in the future, especially in New Zealand, weakening the movement's already marginal influence over future policy decisions. By the late 1990s, New Zealand employers and manufacturers groups (such as the Business Roundtable) were much more influential than trade unions.

In Canada, the union movement and its allies in the CCF/NDP were instrumental in arguing for social-security programs, labour protection, and higher wages. Yet the influence of unions was limited by strong North American sentiments against socialism and by the fact that some 'Canadian' unions were subsidiaries of American ones and were less involved in local politics than Australian unions were. Unlike unions in the other three countries, the Canadian trade union movement aligned itself with a political party (NDP) which has never won a federal election, although it has succeeded at the provincial level. Trade unions were further weakened by the two free-trade agreements between Canada and the United States and among Canada, the United States, and Mexico. For many years, the voice of Canadian unions in social policy was more indirect than in the other three countries, although in the 1960s they were able to influence labour-market policy when labour shortages were most prevalent and were able to promote the introduction of Medicare. Since the late 1970s, Canadian trade unions have been less able than Australian ones to protect their members' wages from being eroded by inflation (White 1993).

In the United Kingdom, the trade unions also fought vigorously for social programs but also supported the family wage and programs delivered to the male breadwinner on behalf of his family (Land 1979; Harding 1996). This support contributed to the fact that the income tax system, employment benefits, and most other social-assistance programs were based on the male-breadwinner family. During the post-1980 restructuring period, the British labour movement was cast in an oppositional mould, ostracized and castigated by the Tories. As was observed in chapter 6, the labour movement has not yet enjoyed a renewed prominence despite the election of New Labour in 1997. The UK Labour Party, long aligned with trade unions and anti-poverty groups, has been an important force in encouraging payment for mothering at home and supporting the choice of mothers to work for pay or care for their children at home. In the late 1990s, however, the Blair Labour government is emphasizing work incentives and employability, with only recent and modest attention to improved childcare services. Depending on the pressure of advocacy groups, mothers with pre-school and school-aged children may continue to be exempted from the new 'welfare-to-work' program.

Women's Groups

The role and influence of women's groups in reforming social policy have been downplayed by mainstream theorists but feminist researchers have demonstrated that these groups have always been influential in the development of social policies affecting women and children (Pedersen 1993; Kaplan 1996; Baker and Phipps 1997; Bashevkin 1998). Women's caucuses within trade unions and political parties (especially Labour) have also been important pressure groups for women's interests, as have government departments or ministries designed to raise the status of women.

Even at the turn of the century, basing social provision on the male-breadwinner family was controversial (Land 1979). Women's groups argued that not all men were breadwinners but some women were, and that women workers were entitled to the same wages and benefits as men (Baker and Robeson 1981). In the United Kingdom, Australia, and Canada, women union members and activists opposed the family-wage system early in the century (Ursel 1992), but union leaders wanted to ensure that women were not competing with men for the same jobs. Conservative politicians were concerned that working women would reject marriage and motherhood and that, consequently, the birth rate would fall, causing future problems for the nation.

Women have been over-represented as employees in social-welfare agencies and as clients of the welfare state, and they have often used this status to argue for continued state provision of welfare benefits. As mothers, care providers, and low-income workers, women stand to lose more than men when entitlement to social programs is cut, benefits are made more residual, and statutory protections are removed.

In Australia, groups such as the Women's Electoral Lobby, the National Council of Women, and feminist bureaucrats ('femocrats') have been influential in fighting for many issues relating to women and families. These include efforts to maintain universal child benefits, to increase childcare funding, to gain employment and pay-equity legislation, to prevent user fees in Medicare, and generally to prevent the erosion of the welfare state (Bacchi 1996; Curtin and Sawer 1996). The childcare lobby and anti-poverty groups, with large numbers of women members, have also been important voices for maintaining the level of government benefits and defeating proposed changes based on economic rationalism (such as the consumption tax in Australia).

In New Zealand, policies to promote women's interests have been supported by the National Council of Women, by women within the

Labour Party, and by employees of the Ministry of Women's Affairs. Efforts to support mothering at home have also been bolstered by relatively high birth rates and a population that is more rural and isolated than that of the other three countries. (High fertility and low urbanization have always been correlated with low rates of labour-force participation and a strong domestic role for women.) An emphasis on women's domestic role is also characteristic of interest groups such as the Plunket Society, which advocates long-term breast-feeding, the establishment of mother-led play groups, and other child-oriented activities that are made more difficult by mothers' full-time employment.

Despite working within a the federal system, the Canadian women's movement has been more cohesive and influential in public policy than the movement in the other three countries. In 1970, the Royal Commission on the Status of Women in Canada continued the strong tradition of women's lobbying and successfully recommended an advisory council and a federal government department devoted to improving women's position. Since then, various interest groups consisting predominantly of women have successfully demanded policies and programs promoting gender equity in the labour force (including maternity benefits, pay equity, subsidies for childcare) (Baker 1997a). Some women's groups have lobbied for a homemaker's wage or allowance, but they have been less successful than the lobby for women's employment rights.[6]

During the 1980s, the Canadian childcare lobby (led by women) successfully pressured government to increase subsidies for childcare spaces and to raise tax benefits for employed parents using childcare services (Friendly 1994). Furthermore, anti-poverty groups also pressed for improved social assistance and social services in the 1970s and 1980s. National voluntary organizations such as the National Action Committee on the Status of Women, the National Association of Women and the Law, Women's Legal Education and Action Fund, as well as the Canadian Advisory Council on the Status of Women,[7] have served as powerful pressure groups (Cohen 1993). In addition, feminist politicians, bureaucrats, and policy advisers have kept equity issues on the agenda (Burt 1993). In 1985 the Charter of Rights and Freedoms was added to the Canadian constitution, leading to pro-feminist court and legislative decisions[8] even during the conservative Mulroney years (Bashevkin 1998, 8).

Although feminism has been an important force in the United Kingdom for over a century, the British feminist movement has not been particularly successful in promoting women's employment rights or individual entitlement to social benefits. Randall (1996) argues that feminist mobilization around childcare has achieved less over the past three decades than in other English-speaking countries. She attributes this to the movement's fragmentation by ideology and social class, changing views about the relevance of children to the women's movement, concerns that state-run childcare would perpetuate patriarchy and capitalism, and disagreements about how parenting and employment for mothers should be organized.

Under the post-1997 New Labour government, more women have been brought into elite positions but feminist priorities have not been made a core part of party policy (Bashevkin 1998, 202). Women's movement activists have accused both the Conservative Party and the Labour Party of using the rhetoric of feminism without much substance, or 'equal opportunism' (ibid., 210). They also criticize Labour for its focus on 'family values' and 'unbounded individualism,' which are both reminiscent of values promoted by the Conservatives. There is little optimism among British feminists that New Labour will dramatically improve social policies for women.

Women's groups, then, have met with varying success in achieving greater gender equality and protecting the gains previously made by women as a result of the expansion of social-welfare systems. They have at times pursued different objectives, with varying strategies, including divergent emphases concerning women's 'choices' to enter paid work and the support that should be provided when they do so.

Major differences are also apparent in the political and cultural environment within which women's groups function. In Canada, that environment favours paid employment and models of motherhood that place less value on full-time care for children at home. This environment is supported structurally by government support for childcare, paid maternity leave, and an equality clause in the Canadian constitution which is absent in the other three countries. In contrast, women's groups in the United Kingdom, Australia, and New Zealand must confront cultural legacies that elevate motherhood and caring to national icons and that widely regard childcare provided outside the home with suspicion. As we pointed out in the country chapters, these legacies have limited the vigour with which women's groups pursue issues surrounding access to paid work and childcare. We also noted that divergent policy environments are related to the economic and labour market conditions in each country.

Business Groups
Employers and manufacturers groups have always formed a powerful lobby for public-policy reform, and in recent years these groups have been particularly influential. Recent Canadian concerns over high public debt and the relative weakening of the political left provided fertile ground for business and economic conservatives to exercise strong influence on federal government policy. None of these groups can be considered vigorous advocates for women's interests and gender equality. Instead, they have lobbied for lower taxes, reduced public spending, and less government regulation of the labour force, and they have been a major force behind the welfare-dependency debate.

Employers groups in the United Kingdom, keenly pro-market in orientation, always played second fiddle to Margaret Thatcher's lead and were eager to reap the benefits of privatizing state assets. The New Labour government has taken great care to enable business to help shape social reforms, including the setting of the minimum wage and the welfare reforms contained in the 1998 budget. Labor governments in Australia have given a slightly cooler reception to neo-liberal ideas, and the business lobbies jockeyed for position with labour groups under the umbrella of the tripartite Accord of 1983. Nevertheless, as we illustrated in the Australian chapter, business groups played a major role in promoting economic-rationalist ideas in that country. The Liberal-National coalition government in power since 1996 has offered strong support for many neo-liberal ideas, including a consumption tax (GST) and income-tax reductions. The coalition government has also made a powerful political statement of its intention to reshape Australian society and social attitudes through its battles in 1998 with the unionized dock workers.

The business lobby has been particularly strong in New Zealand. Chapter 5 showed the ability of business groups and a small cast of ideologically committed politicians and bureaucrats to overturn broadly supported social policies. The role of the Business Roundtable as the political organizing committee of big capital remains to be studied in detail. Nevertheless, its power and skill at articulating a hard neo-liberal line is not doubted (Kelsey 1995). In 1998 the major business groups greeted with enthusiasm the introduction of the proposed Code of Social and Family Responsibility. As we showed in chapter 5, business ideas inspired the Code's emphasis on individual and family responsibility for income security and well-being, as well as its suggestion that benefit levels need to be reduced and made more conditional.

The Varying Strength of Interest Groups

The strength and role of interest groups varies over time in each country. Trade unions played an important role in the early formulation of social-policy and the expansion of welfare states in Britain, Australia, and New Zealand. In the restructuring phase, the labour movement has been an oppositional force in Britain, an incorporated entity in Australia, and a marginalized one in New Zealand. Feminist groups in these countries appear to have had only sporadic roles in policy making, while employers groups are strong and in the ascendance.

The labour movement has been influential in social-policy development but not as directly in Canada as in the other three countries. Furthermore, global markets and technological change have challenged the strength of the labour movement. Restructuring has taken place against the backdrop of continental trade agreements that allow the free movement of capital but not labour and that have encouraged harmonization of Canadian social policies with American standards. Social reform and feminist groups were more influential in family-policy development in the 1960s and 1970s than in the other three countries. Yet this is waning in the 1990s as business and employers groups, and neo-liberal economists and think-tanks, have positioned themselves as the more influential commentators and lobby groups.

Interest groups interact with each other and with political parties within the political and bureaucratic systems, so it is important to acknowledge the orientations of governing parties during the period of restructuring. The pervasiveness and penetration of pro-market philosophies across political parties in the four countries is noteworthy. In Australia and New Zealand, the centre-left parties initiated state restructuring and took tentative steps towards bringing some beneficiaries closer to the labour market. The centre-right government in New Zealand is now in the process of moving employability schemes more rapidly to the forefront, but its Australian counterpart is proceeding somewhat more cautiously. In the United Kingdom, centre-left New Labour has launched potentially far-reaching schemes to bring more 'workless' beneficiaries into employment, in effect, operationalizing some of the rhetoric of Thatcherite Conservatives. This indicates that an emphasis on employability is not the exclusive property of any political party.

In Canada, much of the political activity related to employability occurs at the provincial level and has cut across parties of the right and left. Social democrats in the Parti Québécois promote individual responsibility and the end of 'welfare dependency' through paid work with the same enthusiasm as their ideological opponents in the Ontario Conservative Party. Yet the political pattern at the national level bears some parallels to Britain: the Conservative Party set the ideological tone for employability during its tenure at the outset of welfare-state restructuring, and this has been consolidated by a party that used to be seen as the political left.

We must be careful not to over-emphasize the degree of political convergence within any particular country or political party. The Australian Labor Party, for example, is by no means in full agreement with employability principles, and political opposition to these schemes exists within the other three countries. Nevertheless, the degree of broad political consensus within each country is impressive. Comparatively, despite national divergences of timing and emphasis, a remarkable degree of convergence is apparent among governments in the four countries that neo-liberal principles should form the dominant paradigm for welfare-state reform.

The degree to which each national political culture tolerates the existence of a permanent underclass may also be an important issue in explaining the uneven path of restructuring efforts. Canada's proximity to the United States, with its punitive means-tested welfare system and workfare programs, appears to lead to greater Canadian tolerance of the working poor, of food banks, and of people sleeping in the streets. On the other hand, the Australian culture of giving all citizens a 'fair go' probably moderates radical pro-market tendencies. A similar emphasis existed in New Zealand, although its political and social culture may be changing as the government relies heavily on American political advice and as a generation grows up under neo-liberal reform. In the United Kingdom, a socially immobile lower class has been a feature of society for generations but public discomfort with it remains visible.

Politics, Decision Making, and the Structure of Government

Chapter 2 highlighted the argument of the power-resources tradition that the structure of government can influence the speed and extent of the restructuring of welfare states. This influence can both impede and accelerate change. A nation with one central government can make rapid decisions, while a federation may require time-consuming consultations in order to reach a national consensus. Yet a centralized government may also delay policy reforms, while state or provincial governments may pressure a federal government to act more rapidly.

A bicameral system requires legislation to pass through two decision-making houses, which takes more time and lobbying efforts than passing policy through a unicameral system. In addition, an electoral system based on first-past-the-post sometimes allows one political party to gain a majority of seats even when most voters in the country choose another party. This means that policy opposed by the smaller opposition parties can still be passed into law. And, finally, a government dominated by men, privileged socio-economic classes, or one cultural group may pass legislation that does not represent the wishes of women, the working classes, or cultural minorities.

Our cross-national research certainly reinforces the idea that the structure of government influences the process of policy reform. New Zealand is the prime example of a nation that rapidly changed from state control over much of the economy and labour force to heavy reliance on foreign markets and the private sector for the development of the economy. In a matter of ten years, New Zealand governments dismantled the state and downsized social programs more rapidly and extensively than other industrialized nations. This was facilitated by the government structure: a unicameral system in which mainly the Cabinet generates social and economic policy. There is no Senate, and the pre-1996 first-past-the-post electoral system was dominated by one of two main political parties (National and Labour). In New Zealand, no provincial or state governments serve as institutional bases from which to express opposition to government restructuring or to delay or reconsider decisions. Non-parliamentary opposition (such as the labour movement, community groups, and the media) was sporadic and weak, and the major political opposition after 1990 – the Labour Party – was compromised by its role as the enthusiastic initiator of reform in the 1980s. The result in New Zealand was the effective use of a political system by a small political-bureaucratic-business alliance with an ideologically coherent program in order to make substantive changes in social programs.

The post-1996 proportional-representation system in New Zealand was supposed to act as a political brake on rapid change. Nevertheless, in its 1998 budget the coalition government was able to make extensive changes to work provisions for beneficiaries. This was accomplished within two days by introducing legislation under 'urgency' and bypassing extensive public hearings. The process bears close parallels to the rapidity of reform in the late 1980s and early 1990s. Clearly, political structural change does not necessarily slow the process of welfare-state restructuring.

The British system shows some structural similarities. The single-level government system in the 1980s was further simplified by the Conservatives' abolition of the Greater London Council, which was a major focal point for local political opposition. The internal disorganization and strife of the Labour Party was offset somewhat by the political struggles within the Conservative Party between its hard- and moderate-right wings. Vibrant local organization around specific political issues such as the poll tax also tempered the Thatcherite urge for more radical reform. In comparison to the New Zealand neo-liberal blueprint, British reform led to a more uneven and mixed outcome.

Australia is a federation with active and shifting political coalitions at both federal and state levels. Income-support programs are federal jurisdiction, which enables the federal government to make national welfare reform without discussion with the state governments. The restructuring process under Labor governments also differed from other nations because it incorporated organized labour into a formal agreement, allowing unions more social-policy discussion within government frameworks.

In contrast, Canada is an example of a federation in which the central government's options are often constrained by jurisdictional disputes and the necessity to consult provincial governments. This has been particularly contentious in a political climate of wrangling over Quebec's right to self-determination, and of attempts to keep Quebec within the federation by offering various concessions that were unpalatable to other regions of the country. Yet, despite these constraints, the Canadian federal government has made major changes to 'fiscal federalism' and reduced federal expenditures by changing federal/provincial funding agreements. This policy decision has allowed the federal government to save money while permitting the provinces to gain more control over social programs and to redesign their social-assistance programs in a more cost-effective and ideologically acceptable way.

We have also shown that more subtle changes in the political process can affect the pace and process of welfare-state reform. In chapter 2, we argued that institutional reforms specific to each country could place pressure on the maintenance of existing social-welfare programs, both in levels of benefits and ineligibility. In the country chapters we discussed the importance of these institutional changes and the political mobilization necessary to achieve and solidify them. The New Zealand case, for example, shows how ideologically inspired budget-cutters gained a stronger hand in the Treasury department, and how that department gained ascendance as bureaucratic structures throughout the central government were modernized and rationalized. Tax cuts, diminishing the state's revenue base, further weakened support for social programs. Moreover, the Employment Contracts Act weakened the position of trade unions as advocates for welfare-state retention. The Canadian labour movement was also weakened politically as free trade expanded. The federal Finance department reasserted its traditional role as a dominant force in Canadian policy making, further enhanced by the transformation of some social programs into tax credits. Decentralization of Canadian decision making will promote additional restructuring in the future as many provincial governments seek to resolve their public-debt problems.

Political and decision-making structures pertaining to welfare-state reform are of particular interest to women for at least two reasons. First, women are major users of social-welfare programs as well as being welfare workers, and the policy outcomes of these programs are, as feminist researchers have demonstrated, highly gendered. Second, women have traditionally been marginalized from political decision making in all four countries, and political norms – such as women political candidates not getting their share of 'safe' constituencies to run it – can also inhibit women's participation. Hernes (1987), Waring (1988), and other feminists have argued that the involvement of women (or lack of involvement) in governmental decision making has had an impact on social policy. Variations are apparent in women's representation as elected members of parliament among the four countries in our study, as we indicated in Table 1.4 of chapter 1, but they do not seem to make a noticeable difference in policy reform. Counting parliamentary seats does not provide a full picture of political influence. We should attempt to determine whether the presence of women in key Cabinet positions, in the Senate (in the three countries that have a Senate), as 'femocrats' in high-level public-sector positions, and as members of influential boards altered or influenced policy decisions. This, however, is a task for another study.

Conclusion: Towards a Theory of Welfare-State Restructuring

Considerable research has been devoted to explaining the expansion of welfare states but less to cross-national variations in restructuring. Our study shows that the needs and roles of low-income mothers have been conceptualized differently within the four liberal welfare states and that policy reforms have varied. Yet all four countries have adopted similar strategies of employability to restrict entitlement to social provision. This focus on employability devalues social benefits in maintaining income security and contains ideological assumptions about the importance of work discipline for the moral make-up of beneficiaries.

The integration of beneficiaries into paid employment is a complex and non-uniform process that varies cross-nationally and is influenced by several factors. First, the variables traditionally highlighted by power-resource research – including political ideologies, political structures, and interest-group mobilization – must be retained as important explanatory elements. All four countries have been affected by neo-liberal ideologies about the need to reduce government involvement in the economy, labour markets, communities, and families. Increasingly, political parties and interest groups have to function within a policy framework based on neo-liberalism, and political structures have sometimes been altered to facilitate this ideology.

All four governments are now making direct assaults on the basic tenets of the welfare state and its supporters, which suggests that governments are becoming more confident about broad public support for reducing welfare dependency. In countries such as Canada, there currently seems to be less political risk in combating advocates for the poor than there was in confronting the seniors' lobby in the mid-1980s. The ideological dominance of neo-liberalism has meant that alternative policy initiatives have suffered from lack of political sponsorship. Although significant dissent has taken place at the community level in each country, organized regional and national opposition and promotion of alternative paradigms remain limited. Many policy options to reduce poverty have been discredited as 'politically unfeasible,' such as government job creation or the establishment of a guaranteed annual income.

Second, the restructuring process as it affects low-income mothers is profoundly influenced by trends in labour markets and the wider economy. Labour scarcity in countries such as Australia, New Zealand, and, to a lesser extent, Canada has been replaced by labour surplus. The low-wage end of employment markets has been dramatically affected by the decline of manufacturing jobs and growth in the service sector. Increasingly, the jobs available to low-income mothers are insecure and low paid, and with fewer statutory and union protections. In economies where ethnic and racial minorities have been historically disadvantaged, such as New Zealand, the destruction of traditional employment sources for these minorities constrains their options to seek and retain paid work. Rapid urbanization and the cumulative effects of low educational attainment compounds these forces.

Theories of welfare-state restructuring must include an assessment of women's labour-force participation, which both influences and is influenced by policy decisions. We have shown that, in Canada, the comparatively high rates of full-time labour-force participation of mothers and the need for two-family incomes have created a strong political constituency for publicly funded childcare. The political demand for public childcare in the other countries remains weaker. The dominance of the male-breadwinner model of family continues to reinforce the primary status of women as caregivers rather than wage earners in Australia, New Zealand, and Britain. Consequently, employability programs in these three countries have yet to focus significantly on mothers with pre-school children.

Two other elements, which mainstream researchers have downplayed, need to be stressed in understanding welfare-state reform in relation to low-income mothers. One is the gendered nature of family life, which has been incorporated into social programs. We have indicated that during the formative period of social programs, mainly from the 1940s to the 1970s, patriarchal family models mirrored and perpetuated prevailing gender relations in the family and society. Now, reforms are sometimes based on misleading or inconsistent ideas about how families actually live and what constrains their daily lives (Baker 1990). Similarly, employability initiatives are fraught with contradictions that have gendered origins and implications. This study has deliberately used the term low-income mothers, rather than gender-neutral terms such as low-income parents or one-parent families, to highlight the gendered issues involved.

Historically, women in these four countries have typically become social beneficiaries through maternity or their relationships with men rather than through their labour-force attachment (Baker 1995; Sainsbury 1996). Although economic, social, and demographic conditions have changed, many social programs continue to portray partnered women as men's dependants and lone mothers as primarily mothers rather than potential employees. Canadian social programs are the exception, as women there have moved more rapidly into the full-time employment and become recipients of work-related benefits as well as means-tested social assistance. Yet Canadian family law and new employability programs now overestimate women's opportunities to become self-supporting.

Understanding the process of reforming social provision means that gendered ideologies and practices about family and work must be acknowledged and analysed. Much of women's work has been unpaid and related to caring activities within the home and/or fundraising and caring within the community. Whether or not mothers enter the labour force relates to changing economic conditions, employment opportunities, family arrangements, and trade union agreements, but it is also linked to prevailing ideologies about women's capacities, children's needs, and the social acceptance of non-family childcare.

Women, especially mothers of dependent children, typically enter and leave the labour force under different conditions than most men. They are more likely than men to work part-time, to be employed in the public or voluntary sector, to accept clerical and service positions, and to have low-paid, temporary, and non-unionized jobs. Positions in the public sector and in voluntary organizations have been particularly vulnerable to cutbacks in societies that have governments sympathetic to neo-liberal ideologies. Furthermore, part-time jobs are growing faster than full-time positions, yet these positions seldom lead to independence from social benefits or family assistance. Restructuring has increasingly encouraged part-time work for both men and women, but low-income people, including lone mothers and visible minorities, bear the brunt of restructuring.

Employability programs fail to acknowledge both the diverse needs of beneficiaries and the gendered nature of work, even though these programs sometimes include childcare services and individual counselling. Many beneficiaries are mothers with young children, or persons with disabilities or illnesses that prevent or inhibit them from entering the competitive labour force. If they are to find and retain paid jobs and actually exit from poverty, they will need considerable assistance. Yet employability programs tend to focus on educational achievement, employment skills, work habits, ability to write résumés, interviewing skills, and attitudes. Overlooked or downplayed are the structural barriers to market income: the lack of paid work in some communities, family responsibilities that might interfere with full-time employment, emotional or physical disabilities, and the availability of affordable childcare. Furthermore, employability programs do not accept the idea that raising children is a social responsibility rather than merely a family one.

Employability programs are designed to be gender-neutral, assuming that the labour market treats all individuals equally and that gender (as well as race and class) are not important reasons for unemployment or underemployment. In reality, men and women tend to compete in labour markets on unequal terms. Men typically participate as relatively unencumbered individuals and more closely approximate the 'rational economic actors' of econometric models than do most mothers. Although employability programs still exclude beneficiary mothers with school-aged children in Australia, New Zealand, and the United Kingdom, they are being modified to include mothers with younger children in all four countries. The idea that all adults should become self-supporting wage earners in full-time jobs is less feasible for low-income mothers than for unemployed men or women without dependent children.

Trying to make women into economic actors without addressing their family roles and their relationship to the market and state lays the groundwork for policy failure. Instead, increasing burdens will be placed upon women to manage both low-paid work and unpaid domestic responsibilities. Yet employability schemes in these four countries do not and cannot address the current gender imbalance of responsibility for caring work and household chores.

Gendering the concept of employability, then, requires acknowledgement that drawing low-income people into paid work may have different consequences for them, depending on their gender (as well as social class and culture). Attempts to make mothers more employable have been resisted more strenuously in countries such as Australia, New Zealand, and the United Kingdom, where mothers are expected to care for young children at home. In countries such as Canada, there is a broader acceptance of non-maternal childcare during the workday. While a greater value is now being placed upon paid work for low-income mothers, the devaluation of mothering at home and commodification of childcare varies cross-nationally.

Enhancing the employability of low-income mothers necessarily involves an implicit attempt to reconstruct their personal and social identities, including what it means to be a good mother, carer, paid worker, and citizen. The identity reconstruction demanded by these schemes encourages beneficiary mothers to see themselves more as independent participants in the labour force and less as carers providing unpaid work that is nevertheless socially valued. Paying mothers a social wage is being devalued in each of the four countries, and through this process governments are reshaping social and economic relations.

We have shown that this 'discursive mobilization' varies in emphasis in each country, partly associated with labour-market conditions and dominant social values of what constitutes appropriate motherhood and caring. Beneficiaries are encouraged to modify their identities, accept a revised definition of rights and responsibilities, and change behaviour accordingly. Individually, they become paid workers providing for themselves and their families; collectively, they become more integrated members of the workforce and society. Researchers need to give closer consideration to beneficiaries' responses to initiatives that seek to change their motivations and behaviour, rather than seeing them as passive recipients of change.

Gender is incorporated into employability programs in at least two different ways. In Canada, a full-time worker/mother model of citizenship is supported in principle by public childcare and legal equality. In Australia, New Zealand, and the United Kingdom, the dominant model is mother/part-time worker, reflecting social ambivalence concerning mothers in the labour force and emphasizing difference rather than gender equality (Lister 1996). The emphasis on women working part-time while retaining primary responsibility for caring is an attempt to reconcile the neo-liberal concept of employability with the policy legacy left by the male-breadwinner model of family.

Changing the identity of mothers to workers will, of course, have social consequences. Who will do the caring work in society if low-income women are pushed into the paid labour force? These workers will not be able to afford to pay someone else to care for their children unless the cost of childcare is heavily subsidized, which will raise public costs. The growing policy consensus that most beneficiaries want to work and should work is more problematic than it initially appears.

In these four countries, the evolving shape of social welfare holds mixed prospects for poverty alleviation, especially for low-income mothers. More attention will be given to the conditions of entry into paid work and the removal of barriers that make mothers reluctant to work for pay. Social-safety nets may increasingly be redesigned around periods between paid jobs, while also providing lower levels of income support for those deemed unemployable. To facilitate deeper and longer attachment to paid employment, improvements may be made in such areas as childcare, statutory parental leave, and training and education.

These reforms may represent increased incorporation of gender consid-erations into social program design, but their potential impact is miti-gated by at least three other factors.

First, low-income mothers with caring responsibilities can never fully conform to the economically rationalist behaviour models underlying employability programs. Second, employability is *not* the solution to poverty for all beneficiaries. Total incomes for some mothers may improve through the opportunity to earn income while receiving partial benefits, but this may be offset by low pay, insecure jobs in an unpro-tected labour market, and higher employment expenses. Minimum wages are rarely 'living wages,' and those receiving them have little power to negotiate and make employment choices. Paid work is not always the best path out of poverty. Finally, existing social benefits for the poor may be targeted further, fuelled by strong political pressure in all four countries for tax reductions.

Employability programs appear to be only a partial solution to pov-erty and benefit dependency, since they do not address the problems of low-paid work, structural unemployment, and gender inequalities. In fact, liberal welfare states may have reduced class inequality since the 1940s, but the poverty of low-income mothers and their children was never seriously reduced even during the expansionist phase of welfare states. The outlook for reduced poverty during a period of economic and social-program contraction appears equally bleak. Neither eco-nomic nor social well-being is guaranteed through paid work in an unfettered market, yet ironically, employability schemes are attempting to integrate economic and social policies that have been divided since the 1980s when governments began to grapple with public-debt prob-lems at the expense of social issues.

Understanding restructuring and evolving welfare states remains a daunting challenge but one that will benefit from greater integration of mainstream and feminist research. Theories and typologies that omit women's life experiences are no longer academically acceptable and, if applied to social policy, could lead to policy failure. The links between poverty, social assistance, and employability are deeply gendered and require gendered analytical approaches. The attempt to incorporate gen-der into existing theories and research is sometimes a formidable task because they tend to reflect men's experience and priorities. One prob-lem is gender-neutral research that treats women as rational economic actors who happen to have primary responsibility for taking care of chil-dren and others. Another problem is viewing 'the welfare state' as unitary rather than acknowledging that the development and restructuring of specific social programs and policies will usually differ.

Finally, changes in social policy are usually incremental and done by different governments with different agendas amending existing programs rather than making sweeping reforms. This tendency towards incrementalism, as well as the diverse situations of those affected by social provision, suggests that it may be more prudent to research specific programs or smaller aspects of welfare states, especially in cross-national research. In doing so, researchers must use more complex conceptions of gender, work, and family to gain a better understanding of changing social-welfare systems.

Notes

1 Setting the Stage

1 Senior bureaucrats in the Canadian Department of Finance, which is a focal point for neo-liberal policies in Canada, argued in 1997 that the generosity of Canada's social programs is keeping Canada's 'natural' or 'structural' rate of unemployment several points higher than that of the United States. The difference is supposedly attributable to over-generous unemployment-insurance and welfare payments that discourage the jobless from taking low-wage jobs. *Globe and Mail*, 'Report on Business,' 18 September 1997, B4.
2 Canadian left-wing opposition parties and anti-poverty groups have developed 'alternative budgets' indicating how real changes to social equality could be made in terms of government tax and transfer programs.
3 A recent study in the Canadian province of Quebec suggested that about 50 per cent of the income of single parents is spent on housing alone (McAll et al. 1995).
4 Unfortunately for us, New Zealand does not participate in the LIS data base. In attempting to compare family poverty rates in New Zealand to the other three countries, we are faced with the problem of how disposable income is calculated and how much is allocated for each child. In order to compensate for these differences, we have used a 60 per cent median income for New Zealand and 50 per cent median income for the other countries (personal communication with Bob Stephens, Victoria University of Wellington, 11 June 1998, Stephens and Waldegrave 1995).

2 Gendering the Analysis of Restructuring

1 See, for example, Williams 1989; Lewis 1993; Pedersen 1993; Bryson, Bittman,

and Donath 1994; Everingham 1994; Wennemo 1994; Baker 1995; 1997e;
Gauthier 1993, 1996; Sainsbury 1994a, 1996; Bakker 1996a, 1996b; Phipps 1996;
Silva 1996; Duncan and Edwards 1997; Mahon 1997; Bashevkin 1998; Freiler
and Cerny 1998.

3 Government Debt and Policy Choices: Restructuring in Canada

1 Since 1984, only the Conservatives (centre-right) and Liberals (centre-centre-
  left) have led the government. However, three opposition parties have also
  been important in influencing social policy: the New Democratic Party (NDP)
  (left), the western-based Reform Party (right), and the Quebec-based Parti
  Québécois (sovereigntist and centre-left).
2 These groups include the Business Council on National Issues, the Canadian
  Federation of Independent Business, and influential conservative think-tanks
  such as the C.D. Howe Institute and the Fraser Institute.
3 The federal NDP has never been in power in Ottawa and from 1993 to 1997
  held only nine seats in Parliament, yet provincial NDP governments have
  held office in several provinces over the years. By 1998, however, only British
  Columbia had an NDP government. In the 1997 federal election, as noted later
  in this chapter, the NDP won twenty-one seats in Parliament, mainly in Atlantic Canada.
4 In discussing poverty, both Canadian governments and advocacy groups over
  the past ten years have used the term 'child poverty' to avoid the problems of
  the 'undeserving poor' and to elicit public support for intervention. However,
  this focus allows governments to disconnect poverty from high unemployment rates.
5 This includes a variety of social-support services such as childcare for low-
  income families, visiting homemakers, personal support for seniors and persons with disabilities, respite care, counselling, child-welfare services, rehabilitation for chronically unemployed people, and community-development
  services.
6 This case was brought to the courts by a man using the Canadian Charter of
  Rights and Freedoms to argue that the law does not treat biological and adoptive fathers equally. At this time, biological mothers and adoptive parents (but
  not biological fathers) were entitled to UI benefits.
7 Defined differently by each province but generally including persons with
  disabilities or illnesses who are unable to work and mothers with pre-school
  children.
8 Nova Scotia, Ontario, and Manitoba.
9 Statistics Canada has established low-income cut-offs (LICOs) that vary by
  family size and size of community. These are often referred to as poverty lines.

10 British Columbia and Ontario.
11 EPF is the block-grant program that replaced matched funding for Medicare that was in place from 1966 to 1977.
12 The government initiated further tax-reform measures in 1988, converting other deductions to credits.
13 While this used to be the Department of National Health and Welfare, the Liberals divided that department into two in 1993 and renamed the welfare component 'Human Resources Development Canada.'
14 Apparently these brokers were difficult to find in high-unemployment areas (Philp 1997).
15 The next two sections borrow heavily from Maureen Baker's article 'Entre le pain et les soins: Les pères et la loi canadienne du divorce,' *Liens sociaux et politiques* 37 (1997), 63–74.
16 Quebec has the highest rate of common-law marriages of all the Canadian provinces.
17 Although the Liberals retained their majority, it was reduced to 155 out of 301 seats in the 1997 election and Prime Minister Jean Chrétien's popularity in Quebec remained low. Yet the Bloc Québécois also lost seats to the Liberals in Quebec.
18 Quebec already has a separate income-tax system and its own public pension system, and it funds welfare programs differently than the rest of Canada. All provinces design and administer their own welfare, education, and health-care programs.
19 When Prime Minister Pierre Trudeau 'repatriated' the constitution from the United Kingdom in 1982, Quebec refused to sign it partly because the concept of ten equal provinces, rather than two equal nations, was entrenched and partly because the new Charter of Rights was deemed to encroach on Quebec jurisdiction.
20 Unemployment rates have remained at about 10 per cent for the past five years in Canada.
21 The Fraser Institute and the C.D. Howe Institute have been given strong voices in recent public-policy discussions in Canada.
22 Although parliamentary committees have a legal obligation to consult the public, they do not have a legal obligation to incorporate their views into legislation and policy.

4 From Public to Private Dependency? Reforming Policies in Australia

1 However, Canadian provincial governments pay a social benefit to those without other resources, and parents with children receive more money than individuals.

2 The world's first labour government was elected in Queensland in 1899.
3 These rules vary by the type of beneficiary and age of the client.
4 Initially established by and funded by the Commonwealth government and now part of the government.
5 Represented by the National Association of Community Based Children's Services.
6 Regulated childcare in the providers' home of several children, often in addition to her own.
7 This income test is at the same level as the Basic Family Payment, which in October 1996 was $61,020 for a family with one child.

5 The 'Great Experiment': Restructuring New Zealand's Social Programs

1 A 'dependent' child is under sixteen years old, or under eighteen if still in school.
2 In 1996 the official unemployment rate for Pakeha women was 4.1 per cent, while for Maori women it was 13.6 per cent and for Pacific Island women 14.0 per cent (New Zealand Government, *Household Labour Force Survey 1996*).
3 Maori fertility declined sharply in the 1960s and 1970s and is now just above replacement rate (Shirley et al. 1997, 211). New Zealand's overall teenage birth rate of 32.2/1000 women (1994 data) is the highest of the four countries in this study (Goodger 1997).
4 Canada patterned its GST (created in 1988) after New Zealand's.
5 Provinces were eliminated in 1876 and the Upper House was abolished in 1950 (Cheyne, O'Brien, and Belgrave 1997, 26).
6 The Employment Equity Act, passed by the Labour government in 1990, was declared to be undue interference in the labour market by the new National government, which promptly repealed the act when it took office a few months later.
7 Throughout this section, labour-force participation is defined as the number of full- and part-time workers and unemployed who are actively seeking work, expressed as a percentage of the working-age (fifteen to sixty-four) population.
8 Older widowed or divorced women whose children have left home may also receive the DPB if they stayed at home for years to raise their children.
9 Abatement refers to the income beyond which beneficiaries would begin to see their maximum benefit level reduced.
10 The maximum benefit is paid to those with an annual income before taxes of $4160 or $80 a week. (This would be equivalent to about $3,536 Canadian, or

$68 per week, converted at $.85 Canadian to $1NZ). At earnings of $9,361, 70 cents is deducted for each dollar of income.

11 To be eligible for this benefit, women must have become 'alone' after the age of fifty, must have cared for children for at least fifteen years or cared full-time for a sick or frail relative for at least five years, and must have been supported by a partner for at least five years.

12 Those on a visitor's permit, temporary work permit, or study permit are excluded from this benefit.

13 Rates were reduced by 10.7 per cent for beneficiaries with one child, 8.9 per cent for those with two children, and 16.7 per cent for sole parents.

14 Except for those who have been legally married.

6 The United Kingdom: Restructuring the 'Nanny State'

1 Lone parents comprise about 13 per cent of families with children in France, 15 percent in Germany, and 5 to 6 per cent in Italy and Greece (Millar 1996).

2 Single people and lone parents between the age of sixteen and seventeen receive a lower amount than those eighteen to twenty-four. The highest amount is granted to those aged twenty-five and over.

3 Recipients of IS (and any partner) must not have savings of more than £8,000.

4 Premiums are also paid for other categories of recipients, such as pensioners and persons with disabilities.

5 In the United Kingdom, renters as well as owners paid local council taxes.

6 In 1997 the basic FC rate was £47.65 for one adult (or couple) and an additional amount per child (with a higher rate for older children) per week.

7 FC will not be paid if the household savings exceed £8,000, and savings between £3,000 and £8,000 will reduce the amount payable.

8 The maximum savings of the recipient and partner were £16,000 in 1996.

9 Married women who have retained their right to pay reduced-rate contributions cannot get HRP.

10 The benefit is worth £54.55 if the woman had an employer in the qualifying week or £47.35 if she was not employed or self-employed.

11 Australia was the first to target the family allowance in 1987, but it added a generous supplement for low-income families. New Zealand targeted the FA in 1991 and Canada at the end of 1992.

12 Canada converted exemptions to credits in 1988 but combined child-tax concessions with the Family Allowance in December 1992. Nevertheless, the Married Exemption and the Equivalent to Married Exemption (for lone parents) was left intact.

13 This is an income-tax exemption for a married person supporting a spouse.

272 Notes to pages 207–66

14 The former term 'custodial parent' was replaced with 'parent with care,' while the parent not living with the child was called the 'absent parent.'
15 The British scheme was also based on the Wisconsin model.
16 This also included peace and quiet, or the absence of harassment.
17 That being said, the opposite may also occur. There remains strong public and academic opposition throughout Europe to the alleged macroeconomic rigidities and austerity requirements inherent in the monetary union project (EMU). Most important could be the negative influences on the generosity and expansion of social benefits stemming from requirements of national limitation of debt to GDP levels. In mid-1997, 331 economists from fourteen of the fifteen European Union countries (including sixty-six from Britain) signed an open letter to EU heads of government. This letter denounced deflationary and austerity policies, and the rigidities of the EMU project, calling for economic policies that served human interests and a 'Euro for the people' (*Guardian*, 13 June 1997, 21).

7 Welfare-State Restructuring: The Poverty of Employability

1 Those lone mothers currently receiving the special benefits will not have their incomes reduced, but no new applicants will be accepted.
2 Sole Parent Pension in Australia and the Domestic Purposes Benefit in New Zealand.
3 For example, it was part of the Australian Arbitration Court's *Harvester* judgment of 1907 (Castles, 1985).
4 These tax deductions now reduce total income by $7,000 per pre-school child, with no family maximum, offering a large tax benefit mainly to the middle classes.
5 For example, gender-neutral parental benefits were added to UI in 1990 after a successful Supreme Court challenge using the equality clause.
6 REAL Women of Canada have lobbied unsuccessfully for payments for mothers at home. On the other hand, the National Action Committee on the Status of Women, Women's Legal Education Action Fund, the Canadian Child Care Advocacy Association, and other groups have lobbied more successfully for employment and pay equity and for childcare subsidies for working women.
7 The Canadian government abolished CACSW in 1996 and merged some of its functions with Status of Women Canada, the government department.
8 However, many men have also used the Charter to argue for their own interests.

Bibliography

Abramovitz, Mimi. 1989. *Regulating the Lives of Women*. Boston: South End Press.

Alcock, Peter. 1996. *Social Policy in Britain: Themes and Issues*. London: Macmillan.

Alexander, Liz. 1995. 'Australia's Child Support Scheme.' *Family Matters* 2 (Spring/Summer): 6–11.

Allard, Tom. 1998. 'No Relief from Soaring Child-Care Fees.' *Sydney Morning Herald*, 13 May (internet).

Allen, Douglas. 1993. 'Welfare and the Family: The Canadian Experience.' *Journal of Labor Economics* 11 (1): S201–S223.

Anderton, Jim. 1998. 'Budget Speech.' Press release. 14 May. Wellington: New Zealand.

Armitage, Andrew. 1996. *Social Welfare in Canada Revisited*. Toronto: Oxford University Press.

Armstrong, Hugh, Pat Armstrong, and M. Patricia Connelly. 1997. 'Introduction: The Many Forms of Privatization.' *Studies in Political Economy* 53 (Summer): 3–9.

Armstrong, Pat. 1996. 'The Feminization of the Labour Force: Harmonizing Down in a Global Economy.' In *Rethinking Restructuring: Gender and Change in Canada*, 29–54. Edited by Isabella Bakker. Toronto: University of Toronto Press.

– 1997. 'Restructuring Public and Private: Women's Paid and Unpaid Work.' In *Challenging the Public/Private Divide*, 37–61. Edited by Susan Boyd. Toronto: University of Toronto Press.

Armstrong, Pat, and Hugh Armstrong. 1990. *Theorizing Women's Work*. Toronto: Garamond Press.

Aronson, Jane, and Sheila Neysmith. 1997. 'The Retreat of the State and Long-Term Care Provision: Implications for Frail Elderly People, Unpaid Family Carers and Paid Home Care Workers.' *Studies in Political Economy* 53 (Summer): 37–63.

Australia, Child Care Task Force Interim Report. 1996. *Future Child Care Provision in Australia*. Canberra: Australian Government Publishing Service.

Australia, Department of Industrial Relations. 1996. *Work and Family Resource Kit* (The Work and Family Unit). Canberra, Australia.

Australia, Department of Social Security. 1992. *Social Security and Families with Children*. Canberra: DSS.

– 1996. Various statistics given to Maureen Baker in Canberra during October visit.

Australia, National Family Day Care Council (NFDCC). 1996. *Jigsaw: The Magazine for the NFDCCA*. Issue 3.

Australian Bureau of Statistics. 1991. *Australia's One Parent Families*. Catalogue #2511.0. Canberra: Australian Government.

– 1993. *Working Arrangements Australia*. Catalogue #6342.0. Canberra.

– 1994a. *Focus on Families: Work and Family*. Catalogue #4420.0. Canberra: ABS.

– 1994b. *The Labour Force (Australia)*. Catalogue #6203.0. Canberra: ABS.

– 1994c. *Labour Statistics Australia*. Catalogue #6101.0 (1966–93).

– 1995. *Labour Force Status and Other Characteristics of Families*. Canberra: ABS.

Bacchi, Carol Lee. 1996. *The Politics of Affirmative Action: 'Women,' Equality and Category Politics*. London: Sage.

Baker, Maureen. 1993. *Families in Canadian Society*. 2nd ed. Toronto: McGraw-Hill Ryerson.

– 1994. 'Family and Population Policy in Quebec: Implications for Women.' *Canadian Journal of Women and the Law* 7 (1): 116–32.

– 1995. *Canadian Family Policies: Cross-National Comparisons*. Toronto: University of Toronto Press.

– 1996. 'Social Assistance and the Employability of Mothers: Two Models from Cross-National Research.' *Canadian Journal of Sociology* 21 (4): 483–503.

– 1997a. 'Advocacy, Political Alliances and the Implementation of Family Policies.' In *Child and Family Policy: Struggles, Strategies and Options*. Edited by Jane Pulkingham and Gordon Ternowetsky. Toronto: Fernwood Publishing.

– 1997b. 'Gender Inequality and Divorce Laws: A Canadian Perspective.' *Family Matters* 46: 51–5.

– 1997c. 'Parental Benefit Policies and the Gendered Division of Labor.' *Social Service Review* 71 (1) March: 51–71.

– 1997d. 'Restructuring Welfare States: Ideology and Policies for Low-Income Mothers.' *Social Policy Journal of New Zealand* 8 (March): 37–48.

– 1997e. 'The Restructuring of the Canadian Welfare State: Ideology and Policy.' University of New South Wales, Social Policy Research Centre, Discussion Paper no. 77. June.

- 1997f. 'Women, Family Policies and the Moral Right.' *Canadian Review of Social Policy* Issue 40 (Fall).
Baker, Maureen, and Shelley Phipps. 1997. 'Family Change and Family Policy: Canada.' In *Family Change and Family Policies in Britain, Canada, New Zealand and the U.S.* Edited by Sheila Kamerman and Alfred Kahn. Oxford, UK: Oxford University Press.
Baker, Maureen, and Mary-Anne Robeson. 1981. 'Trade Union Reactions to Women Workers and Their Concerns.' *Canadian Journal of Sociology* 6 (1): 19–31.
Baker, Maureen, and David Tippin. 1997. 'Welfare State Restructuring: Gendering Mainstream Theories.' Paper presented to the British Social Policy Association, Lincoln, UK. 16 July.
Bakker, Isabella. 1996. 'Introduction: The Gendered Fundations of Restructuring in Canada.' In *Rethinking Restructuring. Gender and Change in Canada*, 3–25. Edited by Isabella Bakker. Toronto: University of Toronto Press.
- ed. 1996. *Rethinking Restructuring: Gender and Change in Canada.* Toronto: University of Toronto Press.
Baldock, Cora Vellekoop. 1994. 'The Family and the Australian Welfare State.' *Australian Journal of Social Issues* 29 (2) May: 105–18.
Bane, Mary Jo, and David T. Ellwood. 1994. *Welfare Realities: From Rhetoric to Reform.* Cambridge: Harvard University Press.
Banting, Keith G. 1987. *The Welfare State and Canadian Federalism.* Kingston and Montreal: McGill-Queen's University Press.
- 1992. 'Economic Integration and Social Policy: Canada and the United States.' In *Social Policy in the Global Economy*, 21–44. Edited by Terrance Hunsley. Kingston: Queen's University Press.
Banting, Keith G., and Charles M. Beach, eds. 1995. *Labour Market Polarization and Social Policy Reform.* Kingston, Ontario: Queen's University, School of Policy Studies.
Banting, Keith G., Charles M. Beach, and Gordon Betcherman. 1995. 'Polarization and Social Policy Reform.' In *Labour Market Polarization and Social Policy Reform*, 1–20. Edited by K. Banting and C. Beach. Kingston: Queen's University, School of Policy Studies.
Banting, Keith G., Douglas M. Brown, and Thomas Courchene, eds. 1994. *The Future of Fiscal Federalism.* Kingston, Ontario: Queen's University, School of Policy Studies.
Barbalet, J.M. 1996. 'Developments in Citizenship Theory and Issues in Australian Citizenship.' *Australian Journal of Social Issues* 31 (1) February: 55–72.
Barrett, Gary. 1994. 'The Duration of Income Assistance Spells in British Columbia.' Vancouver: University of British Columbia, Department of Economics.

Bashevkin, Sylvia. 1998. *Women on the Defensive: Living through Conservative Times*. Toronto: University of Toronto Press.

Battle, Ken. 1992. 'White Paper Whitewash: The New Child Benefit.' *Perception* 16 (2,3): 34–40.

– 1995. 'Constitutional Reform by Stealth.' *Caledon Commentary*, May. Ottawa: Caledon Institute of Social Policy.

– 1997. *The National Child Benefit: Best Thing since Medicare or New Poor Law?* Ottawa: Caledon Institute of Social Policy.

Battle, Ken, and Sherri Torjman. 1993. *The Welfare Wall: The Interaction of the Welfare and Tax Systems*. Ottawa: Caledon Institute of Social Policy.

– 1995. *How Finance Re-Formed Social Policy*. Ottawa: Caledon Institute of Social Policy.

Beaujot, Roderic. 1997. 'Parental Preferences for Work and Childcare.' *Canadian Public Policy* 23 (3): 275–88.

Berger, Peter L., and Thomas Luckmann. 1967. *The Social Construction of Reality*. Garden City, NJ: Doubleday.

Bertoia, Carl, and Janice Drakich. 1993. 'The Fathers' Rights Movement: Contradictions in Rhetoric and Practice.' *Journal of Family Issues* 14 (4) December: 592–615.

Beveridge, William. 1942. *Report on Social Insurance and Allied Services*. London: HMSO.

Bittman, Michael. 1991. *Juggling Time: How Australians Use Time*. Canberra: Office of the Status of Women, Department of the Prime Minister and Cabinet.

– 1995. *Recent Changes in Unpaid Work*. Catalogue 4154.0. Canberra: Australian Bureau of Statistics.

Bittman, Michael, and Jocelyn Pixley. 1997. *The Double Life of the Family: Myth, Hope and Experience*. Sydney: Allen and Unwin.

Bolderson, Helen, and Deborah Mabbett. 1991. *Social Policy and Social Security in Australia, Britain and the USA*. Aldershot, England: Avebury.

Boston, Jonathan. 1991. 'The Theoretical Underpinnings of Public Sector Restructuring.' In *Reshaping the State: New Zealand's Bureaucratic Revolution*, 1–26. Edited by J. Boston, J. Martin, J. Pallot, and P. Walsh. Auckland: Oxford University Press.

Boston, Jonathan, and John Uhr. 1996. 'Reshaping the Mechanics of Government.' In *The Great Experiment: Labour Parties and Public Policy Transformation in Australia and New Zealand*, 48–67. Edited by F. Castles, R. Gerritsen, and J. Vowles. Auckland: Auckland University Press.

Boston, Jonathan, Paul Dalziel, and Susan St John. 1998. *Redesigning the Welfare State in New Zealand*. Auckland: Oxford University Press.

Boyd, Monica. 1997. 'Feminizing Paid Work.' *Current Sociology* 45 (2) April: 49–73.

Boyd, Susan. 1989. 'Child Custody, Ideologies and Employment.' *Canadian Journal of Women and the Law* 3 (1): 111–33.
– 1997a. 'Challenging the Public/Private Divide: An Overview.' In *Challenging the Public/Private Divide. Feminism, Law, and Public Policy*, 3–33. Edited by Susan Boyd. Toronto: University of Toronto Press.
– ed. 1997b. *Challenging the Public/Private Divide. Feminism, Law, and Public Policy.* Toronto: University of Toronto Press.
Bradbury, Bruce. 1993. 'Male Wage Inequality before and after Tax: A Six Country Comparison.' Discussion Paper 42, Social Policy Research Centre. Sydney: University of New South Wales.
– 1996. *Income Support for Parents and Other Carers.* Sydney: University of New South Wales, Social Policy Research Centre.
Bradshaw, Jonathan. 1997. 'International Comparisons of Support for Lone Mothers.' Prepared for the conference Private Lives and Public Responses: Lone Parenthood and Future Policy in the UK, University of Bath, 5–6 June.
Bradshaw, Jonathan, and Jane Millar. 1991. *Lone Parent Families in the U.K.* London: Department of Social Security.
Bradshaw, Jonathan, John Ditch, Hilary Holmes, and Peter Whiteford. 1993. *Support for Children: A Comparison of Arrangements in Fifteen Countries.* London: HMSO (Department of Social Security. Research Report 21).
Bradshaw, Jonathan, Steven Kennedy, Majella Kilkey, Sandra Hutton, Anne Corden, Tony Eardley, Hilary Holmes, and Joanne Neale. 1996. *Policy and Employment of Lone Parents in 20 Countries.* The UE Report. Commission of European Communities.
Bray, Mark, and David Neilson. 1996. 'Industrial Relations Reform and the Relative Autonomy of the State.' In F. Castles, R. Gerritsen, and J. Vowles, *The Great Experiment*, 68–87. Auckland: Auckland University Press.
Briar, Celia, and Christine Cheyne. 1997. 'Women and Social/Economic Policy: New Feminist Agendas for Changing Times.' In *Crafting Connections/Defining Difference*. Edited by Rosemary DuPlessis and Lynne Alice. Auckland: Oxford University Press.
Brodie, Janine. 1996a. 'Restructuring and the New Citizenship.' In *Rethinking Restructuring: Gender and Change in Canada*, 126–40. Edited by Isabella Bakker. Toronto: University of Toronto Press.
– ed. 1996b. *Women and Canadian Public Policy.* Toronto: Harcourt Brace.
Brown, Joan. 1992. 'Which Way for Family Policy? Choices for the 1990s.' *Social Policy Review* 4: 154–74.
Brown, Stephanie, J. Lumbley, R. Small, and J. Astbury. 1994. *Missing Voices: The Experience of Motherhood.* Melbourne: Oxford University Press.
Bruce, Rob. 1994. 'A Microdata Analysis of the Behaviour of Income Assistance

Recipients in British Columbia.' Victoria, British Columbia: Ministry of Social
  Services.
Bryson, Alex. 1997. 'Lone Mothers Earnings.' Prepared for the conference Pri-
  vate Lives and Public Responses, University of Bath, 5–6 June.
Bryson, Lois. 1992. *Welfare and the State*. London: Macmillan.
– 1995. 'Two Welfare States: One for Women, One for Men.' In *Women in a
  Restructuring Australia: Workers and Welfare*, 60–76. Edited by Anne Edwards
  and Susan Magarey. Sydney: Allen and Unwin.
Bryson, Lois, Michael Bittman, and Sue Donath. 1994. 'Men's Welfare State,
  Women's Welfare State: Tendencies to Convergence in Practice and Theory?'
  In *Gendering Welfare States*, 118–31. Edited by Diane Sainsbury. London:
  Sage.
Buckingham, Lisa. 1998. 'Brown's Changes Raise Doubts,' *Guardian*, 19 March.
Buckingham, Lisa, and Finch, Julia. 1998. 'Families: Child Care – Breakthrough
  for Poorest Parents.' *Guardian*, 18 March.
Burt, Sandra. 1993. 'The Changing Patterns of Public Policy.' In *Changing Pat-
  terns: Women in Canada*, 212–41. Edited by Sandra Burt, Lorraine Code, and
  Lindsay Dorney. Toronto: McClelland and Stewart.
Bussemaker, Jet, and Kees van Kersbergen. 1994. 'Gender and Welfare States:
  Some Theoretical Considerations.' In *Gendering Welfare States*. Edited by Diane
  Sainsbury. London: Sage.
Caledon Institute of Social Policy. 1996. *Roundtable on Canada Pension Plan
  Reform: Gender Implications*. May 17. Ottawa: Caledon Institute of Social Policy.
Callahan, M., et al. 1990. 'Workfare in British Columbia: Social Development
  Alternatives.' *Canadian Review of Social Policy* 26: 15–25.
Cameron, Duncan. 1997. 'Selling the House to Pay the Mortgage: What Is behind
  Privatization? *Studies in Political Economy* 53 (Summer): 11–33.
Campbell, Gordon. 1997. 'Welfare's Fallout.' *The Listener*, 26 July: 36–9.
Canada, Department of Employment and Immigration. 1985. *Agreement Regard-
  ing Enhancing the Employment Opportunities for Social Assistance Recipients*.
  18 September. Ottawa.
Canada, Department of Justice. 1996. 'Up-Date on Child-Support Legislation'
  (single sheet). Ottawa.
– 1997. 'The Child Support Newsletter.' 20 February. Ottawa.
Canada, Federal/Provincial/Territorial Family Law Committee. 1995. *Report and
  Recommendations on Child Support*. Ottawa: Minister of Public Works and Gov-
  ernment Services Canada.
Canada, Government of. 1994. *Improving Social Security in Canada*. Ottawa:
  Human Resources Development Canada.
Canada, House of Commons Standing Committee on Human Resources Devel-

opment. 1995. *Security, Opportunities and Fairness: Canadians Renewing their Social Programs*. Ottawa: Queen's Printer.

Canada, Human Resources Development. 1994a. *Basic Facts on Social Programs*. Ottawa: Minister of Supply and Services.

– 1994b. *Employment Development Services: A Supplementary Paper*. Ottawa: Minister of Supply and Services.

– 1994c. *Inventory of Income Security Programs in Canada*. Ottawa: Minister of Supply and Services Canada.

– 1997. *Status of Day Care in Canada 1995 and 1996*. Ottawa: Ministry of Supply and Services Canada.

Canada, Ministerial Council on Social Policy Reform and Renewal. 1995. *Report to the Premiers*. December. Ottawa.

Canada, Statistics Canada. 1995. *Women in Canada. A Statistical Report*. 3rd edition. Catalogue #89–503E. Ottawa: Minister of Industry.

Canada, Status of Women. 1997. 'Parliamentary Update.' *Perspectives* 10 (1) Summer: 6–7.

Canadian Council on Social Development. 1996. 'Presentation to the Parliamentary Standing Committee on Human Resources Development on UI.' Ottawa: CCSD.

Carers Association of Australia, Inc. 1996. Press release, 20 October.

Cass, Bettina. 1994. 'Citizenship, Work, and Welfare: The Dilemma for Australian Women.' *Social Politics* 1 (1) Spring: 106–24.

– 1995. 'Gender in Australia's Restructuring Labour Market and Welfare State.' In *Women in a Restructuring Australia. Work and Welfare*, 38–59. Edited by A. Edwards and S. Magarey. Sydney: Allen and Unwin.

Castles, Francis G. 1985. *The Working Class and Welfare: Reflections on the Political Development of the Welfare State in Australia and New Zealand, 1890–1980*. Sydney: Allen and Unwin.

– 1996. 'Needs-Based Strategies of Social Protection in Australia and New Zealand.' In *Welfare States in Transition: National Adaptations in Global Economies*. Edited by G. Esping-Andersen. London: Sage Publications.

Castles, Francis G., and Christopher Pierson. 1995. 'New Convergence? Recent Policy Developments in the United Kingdom, Australia and New Zealand.' *Policy and Politics* 24 (3): 233–45.

Castles, Francis G., and Ian F. Shirley. 1996. 'Labour and Social Policy: Gravediggers or Refurbishers of the Welfare State?' In *The Great Experiment: Labour Parties and Public Policy Transformation in Australia and New Zealand*, 88–106. Edited by F. Castles, R. Gerritsen, and J. Vowles. Auckland: Auckland University Press.

Castles, Francis G., Rolf Gerritsen, and Jack Vowles. 1996. *The Great Experiment:*

Labour Parties and Public Policy Transformation in Australia, and New Zealand.
Auckland: Auckland University Press.

Catalyst. 1993. *Flexible Work Arrangements II: Succeeding With Part-Time Options.*
New York: Catalyst.

Charette, M., and R. Meng. 1994. 'The Determinants of Welfare Participation of
Female Heads of Households in Canada.' *Canadian Journal of Economics* 27 (2):
290–306.

Cheyne, Christine, Mike O'Brien, and Michael Belgrave. 1997. *Social Policy in
Aotearoa New Zealand: A Critical Introduction.* Auckland: Oxford University
Press.

Child Poverty Action Group (Canada). 1986. *A Fair Chance for All Children:
The Declaration on Child Poverty.* Toronto: The Child Poverty Action
Group.

Child Poverty Action Group (UK). 1997. *Poverty* 97 (Summer).

Clark, Christopher. 1998. *Canada's Income Security Programs.* Ottawa: Canadian
Council on Social Development.

Clarke, Karen, Caroline Glendinning, and Gary Craig. 1997. 'Supporting Chil-
dren? The Impact of the Child Support Act on Lone Mothers and Children.'
Prepared for the conference Private Lives and Public Responses, University of
Bath, 5–6 June.

Clarke, L. 1996. 'Demographic Change and the Family Situation of Children.' In
Children in Families: Research and Policy, 66–83. Edited by J. Brannen and M.
O'Brien. London: Falmer Press.

Cohen, Marjorie Griffin. 1993. 'The Canadian Women's Movement.' In *Canadian
Women's Issues Volume 1: Strong Voices,* 1–97. Edited by R.R. Pierson, M.G.
Cohen, P. Bourne, and P. Masters. Toronto: James Lorimer.

Connelly, M. Patricia. 1996. 'Gender Matters: Global Restructuring and Adjustment.' *Social Politics* 3 (1) Spring: 12–31.

Connelly, M. Patricia, and Martha MacDonald. 1996. 'The Labour Market, the
State and the Reorganization of Work: Policy Impacts.' In *Rethinking Restruc-
turing: Gender and Change in Canada,* ch. 3. Edited by Isabella Bakker. Toronto:
University of Toronto Press.

Conseil de la Famille. 1997. *Impact de Certains Aspects de la Reforme de la Securité
du Revenu sur les Familles.* Quebec. March.

Cooper, Glenda. 1997. 'Lone Parents Applaud New Deal as a Step in the Right
Direction.' *Independent,* 3 July: 17.

Courchene, Thomas J., and Arthur E. Stewart. 1992. 'Financing Social Policy:
Observations and Challenges.' In *Social Policy in a Global Economy,* 129–54.
Edited by Terrance M. Hunsley. Kingston, Ontario: Queen's University, School
of Policy Studies.

Cragg, Michael. 1994. 'The Dynamics of Welfare Participation in British Columbia.' New York: Columbia University, Department of Economics.

Crean, Susan. 1988. *In the Name of the Fathers*. Toronto: Amanita Enterprises.

Cuneo, Carl. 1979. 'State, Class and Reserve Labour: The Case of the 1941 Unemployment Insurance Act,' *Canadian Review of Sociology and Anthropology* 16 (2): 147–70.

Curtin, Jennifer, and Marian Sawer. 1996. 'Gender Equity in the Shrinking State: Women and the Great Experiment.' In *The Great Experiment: Labour Parties and Public Policy Transformation in Australia, and New Zealand*, 149–69. Edited by F. Castles, R. Gerritsen, and J. Vowles. Auckland: Auckland University Press.

Dale, Roger. 1994. 'The State and Education.' In *Leap into the Dark*, 68–88. Edited by Andrew Sharp. Auckland: Auckland University Press.

Dannin, Ellen J. 1997. *Working Free: The Origins and Impact of New Zealand's Employment Contracts Act*. Auckland: Auckland University Press.

Davidson, C., and M. Bray. 1994. *Women and Part Time Work in New Zealand*. Christchurch, NZ: Institute for Social Research.

Davies, Lisa (with Jackson, Natalie). 1993. *Women's Labour Force Participation in New Zealand: The Past 100 Years*. Wellington: Social Policy Agency.

Deniger, Marc-André, R.Scott Evans, Viviane Portebois, Monique Provost, André Regimbald, and Jean-Francois Rene. 1995. *Poverty among Young Families and Their Integration into Society and the Work Force: An Ontario-Quebec Comparison*. Ottawa: CCSD.

Denny and Elliott. 1997. 'Labour's Job Plan Is Shown Revolving Door.' *Guardian*, 17 June: 18.

Doherty, Gillian, Martha Friendly, and Mab Oloman. 1998. *Women's Support, Women's Work: Child Care in an Era of Deficit Reduction, Devolution, Downsizing and Deregulation*. Ottawa: Status of Women Canada.

Dominelli, Lena. 1991. *Women across Continents: Feminist Comparative Social Policy*. London: Harvester/Wheatsheaf.

Dooley, Martin. 1995. 'Lone-Mother Families and Social Assistance Policy in Canada.' In *Family Matters: New Policies for Divorce, Lone Mothers, and Child Poverty*, 35–104. By M. Dooley et al. Toronto: CD Howe Institute.

Drakich, Janice. 1988. 'In Whose Best Interest? The Politics of Joint Custody.' In *Family Bonds and Gender Divisions*. Edited by Bonnie Fox. Toronto: Canadian Scholars' Press.

Drover, Glenn, and Patrick Kerans, eds. 1993. *New Approaches to Welfare Theory*. Aldershot: Edward Elgar.

Dulac, Germain. 1989. 'Le Lobby des pères: divorce et paternité.' *Canadian Journal of Women and the Law* 3 (1): 45–68.

Duncan, Simon, and Ros Edwards. 1996. 'Lone Mothers and Paid Work: Neighbourhoods, Local Labour Markets, and Welfare State Regimes.' *Social Politics* 3 (2/3) Summer/Fall: 195–222.

– eds. 1997. *Single Mothers in International Contexts: Mothers or Workers?* London: Taylor and Francis.

Du Plessis, Rosemary. 1992. 'Stating the Contradictions: The Case of Women's Employment.' In *Feminist Voices. Women's Studies Texts for Aotearoa/New Zealand*, 209–23. Auckland: Oxford University Press.

Eardley, Tony, Jonathan Bradshaw, John Ditch, Ian Gough, and Peter Whiteford. 1996a. *Social Assistance in OECD Countries: Synthesis Report.* London: HMSO, Department of Social Security Research Report 46.

– 1996b. *Social Assistance in OECD Countries: Country Reports.* London: HMSO, Department of Social Security Research Report 47.

Easton, Brian. 1993. 'Poverty and Families: Priority or Piety?' Wellington: Economic and Social Trust on New Zealand (unpublished).

– 1997. *In Stormy Seas: The Post-War New Zealand Economy.* Dunedin: University of Otago Press.

Easton, Brian, and Gerritson, Rolf. 1996. 'Economic Reform: Parallels and Divergences.' In *The Great Experiment: Labour Parties and Public Policy Transformation in Australia and New Zealand*, 22–47. Edited by F. Castles, R. Gerritsen, and J. Vowles. Auckland: Auckland University Press.

Edin, Kathryn, and Laura Lein. 1996. 'Work, Welfare and Single Mothers: Economic Survival Strategies.' *American Sociological Review* 61 (February): 253–66.

Edwards, Anne, and Susan Magarey, eds. 1995. *Women in a Restructuring Australia: Work and Welfare.* Sydney: Allen and Unwin

Eichler, Margrit. 1997. *Family Shifts. Families, Policies, and Gender Equality.* Toronto: Oxford University Press.

Elliott, Larry and White, Michael. 1998. 'Brown's Balancing Act.' *Guardian*, 18 March.

Else, Ann. 1992. 'To Market and Home Again: Gender and the New Right.' In *Feminist Voices. Women's Studies Texts for Aotearoa/New Zealand*, 239–51. Edited by Rosemary Du Plessis. Auckland: Oxford University Press.

Ergas, Y. 1990. 'Child-Care Policies in Comparative Perspective: An Introductory Discussion.' In *Lone-Parent Families: The Economic Challenge*, 201–22. Edited by OECD. Paris: OECD.

Ermisch, John. 1991. *Lone Parenthood: An Economic Analysis.* London: Cambridge University Press.

Esping-Andersen, Gøsta. 1990. *The Three Worlds of Welfare Capitalism.* Cambridge: Polity Press.

– 1996a. 'After the Golden Age? Welfare States Dilemmas in a Global Economy.'

In *Welfare States in Transition: National Adaptations in Global Economies*. Edited by G. Esping-Andersen. London: Sage.

– 1996b. 'Welfare States without Work: The Impasse of Labour Shedding and Familialism in Continental European Social Policy.' In *Welfare States in Transition: National Adaptations in Global Economies*, 66–87. Edited by G. Esping-Andersen. London: Sage.

Esping-Andersen, Gøsta, ed. 1996. *Welfare States in Transition: National Adaptations in Global Economies*. London: Sage.

Evans, Patricia. 1984. 'Work and Welfare: A Profile of Low-Income Mothers.' *Canadian Social Work Review*. 81–96.

– 1987. 'A Decade of Change: The FBA Caseload, 1975–1986.' Background paper prepared for the Ontario Social Assistance Review. Toronto.

– 1988. 'Work Incentives and the Single Mother: Dilemmas of Reform.' *Canadian Public Policy* 14 (2): 125–36.

– 1992. 'Targeting Single Mothers for Employment: Comparisons from the United States, Britain, and Canada.' *Social Service Review* 66 (3): 378–98.

– 1993. 'From Workfare to the Social Contract: Implications for Canada of Recent U.S. Welfare Reforms.' *Canadian Public Policy* 19 (1): 54–67.

– 1995. 'Linking Welfare to Jobs: Workfare, Canadian Style.' In *Workfare: Does it Work? Is it Fair?* 75–104. Edited by Adil Sayeed. Montreal: IRPP.

– 1996. 'Single Mothers and Ontario's Welfare Policy: Restructuring the Debate.' In *Women in Canadian Public Policy*, 151–71. Edited by Janine Brodie. Toronto: Harcourt Brace.

– 1997. 'Divided Citizenship? Gender, Income Security, and the Welfare State.' In *Women and the Canadian Welfare State*, 91–116. Edited by P. Evans and G. Wekerle. Toronto: University of Toronto Press.

Evans, Patricia, and Gerde R. Wekerle. 1997. 'The Shifting Terrain of Women Workers: Theory, Discourse and Activism.' In *Women and the Canadian Welfare State*, 3–27. Edited by P. Evans and G. Wekerle. Toronto: University of Toronto Press.

Everingham, Christine. 1994. *Motherhood and Modernity*. Sydney: Allen and Unwin.

Fine, Sean. 1994. 'Ontario Crackdown Shows Cracks.' *Globe and Mail*, 5 April: 1, 6.

Finlay, H., and R. Bailey-Harris. 1989. *Family Law in Australia*. 4th ed. Sydney: Butterworths.

Finlayson, Louise, and Alan Marsh. 1997. 'Lone Parents on the Margins of Work.' Prepared for the conference Private Lives and Public Responses, University of Bath, 5–6 June.

Finnbogason, E., and M. Townson. 1985. *The Benefits and Cost-Effectiveness of a*

Central Registry of Maintenance and Custody Orders. Ottawa: Status of Women Canada.

Finnie, Ross. 1993. 'Women, Men and the Economic Consequences of Divorce: Evidence from Canadian Longitudinal Data.' *Canadian Review of Sociology and Anthropology* 30 (2): 205–41.

– 1996. *Good Idea, Bad Execution: The Government's Child Support Package.* Ottawa: Caledon Institute of Social Policy. June.

Finnie, Ross, et al. 1994. *Child Support: The Guideline Options.* Montreal: Institute for Research on Public Policy.

Folbre, Nancy. 1994. *Who Pays for the Kids? Gender and the Structures of Constraint.* New York: Routledge.

Ford, Reuben. 1997. 'Childcare in the Balance.' Prepared for the conference Private Lives and Public Responses, University of Bath, 5–6 June.

Ford, Reuben, and Jane Millar. 1997. 'Policy Dilemmas Posed by the Growth of Lone Parenthood in the UK.' Prepared for the Conference Private Lives and Public Responses, University of Bath, 5–6 June.

Ford, Reuben, A. Marsh, and L. Finlayson. 1997. *What Happens to Lone Parents.* London: Policy Studies Institute.

Frankel, Boris. 1997. 'Beyond Labourism and Socialism: How the Australian Labour Party Developed the Model of "New Labour."' *New Left Review* 221: 3–33.

Fraser, Nancy. 1997. *Justice Interruptus: Critical Reflections on the 'Postsocialist' Condition.* London: Routledge.

Fraser, Nancy, and Linda Gordon. 1994a. '"Dependency" Demystified: Inscriptions of Power in a Keyword of the Welfare State.' *Social Politics* 1 (1): 4–31.

– 1994b. 'A Genealogy of "Dependency": Tracing a Keyword of the U.S. Welfare State.' *Signs* 19 (2): 309–36.

Frederick, Judith A. 1992. *As Times Goes by ... Time Use of Canadians.* Ottawa: Statistics Canada, Catalogue no. 89–544E.

Freiler, Christa. 1996. 'A National Child Benefit: Promising First Step or Final Gesture in Child Poverty Strategy?' *Canadian Review of Social Policy* 38 (Fall): 109–16.

Freiler, Christa, and Judy Cerny. 1998. *Benefiting Canada's Children: Perspectives on Gender and Social Responsibility.* Ottawa: Status of Women Canada.

Friendly, Martha. 1994. *Child Care Policy in Canada: Putting the Pieces Together.* Toronto: Addison-Wesley.

Funder, Kathleen. 1993. 'Parents, Divorce and Economic Recovery.' In *Settling Down: Pathways of Parents after Divorce*, 1–12. Edited by K. Funder, M. Harrison, and R. Weston. Melbourne: AIFS.

- 1996a. *Remaking Families: Adaptation of Parents and Children to Divorce*. Melbourne: AIFS.
- 1996b. 'Simplified Procedures for Settling the Affairs of Divorcing Couples.' *Family Matters* 43 (Autumn): 48–49.

Funder, Kathleen, and Margaret Harrison. 1993. 'Drawing a Longbow on Marriage and Divorce.' In *Settling Down: Pathways of Parents after Divorce*, 13–32. Edited by K. Funder, M. Harrison, and R. Weston. Melbourne: AIFS.

Funder, Kathleen, Margaret Harrison, and Ruth Weston. 1993. *Settling Down: Pathways of Parents after Divorce*. Melbourne: AIFS.

Galarneau, Diane. 1992. 'Alimony and Child Support.' *Perspectives on Labour and Income* 4 (20): 8–21.

Garfinkel, Irwin, and Patrick Wong. 1990. 'Child Support and Public Policy.' *Lone-Parent Families: The Economic Challenge*, 101–26. Edited by OECD. Paris: OECD.

Gauthier, Anne Hélène. 1993. *Family Policies in OECD Countries*. Oxford: Claredon Press.

- 1996. *The State and the Family: A Comparative Analysis of Family Polices in Industrialized Countries*. Oxford: Clarendon Press.

Ghalam, Nancy Zukewich. 1997. 'Attitudes toward Women, Work and Family.' *Canadian Social Trends* 46 (Autumn): 13–17.

Ginsborg, Paul. 1995. 'Family, Civil Society and the State in Contemporary European History: Some Methodological Considerations.' *Contemporary European History* 4 (3) November: 249–73.

Glendinning, C. 1992. *The Costs of Informal Care: Looking inside the Household*. Published for Social Policy Research Unit, University of York. London: HMSO.

Glezer, Helen. 1993. *Financial Control and Financial Management within Couples in Australia*. Canberra: AIFS.

Globe and Mail, 1999. 'The Social Union Framework,' 5 February, A13.

Goertzel, Ted. G., and John W. Cosby. 1997. 'Gambling on Jobs and Welfare in Atlantic City.' *Society*, May/June: 62–6.

Goetz, Anne Marie. 1994. 'No More Heroes? Feminism and the State in Australia.' *Social Politics* 1 (3): 341–54.

Goldberg, Michael. 1994. 'The Adequacy of Social Assistance.' *Perception* 18.1 (June): 22.

Goodger, Kay. 1997. *New Zealand Social Trends*. Wellington: Social Policy Agency.

- 1998. 'Beyond Assumptions: Informing the Debate on Sole Mothers and Employment in New Zealand.' In *Work, Families and the State: Problems and Possibilities for the 21st Century*. Conference proceedings edited by Celia Briar and Gurjeet Gill. Palmerston North, NZ: Massey University.

Gordon, Linda. 1994. *Pitied, but Not Entitled: Single Mothers and the History of Welfare 1890–1935*. New York: Maxwell MacMillan.

Gorlick, Carolyne A. 1995. 'Listening to Low-Income Children and Single Mothers: Policy Incomes Related to Child Welfare.' In *Child Welfare in Canada: Research and Policy Implications*, 286–97. Edited by Joe Hudson and Burt Galaway. Toronto: Thompson Educational Publishing.

– 1996. *Taking Chances: Single Mothers and Their Children Exiting Social Welfare*. Report Summary. London: University of Western Ontario.

Gorlick, Carolyne A., and D. Alan Pomfret. 1993. 'Hope and Circumstance: Single Mothers Exiting Social Assistance.' In *Single Parent Families: Perspectives on Research and Policy*, 153–270. Edited by J. Hudson and B. Gallaway. Toronto: Thompson Educational Publishing.

Green, David. 1996. *From Welfare State to Civil Society: Towards Welfare That Works in New Zealand*. Wellington: New Zealand Business Roundtable.

Greenspon, Edward. 1997. 'Liberal Unity Agenda Part of Election Debris.' *Globe and Mail* (internet), 3 June.

Group of Eight. 1998a. *Conference on Growth, Employability and Inclusion: Chairman's Conclusions*. London: HM Treasury press release, 22 February.

– 1998b. *The Birmingham Summit*: Final Communiqué. 17 May.

The Guardian. 1998. 'Leader: A Milestone for the Poor.' 19 June (internet).

Gueron, Judith M. 1990. 'Work and Welfare: Lessons from Employment Programs.' *Journal of Economic Perspectives* 4 (1): 79–98.

– 1995. 'Work for People on Welfare.' *Public Welfare* 51 (1): 39–41.

Gueron, Judith, and E. Pauly. 1991. *From Welfare to Work*. New York: Russell Sage Foundation.

Guest, Dennis. 1997. *The Emergence of Social Security in Canada*. 3rd ed. Vancouver: University of British Columbia Press.

Gunn, Michelle. 1997. 'Suffer the Children as Care Slashed.' *The Australian Online*, 14 May.

Habgood, Ruth. 1992. 'On His Terms: Gender and the Politics of Domestic Life.' In *Feminist Voices. Women's Studies Texts for Aotearoa/New Zealand*, 163–79. Edited by Rosemary Du Plessis. Auckland: Auckland University Press.

Hallett, Christine, ed. 1996. *Women and Social Policy: An Introduction*. London: Prentice-Hall/Harvester Wheatsheaf.

Hantrais, Linda, and Marie-Thérèse Letablier. 1996. *Families and Family Policies in Europe*. London: Longman.

Hardina, Donna. 1997. 'Workfare in the U.S.: Empirically-Tested Programs or Ideological Quagmire?' In *Workfare: Ideology for a New Under-Class*, 131–48. Edited by Eric Shragge. Toronto: Garamond.

Harding, Lorraine Fox. 1996. *Family, State and Social Policy*. London: Macmillan.

Harrison, Margaret. 1993. 'The Law's Response to New Challenges.' In *Settling*

Down: Pathways of Parents after Divorce, 33–55. Edited by K. Funder, M. Harrison, and R. Weston. Melbourne: AIFS.

Harrison, Margaret, Gregg Snider, and Rosangela Merlo. 1990. *Who Pays for the Children? A First Look at the Operation of Australia's New Child Support Scheme.* Mongraph 9. Melbourne: AIFS.

Harrison, Margaret, Gregg Snider, G. Merlo, and V. Lucchesi. 1991. *Paying for the Children.* Melbourne: AIFS.

Hay, David I. 1997. 'Campaign 2000: Child and Family Poverty in Canada.' In *Child and Family Policies*, 116–33. Edited by J. Pulkingham and G. Ternowetsky. Halifax: Fernwood Publishing.

Henman, Paul. 1996. 'Constructing Families and Disciplining Bodies: A Socio-Technical Study of Computers, Policy and Governance in Australia's Department of Social Security.' Doctoral thesis, Department of Sociology and Anthropology, University of Queensland, Brisbane.

Herbert, Patricia. 1998. 'Job-Scheme Net Set to Widen.' *New Zealand Herald,* 23 April.

Hernes, Helga Marie. 1987. *Welfare State and Women Power: Essays in State Feminism.* Oslo: Norwegian Press.

Higgins, H.B. 1922. *A New Province for Law and Order.* London: Constable.

Higgins, Jane. 1999. 'From Welfare to Workfare.' In *Redesigning the New Zealand Welfare State*, 260–77. Edited by Jonathon Boston, Paul Dalziel, and Susan St John. Auckland: Oxford University Press.

Hill, Michael. 1990. *Social Security in Britain.* Aldershot, England: Edward Elgar.

Hills, J. 1994. *The Future of Welfare.* London/York: Rowntree/London School of Economics.

Himmelfarb, Gertrude. 1995. *The Demoralizition of Society: From Victorian Virtues to Modern Values.* New York: Alfred A. Knopf.

Hobson, Barbara. 1994. 'Solo Mothers, Social Policy Regimes, and the Logics of Gender.' In *Gendering Welfare States*, 170–87. Edited by Diane Sainsbury. London: Sage.

Holt, H. 1993. 'Making the Workplace Organisation and Culture More Responsive to the Needs of Parents.' In *Parental Employment and Caring for Children: Policies and Services in EC and Nordic Countries.* Denmark: Ministry of Social Affairs.

Hunsley, Terrance. 1997. *Lone Parent Incomes and Social Policy Outcomes: Canada in International Perspective.* Kingston, Ontario: School of Policy Studies, Queen's University.

Hutton, Will. 1997. 'Let Labour Beware the Clintonite Rhetoric,' *Observer*, 1 June: 26.

Hyman, P. 1995. *Women and Economics.* Wellington, NZ: Bridget Williams Books.

International Labour Office (ILO). 1949. *The Cost of Social Security*. Geneva: ILO.
International Social Security Association. 1992. *Social Security and Changing Family Structures*. Studies and Research no. 29: Geneva: ISSA.
Jacobs, Lesley A. 1995. 'What are the Normative Foundations of Workfare?' In *Workfare: Does it Work/Is it Fair?* 13–37. Edited by Adil Sayeed. Montreal: IRPP.
Jamrozik, A. 1994. 'From Harvester to Deregulation: Wage Earners in the Australian Welfare State.' *Australian Journal of Social Issues* 29 (2): 162–70.
Japan, Ministry of International Trade and Industry. 1997. 'Chair's Conclusion,' G8 Jobs Conference, Kobe, Japan, 28–29 November.
Jarvis, Sarah, and Stephen Jenkins. 1997. 'Marital Splits and Income Changes: Evidence for Britain.' Prepared for the conference Private Lives and Public Responses, University of Bath, 5–6 June.
Jenkins, Stephen. 1996. 'Trends in Real Income in Britain: A Microeconomic Analysis.' Working Paper 96–7, ESRC Research Centre on Micro-Social Change, University of Essex, Colchester. Forthcoming in *Empirical Economics*.
Jenson, Jane. 1990. 'Representations in Crisis: The Roots of Canada's Permeable Fordism.' *Canadian Journal of Political Science* 23 (4): 653–83.
– 1993. 'All the World's a Stage: Ideas, Spaces and Times in Canadian Political Economy.' In *Production, Space, Identity*, 143–69. Edited by Jane Jenson, Rianne Mahon, and Manfred Bienefeld. Toronto: Canadian Scholars' Press.
– 1996. 'Introduction: Some Consequences of Economic and Political Restructuring and Readjustment.' *Social Politics* 3 (1) Spring: 1–11.
Jenson, Jane, and Susan D. Phillips. 1996. 'Regime Shift: New Citizenship Practices in Canada.' *International Journal of Comparative Sociology* 14 (Fall): 111–35.
Johnson, Carol. 1996. 'Shaping the Future: Women, Citizenship and Australian Political Discourse.' In *Gender, Politics and Citizenship in the 1990s*, 25–43. Edited by B. Sullivan and G. Whitehouse. Sydney: UNSW Press.
Jones, George. 1997. 'Tories Pitch for the Family.' *Daily Telegraph*, 3 April: 1.
Jones, Helen, and Jane Millar, eds. 1996. *The Politics of Family*. Aldershot: Avebury.
Jones, Michael. 1996. *The Australian Welfare State: Evaluating Social Policy*. Sydney: Allen and Unwin.
– 1997. *Reforming New Zealand Welfare: International Perspectives*. Wellington: Centre for Independent Studies.
Kahn, A.J., and S.B. Kamerman. 1994. 'Family Policy and the Under-3s: Money, Services, and Time in a Policy Package.' *Social Security Review* 47 (3–4): 31–43.
Kamerman, S.B., and A.J. Kahn, eds. 1997. *Family Change and Family Policies in Great Britain, Canada, New Zealand and the United States*. Oxford: Clarendon Press.
Kangas, Olli, and Joakim Palme. 1992–3. 'Statism Eroded? Labor-Market Bene-

fits and Challenges to the Scandinavian Welfare States.' *International Journal of Sociology* 22 (4): 3–24.

Kaplan, Gisela. 1996. *The Meagre Harvest: The Australian Women's Movement 1950–1990s*. Sydney: Allen and Unwin.

Kapsalis, Constantine. 1997. *Social Assistance and the Employment Rate of Lone Mothers: An Analysis of Ontario's Live Experiment*. Ottawa: Data Probe Economic Consulting.

Kedgley, Sue. 1996. *Mum's the Word: The Untold Story of Motherhood in New Zealand*. Auckland: Random House.

Kelsey, Jane. 1995. *Economic Fundamentalism*. London: Pluto Press.

Kelsey, Jane, and Mike O'Brien. 1995. *Setting the Record Straight: Social Developments in Aotearoa/New Zealand*. Wellington: Association of Non Government Organisations of Aotearoa.

Kerstetter, Steve. 1997. 'Fighting Child Poverty with Parental Wage Income Supplements.' In *Child and Family Policies*, 147–56. Edited by J. Pulkingham and G. Ternowetsky. Halifax: Fernwood Publishing.

Keynes, John Maynard. 1936. *The Central Theory of Employment, Interest and Money*. London: Macmillan.

Kiernan, K. 1992. 'Men and Women at Work and at Home.' In *British Social Attitudes Ninth Report*. Edited by R. Jowell. London: SCPR.

Kiernan, K, H. Land, and J. Lewis. 1998. In *Lone Mothers in Twentieth Century Britain: From Footnote to Frontpage*. Oxford: Oxford University Press.

Kitchen, Brigitte. 1990. 'Family Policy.' *Families: Changing Trends in Canada*, 306–29. Edited by Maureen Baker. Toronto: McGraw-Hill Ryerson.

– 1997. 'The New Child Benefit: Much Ado about Nothing.' *Canadian Review of Social Policy* 39 (Spring): 65–74.

Klassen, Thomas R. and Daniel Buchanan. 1997. 'Getting It Backwards? Economy and Welfare in Ontario, 1985–1995.' *Canadian Public Policy*. 23(3): 333–7.

Knijn, Trudie, and Monique Kremer. 1997. 'Gender and the Caring Dimension of Welfare States: Toward Inclusive Citizenship.' *Social Politics* 4 (3): 328–61.

Knijn, Trudie, and Clare Ungerson. 1997. 'Introduction: Care Work and Gender in Welfare Regimes.' *Social Politics* 4 (3): 323–7.

Korpi, Walter. 1983. *The Democratic Class Struggle*. London: Routledge and Kegan Paul.

Kumar, Krishan. 1995. *From Post-Industrial Society to Post-Modern Society: New Theories of the Contemporary World*. Oxford: Blackwell.

Lacroix, Guy. 1997. 'Reforming the Welfare System: In Search of Optimal Policy Mix.' Paper presented to the Institute for Research on Public Policy conference Adapting Public Policy to a Labour Market in Transition, Montreal.

Lambert, Suzanne. 1994. 'Sole Parent Income Support: Cause or Cure of Sole Parent Poverty.' *Australian Journal of Social Issues* 29 (1): 75–97.

Lamont, Leonie. 1998. 'Sole Parent Support to Be Slashed.' *Sydney Morning Herald*, 20 May (internet).

Land, Hilary. 1979. 'The Family Wage.' University of Leeds, Eleanor Rathbone Memorial Lecture.

– 1980. 'The Family Wage.' *Feminist Review* 6: 55–7.

– 1985. 'Who Still Cares for the Family? Recent Developments in Income Maintenance, Taxation and Family Law.' In *Women and Social Policy: A Reader*. Edited by Clare Ungerson. London: Macmillan.

– 1991. 'Time to Care.' In *Women's Issues in Social Policy*, 7–19. Edited by Mavis Maclean and Dulce Groves. London: Routledge.

– 1998a. 'Housing and Lone Mothers.' In *Lone Mothers in Twentieth Century Britain: From Footnote to Frontpage*. By K. Kiernan, H. Land, and J. Lewis. Oxford: Oxford University Press.

– 1998b. 'Lone Mothers, Paid Work and Child Care.' In *Lone Mothers in Twentieth Century Britain: From Footnote to Frontpage*. By K. Kiernan, H.Land, and J. Lewis. Oxford: Oxford University Press.

– 1998c. 'Social Security and Lone Mothers.' In *Lone Mothers in Twentieth Century Britain: From Footnote to Frontpage*. By K. Kiernan, H. Land, and J. Lewis. Oxford: Oxford University Press.

Land, Hilary, and Jane Lewis. 1997. 'The Problem of Lone Motherhood in the British Context.' Prepared for the conference Private Lives and Public Responses, University of Bath, 5–6 June.

LaPointe, Rita E., and C. James Richardson, 1994. *Evaluation of the New Brunswick Family Support Orders Service*. New Brunswick: Department of Justice.

Larner, Wendy. 1993. 'Changing Contexts: Globalisation, Migration and Feminism in New Zealand.' In *Feminism and the Politics of Difference*, 85–102. Edited by S. Gunew and A. Yeatman. Sydney: Allen and Unwin.

– 1995. 'Theorising "Difference" in Aotearoa/New Zealand.' *Gender, Place and Culture* 2 (2): 177–90.

– 1996. 'The "New Boys": Restructuring in New Zealand, 1984–94.' *Social Politics* 3 (1) Spring: 32–56.

– 1997. 'The Legacy of the Social: Market Governance and the Consumer.' *Economy and Society* 26: 373–99.

Laugesen, Ruth. 1998. 'Hated Tax Scrapped.' *Auckland Sunday Star-Times*, 29 March: 1.

Le Grand, Julian. 1997. 'Knights, Knaves or Pawns? Human Behaviour and Social Policy.' *Journal of Social Policy* 26 (2): 149–69.

Leonard, Peter. 1997. *Postmodern Welfare: Reconstructing an Emancipatory Project*. London: Sage.

Lero, Donna, and Lois Brockman. 1993. 'Single Parent Families in Canada: A

Closer Look.' In *Single Parent Families: Perspectives on Research and Policy*, 91–114. Edited by J. Hudson and B. Gallaway. Toronto: Thompson Educational Publishing.

Levine, M., Wyn H., and Asiasiga, L. 1993. *Lone Parents and Paid Work: A Study of Employment Patterns and Barriers, and Options for Change*. Wellington: Social Policy Agency.

Lewis, Jane. 1997. 'Gender and Welfare Regimes: Further Thoughts.' *Social Politics* 4 (2) Summer: 160–77.

– ed. 1993. *Women and Social Policies in Europe: Work, Family and the State*. Aldershott: Edward Elgar.

Lewis, Suzan, and Jeremy Lewis. 1996. *The Work-Family Challenge: Rethinking Employment*. London: Sage.

Lightman, Ernie S. 1995. 'You Can Lead a Horse to Water; but ...: The Case against Workfare in Canada.' In *Helping the Poor: A Qualified Case for 'Workfare,'* 151–83. Edited by John Richards and William G. Watson. Ottawa: C.D. Howe Institute.

– 1997. '"It's Not a Walk in the Park": Workfare in Ontario.' In *Workfare: Ideology for a New Under-Class*, 85–107. Edited by E. Shragge. Toronto: Garamond.

Lister, Ruth. 1996. 'Citizenship Engendered.' In *Critical Social Policy*, 168–74. Edited by David Taylor. London: Sage.

Little, Margaret Hillyard. 1995. 'The Blurring of Boundaries: Private and Public Welfare for Single Mothers in Ontario.' *Studies in Political Economy* 47 (Summer): 89–107.

– 1998. *No Car, No Radio, No Liquor Permit: The Moral Regulation of Single Mothers in Ontario, 1920–1997*. Toronto: Oxford University Press.

Lochhead, Clarence. 1997. 'Identifying Low Wage Workers and Policy Options.' In *Child and Family Policies*, 134–46. Edited by J. Pulkingham and G. Ternowetsky. Halifax: Fernwood Publishing.

Lord, Stella. 1994. 'Social Assistance and 'Employability' for Single Mothers in Nova Scotia.' In *Continuities and Discontinuities: The Political Economy of Social Welfare and Labour Market Policy in Canada*, 191–206. Edited by A.F. Johnson, S. McBride, and P.J. Smith. Toronto: University of Toronto Press.

Low, Will. 1993. 'Work and Welfare: Assessing Earnings Exemption Policies in BC.' Report prepared for the British Columbia Ministry of Social Services. Victoria.

Mackie, Richard. 1994. 'Crackdown on 'Deadbeat Dads' Discussed.' *Globe and Mail*, 4 August: A1.

Maclean, Mavis. 1997a. 'Delegalized Family Obligations.' In *Family Law and Family Policy in the New Europe*, 129–53. Edited by Jacek Kurczewski and Mavis Maclean. Aldershot, UK: Dartmouth.

– 1997b. 'The Origins of Child Support in Britain and the Case for a Strong

Child Support System.' Presented to the conference Private Lives and Public Responses, University of Bath, 5–6 June.

Maclean, Mavis, and Dulce Groves. 1991. *Women's Issues in Social Policy.* London: Routledge.

Mahon, Rianne. 1997. 'Child Care in Canada and Sweden: Policy and Politics.' *Social Politics* 4 (3): 382–418.

Maloney, D. 1994. *Towards 2000: Executive Women in Australia.* Sydney: Korn/Ferry International.

Maloney, Tim. 1997. *Benefit Reform and Labour Market Behaviour in New Zealand.* Wellington: Institute of Policy Studies, Victoria University of Wellington.

Maré, Dave. 1996. 'Labour Market Trends, Cycles, and Outlook.' Paper presented at the Seventh Conference on Labour, Employment and Work. Victoria University, Wellington, 28–29 November.

Marsh, A., R. Ford, and L. Findlayson. 1997. *Lone Parents, Work and Benefits.* London: Policy Studies Institute.

Marsh, Leonard. 1943. *Report on Social Security for Canada.* Ottawa: King's Printer.

Marshall, Barbara L. 1994. *Engendering Modernity. Feminism, Social Theory and Social Change.* Cambridge: Polity Press.

Matthews, Beverly, and Roderic Beaujot. 1997. 'Gender Orientations and Family Strategies.' *Canadian Review of Sociology and Anthropology* 34 (4) November: 415–28.

McAll, Christopher, Jean-Yves Desgagnes, Madlyn Fournier, Lucie Villeneuve. 1995. *Les barrières a la reinsertion sociale et professionnelle des personnes assistées sociales et la reforme du système de la securité du revenu.* Montreal: Université de Montréal avec collaboration avec le Front commun des personnes assistées sociales du Québec.

McClure, Margaret. 1998. *A Civilised Community. A History of Social Security in New Zealand 1989–1998.* Auckland: Auckland University Press.

McDonald, Peter, ed. 1986. *Settling Up: Property and Income Distribution on Divorce in Australia.* Melbourne: AIFS, and Sydney: Prentice-Hall.

McFarland, Joan, and Robert Mullaly. 1995. 'NB Works: Image vs. Reality.' In *Remaking Canadian Social Policy: Staking Claims and Forging Change.* Edited by J. Pulkingham and G. Ternowetsky. Halifax: Fernwood Publishing.

McGilly, Frank. 1998. *Canada's Public Social Services: Understanding Income and Health Programs.* 2nd ed. Toronto: Oxford University Press.

McGrath, Susan. 1997. 'Child Poverty Advocacy and the Politics of Influence.' In *Child and Family Policies,* 172–87. Edited by J. Pulkingham and G. Ternowetsky. Halifax: Fernwood Publishing.

McHugh, Marilyn, and Jane Millar. 1997. 'Sole Mothers in Australia: Supporting Mothers to Seek Work.' In *Single Mothers in International Contexts: Mothers or*

Workers? Edited by S. Duncan and R. Edwards. London: Taylor and Francis.

McKay, Stephen, and Alan Marsh. 1994. *Lone Parents and Work.* London: HMSO (Department of Social Security, Research Report 25).

McKay, Stephen, and Karen Rowlingson. 1997. 'Choosing Lone Parenthood? The Dynamics of Family Change.' Prepared for the conference Private Lives and Public Responses: Lone Parenthood and Future Policy in the UK, University of Bath, 5–6 June.

McKendrick, John. 1997. 'The "Big" Picture: Quality in the Lives of Lone Parents.' Prepared for the conference Private Lives and Public Responses, University of Bath, 5–6 June.

Mendelson, Michael. 1995. *Looking for Mr. Good-Transfer: A Guide to the CHST Negotiations.* Ottawa: Caledon Institute of Social Policy.

– 1996. *The Provinces' Position: A Second Chance for the Social Security Review?* Ottawa: Caledon Institute of Social Policy. June.

– 1998. *To Pay or Not to Pay: Should the Federal Government 'Pay Down' Its Debt?* Ottawa: Caledon Institute of Social Policy.

Middleton, Sue, and Karl Ashworth. 1997. 'Small Fortunes: Spending on Children in One-Parent Families.' Prepared for the conference Private Lives and Public Responses, University of Bath, 5–6 June.

Millar, Jane. 1996. 'Family Obligations and Social Policy: The Case of Child Support.' *Policy Studies* 17 (3): 181–93.

Millar, Jane, and Peter Whiteford. 1993. 'Child Support in Lone-Parent Families: Policies in Australia and the UK.' *Policy and Politics* 21 (1): 59–72.

Millar, Stuart, David Hencke, and Sarah Ryle. 1997. 'Two Million Gain in 1.2bn Tax Plan.' *Guardian*, 3 April: 13.

Milne, S., and M. White. 1998. 'Blair's Virtue: £3.60 Minimum Hourly Pay.' *Guardian*, 19 June.

Mimoto, H., and P. Cross. 1991. 'The Growth of the Federal Debt.' *Canadian Economic Observer* 3 (June): 1–3, 18.

Mishra, Ramesh. 1984. *The Welfare State in Crisis.* Brighton: Wheatsheaf Books.

– 1990. *The Welfare State in Capitalist Society.* Toronto: University of Toronto Press.

Mitchell, Deborah. 1991. *Income Transfers in Ten Welfare States.* Aldershot, UK: Avebury.

– 1992. 'Sole Parents, Work and Welfare: Evidence from the Luxembourg Income Study.' Presentation to the Social Policy Research Centre, University of New South Wales, Sydney.

– 1995. 'Women's Incomes.' In *Women in a Restructuring Australia: Work and Welfare,* 79–94. Edited by A. Edwards and S. Magarey. Sydney: Allen and Unwin.

Mitchell, Deborah, and Geoffrey Garrett. 1996. 'Women and the Welfare State in the Era of Global Markets.' *Social Politics* 3 (2/3) Summer/Fall: 185–194.

Mitchell, Deborah, and Ann Harding. 1993. 'Changes in Poverty Among Families during the 1990s: Poverty Gap versus Poverty Head-Count Measures.' Discussion Paper 2. Canberra, Australia: National Centre for Social and Economic Modelling, University of Canberra.

Morton, Mary E. 1988. 'Dividing the Wealth, Sharing the Poverty: The (Re)formation of "Family" in Law.' *Canadian Review of Sociology and Anthropology* 25 (2): 254–75.

Moylan, Judi. 1996a. Press release from Minister for Family Services (for Carers Week), 19 October.

– 1996b. 'Strengthening Families.' Statement by the Minister for Family Services, 20 August.

Mulgan, Richard. 1997. *Politics in New Zealand*. 2nd ed. Auckland: Auckland University Press.

Mullaly, Robert. 1994. 'Social Welfare and the New Right: A Class Mobilization Perspective.' In *Continuities and Discontinuities*, 76–94. Edited by A.F. Johnson, S. McBride, and P.J. Smith. Toronto: University of Toronto Press.

– 1995. 'Why Workfare Doesn't Work.' *Perception* 18 (3, 4): 9–13.

– 1997. 'The Politics of Workfare: NB Works.' In *Workfare: Ideology for a New Under-Class*, 35–57. Edited by Eric Shragge. Toronto: Garamond Press.

Murphy, Jonathan. 1997. 'Alberta and the Workfare Myth.' In *Workfare: Ideology for a New Under-Class*, 109–29. Edited by Eric Shragge. Toronto: Garamond Press.

Myles, John. 1995. *The Market's Revenge: Old Age Security and Social Rights*. Ottawa: Caledon Institute of Social Policy. November. November.

– 1996. 'When Markets Fail: Social Welfare in Canada and the United States.' In *Welfare States in Transition: National Adaptatons in Global Economies*, 116–40. Edited by G. Esping-Andersen. London: Sage.

Myles, John, and Paul Pierson. 1997. *Friedman's Revenge: The Reform of 'Liberal' Welfare States in Canada and the United States*. Ottawa: Caledon Institute of Social Policy. November.

National Council of Welfare. 1987. *Welfare in Canada. The Tangled Safety Net*. Ottawa: Supply and Services Canada.

– 1992. *Welfare Reform*. Ottawa: Supply and Services Canada.

– 1993. *Incentives and Disincentives to Work*. Ottawa: Minister of Supply and Services.

– 1995a. *Budget and Block Funding*. Ottawa: Minister of Supply and Services.

- 1995b. *Welfare Incomes 1994*. Ottawa: Minister of Supply and Services.
- 1996a. *A Guide to the Proposed Seniors Benefit*. Ottawa: Minister of Supply and Services.
- 1996b. *A Pension Primer*. Ottawa: Minister of Supply and Services.
- 1996c. *Poverty Profile 1994*. Ottawa: Minister of Supply and Services.
- 1997a. *Child Benefits: A Small Step Forward*. Ottawa: Minister of Supply and Services Canada. Spring.
- 1997b. *Welfare Incomes 1995*. Ottawa: Minister of Supply and Services Canada.
Nelson, Hilde Lindemann, ed. 1997. *Feminism and Families*. New York: Routledge.
Newman, Jocelyn. 1996. 'More Choice for Women.' Statement by the Minister for Social Security, 20 August.
New Zealand, Department of Social Welfare. 1995. *Income Support, Strategic Directions 1995–2005*. Wellington.
- 1996. *Strategic Directions*. Post-Election Briefing Paper. Wellington.
- 1997. *Statistics Report*. Wellington.
- 1998. *Towards a Code of Social and Family Responsibility*. Public Discussion Document. Wellington .
New Zealand Government. *Household Labour Force Surveys, 1986, 1991, 1996*.
- 1995. *Focus On Employment: The Government's Response to the Employment Task Force and the Multi-Party Group Memorandum of Understanding*. Wellington.
- 1996a. *Childcare Subsidy. A Guide for Parents and Caregivers*. Wellington. July.
- 1996b. *Domestic Purposes*. Wellington. November.
- 1996c. *Widows and Bereaved Families*. Wellington. November.
- 1998. *Budget: Work Focused Welfare*. Press release. 14 May.
- n.d. 'Domestic Pupuses Benefit and Related Programmes Historical Summary.' Chart. Wellington.
New Zealand Herald. 1998a. 'Brash's Words "Expose Wage Plan as Farce."' 28 May, A3.
- 1986b 'Govt in Retreat on Work Scheme.' 23 July, A1.
New Zealand, Ministry of Education, Education Statistics. 1997. *News-Sheet* 7 (2) April.
New Zealand, Statistics New Zealand. 1993. *All about Women in New Zealand*. Wellington.
- 1995. *Demographic Trends*. Wellington: Statistics NZ.
- 1996a. *Labour Market Statistics 1995*. Wellington: Department of Statistics.
- 1996b. *Key Statistics 1991–1996*. Wellington: Department of Statistics.
- 1997. *1996 Census of Population and Dwellings*. 7 May 1997. Wellington.

Nightingale, Demetra Smith, and Robert H. Haveman, eds. 1994. *The Work Alternative: Welfare Reform and the Realities of the Job Market*. Washington: Urban Institute Press.

Nightingale, Martina. 1995. 'Women and a Flexible Workforce.' In *Women in a Restructuring Australia: Work and Welfare*, 121–38. Sydney: Allen and Unwin.

Oakley, Ann, and A. Susan Williams, eds. 1994. *The Politics of the Welfare State*. London: UCL Press.

Ochiltree, Gay. 1990. *Children in Australian Families*. Melbourne: Longman Chesire and AIFS.

O'Connor, Julia. 1993. 'Citizenship, Class, Gender and Labour Market Participation in Canada and Australia.' In *Gender, Citizenship and the Labour Market: The Australian and Canadian Welfare States*. Edited by Sheila Shaver. Sydney: Social Policy Research Centre, University of New South Wales. August.

Oliker, Stacey. 1995. 'Work Commitment and Constraint among Mothers on Workfare.' *Journal of Contemporary Ethnography* 24 (2): 165–94.

Ontario Government, Ministry of Community and Social Services. 1988. *Transitions*. Report of the Social Assistance Review Committee. Toronto: Queen's Printer.

– 1992. *Time for Action*. Principal Report of the Advisory Group on New Social Assistance Legislation. Toronto: Queen's Printer.

Opie, Anne. 1992. 'Joint Custody, Gender, and Power.' In *Feminist Voices: Women's Studies Texts for Aotearoa/New Zealand*. Edited by Rosemary Du Plessis. Auckland: Auckland University Press.

Organization for Economic Co-Operation and Development (OECD). 1994a. *Employment Outlook: July 1994*. Paris: OECD.

– 1994b. *OECD Economic Survey 1994: Canada*. Paris: OECD.

– 1994c. *The OECD Jobs Study: Facts, Analysis, Strategies*. Paris: OECD.

– 1994d. *Women and Structural Change: New Perspectives*. Paris: OECD

– 1995. *The OECD Jobs Study: Implementing the Strategy*. Paris: OECD.

– 1996a. *Social Expenditure Statistics of OECD Members Countries, Provisional Version*. Labour Market and Social Policy Occasional Papers 17. Paris: OECD.

– 1996b. *Structural Indicators*. Paris: OECD.

– 1997. *OECD Economic Outlook December 1997*. Paris: OECD.

Orloff, Ann. 1993. 'Gender and the Social Rights of Citizenship: The Comparative Analysis of Gender Relations and Welfare States.' *American Sociological Review* 58: 303–28.

– 1996. 'Gendering the Analysis of Welfare States.' In *Gender, Politics and Citizenship in the 1990s*, 81–99. Edited by B. Sullivan and G. Whitehouse. Sydney: UNSW Press.

Pascal. Gillian. 1997. *Social Policy: A New Feminist Analysis*. London: Routledge.

Pask, E. Diane, and L.M. McCall, eds. 1989. *How Much and Why? Economic Implications of Marriage Breakdown: Spousal and Child Support.* Calgary, Alberta: Canadian Research Institute for Law and the Family.

Pearce, Diana. 1990. 'Welfare Is Not for Women: Why the War on Poverty Cannot Conquer the Feminization of Poverty.' In *Women, the State and Welfare.* Edited by Linda Gordon. Madison: University of Wisconsin Press.

Pedersen, Susan. 1993. *Family, Dependence, and the Origins of the Welfare State: Britain and France, 1914–1945.* Cambridge: Cambridge University Press.

Perry, Julia. 1991. *Breadwinners or Childrearers: The Dilemma for Lone Mothers.* Australia: OECD Working Party on Social Policy.

Philp, Margaret. 1997. 'Workfare Begins with a Wimper.' *Globe and Mail,* 4 June (internet).

Phipps, Shelley A. 1995a. Poverty and Labour Market Change: Canada in Comparative Perspective.' In *Labour Market Polarization and Social Policy Reform,* 59–88. Edited by K.G. Banting and C. Beach. Kingston: Queen's University, School of Policy Studies.

– 1995b. 'Taking Care of Our Children: Tax and Transfer Options for Canada.' In *Family Matters: New Policies for Divorce, Lone Mothers, and Child Poverty,* 186–216. By M. Dooley et al. Toronto: CD Howe Institute.

– 1996. 'Lessons from Europe: Policy Options to Enhance the Economic Security of Canadian Families.' In *Family Security in Insecure Times. Vols. II & III.* Edited by David Ross. Ottawa: Canadian Council on Social Development.

Phipps, Shelley A., and Peter S. Burton. 1992. *What's Mine Is Yours? The Influence of Male and Female Incomes on Patterns of Household Expenditure.* Discussion Paper 92-12. Halifax: Dalhousie University, Department of Economics.

– 1996. 'Collective Models of Family Behaviour: Implications for Economic Policy.' *Canadian Public Policy* 22 (2): 129–43.

Pierson, Paul. 1994. *Dismantling the Welfare State? Reagan, Thatcher, and the Politics of Retrenchment.* Cambridge: Cambridge University Press.

Piven, Frances Fox. 1990. 'Ideology and the State: Women, Power, and the Welfare State.' In *Women, the State and Welfare,* 250–64. Edited by L. Gordon. Madison: University of Wisconsin Press.

Pixley, Jocelyn. 1993. *Citizenship and Employment. Investigating Post-Industrial Options.* Cambridge: Cambridge University Press.

Plant, Raymond. 1997. 'Rights, Obligations and the Reform of the Welfare State.' Eleanor Rathbone Lecture, Bristol. 14 May.

Plough, Niels, and Jon Kvist. 1996. *Social Security in Europe: Development or Dismantlement?* The Hague: Kluwer Law International.

Prescott, David, et al. 1986. 'Labour Supply Estimates for Low-Income Female

Heads of Households Using Mincome Data.' *Canadian Journal of Economics* 19 (1): 134–41.

Price, S.J., and P.C. McKenry. 1988. *Divorce. A Major Life Transition.* Sage Publications.

Pringle, Rosemary, and Sophie Watson. 1996. 'Feminist Theory and the State: Needs, Rights and Interests.' In *Gender, Politics and Citizenship in the 1990s.* Edited by Barbara Sullivan and Gillian Whitehouse. Sydney: UNSW Press.

Pulkingham, Jane. 1994. 'Private Troubles, Private Solutions: Poverty among Divorced Women and the Politics of Support Enforcement and Child Custody Determination.' *Canadian Journal of Law and Society* 9 (2): 73–97.

Pulkingham, Jane, and Gordon Ternowetsky, eds. 1996. *Remaking Canadian Social Policy: Social Security in the Late 1990s.* Halifax: Fernwood Publishing.

– 1997a. *Child and Family Policies: Struggles, Strategies and Options.* Halifax: Fernwood Publishing.

– 1997b. 'The Changing Context of Child and Family Policies.' In *Child and Family Policies: Struggles, Strategies and Options*, 14–39. Edited by J. Pulkingham and G. Ternowetsky. Halifax: Fernwood Publishing.

– 1997c. 'The New Canada Child Tax Benefit: Discriminating between the "Deserving" and "Undeserving" Poor Families With Children.' In *Child and Family Policies: Struggles, Strategies and Options.* Edited by J. Pulkingham and G. Ternowetsky. Halifax: Fernwood Publishing.

Pupo, Norene. 1997. 'Women, Unions, and the State: Challenges Ahead.' In *Women and the Canadian Welfare State*, 291–309. Edited by P. Evans and G. Wekerle. Toronto: University of Toronto Press.

Pusey, Michael. 1991. *Economic Rationalism in Canberra: A Nation-Building State Changes Its Mind.* Cambridge: Cambridge University Press.

– 1993. 'Reclaiming the Middle Ground ... from New Right Economic Rationalism.' Public Sector Research Centre, University of New South Wales, Discussion Paper 31.

Quebec Government. 1997. 'La Nouvelle allocation familiale' (pamphlet).

Randall, Vicky. 1996. 'Feminism and Child Daycare.' *Journal of Social Policy* 25 (4): 485–505.

Rank, M. 1994, *Living on the Edge.* New York: Columbia University Press.

Rees, Stuart. 1994. 'Economic Rationalism: An Ideology of Exclusion.' *Australian Journal of Social Issues* 29 (2) May: 171–85.

Rehn, Gosta. 1985. 'Swedish Active Labour Market Policy: Retrospect and Prospect.' *Industrial Relations* 24 (1): 62–89.

Richards, John. 1994. *The Case for Change.* Ottawa: Renouf.

Richards, John, et al. 1995. *Helping the Poor: A Qualified Case for 'Workfare.'* Toronto: CD Howe Institute.

Richardson, C. James. 1988. *Court-Based Divorce Mediation in Four Canadian Cities: An Overview of Research Results.* Ottawa: Minister of Supply and Services.

– 1996. 'Divorce and Remarriage.' In *Families: Changing Trends in Canada* 3rd ed. Edited by Maureen Baker. Toronto: McGraw-Hill Ryerson.

Ringen, Stein, et al. 1997. 'Great Britain.' In *Family Change and Family Policies in Great Britain, Canada, New Zealand and the United States*, 29–102. Edited by S. Kamerman and A. Kahn. Oxford: Clarendon Press.

Rochford, M. 1993. *A Profile of Sole Parents from the 1991 Census.* Research Report Series 15. Wellington, NZ: Social Policy Agency, Research Unit, Department of Social Welfare.

Ross, David P, Katherine Scott, and Mark Kelly. 1996. *Child Poverty: What Are the Consequences?* Ottawa: Centre for International Statistics, Canadian Council on Social Development.

Rudd, Chris. 1997. 'The Welfare State.' In *New Zealand Politics in Transition*, 256–67. Edited by Raymond Miller. Auckland: Auckland University Press.

Rudd, Chris, and Brian Roper, eds. 1997. *The Political Economy of New Zealand.* Auckland: Oxford University Press.

Sainsbury, Diane. 1993. 'Dual Welfare and Sex Segregation of Access to Social Benefits: Income Maintenance Policies in the U.K., the U.S., the Netherlands and Sweden.' *Journal of Social Policy* 22 (1): 69–98.

Sainsbury, Diane, ed. 1994a. *Gendering Welfare States.* London: Sage.

– 1994b. 'Introduction.' In *Gendering Welfare States.* Edited by Diane Sainsbury, 1–7. London: Sage.

– 1994c. 'Women's and Men's Social Rights: Gendering Dimensions in Welfare States.' In *Gendering Welfare States.* Edited by D. Sainsbury, 50–69. London: Sage.

– 1996. *Gender, Equality and Welfare States.* Cambridge: Cambridge University Press.

St John, Susan. 1994. 'The State and Welfare.' In *Leap into the Dark: The Changing Role of the State in New Zealand since 1984*, 89–106. Edited by A. Sharp. Auckland: Auckland University Press.

– 1997. 'The Measure of Success for Beyond Dependency: Aims, Methods and Evaluation.' *Social Policy Journal of New Zealand* 8 (March): 61–6.

Saunders, Peter. 1994. *Welfare and Inequality: National and International Perspectives on the Australian Welfare State.* Cambridge: Cambridge University Press.

Saunders, Peter, and George Matheson. 1991. 'Sole parent Families in Australia.' *International Social Security Review* 34 (3): 51–75.

Sayeed, Adil, ed. 1995. *Workfare: Does it Work? Is it Fair?* Montreal: Institute for Research on Public Policy.

Sharp, Andrew, ed. 1994a. *Leap into the Dark: The Changing Role of the State in New Zealand since 1984*. Auckland: Auckland University Press.
– 1994b. 'The Case for Politics and the State.' In *Leap into the Dark: The Changing Role of the State in New Zealand since 1984*, 1–18. Auckland: Auckland University Press.
Shaver, Sheila. 1993a. 'Citizenship, Gender and the Life Cycle Transition: Sole Parents Whose Youngest Child Is Turning 16.' In *Gender, Citizenship and the Labour Market: The Australian and Canadian Welfare States*. Edited by S. Shaver. Sydney: Social Policy Research Centre, University of New South Wales. August.
– 1993b. *Gender, Citizenship and the Labour Market: The Australian and Canadian Welfare States*. Sydney: Social Policy Research Centre, University of New South Wales. August.
– 1993c. *Women and the Australian Social Security System: From Difference towards Equality*. Sydney: UNSW, Social Policy Research Centre, Discussion Paper 41.
– 1995. 'Women, Employment and Social Security.' In *Women in a Restructuring Australia: Work and Welfare*, 141–57. Edited by A. Edwards and S. Magarey. Sydney: Allen and Unwin.
Shaver, Sheila, and Michael Fine. 1995. *Social Policy and Personal Life: Changes in State, Family and Community in the Support of Informal Care*. Sydney: University of New South Wales, Social Policy Research Centre. Discussion Paper 65.
Shaver, Sheila, Anthony King, Marilyn McHugh, and Toni Payne. 1994. *At the End of Eligibility: Female Sole Parents Whose Youngest Child Turns 16*. Sydney, University of New South Wales, SPRC. Report 117. December.
Shields, John, and Bob Russell. 1994. 'Part-Time Workers, the Welfare State, and Labour Market Relations.' In *Continuities and Discontinuities*, 327–49. Edited by A.F. Johnson, S. McBride, and P.J. Smith. Toronto: University of Toronto Press.
Shipley, Jenny. 1991. *Social Assistance: Welfare That Works*. Wellington: Department of Social Welfare.
Shirley, Ian. 1994. 'Social Policy.' In *New Zealand Society*. 2nd ed. Edited by Paul Spoonley, David Pearson, and Ian Shirley. Palmerston North, NZ: Dunmore Press.
Shirley, Ian, Peggy Koopman-Boyden, Ian Pool, and Susan St John. 1997. 'Family Change and Family Policy in New Zealand.' In *Family Change and Family Policies in Great Britain, Canada, New Zealand and the U.S.* Edited by S. Kamerman and A. Kahn. Oxford: Clarendon Press.
Shragge, Eric, 1997. 'Workfare: An Overview.' In *Workfare: Ideology for a New Under-Class*, 17–34. Edited by E. Schragge. Toronto: Garamond Press.
Shragge, Eric, and Marc-André Deniger. 1997. 'Workfare in Quebec.' In *Workfare: Ideology for a New Under-Class*, 59–83. Edited by E. Shragge. Toronto: Garamond Press.

Shrimsley, Robert. 1997. 'Radical Change behind a Reassuring Smile.' *Daily Telegraph*, 3 April: 8.

Sidel, Ruth. 1992. *Women and Children Last: The Plight of Poor Women in Affluent America*. New York: Penguin Books.

Siim, Birte. 1988. 'Towards a Feminist Rethinking of the Welfare State.' In *The Politics Interests of Gender*, 160–86. Edited by K.B. Jones and A.G. Jonasdottir. London: Sage.

Silva, Elizabeth Bortolaia, ed. 1996. *Good Enough Mothering? Feminist Perspectives on Lone Motherhood*. London: Routledge.

Smart, Carol. 1997. 'Feminist Interventions and State Policy.' In *Women and the Canadian State*, 110–15. Edited by C. Andrew and S. Rodgers. Montreal: McGill-Queen's University Press.

Smithers, Rebecca. 1997a. 'LibDems Pledge to Boost Women's Role.' *Guardian*, 3 April: 13.

–1997b. 'Blair Offers Jobless a New "Bargain."' *Guardian*, 3 June.

Spoonley, Paul. 1994. 'Racism and Ethnicity.' In *New Zealand Society*. 2nd ed. Edited by Paul Spoonley, David Pearson, and Ian Shirley. Palmerston North, NZ: Dunmore Press.

Stanton, David I., and Andrew Herscovitz. 1992. 'Social Security and Sole Parents: Developments in Australia.' In *Social Security and Changing Family Structures*, 157–84. Edited by the International Social Security Association. Geneva: ISSA.

Steinhauer, Paul D. 1995. *The Canada Health and Social Transfer: A Threat to the Health, Development and Future Productivity of Canada's Children and Youth*. Ottawa: Caledon Institute of Social Policy, November.

Stephens, John D. 1996. 'The Scandinavian Welfare States: Achievements, Crisis, and Prospects.' In *Welfare States in Transition*. Edited by G. Esping-Andersen. London: Sage.

Stephens, Robert, and Charles Waldegrave. 1995. 'Measuring Poverty in New Zealand.' *Social Policy Journal of New Zealand* 5 (December).

Strong-Boag, V. 1979. '"Wages for Housework": The Beginnings of Social Security in Canada.' *Journal of Canadian Studies* 14 (1): 24–34.

Struthers, James. 1996. *Can Workfare Work? Reflections from History*. Ottawa: Caledon Institute of Social Policy.

Sullivan, Barbara, and Gillian Whitehouse, eds. 1996. *Gender, Politics and Citizenship in the 1990s*. Sydney: UNSW Press.

Tapper, Alan. 1990. *The Family in the Welfare State*. Sydney: Allen and Unwin.

Taylor, Janet. 1996. 'Life Chances: Longitudinal Research in a Changing Policy Context.' Paper presented at the 5th Australian Family Research Conference, 26–29 November, Brisbane.

Taylor-Gooby, Peter. 1997. 'In Defence of Second-Best Theory: State, Class and Capital in Social Policy.' *Journal of Social Policy* 26 (2): 171–92.

Thane, Pat. 1996. *Foundations of the Welfare State.* 2nd ed. London: Longman.

Thomas, Richard. 1997. 'Freeing Young Jobless from Welfare "Hammock,"' *Guardian,* 15 May: 8.

Titmuss, Richard M. 1974. *Social Policy: An Introduction.* London: Allen and Unwin.

Torjman, Sherri. 1996. *Workfare: A Poor Law.* Ottawa: Caledon Institute of Social Policy.

– 1997. 'The New Handshake Federalism.' Caledon Commentary, September. Ottawa: Caledon Institute of Social Policy.

Toupin, Lynn. 1995. 'Index on Workfare.' *Canadian Forum* 74 (843): 32.

Townson, Monica. 1996. 'The Special Importance of CPP to Women,' in *Round Table On Canada Pension Plan Reform.* Ottawa: Caledon Institute of Social Policy.

Ungerson, Clare. 1997. 'Social Politics and the Commodification of Care,' *Social Politics* 4 (3): 362–81.

United Kingdom, Conservative Party. 1997. *The Conservative Manifesto.* London. April.

United Kingdom, Department of Social Security. 1995a. *Piloting Change in Social Security: Helping People into Work.* London: DSS.

– 1995b. *Social Security Departmental Report.* London: Stationery Office.

– 1996 *Bringing Up Children?* October. London: Benefits Agency.

– 1997. *Social Security Benefit Rates.* NI196. London: Department of Social Security. April.

– 1998. 'New Ambitions for Our Country: A New Contract for Welfare: A Summary.' London: Stationery Office. March.

United Kingdom, Department of Trade and Industry. 1998. *National Minimum Wage: The Government's Evidence to the Low Pay Commission.* London: HM Stationary Office. January.

United Kingdom, HM Treasury. 1998a. *Financial Statement and Budget Report.* March. House of Commons Paper No. HC 620. London: Stationary Office.

– 1998b. *The Modernization of Britain's Tax and Benefit System. 3: Working Families Tax Credit and Work Incentives.* London: Stationery Office.

United Kingdom, HM Treasury Press Office. 1998. Women and the Budget. Budget News Release 9. 17 March.

United Nations. 1992. *UN Demographic Yearbook.* New York: United Nations.

United States, Department of Health and Human Services. 1992. *Social Security Programs Throughout the World – 1991.* Washington: U.S. Government.

Ursel, Jane. 1992. *Private Lives, Public Policy: 100 Years of State Intervention in the Family.* Toronto: Women's Press.

Van den Berg, Axel, and Joseph Smucker, eds. *The Sociology of Labour Markets: Efficiency, Equity, Security.* Scarborough, Ont.: Prentice Hall Allyn and Bacon Canada.

VandenHeuvel, Audrey. 1993. *When Roles Overlap: Workers with Family Responsibilities.* Report of the Findings of the Dependent Care Study. Melbourne: AIFS.

Vanier Institute of the Family. 1994. *Profiling Canadian Families.* Ottawa: Vanier Institute of the Family.

Vrielink, Gerda. 1996. 'The Australian Welfare State Regime: Poverty among Sole Parent Families.' Thesis, University of Twente, Enschede, Netherlands.

Walker, David. 1998a. 'Budget 98 – Help for Low-Paid Families Is More than Doubled.' *Independent*, 18 March.

– 1998b. 'Harman in "Full Monty" Bid to Lure Women into Work.' *Independent*, 11 May.

Ward, Clare, Angela Dale, and Heather Joshi. 1996. 'Combining Employment with Childcare: An Escape from Dependence?' *Journal of Social Policy* 25 (2): 223–47.

Waring, Marilyn. 1988. *Counting for Nothing: What Men Value and What Women Are Worth.* Wellington, NZ: Allen and Unwin and Port Nicholson Press.

Wastell, David. 1997. 'Tories to Pledge Workfare for All Jobless.' *Sunday Telegraph* (London), 23 February: 2.

Watson, Sophie, ed. 1990. *Playing the State: Australian Feminist Interventions.* Sydney: Allen and Unwin.

Webb, Steve, Martin Kemp, and Jane Millar. 1996. 'The Changing Face of Low Pay in Britain.' *Policy Studies*, 17 (4): 255–71.

Wennemo, Irene. 1994. *Sharing the Cost of Children.* Stockholm: Swedish Institute for Social Research.

Wexler, Sherry. 1997. 'Work/Family Policy Stratification: The Examples of Family Support and Family Leave.' *Qualitative Sociology* 20 (2): 311–22.

White, Julie. 1993. *Sisters and Solidarity: Women and Unions in Canada.* Toronto: Thompson Educational Publishing.

White, Michael. 1997. 'Bold PM goes for the gold.' *Guardian*, 3 April: 11.

Whiteford, Peter. 1996. 'Welfare Dependence and Lone Parent Families: A Comparative Analysis.' Presented at the 5th Australian Family Research Conference, Brisbane, 27–29 November.

Whiteford, Peter, and S. Kennedy, 1995. *Incomes and Living Standards of Older People: A Comparative Analysis.* DSS Research Report 34. London: HMSO.

Wiggins, Cindy. 1996. 'Dismantling Unemployment Insurance: The Changes, the Impacts, the Reasons.' *Canadian Review of Social Policy* 37 (Spring): 75–84.

Wilkie, M. 1993. *Women Social Security Offenders: Experiences of the Criminal Justice System in Western Australia*. Research Report 8, Crime Research Centre. Perth: University of Western Australia.

Williams, Fiona. 1989. *Social Policy: A Critical Introduction*. Cambridge: Polity Press.

Wilson, Karen. 1996. 'Women's Paid and Unpaid Labour: Where Is the Choice?' Paper presented at the 5th Australian Family Research Conference, Brisbane, 26–29 November.

Wintour, Patrick. 1997. 'The Delicate Balance: Blair and Clinton Talk the Same Language on the Underclass, but US Solutions May Not Work Here.' *Observer*, 1 June: 20.

Wolcott, Ilene. 1991. *Work and Family: Employers' Views*. Melbourne: AIFS.

– 1993. *A Matter of Give and Take: Small Business Views of Work and Family*. Melbourne: AIFS.

Wolcott, Ilene, and H. Glezer. 1995. *Work and Family Life: Achieving Integration*. Melbourne: AIFS.

Woods, N. 1963. *Industrial Conciliation and Arbitration in New Zealand*. Wellington: Government Printer.

Woolley, Frances, Arndt Vermaeten, and Judith Madill. 1996. 'Ending Universality: The Case of Child Benefits.' *Canadian Public Policy* 22 (1): 24–39.

Yeatman, A. 1990. *Bureaucrats, Technocrats, Femocrats: Essays on the Contemporary Australian State*. Sydney: Allen and Unwin.

Young, Iris Marion. 1990. *Justice and the Politics of Difference*. Princeton, NJ: Princeton University Press.

– 1997. *Intersecting Voices: Dilemmas of Gender, Political Philosophy, and Policy*. Princeton, NJ: Princeton University Press.

Zackin, D. 1994. *Family and Medical Leave: Work-Family Roundtable* 4 (4) Winter. New York: Conference Board.

Zweibel, Ellen B. 1993. 'Canadian Income Tax Policy on Child Support Payments: Old Rationales Applied to New Realities.' In *Single Parent Families: Perspectives on Research and Policy*, 157–84. Edited by J. Hudson and B. Gallaway. Toronto: Thompson Educational Publishing.

– 1995. 'Child Support: From Tax Deduction to Tax Credit.' *Policy Options/ Options Politiques* 16 (10) December: 19–23.

Index

Abramovitz, Mimi, 51, 67
Affirmative Action, Equal Employment Opportunities for Women Act (Australia), 127, 145
Alcock, Peter, 225–6
Alexander, Liz, 137
Allard, Tom, 143
Allen, Douglas, 84
Anderton, Jim, 190
Armitage, Andrew, 74, 111
Armstrong, Hugh, Pat Armstrong, and M. Patricia Connelly, 51
Armstrong, Pat, 12, 14, 19, 57, 63, 102, 231
Armstrong, Pat, and Hugh Armstrong, 49
Aronson, Jane, and Sheila Neysmith, 45
Australia: Accord of 1983, 121–2, 140; business groups, 123, 254; caring responsibilities of women, 16, 117–18, 121, 128, 140–1, 146, 149–52; childcare, 138–43, 152; child support, 125, 133–8, 211–12; coalition government, 141–3, 147–8, 254; demographic trends, 26–8; Dependent Spouse Rebate, 139; divorce and spousal support, 132–5; equality, 118, 120, 146; employability, 15, 129–32, 141; family allowances 125–6, 151; Family Tax Initiative, 148; Home Child Care Allowance (HCCA), 139–40; ideologies of good mothering, 14, 25; Jobs, Education and Training (JET), 125, 130, 151, 227; Job Search Allowance, 130; Labor governments, 25, 121, 124–5, 127, 139, 140, 143, 256; labour-force participation, 21, 124, 126–9, 150; low-paid employment, 22–3; maternity allowances, 118–19, 143, 145; medicare, 122; monitoring of beneficiaries, 132; parental leave, 143–7; Parenting Allowance, 34, 140, 149; part-time employment, 21, 28–9; political decision-making structures 124, 258; poverty rates, 22, 48, 150; social-security review, 124, 130; Sole Parent Pension, 34, 117, 125, 128–30, 151, 238; trade unions, 25, 118, 121–3, 248–9; wage arbitration, 25; women's employment, 127–9; women's movement, 25, 122–4, 140–1, 251

227, 233; interest groups, 205,
210–11; labour-force participation,
21, 218, 239; Labour Party, 8, 16, 26,
192–3, 197, 199, 201, 204–5, 214, 217,
219–24, 227, 250, 253, 255, 258; Liberal Democratic Party, 206, 218, 221;
One (Lone) Parent Benefit, 34, 197,
199, 205; low-paid employment, 23,
217, 221; maternity benefits, 204;
minimum wage, 8–9, 202, 213–18;
moral regulation, 192, 221, 227;
part-time employment, 21, 28–9;
political system, 258; poverty 22,
195–6, 199, 224; trade unions, 196,
205, 250; unemployment benefits,
215–16; welfare spending, 218;
Welfare to Work program, 26, 63,
219–21, 239, 250; widows' benefits,
203–4; women's movement, 205,
252–3; Working Family Tax Credit,
201–2, 214–15, 227
United Kingdom, Department of
Social Security (DSS), 198, 200,
203–4, 213, 217, 218, 221, 223–4
United Kingdom, Department of
Trade and Industry, 202
United Kingdom Employment
Department, 29
United Kingdom General Household
Survey, 27
United Kingdom, HM Treasury,
195–6, 201–2, 203, 205, 215, 218,
221–3, 239
United Nations, 27, 182
United States, 22, 24, 27, 52, 54–63,
67, 72–4, 84, 114–15, 119, 126, 146,
241–2, 250, 256
United States, Department of Health
and Human Services, 215
Ursel, Jane, 11, 77, 79, 251

Van den Berg, A., and J. Smucker, 19
VandenHeuvel, Audrey, 145
Vanier Institute of the Family (Can-
ada), 104
Vrielink, Gerda, 125, 150

Walker, David, 202, 222
Ward, C., A. Dale, and H. Joshi, 213
Waring, Marilyn, 259
Wastell, David, 219
Watson, Sophie, 37
Webb, Steve, Martin Kemp, and Jane
Millar, 21, 22, 46, 62, 194, 217–18,
226–7
welfare state: classifications, 40–1;
expansion, 4–8; generosity of bene-
fits, 42, 52, 70, 120
Wennemo, Irene, 41, 63, 268
Wexler, Sherry, 51
White, Julie, 245, 249–50
White, Michael, 206
Whiteford, Peter, and S. Kennedy, 42
widows' allowances and pensions,
12, 18, 32; in New Zealand, 180,
189; in the United Kingdom, 203–4
Wilkie, M., 132
Williams, Fiona, 267
Wilson, Karen, 149
Wintour, Patrick, 220
Wolcott, Ilene, 146
Wolcott, Ilene, and H. Glezer, 131–2,
139, 143–7
Woods, N., 156

Yeatman, A., 132
Young, Iris Marion, 38

Zackin, D., 146
Zweibel, Ellen B., 80, 107